UNDERSTANDING
DISABILITY LAW
Second Edition

UNDERSTANDING DISABILITY LAW

Second Edition

MARK C. WEBER
Vincent de Paul Professor of Law
DePaul University College of Law

ISBN 978-1-4224-9875-0 (soft cover)

Library of Congress Cataloging-in-Publication Data

Weber, Mark C., 1953-
Understanding disability law / Mark C. Weber. — 2nd ed.
  p. cm.
  Includes index.
  ISBN 978-1-4224-9875-0 (alk. paper)
  1. People with disabilities—Legal status, laws, etc.—United States. 2. Discrimination—Law and legislation—United
States. 3. Discrimination—United States. I. Title.
  KF480.W433 2011
  346.7301'3—dc23
  2011050516

NOTE TO USERS

To ensure that you are using the latest materials available in this area, please be
sure to periodically check the LexisNexis Law School web site for downloadable
updates and supplements at www.lexisnexis.com/lawschool.

Editorial Offices
121 Chanlon Rd., New Providence, NJ 07974 (908) 464-6800
201 Mission St., San Francisco, CA 94105-1831 (415) 908-3200
www.lexisnexis.com

MATTHEW⬧BENDER

DEDICATION

This book is dedicated to the students who assisted me on the project:
Kim Brown, Curtis Gonzalez, Ben Johnson, Elizabeth Powell, and Rachel Milos.

PREFACE

People with disabilities are the largest minority in the United States. In the past forty years, American law has responded vigorously to the problem of discrimination against this group of people. The Rehabilitation Act of 1973 forbade disability discrimination in federally funded activities, and the Americans with Disabilities Act of 1990 outlawed disability discrimination in employment, government services, public accommodations, and telecommunications. In the 1970s, Congress established enforceable rights to special education for children with disabilities. Disability discrimination cases are now an important part of the dockets of the courts, and law schools offer courses on Disability Law and similar topics.

This book discusses the major statutory and constitutional issues relating to disability discrimination. It is designed to help students in Disability Law courses synthesize and apply the materials they are learning. It is also designed to function as a compact treatise for practicing lawyers and others looking for an analysis of the Fourteenth Amendment, the Americans with Disabilities Act, section 504 of the Rehabilitation Act, the Individuals with Disabilities Education Act, the Fair Housing Act Amendments, and other laws, as they relate to legal controversies over disability rights. The book discusses leading cases on the major topics of disability law, and suggests ways of thinking about unresolved questions and debates over legal policy.

The book covers a range of disability discrimination issues: (1) constitutional law bearing on disability discrimination; (2) the controversy over who is a person with a disability for purposes of federal statutes; (3) employment discrimination rights and remedies; (4) educational discrimination, including special education law and higher education for students with disabilities; (5) discrimination in public accommodations; (6) discrimination by federal, state, and local governments; and (7) other topics, including disability discrimination related to housing, transportation, and telecommunications.

Throughout the book, "people-first" terminology is used. That is, the book uses the term "person with disabilities" or "child with disabilities," rather than "disabled person" or "disabled child." This usage follows that of the Americans with Disabilities Act and other recent statutes and is employed to emphasize that a person who has a disability is a human being first, rather than a manifestation of some disabling condition. The book also uses the word "disability" rather than "handicap" because many people consider the latter term stigmatizing. This usage also follows that of recent federal statutes.

Many thanks to those who assisted in this project, notably Kim Brown, Curtis Gonzalez, and Ben Johnson, who provided outstanding research assistance for the original edition and Rachel Milos and Elizabeth Powell for the second edition, and DePaul University College of Law Deans Glen Weissenberger and Gregory Mark, who enthusiastically supported the effort. The project received support from the research fund of the College of Law. Thanks to Keith Moore for his thoughtful editorial work and to Lexis-Nexis for its dedication to the project.

The author would be grateful to readers for advice about how to improve the book. Please direct comments to mweber@depaul.edu.

TABLE OF CONTENTS

Chapter 1   **INTRODUCTION AND CONSTITUTIONAL ISSUES** 1

§ 1.01   OVERVIEW OF DISABILITY LAW 1
  [A]   Medical Models and Civil Rights Models 1
  [B]   Discrimination, Torts, Public Benefits, and Other Legal Topics 2
§ 1.02   OVERVIEW OF DISABILITY DISCRIMINATION 3
  [A]   Forms of Discrimination 3
  [B]   Sources of Law 4
§ 1.03   OVERVIEW OF CONSTITUTIONAL ISSUES 5
  [A]   Equal Protection 5
  [B]   Due Process 9
  [C]   Eighth Amendment 10

Chapter 2   **STATUTORY COVERAGE** 13

§ 2.01   DEFINITIONS OF DISABILITY 13
  [A]   Federal Statutory Provisions 14
  [B]   Alternative Definitions 14
  [C]   Role of Mitigating Measures: The *Sutton* Trilogy and the
          ADA Amendments Act of 2008 17
  [D]   Contagious Diseases 22
  [E]   Exclusion for Current Users of Illegal Drugs 24
  [F]   Other Exclusions 26
§ 2.02   ACTUALLY IMPAIRED 26
  [A]   Physical or Mental Impairment 26
  [B]   Substantially Limits 27
  [C]   Major Life Activities 31
  [D]   Major Life Activity of Working 33
§ 2.03   RECORD OF AN IMPAIRMENT 35
§ 2.04   REGARDED AS HAVING AN IMPAIRMENT 36
§ 2.05   QUALIFIED INDIVIDUAL 39
§ 2.06   ENTITIES AND INDIVIDUALS BOUND BY THE DISABILITY
          DISCRIMINATION LAWS 41
  [A]   ADA Coverage 41
  [B]   Coverage of Section 504 42
  [C]   Coverage of Other Provisions 42

Table of Contents

Chapter 3   **EMPLOYMENT DISCRIMINATION** **45**

§ 3.01   OVERVIEW OF EMPLOYMENT DISCRIMINATION 45
  [A]   Relevant Statutory Provisions 45
  [B]   Covered Entities Under the ADA 48
§ 3.02   QUALIFIED INDIVIDUAL 49
  [A]   Relation of "Qualified Individual" to "Reasonable Accommodation" . . . 50
  [B]   Essential Functions 50
  [C]   Judicial Estoppel 52
§ 3.03   DISPARATE TREATMENT AND LIMITING, SEGREGATING, AND
             CLASSIFYING 54
§ 3.04   STANDARDS, CRITERIA, AND METHODS OF OPERATION WITH
             DISPARATE IMPACTS; TESTS AND SELECTION CRITERIA 57
§ 3.05   FAILING TO PROVIDE REASONABLE ACCOMMODATIONS 62
  [A]   Burdens 63
  [B]   Reasonable Accommodation and Undue Hardship Standards 66
  [C]   Job Restructuring and Reassignment to a Vacant Position 68
  [D]   Interactive Process 71
  [E]   Alcoholism and Use of Illegal Drugs 73
  [F]   Accommodations for Persons Regarded as Disabled 74
§ 3.06   MEDICAL EXAMINATIONS AND INQUIRIES 75
  [A]   Pre-Employment Inquiries 75
  [B]   Medical Examinations After Conditional Offer 77
  [C]   Inquiries and Examinations of Current Employees 78
  [D]   Drug Testing and Related Issues 80
§ 3.07   DISCRIMINATION BY CONTRACTUAL ARRANGEMENT 80
§ 3.08   ASSOCIATIONAL DISCRIMINATION 81
§ 3.09   ADDITIONAL DEFENSES 83
  [A]   Limitations 83
  [B]   Exhaustion of Administrative Remedies 85
  [C]   Direct Threat 86
  [D]   Mandatory Arbitration 90
§ 3.10   REMEDIES 92
  [A]   Compensatory and Punitive Damages 92
  [B]   Backpay, Reinstatement, Injunctions, and Other Equitable Relief 94
  [C]   Attorneys' Fees 95

Chapter 4   **EDUCATIONAL DISCRIMINATION** **97**

§ 4.01   PRIMARY AND SECONDARY EDUCATION 97
  [A]   Overview of the Individuals with Disabilities Education Act 97
  [B]   Eligibility and Evaluation 100
  [C]   Appropriate Education 105

Table of Contents

[D]	Least Restrictive Environment	109
[E]	Procedures and Remedies	112
[F]	Student Discipline	116
§ 4.02	POST-SECONDARY EDUCATION	119
[A]	Overview of Higher Education Discrimination	120
[B]	Qualifications and Reasonable Accommodation	120
[C]	Academic Deference	124
[D]	Specific Issues Regarding Learning Disabilities	127
[E]	Courses and Examinations	130

Chapter 5   PUBLIC ACCOMMODATIONS DISCRIMINATION ... 133

§ 5.01	OVERVIEW OF PUBLIC ACCOMMODATIONS DISCRIMINATION	133
§ 5.02	DEFINING PUBLIC ACCOMMODATIONS	136
§ 5.03	REASONABLE MODIFICATIONS AND AUXILIARY AIDS AND SERVICES	139
[A]	Reasonable Modifications and Fundamental Alteration	139
[B]	Auxiliary Aids and Services and Undue Burden	143
§ 5.04	ACCESSIBILITY STANDARDS AND BARRIER REMOVAL	144
§ 5.05	PLACES OF PUBLIC EXHIBITION OR ENTERTAINMENT	149
§ 5.06	INSURANCE ISSUES	152
§ 5.07	REMEDIES	154

Chapter 6   DISCRIMINATION IN GOVERNMENT SERVICES AND FEDERALLY FUNDED PROGRAMS 159

§ 6.01	OVERVIEW OF DISCRIMINATION IN GOVERNMENT AND FEDERALLY FUNDED PROGRAMS	159
§ 6.02	DISCRIMINATION BY FEDERAL AGENCIES	160
§ 6.03	STATE AND LOCAL GOVERNMENT AND FEDERALLY FUNDED PROGRAMS: DISPARATE IMPACT DISCRIMINATION	163
§ 6.04	STATE AND LOCAL GOVERNMENT AND FEDERALLY FUNDED PROGRAMS: MODIFICATIONS OF POLICIES	166
§ 6.05	STATE AND LOCAL GOVERNMENT AND FEDERALLY FUNDED PROGRAMS: INTEGRATED SERVICES	169
§ 6.06	STATE AND LOCAL GOVERNMENT AND FEDERALLY FUNDED PROGRAMS: SPECIFIC ISSUES AND GENERAL ACCESSIBILITY DUTY	171
[A]	Employment	171
[B]	Voting	173
[C]	Courts	174
[D]	Prisons	175
[E]	Public Benefits and Welfare	176

Table of Contents

[F]	Recreation	177
[G]	Accessibility Requirements in General	178
§ 6.07	STATE AND LOCAL GOVERNMENT AND FEDERALLY FUNDED PROGRAMS: REMEDIES	181
[A]	Exhaustion Issues	181
[B]	Injunctive Relief	181
[C]	Damages Relief	182
[D]	Eleventh Amendment Immunity	183

Chapter 7   HOUSING, TRANSPORTATION, TELECOMMUNICATIONS, AND ADDITIONAL DISCRIMINATION TOPICS 187

§ 7.01	HOUSING DISCRIMINATION	187
[A]	Overview of the FHAA	188
[B]	Facial Discrimination and Disparate Treatment	189
[C]	Reasonable Accommodation and Disparate Impact	192
[D]	Defenses and Exemptions	197
[E]	Remedies	199
§ 7.02	TRANSPORTATION	200
[A]	Ground Transportation	200
[B]	Air Transportation	207
§ 7.03	TELECOMMUNICATIONS	210
[A]	Telecommunications Relay Systems	210
[B]	Internet Sites and Other Means of Telecommunication	211
§ 7.04	ADDITIONAL DISCRIMINATION ISSUES	213
[A]	Retaliation	213
[B]	Disability Harassment	215
[C]	International and Comparative Law Issues	218
Table of Cases		TC-1
Table of Statutes		TS-1
Index		I-1

Chapter 1

INTRODUCTION AND CONSTITUTIONAL ISSUES

§ 1.01 OVERVIEW OF DISABILITY LAW

An understanding of disability law has to begin by coming to grips with disability itself, as well as by learning how disability relates to the universe of law. The understanding of disability in society has evolved over time, and is characterized by the recent appearance of a civil rights model of disability. The relation of disability and law has also changed over time, and it includes not only legal responses to discrimination but also legal responses to the fact of disability and to social attitudes about disability.

[A] Medical Models and Civil Rights Models

In a pathbreaking 1966 law review article, Jacobus tenBroek and Floyd Matson observed that the paradigm for disability law was shifting from what they called "custodialism" to what they termed "integrationism."[1] The custodial model of disability was a medically oriented one. It gave primary attention to the physical or mental defects of persons with disabilities and studied the social and legal mechanisms by which society cared for, protected, and frequently segregated and kept itself from, persons whose medically determinable conditions made them different from others. The disabled were the other, to be cured, or if they could not be cured, to be isolated and sheltered. The authors contrasted this custodial approach with one being developed by civil rights activists working on behalf of persons with disabilities. These individuals were pressing not for protection or caretaking, but for equality and access. They desired not separation from, but integration into, the larger society, integration on a plane where they could participate and compete equally. Their attention was on removing the physical and attitudinal barriers that stood in their way — often literally, as with unramped steps, narrow doorways, and curbs without cuts, blocking the path of a person using a wheelchair for mobility.

Other writers developed these and similar ideas into a comprehensive civil rights model of disability. They pointed out that persons with disabilities are members of a minority group, sharing common interests and kept from integrating

---

[1] Jacobus tenBroek & Floyd W. Matson, *The Disabled and the Law of Welfare*, 54 CAL. L. REV. 809 (1966). Professor tenBroek was blind and a disability rights activist. His work also had a profound effect in other fields, particularly his historical work on the Fourteenth Amendment, which influenced the Warren Court's equal protection jurisprudence. *See* JACOBUS TENBROEK, THE ANTISLAVERY ORIGINS OF THE FOURTEENTH AMENDMENT (1951); Joseph Tussman & Jacobus tenBroek, *The Equal Protection of the Laws*, 37 CAL. L. REV. 341 (1949).

fully into society not by their disabilities but by society's failure to respond properly to human difference.[2] A central insight of the movement was that physical or mental conditions do not necessarily disable, were it not for the human-created environment of physical, legal, and attitudinal obstacles. Thus disability is both human-created and contingent on social actions and attitudes. Many variations on, and some critiques of, civil rights models have appeared over the years,[3] but embrace of civil rights approaches and rejection of narrow medical models of disability are central to social mobilization and legal reform challenging disability discrimination. The Americans with Disabilities Act might be viewed as the culmination of activism and political efforts inspired by a civil rights, integrationist approach to disability.[4]

[B] Discrimination, Torts, Public Benefits, and Other Legal Topics

With the emergence of a civil rights approach to disability, disability discrimination has become the primary topic of discussion in law school Disability Law courses and in discussions among academics and practitioners on disability law issues. Of course, other areas of the law have special effects on persons with disabilities and the interaction of disability and society. Some topics are familiar from first-year Torts: Should the reasonable-person standard adapt for the physical or mental disabilities of a given individual? Traditionally, the answer has been yes for physical disabilities, but no for mental disabilities.[5] Similarly, mental disability affects matters of Contracts, Wills and Trusts, Criminal Law, and other fields, to the point where separate law school courses on Mental Disability Law are common. Disability has serious economic effects, particularly given the maladaptation of much of the workplace to persons with disabilities, to the point where people with disabilities have labor force non-participation rates of around 65% and poverty rates three times those of people without disabilities.[6]

---

[2] Not all of this commentary was from lawyers or focused exclusively on law. *See, e.g.,* Michelle Fine & Adrienne Asch, *Disability Beyond Stigma: Social Interaction, Discrimination and Activism,* 44 J. Soc. Issues 3 (1988) (highly influential article developing minority group model); *see also* James A. Charlton, Nothing About Us Without Us: Disability Oppression and Empowerment 127 (1998) (defending continued relevance of civil rights approaches to disability); The Disability Studies Reader (Lennard J. Davis ed. 1997) (collecting essays on minority group-civil rights approaches to disability).

[3] Partial critiques include Marta Russell, *Backlash, the Political Economy, and Structural Exclusion,* 21 Berkeley J. Emp. & Lab. L. 335 (2000); Bonnie Poitras Tucker, *The ADA's Revolving Door: Inherent Flaws in the Civil Rights Paradigm,* 62 Ohio St. L.J. 335 (2001); Mark C. Weber, *Disability and the Law of Welfare: A Post-Integrationist Examination,* 2000 U. Ill. L. Rev. 889.

[4] *See, e.g.,* Joseph P. Shapiro, No Pity: People with Disabilities Forging a New Civil Rights Movement (1993); Robert L. Burgdorf, Jr., *The Americans with Disabilities Act: Analysis and Implications of a Second-Generation Civil Rights Statute,* 26 Harv. C.R.-C.L. L. Rev. 413 (1991); Timothy M. Cook, *The Americans with Disabilities Act: The Move to Integration,* 64 Temp. L. Rev. 393 (1991).

[5] *See* Restatement (Third) of Torts ch. 3 § 11 (2010); Restatement (Second) of Torts §§ 283B–283C (1965). For illuminating discussions of disability and tort law, see Adam A. Milani, *Living in the World: A New Look at the Disabled in the Law of Torts,* 48 Cath. U. L. Rev. 323 (1999); Jacobus tenBroek, *The Right to Live in the World: The Disabled in the Law of Torts,* 54 Cal. L. Rev. 841 (1966).

[6] According to the Kessler Foundation-National Organization for Disabilities 2010 survey of Americans with disabilities, 21% of working-aged people with disabilities report that they are employed,

Accordingly, Poverty Law and the law that relates to public benefits and social insurance have keen relevance to people with disabilities. Issues of access to health care and other supports for social participation may turn out to be "The Future of Disability Law."[7]

§ 1.02   OVERVIEW OF DISABILITY DISCRIMINATION

The discussion of disability discrimination includes both the conduct that fits under that general heading and the legal responses to it. Because disability discrimination has characteristics somewhat distinct from other forms of unfair treatment, it merits systematic discussion before delving into the sources of law that may address it.

[A]   Forms of Discrimination

In commenting on one disability discrimination statute, section 504 of the Rehabilitation Act of 1973, Justice Thurgood Marshall observed, "Discrimination against the handicapped was perceived by Congress to be most often the product, not of invidious animus, but rather of thoughtlessness and indifference — of benign neglect."[8] The insight that failure to adjust mental attitudes and environmental conditions need not have an evil intent behind it is crucial to understanding the forms of discrimination that persons with disabilities experience. The failure to adapt or make accommodations and the maintenance of rules that apply across the board but harm persons with particular disabilities disproportionately and lack adequate justification constitute much of disability discrimination. If every prospective law student, seeing or blind, must take the same paper and pencil law school admissions test, the treatment is in a sense equal, but it discriminates against the person who needs Braille or a computerized reading system to compete fairly. Similarly, if class is held in the same classroom for everyone, but the room is up a step from ground level, persons using wheelchairs cannot participate.

Beyond the simple failure to accommodate and maintenance of rules and practices that have disparate impacts, discriminatory conduct may take the form of paternalism — keeping a person with a chronic disease out of a dangerous job for his or her own safety when the person would prefer to make the decision which risks to take — or it may take the form of stereotyping — assuming that a person with depression or another mental impairment cannot be relied on to perform a critical function. Sympathy in the form of pity or condescension may lead to systematic underestimation of the capabilities of individuals with disabilities; discomfort in dealing with someone who is physically or mentally different may

---

compared to 59% of similarly-aged people who do not have disabilities, and people with disabilities are twice as likely as people with disabilities to report that they have a household income of $15,000 or less. The ADA, 20 Years Later, at 10-12 (July, 2010), available at http://www.2010disabilitysurveys.org/pdfs/surveyresults.pdf.

[7] *See* Samuel R. Bagenstos, *The Future of Disability Law*, 114 Yale L.J. 1, 4 (2004) ("In short, the future of disability law lies as much in social welfare law as in antidiscrimination law."); *see also* Mark C. Weber, *Disability Rights, Welfare Law*, ___ Cardozo L. Rev. ___ (forthcoming 2011) (discussing public benefits issues for persons with disabilities).

[8] Alexander v. Choate, 469 U.S. 287, 295 (1985).

lead to social avoidance that closes off avenues of advancement at work or school for persons with disabling conditions.

Some disability discrimination, however, comes in traditional animus-driven form. People with disabilities frequently experience harassment at school, at work, and in other settings. Negative attitudes towards persons with disabilities are common, and are continually fueled by the regular depiction of villains in movies and literature as persons with disfigurements, other visible disabilities, or mental illness.[9] If the law is to respond to disability discrimination, it must address both thoughtless indifference and invidious animus.

[B]   Sources of Law

Numerous legal sources relate to disability discrimination issues. Constitutional provisions, statutes, and even international conventions bear on disability law. The primary statutory provisions that will be discussed in this book are section 504 of the Rehabilitation Act of 1973 ("section 504")[10] and the Americans with Disabilities Act of 1990 ("ADA").[11]

Section 504 provides that no otherwise qualified individual with a disability may be subject to discrimination under, excluded from, or denied the benefits of, any program or activity receiving federal financial assistance, solely on the basis of his or her disability. It also bars discrimination by federal executive agencies and the United States Postal Service.

The ADA forbids discrimination against individuals with disabilities in a number of different contexts and settings. Title I bars employment discrimination against qualified individuals with disabilities. Title II prohibits disability discrimination in state and local government activities. Title III forbids discrimination in privately operated places of public accommodation, such as stores and business offices. Title IV requires the provision of communication services that are accessible to persons with disabilities. Title V contains general provisions. Findings and definitions are contained in the opening sections of the statute.[12]

Unlike some other anti-discrimination laws, neither section 504 nor the ADA outlaws discrimination on a given basis across the board, for everyone. Generally, only a person who meets the definition of a person with a disability is protected by

---

[9] *See, e.g.,* LENNARD J. DAVIS, BENDING OVER BACKWARDS: DISABILITY, DISMODERNISM & OTHER DIFFICULT POSITIONS 52 (2002) (noting classic literature's use of deformity as sign of evil); Hugh Gregory Gallagher, *"Slapping Up Spastics": The Persistence of Social Attitudes Toward People with Disabilities,* 10 ISSUES L. & MED. 401 (1995) (discussing negative attitudes toward persons with disabilities); *see also* Ann Hubbard, *The ADA, the Workplace, and the Myth of the "Dangerous Mentally Ill,"* 34 U.C. DAVIS L. REV. 849, 850–52 (2001) (discussing widespread fear of persons with mental illness).

[10] 29 U.S.C. § 794 (2006).

[11] 42 U.S.C.S. §§ 12101–12213 (LexisNexis 2011). Title IV of the ADA is codified outside this framework and instead included in the telecommunications laws. 47 U.S.C. § 225 (2006). The ADA Amendments Act of 2008, Pub. L. 110-325, 122 Stat. 3553, made major changes in the coverage of the ADA as interpreted by the courts. It is discussed in depth *infra,* Chapter 2.

[12] 42 U.S.C.S. §§ 12101–12102 (LexisNexis 2011).

the statute and able to benefit from the anti-discrimination provisions.[13] Thus there is no such thing as a reverse-discrimination case under the ADA.

Other federal statutes carrying great significance for disability discrimination cases but with somewhat narrower application are (1) the Individuals with Disabilities Education Act (originally passed in 1975),[14] which requires states receiving special education funding from the federal government to guarantee that all children with disabilities receive a free, appropriate public education, in settings with children without disabilities to the maximum extent appropriate; (2) the Fair Housing Act Amendments of 1988,[15] which forbid various forms of disability discrimination in housing and establish accessibility requirements; and (3) the Air Carrier Access Act of 1986,[16] which bans discrimination in commercial air transportation and mandates accessibility.

In addition to these federal provisions are state constitutions, statutes, and common law. Because these sources of law are so varied, they will be cited in this book only in the context of discussing specific disability discrimination topics.

§ 1.03   OVERVIEW OF CONSTITUTIONAL ISSUES

Numerous issues of constitutional law come into play in disability discrimination cases. A major topic, that of Eleventh Amendment and related immunities, applies to cases against state government defendants, and so will be addressed in Chapter 6 of this book. Other constitutional issues of salience, however, are introduced here. They concern equal protection and due process of law guaranteed by the Fourteenth Amendment (and for the federal government, the Fifth Amendment), as well as protection against cruel and unusual punishment in the Eighth Amendment.

[A]   Equal Protection

In the period since the emergence in Supreme Court case law of different levels of equal protection and substantive due process scrutiny for laws that target certain classes of people, courts have asked whether people with disabilities, or at least some categories of persons with disabilities, are a "suspect class"[17] and whether laws that use a disability classification should be subject to elevated scrutiny. In *City of Cleburne v. Cleburne Living Center, Inc.*, the Supreme Court considered that issue in an action over denial of a permit to open a group home for persons with mental retardation, and said no.[18] Cleburne Living Center proposed

---

[13] There are exceptions, as with the provisions barring retaliation and coercion, and some other provisions.

[14] 20 U.S.C.S. §§ 1400–1487 (LexisNexis 2011).

[15] 42 U.S.C. §§ 3601–3614 (2006).

[16] 49 U.S.C. § 41705 (2006).

[17] The ADA Amendments Act, however, removed language in the original preamble to the ADA declaring that "individuals with disabilities are a discrete and insular minority who have been faced with restrictions and limitations, subjected to a history of purposeful unequal treatment, and relegated to a position of powerlessness in our society . . ." 42 U.S.C. § 12101(a)(7) (2006) (repealed 2008).

[18] 473 U.S. 432 (1985). Because of its negative connotations, the term "mental retardation" has fallen

to open a group home for 13 men and women with mental retardation, but the city denied a special use permit and the Center sued, claiming a denial of equal protection. The district court ruled for the city, but the court of appeals reversed, holding that mental retardation is a quasi-suspect classification and that therefore the zoning ordinance barring operation of the home was subject to intermediate-level scrutiny. It failed the equal protection test because it did not substantially further any important governmental interest.

In an opinion by Justice White, the Supreme Court affirmed the invalidation of the zoning ordinance as applied to the proposed group home, but it vacated the court of appeals' judgment in all other respects. In defending its application of a rational-relationship test instead of one demanding heightened scrutiny, the Court first said that mental retardation reduces the ability to function in the everyday world, and there is a great deal of diversity in levels of functioning. The difference between persons with mental retardation and others was said to make the states' interest in dealing with and providing for them a legitimate one. Professional judgment guiding legislators would perhaps be superior to the less informed views of the judiciary. As a second argument, the Court pointed to the fact that legislators have addressed the unique problems of persons with mental retardation by outlawing discrimination in federally funded activity in section 504 of the Rehabilitation Act; affirming a right to treatment, services, and habilitation in the Developmental Disabilities Assistance and Bill of Rights Act; conditioning federal education funding on rights to special education in integrated settings in the special education law; and providing hiring preferences for the federal civil service. State law also provided some rights and benefits for persons with mental retardation. This legislation supported the conclusion that relevant differences exist between persons with mental retardation and others, and so legislation employing the category was not suspect on that account. Employing a higher level of scrutiny to evaluate legislation using the category might discourage government from taking actions that favor persons with mental retardation. Third, the beneficial legislation shows that persons with metal retardation are not powerless in the legislative process, thus needing special protection from the judiciary. Finally, many other groups with immutable conditions might also be able to make claims to heightened equal protection scrutiny for legislation affecting them if persons with mental retardation were able to do so.

The Court stressed that legislation nevertheless had to meet a rational relationship test, which, it said "affords government the latitude necessary both to pursue policies designed to assist the retarded in realizing their full potential, and to freely and efficiently engage in activities that burden the retarded in what is essentially an incidental manner."[19] It said that the zoning ordinance, as applied, failed to meet the test. The city did not require a special use permit for apartment houses, multiple dwellings, boarding houses, fraternity houses, dormitories, apartment hotels, sanitariums, nursing homes for convalescents or the aged. The Court found no rational basis for believing the group home would threaten the city's legitimate interests. The reasons that the district court found to support the

---

into disfavor; many authorities now prefer the term "intellectual disability."

[19] *Id.* at 446.

permit requirement were fears of neighboring property owners and elderly residents, but negative attitudes and unsubstantiated fears are not permissible bases for treating a group home for persons with mental retardation differently. Two other justifications advanced by the city council also did not stand up. The council professed to be concerned that students at a junior high school across the street might harass the group home residents, but the school itself had mentally retarded students, and the vague fears were insufficient to support the discrimination. Also, the council's concern that the location was on a 500-year flood plain did not justify distinguishing the treatment of the group home from that nursing homes, hospitals, or sanitariums. Additional concerns about liability for potential actions of the residents of the home did not distinguish the group home from, say, a fraternity house, and the size and occupancy level of the house could not justify different treatment when residences for others could be as large or larger. The same fact applied to concerns over concentration of population and congestion or fire hazards. The Court concluded that "requiring the permit in this case appears to us to rest on an irrational prejudice against the mentally retarded," and so the city's action violated equal protection.[20]

Justice Stevens, joined by Chief Justice Burger, concurred in the judgment, stating doubts about the wisdom of using a rigid three-tier system in equal protection cases, in which some cases receive strict scrutiny, some intermediate, and some only rational-basis. The opinion suggested that the rational-basis test in fact embraced all categories of cases; some government classifications are presumptively irrational, while others, including those that place persons with mental retardation in a special class are not. The justifications advanced by the city for the classification here were utterly unconvincing, and so the government's conduct was irrational and a violation of equal protection.

Justice Marshall, joined by Justices Brennan and Blackmun, concurred in the judgment in part and dissented in part. The opinion said that the law would be considered valid if ordinary rational-basis review were applied. In fact, the majority was applying a more exacting standard. Under rational-basis review, government may approach a problem one step at a time, addressing first that part of a problem viewed as most acute. Precision of categories is not required. The opinion said that "the level of scrutiny employed in an equal protection case should vary with 'the constitutional and societal importance of the interest adversely affected and the recognized invidiousness of the basis upon which the particular classification is drawn.'"[21] According to Justice Marshall, the interest of persons with mental retardation in establishing group homes is substantial: The right to a home is a fundamental liberty protected by due process. Moreover, classification based on mental retardation is invidious: Persons with mental retardation have been subjected to a lengthy and tragic history of segregation and discrimination. Historically, Social Darwinism and eugenics led to a "regime of state-mandated segregation and degradation soon emerged that in its virulence and bigotry rivaled,

---

[20] *Id.* at 450.

[21] *Id.* at 460 (Marshall, J., concurring in the judgment in part and dissenting in part) (quoting San Antonio Indep. Sch. Dist. v. Rodriguez, 411 U.S. 1, 99 (1973) (Marshall, J., dissenting)).

and indeed paralleled, the worst excesses of Jim Crow."[22] Custodial institutions devoted to warehousing persons with mental retardation and measures to halt their reproduction through sterilization were part of this legacy. The importance of the interest in the case and the history of discrimination were said to justify searching scrutiny of the restrictions on group homes for persons with mental retardation. Marshall also noted that heightened scrutiny had been applied to classifications like gender, which related to real differences for which different treatment may be justified. "In light of the scrutiny that should be applied here, Cleburne's ordinance sweeps too broadly to dispel the suspicion that it rests on a bare desire to treat the retarded as outsiders, pariahs who do not belong in the community."[23]

Tracking much of the argument in Justice Marshall's opinion, prominent commentators have described the *Cleburne* decision as in fact the application of something stricter than ordinary rational-basis equal protection review.[24] Nevertheless, in a later case, the Supreme Court applied an ordinary rational-relationship test when sustaining a law that treated persons subject to civil commitment on the basis of mental retardation less favorably than persons subject to civil commitment on the basis of mental illness.[25] More recently, in *Board of Trustees of the University of Alabama v. Garrett*,[26] the Court declared that *Cleburne* established no higher scrutiny than the rational-basis test for the disability classification it considered. The Court used this view of *Cleburne* to support its conclusion that permitting ADA damages claims against state governments in employment cases violates principles of Eleventh Amendment immunity. The Court reasoned that Congress cannot provide damages against states for violating a law unless that law is proportional to and congruent with a violation of the Fourteenth Amendment. Relying on *Cleburne*, it concluded that the Fourteenth Amendment forbids only irrational discrimination on account of disability. Thus, failure to provide accommodations does not violate equal protection and cannot supply the basis for damages against a state.[27]

Even if laws that disadvantage persons on the basis of intellectual disability or disability in general are currently not viewed as subject to elevated scrutiny, equal protection still plays an important role in disability law. Not only does the equal protection issue affect the debate over the application of Eleventh Amendment immunity to state agency defendants in contexts other than employment, but equal protection claims continue to be a basis for actions challenging government-enabled harassment and irrational government policies.

---

[22] *Id.* at 462.

[23] *Id.* at 473.

[24] *E.g.,* ERWIN CHEMERINSKY, CONSTITUTIONAL LAW: PRINCIPLES AND POLICIES § 9.2.3, at 705 (4th ed. 2011) ("Although the Court expressly declared that it was applying rational basis review, it appears that there was more 'bite' to the Court's approach than usual for this level of scrutiny.").

[25] Heller v. Doe, 509 U.S. 312 (1993).

[26] 531 U.S. 356 (2001).

[27] *See generally infra* Chapter 6 (discussing disability discrimination cases involving Eleventh Amendment immunity, including *Garrett*).

[B]　Due Process

Issues of procedural due process frequently arise in cases dealing with disability discrimination. For example, a person may not be subjected to civil commitment on the basis of mental illness without the use of adequate procedures,[28] a right that applies even to a prison inmate whose liberty interest is significantly diminished due to penal confinement.[29] Crucial to that conclusion is the recognition of the massive curtailment of liberty that civil commitment for mental illness entails, as well as the "stigmatizing consequences of a transfer to a mental hospital for involuntary psychiatric treatment."[30] Similar principles come into play in claims that children may not be excluded from educational placements on account of disability-related behavior or conditions without notice and the right to be heard.[31]

Substantive due process issues are perhaps even more prominent in the disability case law than procedural due process issues are. Quite apart from those concerns of substantive due process that overlap with equal protection, special substantive due process concerns apply when persons are institutionalized, as frequently occurs for persons with disabling mental conditions. For example, in *Youngberg v. Romeo*, the Supreme Court interpreted due process obligations with regard to persons involuntarily committed on account of mental retardation to include provision of adequate food, shelter, clothing, medical care, and reasonable safety.[32] The Court said that restraint is not to be used unless professional judgment deems it necessary, and that the government has a duty to provide training and habilitation to the extent that an appropriate professional would consider reasonable to permit the person who is committed to enjoy reasonable safety and the ability to function without restraint. The tenor of the Court's reasoning was that freedom is taken away from a person who is involuntarily committed to an institution for persons with mental retardation. Reasonable safety and habilitation must be provided in return.

Civil commitment for persons who are mentally ill must also be tied to a valid governmental interest. The Court in *O'Connor v. Donaldson* ruled that a person who was not dangerous who is mentally ill cannot simply be involuntarily confined when capable of surviving safely in freedom either on his or her own or with family and friends.[33] Nevertheless, confinement of persons with mental disorders, even long-term confinement, is permitted under due process principles when required for the safety of society.[34]

Other deprivations of life, liberty or property besides civil commitment may also be visited on persons with disabilities, and objections based on due process of law

---

[28] *See, e.g.,* Zinermon v. Burch, 494 U.S. 113 (1990); Addington v. Texas, 441 U.S. 418 (1979).

[29] Vitek v. Jones, 445 U.S. 480 (1980).

[30] *Id.* at 494.

[31] *See, e.g.,* Mills v. Board of Educ., 348 F. Supp. 866 (D.D.C. 1972).

[32] 457 U.S. 307 (1982).

[33] 422 U.S. 563 (1975).

[34] Kansas v. Hendricks, 521 U.S. 346 (1997) (permitting civil confinement of person likely to commit sex crimes on account of mental abnormality or disorder).

may be raised. One deprivation of liberty is forced sterilization. In *Buck v. Bell*, the Supreme Court upheld the compulsory sterilization of a woman who was deemed "feeble minded" against a challenge that the practice violated substantive due process and equal protection.[35] Justice Holmes' opinion fit well with the principles of the Eugenics Movement, which postulated that the human population could be improved by excluding physically or mentally unfit persons from social life by confining them, sterilizing them, or even killing them. The premise was that physical or mental weakness (or its converse) is inherited and that if persons with impairments propagated, the population would be "swamped with incompetence."[36] Holmes upheld the statute after citing its eugenic purpose, declaring that "Three generations of imbeciles are enough."[37] In fact, *Buck v. Bell* was a sham case in which the attorney for the woman to be sterilized was cooperating with proponents of eugenics in order to get Supreme Court approval for eugenic sterilization.[38] Although eugenics fell out of favor as its scientific support was discredited and as revulsion grew over its links to racism and nativism, compulsory sterilization of persons with mental disabilities continues today and remains a source of controversy.[39]

[C]   Eighth Amendment

In *Atkins v. Virginia*, the Supreme Court ruled that a person with mental retardation is not subject to the death penalty.[40] Atkins and another person abducted their victim, robbed him, drove him to an automatic teller machine where they had him withdraw more cash, then took him to an isolated location and shot him. The accomplice testified that Atkins committed the shooting (although Atkins said the accomplice did it), and the jury apparently credited the accomplice's account. The jury sentenced Atkins to death despite hearing evidence that he was mentally retarded. For technical reasons, a resentencing was ordered, where the jury heard conflicting evidence about whether Atkins was mentally retarded, and Atkins again received a death sentence. The Supreme Court ruled that the Eighth Amendment's protection against cruel and unusual punishment would be measured by contemporary standards, not those applicable at the time of adoption, and noted that, in the years since the Court had ruled that execution of a mentally retarded defendant was not categorically prohibited by the Amendment,[41] sixteen states had prohibited execution of mentally retarded defendants. Those jurisdictions joined the federal government and two others that had rejected the capital punishment for persons with mental retardation at the time of *Penry*. Emphasizing the trend in the developments and observing as well that several states permitting the penalty

---

[35]   274 U.S. 200, 205 (1927).

[36]   *Id.* at 207.

[37]   *Id.*

[38]   Paul A. Lombardo, *Three Generations, No Imbeciles: New Light on* Buck v. Bell, 60 N.Y.U. L. REV. 30, 56 (1985).

[39]   *See* Roberta Cepko, *Involuntary Sterilization of Mentally Disabled Women*, 8 BERKELEY WOMEN'S L.J. 122 (1993).

[40]   536 U.S. 304 (2002).

[41]   *See* Penry v. Lynaugh, 492 U.S. 302 (1989).

had not imposed it on a person with mental retardation for decades, the Court found that the practice had become truly unusual and a national consensus had emerged against it.

The Court further supported the conclusion that the penalty was unconstitutional by stressing that diminished capacities to understand, to communicate, learn from experience, act logically, control impulses, and understand others' conduct diminish personal culpability. The Court also relied on the fact that reduced mental capacity of persons with mental retardation might lead to inaccurate impositions of death sentences due to failure to give meaningful assistance to counsel, poor demeanor, or even the possibility of false confessions. The Court left to the states the job of applying the ruling. Justice Scalia dissented, protesting that the Court's approach lacked support in the text or history of the Eighth Amendment, that mental retardation can be feigned, and that mental retardation should simply be considered as another factor in determining if mitigation is appropriate.

There may be some tension between *Atkins'* approach to the legal treatment of disability and that advanced by proponents of civil rights models. The advocate for the person with mental retardation was arguing for different treatment on account of disability, rather than treatment that is the same, and the different treatment sought was not a removal of or compensation for physical or attitudinal barriers. Instead, it was an excuse, an escape from a penalty that would otherwise be appropriate given the nature of the criminal act. Determination of what level of mental retardation is needed to trigger the ruling's application brings the question of disability rights into the study of defects and deviation from the norm, rather than the study of what needs to be done to adapt conventional ways of doing things to accommodate the whole spectrum of society. It might nevertheless be argued that the Court's opinion does show sensitivity to barriers presented by the legal system for a defendant with mental retardation: the difficulty of that person to negotiate trial process, for example. Perhaps the case may be viewed as a partial adaptation of the legal system to what would otherwise be an unthinking imposition of the same treatment on persons who are relevantly different.

Chapter 2

STATUTORY COVERAGE

§ 2.01 DEFINITIONS OF DISABILITY

The Americans with Disabilities Act and section 504 are unusual among civil rights statutes in that generally they protect only a limited class of persons. Unlike title VII of the Civil Rights Act of 1964, which says that all persons are to be free from discrimination based on grounds of race, ethnic origin, religion, and sex, the ADA and section 504 provide that individuals with disabilities are the only ones protected by those laws from disability discrimination.[1] At first glance, the difference may not seem significant. Who but a person with a disability would be discriminated against on grounds of disability? Courts, however, have interpreted the laws to permit defendants to challenge at the outset of a case whether the person bringing the suit has a disability so as to satisfy the statutory definition. And in very many cases, courts have dismissed suits on the ground that disability has not been established under the statute, without making any inquiry whether the plaintiff was discriminated against on grounds of disability. Because title VII covers persons of all races, ethnicities, religions, and both sexes, there has been little litigation whether a person is, for example, a member of a given racial group. Cases instead proceed directly to the issue of whether prohibited discrimination took place.

The ADA and section 504 spell out who is a person with a disability so as to achieve protection, and the definition is broader than might be anticipated. Other approaches to defining the class of protected individuals exist as well, and are applied in other federal laws and some state laws. Moreover, courts and Congress have answered a number of important questions about how the definitions are to be interpreted, most importantly, whether to protect persons with impairments that are amenable to treatment or amelioration. There also is a statutory exclusion in the federal law for current users of illegal drugs, and that provision requires some explanation.

---

[1] Another prominent example of a civil rights law that protects only limited classes of individuals is the Age Discrimination in Employment Act, which protects persons over age 40 from employment discrimination on the basis of age. There are a limited number of provisions in the disability discrimination statutes that have always applied to people who do not have disabilities, and these will be discussed in the context of particular aspects of the law. The medical examination and the retaliation sections of the ADA are examples. Moreover, some parts of the ADA Amendments of 2008 may be read as expanding ADA coverage more broadly to people without disabilities. *See* § 3.04, *infra* (discussing employment discrimination in relation to standards, criteria, and methods of operation); *see also* § 2.04, *infra* (discussing individuals regarded as having a disability and the application of 42 U.S.C.S. § 12102(3)(A) (LexisNexis 2011)).

[A] Federal Statutory Provisions

The ADA protects qualified individuals with a disability. The General Provisions of the law state that the term "disability" means (1) "a physical or mental impairment that substantially limits one or more of the major life activities" of the individual; (2) "a record of such an impairment;" or (3) "being regarded as having such an impairment."[2] Persons who have disabilities that fall in the first category are sometimes referred to as "actually impaired." The second and third categories are commonly known as "record-of" and "regarded-as." For section 504, the terms "disability"[3] and "individual with a disability"[4] have the same meaning as they do in the ADA.

[B] Alternative Definitions

Disability is defined differently in various federal laws and programs, and in many state anti-discrimination laws. The Social Security Disability Insurance and Supplemental Security Income programs furnish monthly financial support to persons who are disabled, using the definition of persons who are unable "to engage in any substantial gainful activity by reason of any medically determinable physical or mental impairment which can be expected . . . to last for a continuous period" of a year or more.[5] If a person has one of a set of listed impairments or the impairment's equivalent, and is not working, these programs presume that the person is disabled and potentially eligible for benefits. A number of writers, especially around the time of the passage of the ADA, argued for the use of a set of impairment listings or some other seemingly objective standard for determining who has a disability and ought to be protected by the anti-discrimination laws.[6] They drew support from the idea that there is a long history of use of these methods in determining eligibility for benefits from Social Security, the Veterans Administration, and some private insurance programs. However, the response was advanced that this position fits better with a medicalized concept of disability than a social one, and so does not fit with the underlying goals of the ADA. Moreover, attitudes and physical conditions that operate as barriers to employment, enjoyment of public services, and participation in the economy are the subject of the ADA, and many of these barriers apply to persons who lack medically determinable conditions. The differences between the definitions of disability for social insurance and for anti-discrimination laws reflect the differing purposes of the programs, as well as the evolution of attitudes towards disability over time.[7]

---

[2] 42 U.S.C.S. § 12102(2) (LexisNexis 2011).

[3] 29 U.S.C.S. § 705(9)(B) (LexisNexis 2011).

[4] 29 U.S.C.S. § 705(20)(B) (LexisNexis 2011).

[5] 42 U.S.C.S. §§ 423(d)(1)(A) (2006) (Social Security), 1382(c)(3)(A) (2006) (Supplemental Security Income). Social Security Disability Insurance provides what is usually a higher level of income, with the amounts based on earnings prior to disability. Supplemental Security Income is a means-tested program that does not require prior work history.

[6] E.g., Mary Crossley, *The Disability Kaleidoscope*, 74 NOTRE DAME L. REV. 621, 714–15 (1999) (discussing debates over having ADA include list of impairments).

[7] See Mark C. Weber, *Disability and the Law of Welfare: A Post-Integrationist Approach*, 2000 U. ILL. L. REV. 889, 894. The regulations adopted by the EEOC for employment cases following the ADA

The federal special education law, titled the Individuals with Disabilities Education Act (IDEA), has a definition of children with disabilities that conditions a child's eligibility on having one or more named disabilities and needing special education because of that condition.[8] At one point, IDEA defined learning disability in a unique way as well. Unlike the ADA and section 504 definitions of impairment, which are sometimes considered to embody a comparison to the typical individual's capacities,[9] prior to the most recent revision the special education regulations' definition of learning disabilities compared the performance of the individual with his or her own potentials:

A team may determine that a child has a specific learning disability if —

(1) The child does not achieve commensurate with his or her age and ability levels in one or more of [specified] areas, if provided with learning experiences appropriate for the child's age and ability levels; and

(2) The team finds that a child has a severe discrepancy between achievement and intellectual ability in one or more of [specified] areas. . . .[10]

Some authorities would advocate an approach to learning disabilities for purposes of the anti-discrimination laws that looks more to the discrepancy between an individual's potential and achievement and less to comparisons of achievement between the individual and the general population.[11] Nevertheless, there are authorities who challenge whether the law ought to take account of learning

---

Amendments Act did, however, add a list of types of impairments for which "it should easily be concluded" that they will substantially limit major life activities. These include deafness, blindness, intellectual disability (formerly termed mental retardation), partially or completely missing limbs or mobility impairments requiring the use of wheelchair, autism, cancer, cerebral palsy, diabetes, epilepsy, HIV infection, multiple sclerosis, muscular dystrophy, major depressive disorder, bipolar disorder, and schizophrenia. 29 C.F.R. § 1630.2(j)(3)(iii) (2011).

[8] 20 U.S.C.S. § 1401(3)(A) (2006) ("The term 'child with a disability' means a child (i) with mental retardation, hearing impairments (including deafness), speech or language impairments, visual impairments (including blindness), serious emotional disturbance . . ., orthopedic impairments, autism, traumatic brain injury, other health impairment, or specific learning disabilities; and (ii) who, by reason thereof, needs special education and related services."). There is an exception allowing children ages three through nine to be found eligible simply on the basis of developmental delay and the consequent need for special education. § 1401(3)(B). The specification of impairments thus bears some similarity to the listing of impairments in the social insurance laws just discussed.

[9] *See, e.g.*, Betts v. Rector & Visitors of the Univ. of Va., 113 F. Supp. 2d 970 (W.D. Va. 2000); *see also* 29 C.F.R. § 1630.2(j)(1)(ii) (2011) (applicable to ADA title I) ("An impairment is a disability within the meaning of this section if it substantially limits the ability of an individual to perform a major life activity as compared to most people in the general population."). *But see* Bartlett v. New York State Bd. of Law Exam'rs, 156 F.3d 321 (2d Cir. 1998) (employing comparison to persons of similar abilities in determining disability under ADA and section 504), *vacated and remanded*, 527 U.S. 1031 (1999). This topic is discussed at greater length *infra* § 2.02[B]. Regarding learning disabilities' treatment under title I of the ADA, see ADA Title I EEOC Interpretive Guidance, 29 C.F.R. pt. 1630, app., § 1630.2(j)(4) (2011) (employing limited comparison of individuals to general population).

[10] 34 C.F.R. § 300.541(a) (2005). The regulation was revised in light of 2004 amendments to IDEA to eliminate the achievement-ability discrepancy criterion. 34 C.F.R. § 300.309(a) (2011).

[11] *E.g.*, Susan M. Denbo, *Disability Lessons in Higher Education: Accommodating Learning-Disabled Students and Student-Athletes Under the Rehabilitation Act and the Americans with Disabilities Act*, 41 AM. BUS. L.J. 145, 169 (2003).

disability at all.[12]

State law may protect categories of persons that differ from those protected by the ADA. Many state laws are broader in their coverage. For example, the Maine Human Rights Act's definition of physical or mental disability includes a list of conditions that are considered disabilities without regard to severity.[13] Some states have long excluded consideration of mitigating measures when determining whether a person has a disability so as to be covered by the state anti-discrimination law.[14] These provisions applied even during the pre-ADA Amendments Act period when the ADA's interpretation was governed by *Sutton v. United Air Lines, Inc.*[15] and related cases holding that the effects of impairments ameliorated by medication, appliances, or the body's own processes have to be evaluated after mitigation.[16]

Finally, a number of academic authorities have suggested alternate approaches to the definition of person with a disability under the ADA. Professor Bagenstos would have the courts employ an approach that asks whether the claimant is subject to subordination on the basis of the condition.[17] Professor Burgdorf contends that courts should focus on the nature of the discrimination rather than the characteristics of the disability.[18] Professor Korn has suggested approaches that do away with requiring any need to prove disability altogether and that emphasize the stigma of a given condition in determining whether it places a person under the

---

[12] *See* MARK KELMAN & GILLIAN LESTER, JUMPING THE QUEUE: AN INQUIRY INTO THE LEGAL TREATMENT OF STUDENTS WITH LEARNING DISABILITIES (1997); Craig S. Lerner, *"Accommodations" for the Learning Disabled: A Level Playing Field or Affirmative Action for Elites?*, 57 VAND. L. REV. 1043 (2004).

[13] ME. REV. STAT. ANN. tit. 5, § 4553-A (2010) ("Without regard to severity unless otherwise indicated: absent, artificial or replacement limbs, hands, feet or vital organs; alcoholism; amyotrophic lateral sclerosis; bipolar disorder; blindness or abnormal vision loss; cancer; cerebral palsy; chronic obstructive pulmonary disease; Crohn's disease; cystic fibrosis; deafness or abnormal hearing loss; diabetes; substantial disfigurement; epilepsy; heart disease; HIV or AIDS; kidney or renal diseases; lupus; major depressive disorder; mastectomy; mental retardation; multiple sclerosis; muscular dystrophy; paralysis; Parkinson's disease; pervasive developmental disorders; rheumatoid arthritis; schizophrenia; and acquired brain injury"). *See generally* Rooney v. Sprague Energy Corp., 519 F. Supp. 2d 131, 133–35 (D. Me. 2007) (discussing definition).

[14] *E.g.*, CAL. GOV'T CODE § 12926.1(c) (Deering 2011) ("Under the law of this state, whether a condition limits a major life activity shall be determined without respect to any mitigating measures, unless the mitigating measure itself limits a major life activity, regardless of federal law under the Americans with Disabilities Act of 1990."); Dahill v. Police Dep't, 748 N.E.2d 956 (Mass. 2001) (holding that statute defining "handicap," MASS. GEN. LAWS ch. 151B § 1(17) (2001), does not require consideration of mitigating or corrective devices).

[15] 527 U.S. 471 (1999).

[16] *See generally infra* § 2.01[C] (discussing controversy).

[17] Samuel R. Bagenstos, *Subordination, Stigma, and "Disability,"* 86 VA. L. REV. 397 (2000). This approach focuses on stigma and social deprivation of opportunity. *Id.* at 445–50. In later writing, Professor Bagenstos has rejected his earlier view, declaring that "Disability identity is too multifarious, society's responses to conditions identified as disabilities too diverse, for the notion of a societally created disability category to offer much traction." SAMUEL R. BAGENSTOS, LAW AND THE CONTRADICTIONS OF THE CIVIL RIGHTS MOVEMENT 50 (2009).

[18] Robert L. Burgdorf, Jr., *"Substantially Limited" Protection from Disability Discrimination: The Special Treatment Model and Misconstructions of the Definition of Disability*, 42 VILL. L. REV. 409, 449–51 (1997).

protection of the discrimination law.[19]

[C]   Role of Mitigating Measures: The *Sutton* Trilogy and the ADA Amendments Act of 2008

The ADA Amendments Act of 2008 responds to — and effectively overrules — the Supreme Court's *Sutton* trilogy. In the three 1999 cases that collectively bear that name, the Supreme Court ruled that in determining whether a person is substantially limited with regard to a major life activity, mitigating measures must be taken into account. Mitigating measures include medication, appliances, even the body's own compensating systems.

In *Sutton v. United Air Lines, Inc.*, the lead case, the defendant had denied the job of commercial airline pilot to twin sister applicants on the ground that their uncorrected vision fell below United's usual standard.[20] If the plaintiffs used eyeglasses or contact lenses, they had normal or better vision, but uncorrected their vision was 20/200 or worse in one eye and 20/400 or worse in the other.[21] The district court dismissed the complaint on the ground that the plaintiffs were not disabled under the ADA, and the Tenth Circuit affirmed the dismissal. The Supreme Court affirmed in an opinion by Justice O'Connor. After reciting the definition of qualified person with a disability, the Court pointed out that no administrative agency was given explicit authority to issue regulations interpreting the general provisions of the ADA, of which the definition is a part. Although the EEOC and Department of Justice guidelines called for disregarding corrective measures in determining of whether an impairment is substantially limiting, the Court ruled that the agencies' interpretation was not a permissible interpretation of the ADA. The Supreme Court reasoned (1) that the ADA defines disability as an impairment that substantially limits a major life activity, a present tense form denoting actual, not hypothetical limit, (2) that the ADA definition requires evaluation with respect to the individual, whereas a judging a person in an unmitigated state would not be individualized and would lead to disregard of negative side effects of the use of mitigating measures, and "critically," (3) the congressional finding of 43 million Americans with disabilities would be far too low if individuals' impairments were considered in their unmitigated state.[22] The Court concluded that with mitigating measures applied, the plaintiffs were not substantially limited in any major life activity.

---

[19] Jane Byeff Korn, *Cancer and the ADA: Rethinking Disability*, 74 S. Cal. L. Rev. 399, 449–52 (2001).

[20] 527 U.S. 471, 476 (1999).

[21] *Id.* at 475.

[22] The Court cited a National Council on Disability statistic of over 160 million Americans with disabilities if all health conditions that impair health or normal functioning are considered, and surmised that Congress applied a National Council number of 37.3 million noninstitutionalized persons over age 15 with functional limitations when using special aids, then added 5.7 million to embrace those younger and those in institutions. The Court said that the 43 million number thus reflected an understanding that persons whose impairments are corrected were not to be included as having disabilities under the ADA. By contrast, 100 million Americans have vision impairments. *Id.* at 484–86.

The Court went on to consider whether the sisters were "regarded" as having a disability, and so covered under the ADA's definition regardless of whether they actually had a disability.[23] Saying that the plaintiffs did not make the "obvious" argument that they were regarded as substantially limited in the major life activity of seeing, the Court considered whether United mistakenly believed that their impairment limited them in the major life activity of working.[24] Relying on an EEOC interpretation that with regard to working, "substantially limits" means unable to work in a broad class of jobs, the Court concluded that the allegation United considered them unable to do the single job of "global airline pilot" did not meet the regarded-as standard.

In dissent, Justice Stevens argued that under the Court's interpretation, the "record of" part of the definition would play a bizarre role: A person with a cured impairment would be covered while one with a merely treatable one would not be. He said that the various provisions of the statute read separately by the majority needed to be read together to avoid "the counterintuitive conclusion that the ADA's safeguards vanish when individuals make themselves more employable by ascertaining ways to overcome their physical and mental limitations." He would have relied on the legislative history of the definitional provision, which clearly supported an understanding that conditions are evaluated in their unmitigated state, and the administrative agencies' guidances, which took the same position. The dissent minimized the significance of the 43 million figure, saying that the number was not intended to be a cap and that the larger numbers cited by the Court for mitigated impairments in fact included many persons with impairments that are not substantially limiting.

In *Albertsons, Inc. v. Kirkingburg*, decided on the same day as *Sutton*, the Supreme Court said that "[t]hough we do not need to speak to the issue whether Kirkingburg was an individual with a disability in order to resolve this case,"[25] the lower court had been too quick to find a disability by, among other things, failing to consider whether the amblyopia[26] that the plaintiff, a truck driver, experienced, rendered him a person with a disability. The lower court acknowledged that Kirkingburg had developed unconscious mental mechanisms to cope with the monocular vision that his condition caused, but failed to consider whether in light of those mechanisms he was a person with a disability. "We see no principled basis for distinguishing between measures undertaken with artificial aids, like medications and devices, and measures undertaken, whether consciously or not, with the body's own systems." The Court nevertheless stated that a brief examination of the medical literature indicated that people with monocular vision

---

[23] The regarded-as holding is developed in greater detail *infra* § 2.04.

[24] The Court noted "some conceptual difficulty" defining working as a major life activity, suggesting that it argues in a circle to deem that exclusion from work constitutes a disability when asking whether a disability exists in the first place. *Id.* at 492. *See generally infra* § 2.02[D] (discussing work as major life activity).

[25] 527 U.S. 555, 562 (1999).

[26] Amblyopia means unequal vision in the two eyes; the plaintiff's vision of 20/200 vision in the left eye produced the effect of monocular vision, that is, vision as of only one eye. *Id.* at 559.

ordinarily will meet the ADA's definition of disability.[27]

Murphy v. United Parcel Service, Inc., also decided the same day, ruled that a mechanic terminated from his job on account of high blood pressure did not meet the definition of a person with a disability under the ADA.[28] The plaintiff's job required that he be able to drive a commercial motor vehicle, and Department of Transportation health requirements barred him from that role if he had high blood pressure; upon a retest after he was erroneously granted certification, his blood pressure exceeded the Department's standard. Nevertheless, when medicated for his blood pressure, the plaintiff had no restrictions on his activities other than that he not lift heavy objects. The Court stated that it was not considering whether the plaintiff was disabled due to limitations that persisted despite the medication or side effects of the medication. On the question on which certiorari had been granted, whether the determination if an individual's impairment "substantially limits" one or more major life activity must be made with regard to mitigating measures, the Court answered yes, and so affirmed the court of appeals' affirmance of the district court's grant of summary judgment to the defendant.[29] The Court further held that United Parcel Service did not regard the plaintiff as substantially limited in the major life activity of working, because there was no indication that he had been regarded as unable to perform any but the specific job of a mechanic who needs Department of Transportation certification for driving a commercial motor vehicle.[30]

Many scholars criticized the *Sutton* trilogy's approach to mitigating measures, emphasizing its inconsistency with the legislative history of the statute and the EEOC regulations,[31] and noting the perverse results it created when someone who mitigated an impairment fell outside the law's scope while someone who chose not to mitigate was entitled to reasonable accommodations and otherwise enjoyed rights under the law.[32] The Supreme Court was accused of creating a Catch-22 situation[33] in which someone like Murphy could be terminated from work because of his high blood pressure in its uncorrected state but could not seek the protection

---

[27] *Id.* at 565–66. The Court disposed of the case by ruling that the employer could apply a Department of Transportation requirement that truck drivers have adequate acuity in each eye and adequate binocular vision, and, as a matter of law, did not need to consider the possibility of obtaining a waiver of the requirement under the Department's experimental waiver program. *Id.* at 571.

[28] 527 U.S. 516 (1999).

[29] *Id.* at 521.

[30] *Id.* at 524.

[31] *See, e.g.*, Bonnie Poitras Tucker, *The Supreme Court's Definition of Disability Under the ADA: A Return to the Dark Ages*, 52 ALA. L. REV. 321, 325–26 (2000).

[32] *See id.* at 335–70 (discussing hypothetical case of Amy and Betty, two sisters with identical hearing impairments, one who mitigates by having cochlear implant, and one who does not).

[33] Elizabeth A. Pendo, *Substantially Limited Justice?: The Possibilities and Limits of a New Rawlsian Analysis of Disability-Based Discrimination*, 77 ST. JOHN'S L. REV. 225, 261–62 (2003) ("The trilogy also creates a 'Catch-22' — a worker with an undisputed impairment who is rejected because of that impairment has no standing to challenge the rejection if it so happens that the impairment can be mitigated or corrected. This is true even if the impairment does not affect the worker's ability to do her job. Thus, employers are free to reject fully capable workers with correctable impairments without fear of an ADA claim because those workers are not 'disabled' as defined by the Court." (footnote omitted)).

of the law because his blood pressure in its corrected state imposed no significant restrictions on his activities. Similarly, the *Sutton* plaintiffs were ruled to be too impaired to be considered for the job of commercial pilot, but were not impaired enough to challenge the validity of United's restrictions.

The ADA Amendments Act specifically disapproved the *Sutton* trilogy, declaring in the Act's findings that "the holdings of the Supreme Court in *Sutton v. United Air Lines, Inc.* . . . and its companion cases have narrowed the broad scope of protection intended to be afforded by the ADA, thus eliminating protection for many individuals whom Congress intended to protect."[34] As a purpose of the Act, Congress listed "to reject the requirement enunciated by the Supreme Court in *Sutton* . . . and its companion cases that whether an impairment substantially limits a major life activity is to be determined with reference to the ameliorative effects of mitigating measures."[35] Additional purposes are "to convey that it is the intent of Congress that the primary object of attention in cases brought under the ADA should be whether entities covered under the ADA have complied with their obligations," as well as "to convey that the question of whether an individual's impairment is a disability under the ADA should not demand extensive analysis."[36] A rule of construction has been adopted that the "definition of disability . . . shall be construed in favor of broad coverage of individuals . . . to the maximum extent permitted by the terms" of the statute.[37]

Specifically with regard to mitigating measures, the law now provides "that determination of whether an impairment substantially limits a major life activity shall be made without regard to the ameliorative effects of mitigating measures."[38] It goes on to list examples of mitigating measures to be disregarded, including medication and medical equipment,[39] assistive technology, reasonable accommodations or auxiliary aids and services, and learned behavioral or adaptive neurological modifications.[40]

The Act contains an exception for ordinary eyeglasses and contact lenses,[41] so that everyone whose vision is substantially limited without glasses is not automatically covered as a person with an actual impairment. The term "ordinary eyeglasses or contact lenses" is defined to mean "lenses that are intended to fully correct visual acuity or eliminate refractive error."[42] Low-vision devices are

---

[34] Pub. L. No. 110-325 § 2(a)(4) (2008).

[35] § 2(b)(2).

[36] § 2(b)(5). The findings and purposes of the ADA Amendments Act are codified at 42 U.S.C.S. § 12101 note (LexisNexis 2011).

[37] 42 U.S.C.S. § 12102(4)(A) (LexisNexis 2011).

[38] § 12102(4)(E)(i).

[39] The medical mitigating measures are those "such as medication, medical supplies, equipment, or appliances, low-vision devices (which do not include ordinary eyeglasses or contact lenses), prosthetics including limbs and devices, hearing aids and cochlear implants or other implantable hearing devices, mobility devices, or oxygen therapy equipment and supplies." § 12102(4)(E)(i)(I).

[40] § 12102(4)(E)(i)(II)–(IV). Auxiliary aids and services are defined at § 12103(1) and include, among other items, interpreters, readers, acquisition of equipment, and similar services and actions.

[41] § 12102(4)(E)(i)(I).

[42] § 12102(4)(E)(iii)(I).

distinguished from ordinary glasses or contact lenses and are on the list of mitigating measures to be disregarded. The term "low-vision devices" means "devices that magnify, enhance, or otherwise augment a visual image."[43]

Although the need for eyeglasses or contact lenses does not confer automatic coverage under the statute, the employment provisions of the ADA now provide that employers and other entities covered by the employment title "shall not use qualification standards, employment tests, or other selection criteria based on an individual's uncorrected vision unless the standard, test, or other selection criteria, as used by the covered entity is shown to be job-related for the position in question and consistent with business necessity."[44] Since the employment title has also been amended to ban discrimination against "a qualified individual" and not just a qualified individual with a disability,[45] a person who has no condition other than the need for corrective lenses would appear to be able to recover for employment discrimination in violation of this uncorrected-vision section of the law.

Effective January 1, 2009, the ADA Amendments Act opens up the field for disability discrimination claims by a much wider range of individuals than would have been able to sue before. It remains to be seen how much the Act will affect case results. Sources have suggested that the focus of litigation will shift to causation, that is, whether discrimination actually took place on the basis of disability, and to the question of what constitutes a reasonable accommodation.[46]

Some sources have argued that there ought to be a duty to take advantage of mitigating measures,[47] but no obligation to mitigate is found in the ADA or section 504.[48] Among the odd effects of the *Sutton* series of cases was that a person who did not use available mitigating measures for an impairment could have a greater likelihood of success in an employment discrimination suit than one who did, provided that person could perform the essential functions of the job with or without reasonable accommodations, and so meet the test for being a "qualified" individual with a disability.[49]

---

[43] § 12102(4)(E)(iii)(II).

[44] § 12113(c).

[45] § 12112(a); *see* Pub. L. No. 110-325 § 5(a)(1) (2008).

[46] On these topics, see Cheryl L. Anderson, *What is Because of Disability Under the Americans with Disabilities Act? Reasonable Accommodation, Causation, and the Windfall Doctrine*, 27 BERKELEY J. EMP. & LAB. L. 323 (2006), and Mark C. Weber, *Unreasonable Accommodation and Due Hardship*, 62 FLA. L. REV. 1119 (2010).

[47] *See* Jill Elaine Hasday, *Mitigation and the Americans with Disabilities Act*, 103 MICH. L. REV. 217 (2004) (proposing limited mitigation duty); *see also* Hooper v. St. Rose Parish, 205 F. Supp. 2d 926, 929 (N.D. Ill. 2002) (imposing duty to mitigate).

[48] *See* Nawrot v. CPC Int'l, 277 F.3d 896, 904 (7th Cir. 2002) (evaluating disability in current state when plaintiff did not mitigate).

[49] *See* Tucker, *supra* note 31, at 335–70 (discussing hypothetical case of Amy and Betty, two sisters with identical hearing impairments, one who mitigates by having cochlear implant, and one who does not).

[D] Contagious Diseases

There is no exclusion in the ADA or section 504 for persons with contagious diseases, and it is easy to imagine how these conditions could disable. In *School Board v. Arline*, a teacher with tuberculosis claimed that the school system discriminated against her in violation of section 504.[50] The district court said that Congress had not intended contagious diseases to be covered by the statute, but the court of appeals reversed, and the Supreme Court affirmed that decision. The Supreme Court found that tuberculosis met the definition of a physical impairment under the section 504 regulations, for it is a physiological disorder or condition affecting the respiratory system. The plaintiff's hospitalization was enough to establish that the impairment substantially limited one or more of her major life activities.[51]

If a person with a contagious disease may be a person with a disability, there remains the question whether that person is considered a "qualified" individual ("otherwise qualified" in the language of section 504). Being a qualified individual means meeting essential eligibility requirements with or without reasonable modifications in public services cases or being able to do the essential functions of a job with or without reasonable accommodations in employment cases.[52] The *Arline* Court said that whether the plaintiff was otherwise qualified for the position of elementary school teacher depended on an individualized inquiry and findings of fact. The Court agreed with a statement by the American Medical Association in its brief amicus curiae that in the context of employment of a person with a contagious disease, the inquiry had to include "facts, based on reasonable medical judgments . . . about (a) the nature of the risk (how the disease is transmitted), (b) the duration of the risk (how long is the carrier infectious), (c) the severity of the risk (what is the potential harm to third parties), and (d) the probabilities the disease will be transmitted and will cause varying degrees of harm."[53] The Court said that in making the findings, courts normally should defer to reasonable medical judgments by public health officials, then evaluate, in light of the medical findings, whether the employer could reasonably accommodate the employee. The Court remanded the case for the district court to determine if Arline was otherwise qualified.

---

[50] 480 U.S. 273 (1987).

[51] *Id.* at 281 ("This impairment was serious enough to require hospitalization, a fact more than sufficient to establish that one or more of her major life activities were substantially limited by her impairment. Thus, Arline's hospitalization for tuberculosis in 1957 suffices to establish that she has a "record of . . . impairment" within the meaning of 29 U.S.C.S. § 706(7)(B)(ii), and is therefore a handicapped individual.").

[52] Because questions of what is essential to a job or a program and what accommodations and modifications are considered reasonable are so central to this determination, the qualified-individual term will be discussed with the other provisions of the ADA relating specifically to employment and public services discrimination. But the *Arline* case did make comments specifically on the topic of when a person with a contagious disease is considered a qualified individual, and those comments are discussed here.

[53] *Arline*, 480 U.S. at 288 (quoting brief of American Medical Association).

After *Arline* and following the passage of the ADA, Congress created a specific exclusion of individuals with some contagious disease from coverage under section 504 in employment cases. The exclusion embodies an idea of direct threat to others or inability to perform job responsibilities. It excludes from the definition of person protected by section 504 "an individual who has a currently contagious disease or infection, and who, by reason of such disease or infection, would constitute a direct threat to the health or safety of other individuals or who, by reason of the currently contagious disease or infection, is unable to perform the duties of the job."[54]

In *Bragdon v. Abbott*, a 1998 case, the Supreme Court applied *Arline's* section 504 principles about both impairment and being a qualified individual to an ADA public accommodations claim of a person with an asymptomatic HIV infection.[55] In that case, a woman whose HIV had not yet progressed to what is termed the symptomatic phase tried to get a cavity filled from her dentist, but the dentist refused to perform the work unless she agreed to have it done at a hospital. The plaintiff won summary judgment in the district court, and the court of appeals affirmed. The Supreme Court's grant of certiorari included the question whether HIV infection is a disability under the ADA when it has not reached the symptomatic phase, and whether the record included enough material to support a grant of summary judgment on the proposition that the HIV infection posed no direct threat to the health and safety of the dentist. The Court affirmed the lower court with regard to the question whether the infection was a disability, but remanded for further consideration on the direct threat issue.

In determining that asymptomatic HIV constituted an disability, the Court applied the three step approach called for in the statute by asking: Is there a physical or mental impairment; is the life activity it limits a major one; and does the impairment substantially limit the activity? The Court reasoned first that the infection constituted a physical impairment, saying that it fit under a definition of impairment found in regulations promulgated to interpret section 504, and pointing out that the term "asymptomatic" is a misnomer due to clinical features that include migration of the infection from the circulatory to the lymphatic system and damage to infected person's white blood cells during that phase. Second, the impairment affects the life activity of reproduction, which should be considered major because of its centrality to the life process itself. Nothing in the statute limits major life activities to those of a character that is public, economic, or daily.[56]

---

[54] 29 U.S.C.S. § 705(20)(D) (LexisNexis 2011) (section 504). The ADA also includes a provision relating to contagious disease in connection with food handling, stating that when a person has an infectious or communicable disease that is transmitted though the handling of food and is included on a list developed by the Secretary of Health and Human Services, an employer may refuse to assign or continue to assign the individual to a job involving food handling if the transmission cannot be eliminated by reasonable accommodation. 42 U.S.C.S. § 12113(e)(2) (LexisNexis 2011).

[55] 524 U.S. 624 (1998).

[56] Four members of the Court dissented on that interpretation, with Chief Justice Rehnquist, joined by Justices Scalia and Thomas, emphasizing that the activity must be a major one for the relevant individual and preferring an approach that looks to activities repetitively performed and essential in the daily life of the individual, and further contending that a person with asymptomatic HIV is not substantially limited in reproduction when she can still engage in intercourse and give birth. *See id.* at 660–61 (Rehnquist, C.J. concurring in judgment in part and dissenting in part). Justice O'Connor agreed that the importance of the life activity should be evaluated individually and that reproduction was not of

The limits the impairment imposed on reproduction were substantial, because of the risk that a woman with HIV imposes on her partner and on the child if she tries to conceive. The Court noted that conception and childbirth are not impossible for someone with an HIV infection, but concluded that the danger to public health and the negative economic and legal consequences impose substantial limits. Administrative interpretations and legislative history further support the conclusion that persons with asymptomatic HIV fall under the ADA's protection.

On the direct threat defense to liability under the ADA, the Court looked to *Arline*, noting that the approach to being a qualified person that *Arline* applied to infectious disease resulted in the direct threat provision of the ADA. The Court said that a risk must be significant and must be based on medical or other objective evidence. The views of public health authorities carry special weight, but are not conclusive. The Court found two sources relied on by the lower court to carry less authority than thought, and so called for a remand.

Beyond affirming the basic proposition that an infectious disease may constitute a disability for purposes of the ADA and section 504, *Bragdon* further reinforces the three step approach courts need to apply, gives a broad reading to what is a major life activity, and demonstrates that if an impairment makes a major life activity risky, without making it physically difficult, the impairment still substantially limits the activity. Moreover, the case establishes as a matter of law that HIV infection constitutes an impairment from the moment of infection and would appear to establish that the condition is a disability for purposes of the ADA and section 504 from that moment as well. The Court's conclusion is reinforced by the amended ADA's listing of "functions of the immune system" as an operation of a major bodily function deemed to be a major life activity.[57]

[E]   Exclusion for Current Users of Illegal Drugs

The ADA[58] and the definitions applicable to section 504[59] exclude current users of illegal drugs from the definition of individuals with disabilities who are protected by those laws. Under the ADA, an illegal drug is one whose possession or distribution is unlawful under the Controlled Substances Act[60] or other provisions of federal law.[61]

---

the same character as the other activities listed in the regulations, such as caring for one's self, walking, seeing, etc. *See id.* at 664–65 (O'Connor, J., concurring in the judgment in part and dissenting in part). Both minority opinions argued that public health authorities deserved no special deference on the direct threat issue and that there was enough evidence of risk in the record to avoid summary judgment against the dentist on that issue.

[57]   42 U.S.C.S. § 12102(2)(B) (LexisNexis 2011). The ADA regulations applicable to employment state "it should easily be concluded" that HIV infection "substantially limits immune function." 29 C.F.R. § 1630.2(j)(3)(iii) (2011).

[58]   42 U.S.C.S. § 12210 (LexisNexis 2011); *see* 42 U.S.C.S. § 12114 (LexisNexis 2011) (comparable provision regarding employment).

[59]   29 U.S.C.S. § 705(20)(C)(i) (LexisNexis 2011).

[60]   21 U.S.C.S. §§ 801, et seq. (2006).

[61]   42 U.S.C.S. §§ 12111(6), 12210(d) (LexisNexis 2011); *see* 29 U.S.C.S.§ 705(10)(B) (LexisNexis 2011) (comparable provision for section 504).

Both the ADA and section 504 contain elaborate provisions barring any exclusion from coverage for persons who are no longer engaging in drug use who have completed or are engaging in a rehabilitation program, though the provisions also specifically permit reasonable drug policies, including drug testing.[62] The definition that pertains to section 504 forbids exclusion even of current drug users from services under specified programs if they are otherwise entitled to the services,[63] as does the ADA with regard to health services and, sensibly, drug rehabilitation services.[64]

Alcoholics may be covered under the law, although exclusions exist from the definitions of what constitutes illegal employer conduct with regard to persons who use alcohol. Title I of the ADA provides that covered entities may prohibit the illegal use of drugs and the use of alcohol at the workplace by all employees,[65] may require that employees not be under the influence of alcohol or be illegally using drugs at the workplace,[66] and may hold an employee who engages in the illegal use of drugs or who is an alcoholic to the same qualification standards and behavior that other employees are held to, even if the unsatisfactory performance or behavior is related to the employee's drug use or alcoholism.[67] The illegality of the conduct in the drug situation most plausibly explains the difference in protection for drug and alcohol abusers, although the difference may have more to do with the greater stigma attached to drug abuse than alcohol abuse.

Various other provisions in the ADA specifically allow employers to conform to the requirements of the Drug-Free Workplace Act,[68] and to comply with federal regulations concerning alcohol and the illegal use of drugs, specifically those established by the Department of Defense, Nuclear Regulatory Commission, and Department of Transportation for industries to which those agencies' regulations are applicable.[69] A provision in title I on drug testing states that a test to determine the illegal use of drugs is not considered a medical examination, and that the law is not to be construed to prohibit the conducting of testing for illegal use of drugs by job applicants or employees or making employment decisions based on the test results.[70]

---

[62] 42 U.S.C.S. § 12210(b) (LexisNexis 2011); *see* 29 U.S.C.S. § 705(20)(C)(ii) (LexisNexis 2011) (comparable provision for section 504).

[63] 29 U.S.C.S. § 705(20)(C)(iii) (LexisNexis 2011).

[64] 42 U.S.C.S. § 12210(c) (LexisNexis 2011).

[65] 42 U.S.C. S. § 12114(c)(1) (LexisNexis 2011).

[66] § 12114(c)(2).

[67] § 12114(c)(4). *See generally* Pernice v. City of Chicago, 237 F.3d 783 (7th Cir. 2001) (upholding discharge for use of drugs off job; collecting cases).

[68] § 12114(c)(3).

[69] § 12114(c)(5).

[70] § 12114(d). The language says that the law shall not be construed "encourage, prohibit, or authorize" the drug testing or making employment decisions based on the results of the testing. § 12114(d)(2).

[F] Other Exclusions

Whether conceptually justifiable or not, there are other exclusions from the definition of person with a disability. The ADA and section 504 provide that disability does not include homosexuality, bisexuality, transvestitism, transsexuality, pedophilia, exhibitionism, voyeurism, gender identity disorders not resulting from physical impairments, other sexual behavior disorders, compulsive gambling, kleptomania, pyromania, or psychoactive substance abuse disorders resulting from current illegal use of drugs.[71] The ADA in fact excludes transvestites twice.[72]

§ 2.02 ACTUALLY IMPAIRED

As noted above, the ADA and section 504 define a disability as a physical or mental impairment that substantially limits one or more major life activities, having a record of such an impairment, or being regarded as having such an impairment. Those persons who currently have real impairments, as opposed to those who have records of the impairments or are regarded as having the impairments, are sometimes called "actually impaired." Development of the topic of actual impairment requires explanation of each of the three terms of the definition: (1) a physical or mental impairment that (2) substantially limits (3) one or more major life activities.

[A] Physical or Mental Impairment

Regulations applicable to title I of the ADA define physical or mental impairment as:

> (1) Any physiological disorder, or condition, cosmetic disfigurement, or anatomical loss affecting one or more body systems, such as neurological, musculoskeletal, special sense organs, respiratory (including speech organs), cardiovascular, reproductive, digestive, genito-urinary, immune, circulatory, hemic, lymphatic, skin, and endocrine; or

> (2) Any mental or psychological disorder, such as an intellectual disability (formerly termed "mental retardation"), organic brain syndrome, emotional or mental illness, and specific learning disabilities.[73]

The title II and III regulations go on to specify that the phrase "includes, but is not limited to, such contagious and noncontagious diseases and conditions as orthopedic, visual, speech and hearing impairments, cerebral palsy, epilepsy,

---

[71] ADA: 42 U.S.C.S. §§ 12211(a) (LexisNexis 2011) (homosexuality and bisexuality), (b) (other conditions); section 504: 29 U.S.C.S. § 705(20)(E) (LexisNexis 2011) (homosexuality and bisexuality), (F) (other conditions).

[72] 42 U.S.C.S. §§ 12208, 12211(b)(1) (LexisNexis 2011).

[73] 29 C.F.R. § 35.1630.2(h) (2011) (EEOC title I regulations). The title II and III and section 504 regulations are similar. 28 C.F.R. § 35.104 (2011) (Department of Justice title II regulations); 28 C.F.R. § 36.104 (2011) (Department of Justice title III regulations); 29 C.F.R. § 32.3 (2011) (Department of Labor section 504 regulations).

muscular dystrophy, multiple sclerosis, cancer, heart disease, diabetes, mental retardation, emotional illness, specific learning disabilities, HIV disease (whether symptomatic or asymptomatic), tuberculosis, drug addition, and alcoholism."[74]

In *Bragdon v. Abbott*, the Supreme Court gave a broad reading to the physical impairment term by applying it to an asymptomatic HIV infection even before the regulations specifically listed the condition.[75] The Court noted the immediate and detrimental effects of having the disorder. Bisexuality and homosexuality are not considered impairments under section 504 and the ADA, and the EEOC's Interpretive Guidance on ADA title I states that impairment does not include left-handedness, height, weight, or muscle tone that are within a normal range and not the result of physiological disorder, nor pregnancy.[76]

[B] Substantially Limits

Bragdon developed the idea of substantially limits by reasoning the impairment may limit an activity because of the risk that engaging in the activity imposes on others — in the case of a woman with HIV infection, the risk that trying to engage in reproduction imposes on the man involved and on any child born from the union. The Court said that even though some technologies may lower the risk of perinatal infection to 8%, "it cannot be said as a matter of law that an 8% risk of transmitting a dread and fatal disease to one's child does not represent a substantial limit on reproduction."[77] As the Court emphasized, "The Act addresses substantial limits on major life activities, not utter inabilities."[78] The Court concluded that "the disability definition does not turn on personal choice" to engage in a major life activity. "When significant limitations result from the impairment, the definition is met even if the difficulties are not insurmountable."[79]

The Court's conclusion in *Bragdon* may seem obvious. As shown in the scene from the movie spoof *Spy Hard* that has Ray Charles driving a bus, there are many things that a person with an impairment can do, but not do safely. According to the

---

[74] 28 C.F.R. § 35.104 (2011) (Department of Justice title II regulations); 28 C.F.R. § 36.104 (2011) (Department of Justice title III regulations); *see also* 29 C.F.R. § 32.3 (similar section 504 regulation for Department of Labor).

[75] 524 U.S. 624, 632–36 (1998). The case is discussed *supra*, § 2.01[D].

[76] 29 U.S.C.S. § 705(20)(E) (LexisNexis 2011) (section 504); 42 U.S.C.S. § 12211(a) (LexisNexis 2011) (ADA); ADA Title I EEOC Interpretive Guidance, 29 C.F.R. pt. 1630, app. § 1630.2(h) (2011). The Guidance further states that "a pregnancy-related impairment that substantially limits a major life activity is a disability under the first prong of the definition," or may constitute a record of impairment or cause coverage under the regarded-as provision. Obesity has generally not been considered a disability under the ADA, *see, e.g.,* EEOC v. Watkins Motor Lines, 463 F.3d 436 (6th Cir. 2006) (holding that non-physiological morbid obesity does not constitute impairment under ADA), but that position is subject to question after the ADA Amendments Act, *see* Lowe v. Am. Eurocopter, LLC, No. 1:10CV24-A-D, 2010 U.S. Dist. LEXIS 133343 (N.D. Miss. Dec. 16, 2010) (denying motion to dismiss in ADA case brought by overweight individual). Even before the ADA Amendments Act, some sources argued that obesity should be considered at least a perceived disability. *See, e.g.,* Jane Byeff Korn, *Fat,* 77 B.U. L. Rev. 25 (1997).

[77] *Bragdon,* 524 U.S. at 641.

[78] *Id.*

[79] *Id.*

Arline majority, those limits need to be considered in determining who meets the definition of a person with a disability. Chief Justice Rehnquist, however, ascribed the decision not to engage in the risky action to personal choice, rather than disability. He stated: "While individuals infected with HIV may choose not to engage in [reproductive] activities, there is no support in language, logic, or our case law for the proposition that such voluntary choices constitute a 'limit' on one's own life activities."[80]

Although *Bragdon* fits well with the ADA Amendments Act, much of the rest of the pre-Amendments caselaw does not. In *Albertson's, Inc. v. Kirkingburg*, the case involving the truck driver with monocular vision, the Court made comments about what "substantially limits" means.[81] The Court, following an EEOC interpretation, required significant restriction, rather than simple difference in how an activity is performed.[82] In *Toyota Motor Manufacturing v. Williams*, the Supreme Court expanded on the interpretation in *Albertson's* by citing dictionary definitions of "substantially" to denote "considerable" or "to a large degree" and by insisting that the ADA requires a strict reading of the term.[83]

The ADA Amendments Act says that "the term 'substantially limits' shall be interpreted consistently with the findings and purposes" of that Act.[84] The findings state that *Toyota* incorrectly narrowed the scope of the ADA's protection, and in particular, it "interpreted the term 'substantially limits' to require a greater degree of limitation than was intended by Congress."[85] The findings in the Act also disapprove the then-current EEOC regulations defining substantially limits as "significantly restricted," saying that standard was too high.[86] The purposes include rejecting the Supreme Court's position in *Toyota* that the terms "substantially" and "major" need to be interpreted strictly to create a demanding standard of disability.[87] The purposes section further rejected *Toyota*'s use of the phrase "prevents or severely restricts." *Toyota* was declared to have "created an inappropriately high level of limitation" when interpreting "substantially limits."[88]

The EEOC's regulations for the employment title of the ADA follow the ADA Amendment Act's text by saying that substantially limits must be construed broadly in favor of expansive coverage; that the term is not meant to be a demanding standard; that an impairment need not prevent, or significantly or severely restrict the individual from performing a major life activity; and that substantially limits shall be interpreted and applied to require a degree of functional limitation that is lower than the standard applied before the ADA

---

[80] *Id.* at 661 (Rehnquist, C.J., concurring in judgment in part and dissenting in part).

[81] Albertson's, Inc. v. Kirkingburg, 527 U.S. 555 (1999).

[82] *Id.* at 565.

[83] 534 U.S. 184, 196–97 (2002). This case is discussed at greater length *infra* § 2.02[C].

[84] 42 U.S.C.S. § 12102(4)(B) (LexisNexis 2011).

[85] Pub. L. No. 110-325, § 2(a)(7) (2008).

[86] § 2(a)(8).

[87] § 2(b)(4).

[88] § 2(b)(5).

Amendments Act.[89] Nevertheless, "not every impairment will constitute a disability within the meaning of this section."[90] For coverage under the regarded-as part of the disability definition, the impairment need not substantially limit a major life activity at all.[91]

Nothing in the ADA or section 504 definitional provisions specifies a minimum duration that the disabling condition has to last to cause a person to be protected by the law. The ADA Amendments Act excludes impairments that are transitory and minor from consideration under the regarded-as having a disability prong of the Act's definition, but this provision does not apply to actual disability or record of disability, and the EEOC's regulations on employment say just that.[92] The EEOC's comments to the regulations state that even before the Amendments, the Commission took the view that several months duration would be sufficient for an impairment to substantially limit a major life activity, and six months is longer than what the Commission had previously required or what Congress intended in the Amendments; the Commission emphasized that duration is only one factor in determining if an impairment substantially limits a major life activity, and impairments lasting only a short period may be sufficient if severe enough.[93] In a 2002 case decided under the employment provisions of the ADA, the Supreme Court commented that in order for a person to be an individual with a disability under the Act, the impact of the person's impairment must be permanent or long-term, but this case is one that was specifically disapproved in the ADA Amendments Act findings and purposes.[94] The ADA Amendments Act also provides that an impairment that is episodic or in remission is a disability if it substantially limits a major life activity when it is active.[95]

If at least some restriction of a major life activity is still required for coverage under the actual-impairment part of the disability definition, the question becomes restriction in comparison to what. Is it a restriction from the individual's previous abilities to perform the activity, or perhaps a restriction in comparison to other persons who perform the activity in the same job or some other relevant set of individuals? The EEOC regulation pertaining to the employment title of the ADA states "An impairment is a disability within the meaning of this section if it substantially limits the ability of an individual to perform a major life activity as compared to most people in the general population."[96] Many courts have applied

---

[89] 29 C.F.R. § 1630.2(j)(1) (2011).

[90] § 1630.2(j)(1)(ii).

[91] § 1630.2(j)(2).

[92] 29 C.F.R. § 1630.2(j)(2))(ix) (2011) ("The six-month 'transitory' part of the 'transitory and minor' exception to 'regarded as' coverage in § 1630.15(f) does not apply to the definition of 'disability' under paragraphs (g)(1)(i) (the 'actual disability' prong) or (g)(1)(ii) (the 'record of' prong) of this section. The effects of an impairment lasting or expected to last fewer than six months can be substantially limiting within the meaning of this section.").

[93] 76 Fed. Rev. 16982 (Mar. 25, 2011).

[94] Toyota Motor Mfg. v. Williams, 534 U.S. 184, 198 (2002); see ADA Amendments Act of 2008, Pub. L. No. 110-325 § 2(a)(5)(b)(4)–(5).

[95] 42 U.S.C.S. § 12102(4)(D) (LexisNexis 2011).

[96] 29 C.F.R. § 1630.2(j)(1)(ii) (2011).

this comparison-to-the-general-population approach even in cases outside the reach of title I of the ADA. For example, in *Wong v. Regents of the University of California*, the Ninth Circuit Court of Appeals ruled that a medical student with learning disabilities was unable to show that the impairment substantially limited the major life activities of learning or reading.[97] The court noted the student's record of success in previous schooling without accommodations and said that he could not be considered significantly restricted in those activities in comparison to the general population. The medical student read at an eighth grade level under time constraints, but his comprehension was at the 99.5 percentile when he was allowed to read without time limits.[98] The dissent pointed out that the majority's approach would exclude from the protection of the ADA large numbers of persons with learning disabilities who read or otherwise learn at a satisfactory level in comparison to the general population but whose impairments restrict them significantly in comparison to students in the same educational program.[99] Thus students like Wong who can benefit dramatically from simple accommodations such as untimed tests never gain the protection of the law that permits them to demand the accommodations. Despite the arguments of the *Wong* dissent, many courts employed general population comparisons even in cases not covered by title I of the ADA.[100]

The EEOC's current Interpretive Guidance to the employment regulations disapproves *Wong* and similar cases, but without rejecting the use of comparisons to the general population.[101] It states that "someone with a learning disability may achieve a high level of academic success but may nevertheless be substantially limited in the major life activity of learning because of the additional time or effort he or she must spend to read, write, or learn compared to most people in the general population."[102] This approach is consistent with the regulations' general approach to "substantially limits." The regulations say that "in determining whether an individual is substantially limited in a major life activity, it may be useful in appropriate cases to consider, as compared to most people in the general population, the condition under which the individual performs the major life activity; the manner in which the individual performs the major life activity; and/or the duration of time it takes the individual to perform the major life activity, or for which the individual can perform the major life activity."[103] Relevant considerations include: difficulty, effort, time taken, pain experienced, and effects on major bodily functions.[104] The focus should be on how the activity is substantially limited and

---

[97] 410 F.3d 1052 (9th Cir. 2005).

[98] *Id.* at 1066.

[99] *Id.* at 1071 (Thomas, J., dissenting).

[100] *Compare* Betts v. Rector & Visitors of the Univ. of Va., 113 F. Supp. 2d 970 (W.D. Va. 2000) (comparing to general population), *and* Gonzalez v. National Bd. of Med. Exam'rs, 60 F. Supp. 2d 703 (E.D. Mich. 1999) (same), *with* Vinson v. Thomas, 288 F.3d 1145 (9th Cir. 2002) (not employing general population comparison).

[101] ADA Title I EEOC Interpretive Guidance, 29 C.F.R. pt. 1630, app. § 1630.2(j)(4) (2011).

[102] *Id.*

[103] 29 C.F.R. § 1630.2(j)(4)(i) (2011).

[104] § 1630.2(j)(4)(ii).

not on the outcomes achieved by additional effort in comparison to most people in the general population.[105]

In keeping with the ADA Amendment Act's purpose to convey "the intent of Congress that the primary object of attention in cases brought under the ADA should be whether entities covered under the ADA have complied with their obligations, and to convey that the question of whether an individual's impairment is a disability under the ADA should not demand extensive analysis,"[106] the EEOC's employment regulations contain a helpful list of types of impairments for which "it should easily be concluded" that they will substantially limit major life activities. These include deafness, blindness, intellectual disability (formerly termed mental retardation), partially or completely missing limbs or mobility impairments requiring the use of wheelchair, autism, cancer, cerebral palsy, diabetes, epilepsy, HIV infection, multiple sclerosis, muscular dystrophy, major depressive disorder, bipolar disorder, and schizophrenia.[107]

[C]　Major Life Activities

The ADA does not have a definition of major life activities, but as a result of the ADA Amendments Act it now has two lists of activities that are considered major life activities "in general" and with regard to major bodily functions. The general list draws in part from earlier EEOC employment regulations and includes, "but is not limited to . . . caring for oneself, performing manual tasks, seeing, hearing, eating, sleeping, walking, standing, lifting, bending, speaking, breathing, learning, reading, concentrating, thinking, communicating, and working."[108] The current EEOC employment regulation adds sitting, reaching, and interacting with others.[109]

A signal change in the law's approach to major life activities is the addition in the statute of a list of major bodily functions that are deemed to be major life activities. These include, but are not limited to, "functions of the immune system, normal cell growth, digestive, bowel, bladder, neurological, brain, respiratory, circulatory, endocrine, and reproductive functions."[110] The employment regulation adds functions of special sense organs and skin, and genitourinary, cardiovascular, hemic, lymphatic, and musculoskeletal functions.[111]

In *Bragdon v. Abbott*, the ADA title III case in which the dentist refused to fill the cavity of the patient with HIV, the Court had to determine whether the patient's infection substantially limited any major life activity.[112] The Court ruled that even asymptomatic HIV substantially limits the major life activity of

---

[105]　§ 1630.2(j)(4)(iii).

[106]　Pub. L. No. 110-325 § 2(b)(5)(2008).

[107]　29 C.F.R. § 1630.2(j)(3)(iii) (2011).

[108]　42 U.S.C.S. § 12102(2)(A) (LexisNexis 2011).

[109]　29 C.F.R. § 1630.2(i)(1)(i) (2011).

[110]　42 U.S.C.S. § 12102(2)(B) (LexisNexis 2011).

[111]　29 C.F.R. § 1630.2(i)(1)(ii) (2011).

[112]　524 U.S. 624 (1998).

reproduction. The majority said it had little difficulty concluding that reproduction is a major life activity. "Reproduction and the sexual dynamics surrounding it are central to the life process itself."[113] The Court rejected the argument that the ADA's term covers only aspects of life that have a public, economic, or daily character. The dissent responded that the major life activity had to be that of the individual in the case at hand and insisted that the meaning of "major" in the statute refers to frequency of the activity rather than its importance.[114] The majority preferred to take a more inclusive approach, one that employed a common sense definition of the term. Neither the majority nor the dissent required that the major life activity affected by the impairment have anything to do with the discrimination alleged in the case. The major life activity of human reproduction need not have any relationship to the refusal to perform dental work. The definition provision merely permits a person to claim protection from the law.

In *Toyota Motor Manufacturing v. Williams*, which the ADA Amendments Act disapproves, the Supreme Court gave a restrictive meaning to the major life activity of performing manual tasks and what it is to have substantial limits on that activity.[115] The Court overturned a direction to grant partial summary judgment to an automotive worker on her claim that she met the definition of person with a disability on the ground that she had impairments that substantially limited her major life activity of performing manual tasks.[116] Williams had carpal tunnel syndrome and other orthopedic difficulties that prevented her from lifting more than 20 pounds or frequently lifting or carrying objects up to 10 pounds, repetitively extending or flexing her wrists or elbows, or doing overhead work. After a recasting of duties of workers in her unit, she was assigned to spread oil on new cars with a sponge attached to a block of wood and inspect the finish for flaws. This required her to hold her hands and arms at shoulder height for hours at a time, and she developed inflammation of the muscles and tendons around both shoulder blades and in her forearms as well as nerve irritation and a back condition leading to pain in her arms. She requested an accommodation to return to her previous duties on the unit, which did not entail the oil-spreading job. Eventually, she was discharged. The trial court granted the employer's summary judgment motion on the ground that Williams could not show that the she was substantially limited in any major life activity, but the court of appeals ruled that she should have been found disabled on the ground that her impairment substantially limited the major life activity of performing manual tasks.

The Supreme Court commented that, " 'Major life activities'. . . refers to those activities that are of central importance to daily life."[117] If performing manual tasks were to fit into the same category as walking, seeing, and hearing (all major life

---

[113] *Id.* at 638.

[114] *Id.* at 660 (Rehnquist, C.J., dissenting).

[115] 534 U.S. 184 (2002).

[116] *Id.* at 202. The Court refused to reinstate the district court's grant of summary judgment in favor of Toyota on the issue of whether Williams was disabled, saying the question was not properly before it. *Id.* at 202–03.

[117] *Id.* at 197.

activities listed in the EEOC regulations),[118] the manual tasks had to be those central to daily life, with the tasks considered either together or separately. The Court insisted that the Act's definitional "terms need to be interpreted strictly to create a demanding standard for qualifying as disabled," citing, as it had in *Sutton*, the congressional finding that 43 million Americans have disabilities, rather than some larger number that might have less severe impairments.[119] The Supreme Court held that the court of appeals erred by focusing on the class of manual activities associated only with the job Williams performed. Manual tasks specific to any given job are not necessarily those that are important parts of most people's lives. The lower court should not have disregarded evidence that Williams could perform household and personal chores and tend to her own hygiene when "household chores, bathing, and brushing one's teeth are among the types of manual tasks of central importance to people's daily lives, and should have been part of the assessment of whether respondent was substantially limited in performing manual tasks."[120] The Court said that the evidence that Williams avoided sweeping, quit dancing, occasionally needed help dressing, and reduced how often she played with her children, gardened, and drove long distances did not establish a manual-task disability as a matter of law. The Court reversed the grant of partial summary judgment in favor of the worker and remanded for further proceedings.

The ADA Amendments Act rejected the Supreme Court's approach to major life activities in *Toyota*,[121] and the EEOC's employment regulation emphasizes that in determining other examples of major life activities, "major" is not to be "interpreted strictly to create a demanding standard for disability," and whether an activity is a major life activity "is not determined by reference to whether it is of central importance to daily life."[122]

[D]   Major Life Activity of Working

In *Sutton v. United Air Lines*, the Court discussed the major life activity of working, which was listed and described in the then-current EEOC regulations, but not actually included in the ADA's list of major life activities:

> To be substantially limited in the major life activity of working, . . . one must be precluded from more than one type of job, a specialized job, or a particular job of choice. If jobs utilizing an individual's skills (but perhaps not his or her unique talents) are available, one is not precluded from a substantial class of jobs. Similarly, if a host of different types of jobs are

---

[118] The Court assumed without deciding that the EEOC title I regulations interpreting the definition of disability applied and also cited interpretations of the Rehabilitation Act that Congress had relied on in drafting the ADA. The Court noted, as it had in *Sutton v. United Air Lines*, that the EEOC was never given explicit authority to interpret the definitional terms of the Act that are not found in title I. *Id.* at 194 (citing *Sutton*, 527 U.S. at 479).

[119] *Id.* at 197.

[120] *Id.* at 202.

[121] Pub. L. No. 110-325 § 2(b)(4) (2008).

[122] 29 C.F.R. § 1630.2(i)(2) (2011).

available, one is not precluded from a broad range of jobs.[123]

The Court applied its interpretation by holding that United Air Lines could not be said to have regarded the plaintiffs as having an impairment that substantially limited them in the major life activity of working when they alleged only that the defendant regarded their poor vision as keeping them from holding the position of "global airline pilot." The Court said that this was a single job, and that other positions using the plaintiffs' skills, such as regional pilot and pilot instructor, remained available. Thus the plaintiffs were not regarded as having an impairment that substantially limited the major life activity of work.[124] Similarly, in *Murphy v. United Parcel Service*, another case in the *Sutton* trilogy, the Court said that when the employer regarded the plaintiff as unable to obtain Department of Transportation certification as a mechanic who drives commercial motor vehicles, it could not be said to have regarded him as substantially limited in the major life activity of working.[125]

In her majority opinion in *Sutton*, Justice O'Connor expressed skepticism about whether working should be considered a major life activity for purposes of the ADA disability definition. She said that "there may be some conceptual difficulty in defining 'major life activities' to include work, for it seems 'to argue in a circle to say that if one is excluded, for instance, by reason of [an impairment, from working with others] . . . then that exclusion constitutes an impairment, when the question you're asking is, whether the exclusion itself is by reason of handicap.' "[126]

Nevertheless, the response might be made that working is obviously a major life activity in that it is what most adults spend vast amounts of their time doing and, generally speaking, cannot survive without doing. Working is thus of central importance to daily life, which is the test of a major life activity imposed by Justice O'Connor's opinion for the Court in *Toyota*.

In keeping with its effort to wholly displace *Sutton*'s approach to defining disability, the ADA Amendments Act explicitly includes working as a major life activity. The EEOC for its part has kept working in the regulations' list of major life activities, and it has removed the more elaborate discussion of working that was previously in the regulations, thus signaling that working will be treated the same as any other major life activity. The Interpretive Guidance comments that an individual may demonstrate a substantial limit on working by showing that an impairment "substantially limits his or her ability to perform a class of jobs or broad range of jobs in various classes as compared to most people having comparable training, skills, and abilities." The standard is supposed to be lower than before the Amendments, and the determination should not require extensive assessment.

---

[123] 527 U.S. 471, 492 (1999). The Court said it was not determining the validity of the EEOC regulations on the topic, because both sides accepted working as a major life activity. *Id.*

[124] *Id.* at 493. *See generally supra* § 2.02[B] (summarizing point in discussing definition of "substantially limits").

[125] 527 U.S. 516 (1999).

[126] 527 U.S. 471, 492 (1999) (quoting transcript of oral argument in School Bd. v. Arline, 480 U.S. 273 (1987)); *see also Toyota*, 534 U.S. at 200 (2002) ("Because of the conceptual difficulties inherent in the argument that working could be a major life activity, we have been hesitant to hold as much, and we need not decide this difficult question today.").

Nevertheless, "[d]emonstrating a substantial limitation in performing the unique aspects of a single specific job is not sufficient to establish that a person is substantially limited in the major life activity of working." The Guidance also comments that given the expanded definition of disability, the major life activity of working "will be used only in very targeted situations," since "impairments that substantially limit a person's ability work usually substantially limit one or more other major life activities."[127]

§ 2.03   RECORD OF AN IMPAIRMENT

The term disability includes not only an actual, current impairment that substantially limits a major life activity, but also a record of such and impairment and being regarded as having such an impairment.[128] In *School Board v. Arline*, discussed above in connection with contagious diseases, the Supreme Court declared that the plaintiff's tuberculosis "was serious enough to result in her hospitalization, a fact more than sufficient to establish that one or more of her major activities were substantially limited by her impairment."[129] According to the Court, "Arline's hospitalization for tuberculosis in 1957 suffices to establish that she has a 'record of . . . impairment' within the meaning of [the definition applicable to section 504], and is therefore a handicapped individual."[130] Even after *Arline*, however, courts were reluctant to permit any impairment that has ever resulted in the individual's hospitalization to support a claim of having a record of an impairment that substantially limits a major life activity.[131] Nevertheless, a number of cases have applied the record-of provision to uphold claims of disability.[132]

---

[127] ADA Title I EEOC Interpretive Guidance, 29 C.F.R. pt. 1630, app. § 1630.2(j) (2011).

[128] 42 U.S.C.S. § 12102(1)(B)–(C) (LexisNexis 2011); *see* 29 U.S.C.S. § 705(9)(B) (LexisNexis 2011) (provision applicable to section 504 adopting ADA definition of disability).

[129] 480 U.S. 273, 281 (1987).

[130] *Id.* The tension between this rule and the rule in the *Sutton* cases that an impairment should be evaluated in its mitigated state is apparent. Perhaps not everyone whose medication, appliances, or bodily systems mitigate an otherwise substantially limiting impairment has a record of the impairment before it was mitigated, but many do. The plaintiff in *Murphy v. United Parcel Service, Inc.*, 527 U.S. 516 (1999), could certainly have argued that the history of his high blood pressure reading prior to medication was a record of an impairment that substantially limited a major life activity. In fact, it would appear that the *Sutton* plaintiffs themselves must have had a record of their poor vision before it was corrected, placing them squarely under the statute due to the record-of provision.

[131] *See, e.g.*, Sorenson v. University of Utah Hosp., 194 F.3d 1084 (10th Cir. 1999); Cowell v. Suffolk County Police Dep't, 158 F.3d 635 (2d Cir. 1998); Taylor v. United States Postal Serv., 946 F.2d 1214 (6th Cir. 1991). *But see* EEOC v. R.J. Gallagher Co., 181 F.3d 645 (5th Cir. 1999) (relying on factors including thirty-day hospitalization to support inference that record of cancer now in remission constituted record of impairment substantially limiting major life activity). A brief hospitalization may indicate only a temporary limit on major life activities, something that courts have been reluctant to consider a substantial limit. *See supra* § 2.01[D] (discussing temporary impairments).

[132] *See, e.g.*, MX Group v. City of Covington, 293 F.3d 326 (6th Cir. 2002) (finding that methadone users met disability definition under record of impairment of drug addiction); Davidson v. Midelfort Clinic, Ltd., 133 F.3d 499 (7th Cir. 1998) (finding no current actual disability but holding that plaintiff could be considered disabled on basis of record of impairment with regard to her attention deficit disorder).

The ADA Amendments Act did not change the record-of provision, and the EEOC's current employment regulations add only that "[a]n individual has a record of a disability if the individual has a history of, or has been misclassified as having, a mental or physical impairment that substantially limits one or more major activities."[133] The regulation goes on to state that whether a person "has a record of an impairment that substantially limited a major life activity is to be construed broadly to the maximum extent permitted by the ADA and should not demand extensive analysis."[134] By covering impairments that are episodic or in remission, and by giving consideration to impairments in their unmitigated state, the ADA Amendments Act brings under the protection of the ADA's actual impairment category a significant number of persons who might previously have been forced to argue they had a record of impairment.

An individuals who is covered under the record-of provision is entitled to reasonable accommodations. The EEOC regulation gives the example of an employee with an impairment that previously limited a major life activity who may need a leave or schedule change for follow-up medical appointments or monitoring.[135]

§ 2.04 REGARDED AS HAVING AN IMPAIRMENT

Being regarded as having an impairment that substantially limits a major life activity makes a person an individual with a disability for the ADA and section 504.[136] Moreover, a person meets that standard if subjected to an action prohibited by the ADA because of an actual or perceived physical or mental impairment, whether or not the impairment limits or is perceived to limit a major life activity, unless the impairment is transitory and minor.[137] Thus the "substantially limits" requirement disappears in regarded-as situations.

The EEOC title I regulation aids in understanding the term by saying that the following principles apply to the regarded-as prong:

(1) Except as provided in § 1630.15(f), an individual is "regarded as having such an impairment" if the individual is subjected to a prohibited action because of an actual or perceived physical or mental impairment, whether or not that impairment substantially limits, or is perceived to substantially limit, a major life activity. Prohibited actions include but are not limited to refusal to hire, demotion, placement on involuntary leave, termination, exclusion for failure to meet a qualification standard, harassment, or denial of any other term, condition, or privilege of employment.

(2) Except as provided in § 1630.15(f), an individual is "regarded as

---

[133] 29 C.F.R. § 1630.2(k)(1) (2011).

[134] § 1630.2(k)(2).

[135] § 1630.2(k)(3).

[136] 42 U.S.C.S. § 12102(1)(C) (LexisNexis 2011); see 29 U.S.C.S. § 705(20)(B) (LexisNexis 2011) (provision applicable to section 504 adopting ADA definition of disability).

[137] 42 U.S.C.S. § 12102(3) (LexisNexis 2011).

having such an impairment" any time a covered entity takes a prohibited action against the individual because of an actual or perceived impairment, even if the entity asserts, or may or does ultimately establish, a defense to such action.

(3)   Establishing that an individual is "regarded as having such an impairment" does not, by itself, establish liability. Liability is established under title I of the ADA only when an individual proves that a covered entity discriminated on the basis of disability within the meaning of section 102 of the ADA, 42 U.S.C.S. 12112.[138]

The coverage of persons who are regarded as having disabilities stems from congressional concern over mistaken beliefs, fears, myths, and prejudices that can be as disabling as actual impairments. Examples of individuals protected by this provision include those falsely believed to have disabling conditions or who have conditions falsely believed to be disabling. There are conditions may cause no limit on life activities at all, but may trigger negative reactions in bosses or others, such as having skin graft scars or other disfigurements. The EEOC Interpretive Guidance comments that "[c]overage under the 'regarded as' prong of the definition of disability should not be difficult to establish," and goes on to say that the underlying claim need not be complicated to present even though the claimant must show discrimination on the basis of an actual or perceived impairment:

> The fact that the "regarded as" prong requires proof of causation in order to show that a person is covered does not mean that proving a "regarded as" claim is complex. While a person must show, for both coverage under the "regarded as" prong and for ultimate liability, that he or she was subjected to a prohibited action because of an actual or perceived impairment, this showing need only be made once. Thus, evidence that a covered entity took a prohibited action because of an impairment will establish coverage and will be relevant in establishing liability, although liability may ultimately turn on whether the covered entity can establish a defense.[139]

In *Sutton v. United Air Lines*, the Supreme Court said that the original ADA established "two apparent ways" in which persons are considered individuals with disabilities under the regarded-as provision: "(1) a covered entity mistakenly believes that a person has a physical impairment that substantially limits one or more major life activities, or (2) a covered entity mistakenly believes that an actual, nonlimiting impairment substantially limits one or more major life activities."[140] The Court said that in both cases the defendant had to have misperceptions about the individual, either with respect to the existence of the impairment or the substantially limiting effect of the impairment. Applying these interpretations to the facts of the case, the Court noted that there was no dispute that the plaintiffs had an impairment, rather the dispute was whether the defendant mistakenly

---

[138] 29 C.F.R. § 1630.2(*l*) (2011). Section 1630.15(f) states that when the individual claims disability under the regarded-as prong of the definition, a respondent may assert the defense that the impairment or perceived impairment is "transitory and minor." *See infra* this section (discussing defense).

[139] ADA Title I EEOC Interpretive Guidance, 29 C.F.R. pt. 1630, app. § 1630.2(l) (2011).

[140] 527 U.S. 471, 489 (1999).

believed that the impairment substantially limited a major life activity. Because the only major life activity that the plaintiffs relied upon was that of working, the Court focused on whether United regarded them as substantially limited in working because of their visual impairments. The Court stressed that under the ADA, an employer may prefer job applicants with some physical or mental characteristics over others (if searching for manual laborers, it may choose the brawniest or if searching for professors it may choose the brainiest), as long as it does not discriminate on the basis of a person's having an impairment that substantially limits a major life activity. The Court went from that observation to the make the point, discussed above, that if the employer is said to regard the plaintiff as substantially limited in the major life activity of working, the substantial limit must mean unable to work in a broad class of jobs, not just a single one. Because there was no evidence United believed the plaintiffs unable to perform any job but the single one of global airline pilot, the regarded-as argument failed under the law as it stood at the time.[141]

In *Sutton*, the plaintiffs relied only on being regarded as having limits on working. As the Court said, the plaintiffs did not make the "obvious" argument that United regarded their impairments as substantially limiting the major life activity of seeing.[142] Had they done so, the result in the case may well have been different. The *Sutton* Court's comment about the employer's freedom to reject applicants or employees with some physical characteristics short of disability (the less brawny or less brainy) suggests that it was worried that an interpretation allowing inferences to be based on a decision about the single job applied for or discharged from would lead to an excessive number of claims by persons with lesser physical or mental abilities than others but not with the impairments — real or only in the view of the employer — that fit the Court's own view of what a disability is. The result, however, was the need on the part of the plaintiff to make an elaborate effort to prove the state of the defendant's mind with regard to the plaintiff's characteristics and show what the dynamic was between that mental state and the availability of employment in the relevant job market. The ADA Amendments Act and the current EEOC regulations eliminate the problems the Court's interpretation created.

The regarded-as provision does not apply to impairments that are transitory and minor, with transitory being defined as having an actual or expected duration of six months or less.[143] The EEOC's employment regulations frame this exception as a defense, providing that "It may be a defense to a charge of discrimination by an individual claiming coverage under the 'regarded as' prong of the definition . . . that the impairment is (in the case of an actual impairment) or would be (in the case of a perceived impairment) 'transitory and minor.' " In order to establish the defense, the employer or other respondent must demonstrate that the impairment is both transitory and minor, and that question is to be viewed objectively, not simply by showing that the respondent subjectively believed the impairment was transitory and minor.[144]

---

[141] *Id.* at 493.

[142] *Sutton*, 527 U.S. at 490.

[143] 42 U.S.C.S. § 12102(3)(B) (LexisNexis 2011).

[144] 29 C.F.R. § 1630.15(f) (2011).

When adding the new regarded-as provisions, Congress codified caselaw establishing that persons protected under the statute solely by virtue of being regarded as having a disability are not entitled to reasonable accommodations.[145] Although many courts took this position, it is not entirely logical.[146] Take the example of the person with skin graft scars or other disfigurements. It would strike many as a form of disability discrimination if an employer refused to make an exception to a requirement that all workers wear a uniform that left affected parts of the worker's body uncovered when the individual would prefer them to be covered, as with long sleeves rather than short, or a higher neckline, or trousers rather than a skirt. If the person claims statutory coverage solely on the basis of the regarded-as part of the definition, however, he or she would be not be able to demand the accommodation. Nonetheless, many such individuals will be protected as well under the actual impairment or record of impairment parts of the definition, and in that case, they may demand reasonable accommodations.

§ 2.05 QUALIFIED INDIVIDUAL

Title I of the ADA protects "qualified" individuals[147] Title II (the state and local government services title) and section 504 cover "qualified" and "otherwise qualified" individuals with disabilities, respectively.[148] For title I, the employment title, a qualified individual is one "who, with or without reasonable accommodation, can perform the essential functions of the employment position that such individual holds or desires."[149] For title II, a qualified individual is one "who, with or without reasonable modifications to rules, policies, or practices, the removal of architectural, communication, or transportation barriers, or the provision of auxiliary aids and services meets the essential eligibility requirements for the receipt of services or the participation in programs or activities provided by a public entity."[150] The Department of Labor regulations under section 504 embody similar definitions.[151] Because the definition of qualified entails consideration of what accommodations and rules modifications are reasonable at work and in governmental services, a more thorough discussion of the meaning of qualified individual will be deferred to the chapters specifically devoted to titles I and II. Nevertheless, the Supreme Court provided general guidance on the topic of who is qualified in a very early section 504 case, *Southeastern Community College v. Davis*,[152] and that case merits discussion

---

[145] 42 U.S.C.S. § 12201(h) (LexisNexis 2011); *see* 29 C.F.R. § 1630.2(o)(4) (2011) (employment regulation). Cases on the issue were in conflict, though the no-accommodations cases appeared to predominate. *Compare* Weber v. Strippit, Inc., 186 F.3d 907 (8th Cir. 1999) (no accommodations), *with* D'Angelo v. ConAgra Foods, Inc., 422 F.3d 1220 (11th Cir. 2005) (accommodations required).

[146] *See* Lawrence D. Rosenthal, *Reasonable Accommodations for Individuals Regarded as Having Disabilities Under the Americans with Disabilities Act? Why "No" Should Not Be the Answer*, 36 SETON HALL L. REV. 895 (2006).

[147] 42 U.S.C.S. § 12112(a) (LexisNexis 2011).

[148] 42 U.S.C.S § 12132 (LexisNexis 2011) (ADA title II); 29 U.S.C.S. § 794 (2006).

[149] 42 U.S.C.S. § 12111(8) (LexisNexis 2011).

[150] 42 U.S.C. § 12131 (2006).

[151] 29 C.F.R. § 32.3 (2011).

[152] 442 U.S. 397 (1979).

here.

Davis involved a student with a serious hearing disability who used lipreading to communicate. A community college denied her admission to its registered nurse training program, and the Supreme Court upheld a decision in favor of the college on her claim under section 504. The Court relied on evidence that it would be impossible for the student to participate safely in the normal clinical training program (as in situations when doctors and nurses wear facial masks), and that to adjust the program would keep her from education that met the objectives of the program. The Court rejected the view of the court of appeals that qualified means meeting all of the requirements of a program except those imposed by the disability, saying that necessary physical requirements may be imposed: "An otherwise qualified person is one who is able to meet all of a program's requirements in spite of his handicap."[153]

This Court's statement, of course, must itself be qualified. Although the individual must be able to perform the essential functions of a job or meet the essential eligibility requirements of a program, the person need not be able to perform or meet non-essential or peripheral functions and requirements: the *Davis* Court referred to "necessary physical qualifications."[154] Moreover, the performance or satisfaction of requirements may be done with reasonable accommodations. *Davis* said that deletion of the clinical portions of the nursing program would be "a fundamental alteration in the nature of a program," something "far more than the 'modification' that the [applicable] regulation requires,"[155] but commented that "situations may arise where a refusal to modify an existing program might become unreasonable and discriminatory."[156] In subsequent case law, the Supreme Court read *Davis* to have defined "qualified" as being able to meet essential standards with the provision of reasonable accommodations.[157] This understanding was written into the language of the ADA, and further reinforces the conclusion that the "qualified" term of the law cannot be understood without analyzing the duty to provide reasonable accommodation in the context of the case.[158]

---

[153] *Id.* at 406. The then-current version of section 504 used the term "handicap" rather than disability, and the word is still found in some section 504 regulatory provisions.

[154] *Id.* at 407.

[155] *Id.* at 410.

[156] *Id.* at 412–13.

[157] *See* School Bd. v. Arline, 480 U.S. 273, 287 n.17 (1987); Alexander v. Choate, 469 U.S. 287, 300–01 & n.20 (1985).

[158] *See Choate*, 469 U.S. at 300 n.19 ("[T]he question of who is 'otherwise qualified' and what actions constitute 'discrimination' under the section would seem to be two sides of a single coin; the ultimate question is the extent to which a grantee is required to make reasonable modifications in its programs for the needs of the handicapped.").

§ 2.06   ENTITIES AND INDIVIDUALS BOUND BY THE DISABILITY DISCRIMINATION LAWS

The entities and persons who must obey the disability discrimination laws vary with each enactment, sometimes with each portion of each enactment. Accordingly, the chapters of this book specific to particular disability discrimination laws and topics will develop a number of coverage issues at greater length than is practical at this point. But meriting brief discussion here are general considerations as to coverage of the ADA, section 504, and a few other provisions such as the Fair Housing Act Amendments.

[A]   ADA Coverage

Coverage under the ADA varies with each subchapter of the statute. Briefly, title I binds employers, employment agencies, labor organizations, and joint labor management committees.[159] An employer is defined as a person "engaged in an industry affecting commerce who has 15 or more employees for each working day in each of 20 or more calendar weeks in the current or preceding calendar year, and any agent of such person"[160] but does not include the federal government, federally owned corporations, Indian tribes, or some private membership clubs.[161] Due to a phase-in, for the first two years following its effective date, title I covered only larger employers.[162] Title II of the ADA covers every "public entity," defined as any state or local government, any department, agency, special purpose district, or other instrumentality of a state or states or local government, the National Railroad Passenger Corporation (Amtrak), and commuter transportation authorities.[163] Title III covers private entities affecting commerce that own, lease, lease to, or operate places of public accommodations, including those that provide nearly all everyday goods and services,[164] but it exempts private clubs and religious organizations, including places of worship.[165] Title IV, the telecommunications chapter, binds common carriers engaged in interstate communication by wire or radio.[166] Title V of the ADA, which contains a variety of general provisions, including ones forbidding retaliation and harassment, generally binds everyone without restriction, and contains a specific provision imposing ADA obligations on the Government Accountability Office, the Government Printing Office, and the Library of Congress.[167]

---

[159] 42 U.S.C.S. § 12111(2) (LexisNexis 2011).

[160] 42 U.S.C.S. § 12111(5)(A).

[161] 42 U.S.C.S. § 12111(5)(B).

[162] 42 U.S.C.S. § 12111(5)(A).

[163] 42 U.S.C.S. § 12131(1) (2006).

[164] 42 U.S.C.S. § 12181(7).

[165] 42 U.S.C.S. § 12187.

[166] 47 U.S.C.S. § 225 (2006).

[167] 42 U.S.C.S. § 12209(4) (2006).

[B] Coverage of Section 504

Section 504 covers programs or activities receiving federal financial assistance, whether they be public, such as state and local governments that receive federal conditional spending or other grants, or private, such as universities that receive federal financial aid and research money.[168] Section 504 also imposes duties not to discriminate on agencies of the executive branch and the United States Postal Service.[169] Section 501 of the Rehabilitation Act further requires federal agencies to engage in affirmative action on behalf of people with disabilities.[170] These affirmative action obligations exceed the simple duty to provide reasonable accommodations.[171]

[C] Coverage of Other Provisions

Laws other than the ADA that prohibit disability discrimination have their own provisions setting out who must obey them. The Fair Housing Act Amendments pertain to residential discrimination and related matters. The language of the Amendments consists primarily of general prohibitions that would appear to cover everyone, but the law contains a number of subject matter and other exemptions, leaving aside much single-family housing and some owner-occupied units and exempting most religious organizations and private clubs that give preference to their own members in providing housing.[172] The Amendments also apply to governments whose conduct, such as zoning regulation, may make dwellings unavailable on the basis of disability.[173] The Air Carrier Access Act applies to persons undertaking by any means, directly or indirectly, to provide air transportation,[174] generally including foreign carriers.[175] The Individuals with Disabilities Education Act binds states[176] that receive federal special education funding and the local education agencies (generally speaking, the public school districts)[177] in them. Non-federal law is also of relevance. The coverage of state and local laws may differ from that of the parallel federal laws. For example, the enactments may cover employers with fewer than fifteen employees, and may

---

[168] 29 U.S.C.S. § 794(b) (2006). Hence, state and local government agencies receiving federal funds will be bound by both ADA title II and section 504.

[169] 29 U.S.C.S. § 794(a) (2006).

[170] 29 U.S.C.S. § 791 (LexisNexis 2011).

[171] *See generally* Mark C. Weber, *Beyond the Americans with Disabilities Act: A National Employment Policy for People with Disabilities*, 46 Buff. L. Rev. 123, 147–66 (1998) (describing federal government's affirmative action obligations and proposing extension to other categories of employers).

[172] *See* 42 U.S.C.S. § 3603(a)–(b) (2006).

[173] *See, e.g.,* City of Edmonds v. Oxford House, Inc., 514 U.S. 725 (1995) (ruling that provision of Amendments could apply to definition of family regarding zoning for single-family units).

[174] 49 U.S.C.S. § 40102(a)(2) (LexisNexis 2011).

[175] 49 U.S.C.S. § 41705 (2006).

[176] 20 U.S.C.S. § 1412(a) (2006). Territories and outlying areas and the Secretary of the Interior (in connection with Bureau of Indian Affairs programs) are also covered. 20 U.S.C.S. § 1411(b), (h)(2), (i).

[177] 20 U.S.C.S. § 1413(a).

impose obligations on operations run by religious organizations that would not be covered under ADA title III.

Chapter 3

EMPLOYMENT DISCRIMINATION

§ 3.01 OVERVIEW OF EMPLOYMENT DISCRIMINATION

Working occupies a large portion of life, and a job not only provides the means to support the person working and dependents, but also establishes an identity for the employee and a place for that person in society. Nevertheless, many people with disabilities are out of the workforce altogether or work at jobs that do not lift them out of poverty.[1] Legal provisions that bar employment discrimination on the basis of disability hold the promise of changing those conditions, though as this chapter demonstrates, the controversies over the application of the provisions are many. Two preliminary matters are the sources of law and the character of the entities to which the employment discrimination provisions apply.

[A] Relevant Statutory Provisions

Title I of the ADA addresses employment discrimination, and contains the basic prohibition of discrimination against a qualified individual on the basis of disability with regard to job application procedures, hiring, advancement or discharge, compensation, training, and other terms and conditions of employment.[2] The title I regulations clarify that these prohibitions extend to:

- Recruitment, advertising, and job application procedures;

- Hiring, upgrading, promotion, tenure awards, demotion, transfer, layoff, termination, right of return after layoff, and rehiring;

- Rates of pay or any other form of compensation and compensation changes;

- Job assignments, classifications, organizational structures, position descriptions, lines of progression, and seniority lists;

- Leaves of absence, sick leave, or any other leaves;

- Fringe benefits, whether or not administered by the covered entity;

- Selection and support for training, including apprenticeships, professional

---

[1] According to the Kessler Foundation-National Organization for Disabilities 2010 survey of Americans with disabilities, 21% of working aged people with disabilities report that they are employed, compared to 59% of similarly aged people who do not have disabilities, and people with disabilities are twice as likely as people with disabilities to report that they have a household income of $15,000 or less. The ADA, 20 Years Later, at 10–12 (July, 2010), *available at* http://www.2010disabilitysurveys.org/pdfs/surveyresults.pdf.

[2] 42 U.S.C.S. § 12112(a) (LexisNexis 2011).

meetings, conferences, and other related activities, and selection for leaves of absence to pursue training;

- Activities sponsored by the covered entity, including recreational and social programs; and

- Any other term, condition, or privilege of employment.[3]

In addition to outlawing discrimination in general, the statutory language in title I specifically defines discrimination to include limiting, segregating, or classifying job applicants or employees in a way that adversely affects the opportunities or status of the individual because of that person's disability;[4] using standards, criteria, or methods of administration that have the effect of discrimination on the basis of disability or that perpetuate the discrimination of others who are subject to common administrative control;[5] not making reasonable accommodations to the known physical or mental limitations of an otherwise qualified individual with a disability, unless the covered entity can demonstrate that the accommodation would impose an undue hardship on the operation of the business of the covered entity;[6] using qualification standards, employment tests, or other selection criteria that screen out or tend to screen out an individual with a disability or a class of individuals with disabilities unless the standard, test, or other selection criterion, as used by the covered entity, is shown to be job-related for the position in question and consistent with business necessity;[7] and failing to select and administer employment tests in the most effective manner to ensure that, when the test is administered to a job applicant or employee with sensory, manual, or speaking impairments, the test results accurately reflect the skills, aptitude, or whatever other factor of the applicant or employee that the test is supposed to measure.[8] These topics will be developed further in this chapter.

Title I also forbids participation in a contractual or other arrangement that has the effect of subjecting a qualified applicant or employee with a disability to otherwise prohibited discrimination,[9] and excluding or denying equal jobs or benefits to a qualified individual because of the known disability of someone with whom the qualified individual is known to have a relationship or association.[10] Title V of the ADA forbids retaliation, as well as interference, coercion, or intimidation in connection with the exercise of ADA rights.[11] These topics will also be developed further.

---

[3] 29 C.F.R. § 1630.4 (2011).

[4] 42 U.S.C.S., § 12112(b)(1) (LexisNexis 2011).

[5] § 12112(b)(3).

[6] § 12112(b)(5)(A). The prohibition extends to denying employment opportunities to an applicant or employee who is an otherwise qualified individual with a disability if the denial is based on the need to make reasonable accommodations. § 12112(b)(5)(B).

[7] § 12112(b)(6).

[8] § 12112(b)(7).

[9] § 12112(b)(2).

[10] § 12112(b)(4).

[11] § 12203(a)–(b); *see* 29 C.F.R. § 1630.12 (regulation applicable to employment). This topic is discussed *infra* § 7.04.

Although title I is the portion of the ADA that directly concerns employment discrimination, it is not the only statutory provision, or even the only ADA provision, of relevance to the topic. Title II forbids discrimination against qualified individuals with disabilities by units of state and local government,[12] and that prohibition extends to employment discrimination.[13] Generally speaking, employees of state and local government may assert employment discrimination claims under both title I (employment) and title II (state and local government) of the ADA.[14] In amendments to the law passed after the ADA was enacted, Congress harmonized the standards for employer conduct under the ADA and section 504.[15] Accordingly, the current Department of Justice regulation applicable to title II provides that "the requirements of title I . . . as established by the regulations of the Equal Employment Opportunity Commission . . . apply to employment in any service, program, or activity conducted by a public entity if that public entity is also subject to the jurisdiction of title I."[16] In addition, the regulation provides that the requirements of section 504, as established by the Department of Justice section 504 regulations, "apply to employment in any service, program, or activity conducted by a public entity if that public entity is also subject to the jurisdiction of [ADA] title I."[17]

Although title II and section 504 incorporate the same requirements for employer conduct toward workers with disabilities as title I does, these statutory provisions say nothing about any requirement to file charges of employment discrimination with the EEOC or otherwise exhaust administrative remedies. The traditional rule is that section 504 does not require exhaustion prior to bringing a claim, and title II incorporates section 504's remedies. Hence, courts generally have held that employment discrimination claims under title II and section 504 do not need to be exhausted through the EEOC.[18]

State statutes also may forbid employment discrimination on the basis of disability. Because these laws are so varied in their coverage and terms, and

---

[12] 42 U.S.C. § 12132 (2006).

[13] 28 C.F.R. § 35.140(a) (2011) ("No qualified individual with a disability shall, on the basis of disability, be subjected to discrimination in employment under any service, program, or activity conducted by a public entity."). Title II gives the Attorney General blanket authority to promulgate regulations to implement the general language found in § 12132. 42 U.S.C. § 12134(a) (2006). However, the Ninth Circuit has found employment not covered at all under title II. Zimmerman v. Oregon Dep't of Justice, 170 F.3d 1169 (9th Cir. 1999). *Contra* Bledsoe v. Palm Beach Soil & Water Conservation Dist., 133 F.3d 816 (11th Cir. 1998) (relying on legislative history and regulation).

[14] The exception to this rule is if the governmental unit has fewer than fifteen employees, in which case the claim will lie only under title II, or, if that unit also receives federal monetary assistance, under title II and section 504. *See infra* § 3.01[B].

[15] *See* 29 U.S.C. § 794(d) (2011) ("The standards used to determine whether this section has been violated in a complaint alleging employment discrimination under this section shall be the standards applied under title I of the Americans with Disabilities Act of 1990 . . . and the provisions of . . . [title V of the ADA] . . . as such sections relate to employment.").

[16] 28 C.F.R. § 35.140(b)(1) (2011).

[17] 28 C.F.R. § 35.140(b)(2) (2011).

[18] Peterson v. University of Wis., Bd. of Regents, 818 F. Supp. 1276 (W.D. Wis. 1993); *see* Bledsoe v. Palm Beach Soil & Water Conservation Dist., 133 F.3d 816, 824 (11th Cir. 1998). *See generally infra* § 3.09[B] (discussing exhaustion defense).

because in many instances the state courts look to the ADA for guidance in state law interpretation,[19] they will not be discussed in any detail here.[20] There also are possible causes of action under common law for discriminatory conduct, such as actions for emotional distress when an employer harasses an employee because of the employee's disability.[21] These claims are discussed in Chapter 7 under the topic of disability harassment.

[B]   Covered Entities Under the ADA

Title I of the ADA applies to employers, employment agencies, labor organizations, and joint labor management committees.[22] Being an employer means being engaged in an industry affecting commerce and having fifteen or more employees for each working day in each of twenty or more calendar weeks in the current or preceding calendar year, or being the agent of such an employer.[23] The term, however, does not include the federal government, federally owned corporations, Indian tribes, or, generally speaking, private membership clubs.[24]

As noted in the previous section, employers that are units of state and local government and have more than fifteen employees are covered under both title I and title II of the ADA. Title II covers every "public entity," defined as any state or local government, any department, agency, special purpose district, or other instrumentality of a state or states or local government, the National Railroad Passenger Corporation (Amtrak), and commuter transportation authorities.[25] Units of state and local government that have fewer than fifteen employees will be covered only by title II of the ADA.[26]

Some public and private employers will be covered as well by section 504 of the Rehabilitation Act of 1973, which applies to programs or activities receiving federal financial assistance, whether they are state and local governments that receive federal conditional spending or other grants, or private entities, such as universities that receive federal financial aid and research money.[27] Section 504

---

[19] *See, e.g.*, Robel v. Roundup Corp., 59 P.3d 611, 615–16 (Wash. 2002) (looking to ADA for support in interpreting state disability discrimination statute to include cause of action for hostile environment).

[20] On some topics, the contrasts between state law and the ADA deserve mention. *See, e.g., supra* Chapter 2 (discussing different definitions of disability in state and federal laws).

[21] *See* Mark C. Weber, *The Common Law of Disability Discrimination*, 2012 UTAH L. REV. (forthcoming) (discussing contract and tort theories supporting claims of disability discrimination).

[22] 42 U.S.C.S. § 12111(2) (LexisNexis 2011).

[23] § 12111(5)(A). The statute phased in, so that for the first two years following its effective date, title I covered only employers with twenty-five or more employees for each working day in each of twenty or more calendar weeks. *Id.*

[24] § 12111(5)(B).

[25] § 12131(1).

[26] If they receive federal funding, however, section 504 will also bind them.

[27] 29 U.S.C. § 794(b) (2006). A funded program can be viewed in a narrow or a broad sense, as with a university that receives federal funding for financial aid. Is only the financial aid program bound not to discriminate under statutes such as section 504? *Grove City College v. Bell*, 465 U.S. 555 (1984), read the program term narrowly in interpreting a statute with wording identical to that in section 504, but Congress overruled that decision in the Civil Rights Restoration Act of 1987, barring discrimination in

applies to any size of entity, even those with fewer than fifteen employees.

Section 504 also imposes duties not to discriminate on agencies of the federal executive branch and the United States Postal Service, and these duties extend to employment as well as other activities.[28] Section 501 of the Rehabilitation Act requires federal agencies to engage in affirmative action on behalf of people with disabilities.[29] These affirmative action obligations exceed the simple duty to provide reasonable accommodations.[30]

Title I of the ADA covers religious organizations, but a section of the statute spells out that the title does not prohibit a religious entity from giving preference in employment to individuals of a particular religion to perform work connected with the entity's activities, and it further provides that the religious organization may require all applicants and employees to conform to the religious tenets of the organization.[31]

§ 3.02 QUALIFIED INDIVIDUAL

"No covered entity shall discriminate against a qualified individual on the basis of disability . . . ."[32] So begins the principal section of the ADA's title regarding employment. Only "qualified" individuals receive the protection against discrimination. A "qualified individual" is defined as "an individual who, with or without reasonable accommodation, can perform the essential functions of the employment position that such individual holds or desires."[33] The critical terms of that definition are reasonable accommodations, that is, the steps towards accessibility and modifications of current activities to enable individuals to succeed at work and other activities; and the essential functions of the job that the person must be able to do (with or without reasonable accommodations) to be deemed qualified. Moreover, the application of the definition is affected by a line of authority holding that some conduct by plaintiffs estops them from maintaining that they are qualified at being able to perform the essential functions of the job with or without reasonable accommodations.

---

the entirety of the agency or institution that receives federal funds, with the exception of private entities when assistance is extended to a geographically separate facility. *See* 29 U.S.C. § 794(b)(3)(B) (2006) (provision applicable to disability discrimination).

[28] 29 U.S.C. § 794(a) (2006).

[29] 29 U.S.C. § 791(b) (2006).

[30] *See generally* Mark C. Weber, *Beyond the Americans with Disabilities Act: A National Employment Policy for People with Disabilities*, 46 Buff. L. Rev. 123, 147–66 (1998) (describing federal government's affirmative action obligations and collecting authorities).

[31] 42 U.S.C.S. § 12113(d) (LexisNexis 2011).

[32] § 12112(a).

[33] § 12111(8).

[A]   Relation of "Qualified Individual" to "Reasonable Accommodation"

A potential source of confusion is that reasonable accommodation is found in two separate parts of title I, both in the definition of who is qualified, and thus protected against discrimination, and also in the definition of what discrimination is. A qualified individual is one "who, with or without reasonable accommodation, can perform the essential functions" of the job,[34] and discrimination includes, among other things, "not making reasonable accommodations to the known physical or mental limitations of an otherwise qualified individual with a disability who is an applicant or employee," unless the employer or other "covered entity can demonstrate that the accommodation would impose an undue hardship on the operation of the business of such covered entity."[35] In analyzing a case in which the plaintiff alleges a failure to provide reasonable accommodations, the issue appears twice, first in establishing that the plaintiff is a person protected by the statute, along with the demonstration that the person has a disability, and second, when proving that the defendant has in fact discriminated against the plaintiff by failing to provide the accessibility measures or rules modifications with which the plaintiff could perform the essential functions of the job. Ordinarily, there is no problem when the same issue arises in more than one part of plaintiff's case. The same behavior on the part of the defendant may support plaintiff's claims both of constructive discharge and of discrimination, for example. Matters are somewhat more complicated with respect to disability discrimination for failure to provide reasonable accommodations, however, because the statute is silent with regard to the burden of proof on the issue of whether an individual is qualified, but appears to put the burden of proof on the defendant regarding whether a reasonable accommodation imposes an undue hardship on the defendant's business.[36] Additional discussion of that topic is provided below.[37]

[B]   Essential Functions

Title I provides that "consideration shall be given to the employer's judgment as to what functions of a job are essential, and if an employer has prepared a written description before advertising or interviewing applicants for the job, this description shall be considered evidence of the essential functions of the job."[38] The EEOC Regulations expand on this provision by stating that essential functions are not marginal ones, by noting various reasons that a function may be essential, and by specifying some types of evidence that a function is essential.[39] The reasons a function may be essential include that the job may exist to perform the function, that there are a limited number of employees available among whom to distribute performance of the function, and that the function may be highly specialized, with

---

[34] *Id.*

[35] § 12112(a)(5)(A).

[36] *See id.* ("unless such covered entity can demonstrate").

[37] *See generally infra* § 3.05 (discussing burdens with regard to reasonable accommodation).

[38] 42 U.S.C.S. § 12111(8) (LexisNexis 2011).

[39] 29 C.F.R. § 1630.2(n) (2011).

the person holding the job being hired for expertise or ability in performing the function. The list of reasons is not considered exclusive. A non-exclusive list of the evidence relevant to whether a particular function is essential includes: the employer's judgment as to which functions are essential; written job descriptions prepared before advertising or interviewing applicants for the job; the amount of time spent on the job performing the function; consequences of not having the person in the job perform the function; terms of a collective bargaining agreement; work experience of previous holders of the job; and current work experience of holders of similar jobs.[40]

Courts applying these rules have frequently deferred to the employer's judgment on which functions are essential, as long as all the employees in a given position actually perform those tasks.[41] This approach mirrors that of the EEOC Interpretive Guidance, which comments that "the inquiry into essential functions is not intended to second guess an employer's business judgment with regard to production standards, whether qualitative or quantitative, nor to require employers to lower such standards."[42] Nevertheless, courts have found issues of fact to exist on whether functions claimed by the employer to be essential were indeed so.[43] This also mirrors the Guidance, which notes that the employer "will have to show that it actually imposes such requirements on its employees in fact, and not simply on paper."[44] An example of this approach is *Miller v. Illinois Department of Transportation*, in which the Seventh Circuit ruled that working at heights above 25 feet in an extreme or exposed position was not an essential function of the job of a highway bridge crew worker who had a fear of heights.[45] The court noted that the bridge crew worked as a team that accommodated the various skills, abilities, and limits of individual members, and that having other team members substitute for tasks performed at high heights could be deemed reasonable. The *Miller* case reinforces the lesson that the test for whether a worker is qualified is whether the worker can perform the essential functions *with or without reasonable accommodations*. Thus even if a function is deemed essential and the individual cannot do it unassisted, the individual may still be qualified if a reasonable accommodation would permit him or her to do the function.[46]

---

[40] 29 C.F.R. § 1630.2(n)(3) (2011).

[41] *E.g.*, Basith v. Cook County, 241 F.3d 919, 929 (7th Cir. 2001) ("But an essential function need not encompass the majority of an employee's time, or even a significant quantity of time, to be essential."); DePaoli v. Abbott Labs., 140 F.3d 668, 674 (7th Cir. 1998) ("Although we look to see if the employer actually requires all employees in a particular position to perform the allegedly essential functions . . . , we do not otherwise second-guess the employer's judgment in describing the essential requirements for the job.").

[42] ADA Title I EEOC Interpretive Guidance, 29 C.F.R. § 1630, App. § 1630.2(n) (2011).

[43] *E.g.*, Skerski v. Time Warner Cable Co., 257 F.3d 273, 281 (3d Cir. 2001) (noting importance of looking to employee's own experience as well as that of other employees and finding issue of fact whether climbing constituted essential function of installer technician despite its listing in written job description); Riel v. Electronic Data Sys., 99 F.3d 678, 683 (5th Cir. 1996) (finding issue of fact whether meeting "milestone deadlines" on projects constituted essential function of systems engineer position).

[44] ADA Title I EEOC Interpretive Guidance, 29 C.F.R. § 1630, App. § 1630.2(n) (2011).

[45] 643 F.3d 190, 197–200 (7th Cir. 2011).

[46] *See generally supra* § 3.02[A] (discussing relation of qualified individual and reasonable

Many courts have said that regular attendance is an essential part of most jobs,[47] though some positions, such as that of a medical transcriptionist, may well be successfully performed from home and so working from home may be a reasonable accommodation in those situations.[48] Advances in technology may greatly increase the number of jobs for which daily attendance at an office, factory, or other workplace is not an essential function of the position.[49]

[C] Judicial Estoppel

The government and some private sources provide benefits for persons who are disabled. In making the application for disability insurance from the Social Security Administration or similar benefits from other sources, the person typically will swear that he or she is totally unable to work, permanently or for some protracted period of time. Defendants in ADA cases have frequently argued that plaintiffs cannot maintain to the court that they are qualified in the sense of being able to perform the essential functions of a job because they made statements to the Social Security Administration or a private insurance company that they cannot work at all. Nevertheless, from early on, the EEOC recognized that the situation was not so simple. In a title I interim enforcement guidance issued in 1997, the EEOC said that representations about the ability to work made in the course of applying for Social Security, workers' compensation, private disability insurance, and other benefits do not bar the filing of an ADA charge, and are never an absolute bar to success on the claim.[50] The EEOC reasoned that the ADA definition of qualified always demands an individualized assessment of the individual and the job, whereas Social Security and other benefits programs frequently allow presumptions about impairments and jobs. The EEOC noted, for example, that Social Security considers a person who has lost vision in both eyes and is not working to be disabled, even though such an individual can do the essential functions of many jobs. Social Security and other benefits programs also look to all functions of jobs, in contrast to the ADA, which considers only the essential functions of a particular job. Moreover, the ADA definition of qualified

---

accommodations) and *infra* § 3.05 (discussing reasonable accommodations and undue hardship standards).

[47] *E.g.*, Tyndall v. Nat'l Educ. Ctrs., 31 F.3d 209 (4th Cir. 1994); *see also* Carr v. Reno, 23 F.3d 525 (D.C. Cir. 1994) (section 501–504 case involving federal employment). Additional cases are cited *infra* § 3.05[B].

[48] *See* Humphrey v. Memorial Hosps. Ass'n, 239 F.3d 1128, 1136 (9th Cir. 2001) ("There is at least a triable issue of fact as to whether Humphrey would have been able to perform the essential duties of her job with the accommodation of a work-at-home position. Working at home is a reasonable accommodation when the essential functions of the position can be performed at home and a work-at-home arrangement would not cause undue hardship for the employer. EEOC Enforcement Guidance: Reasonable Accommodation and Undue Hardship Under the Americans with Disabilities Act, FEP (BNA) 405:7601, at 7626 (March 1, 1999)."); *see also* cases cited *infra* § 3.05[B].

[49] *See* Vande Zande v. Wisconsin Dep't of Admin., 44 F.3d 538, 544 (7th Cir. 1995) ("Most jobs in organizations public or private involve team work under supervision rather than solitary unsupervised work, and team work under supervision generally cannot be performed at home without a substantial reduction in the quality of the employee's performance. This will no doubt change as communications technology advances, but is the situation today.").

[50] EEOC Enforcement Guidance No. 915.002 (Feb. 12, 1997).

requires consideration of reasonable accommodations, an approach much different from that of benefits programs, which do not ask about accommodations at all. Many individuals cannot work without reasonable accommodations, but can perform the essential functions of a particular job with them. The EEOC recognized that representations made while applying for benefits may be relevant to the determination of whether a person is qualified, but said that context and timing needed to be evaluated, and that summary judgment decisions based on the representations are inappropriate.

In *Cleveland v. Policy Management Systems Corp.*,[51] the Supreme Court unanimously held that representations made in applying for Social Security benefits do not necessarily conflict with the claim that an individual is qualified, and therefore no special presumption should operate against a plaintiff who has applied for and received benefits. To survive a motion for summary judgment, however, the plaintiff must offer a sufficient explanation why the claim to Social Security of total disability is consistent with the claim under the ADA that the plaintiff can perform the essential functions of the job, at least with reasonable accommodation.[52]

The case involved Carolyn Cleveland, who had a stroke and lost her job; she applied for and obtained Social Security disability benefits. She sued her former employer, alleging that she had been terminated after being denied reasonable accommodations such as training and additional time to complete tasks. The district court granted summary judgment for the employer, holding that by applying for and receiving the benefits, plaintiff conceded she was totally disabled, and thus not able to perform the essential functions of her job. The court of appeals affirmed. The Supreme Court vacated, stressing that the Social Security disability program does not take into account the possibility of reasonable accommodations, that it makes broad presumptions about a person's ability to work based on the existence of specific medical conditions, and that under various work incentive programs, persons can receive benefits and still work. Nevertheless, the Court said that in some cases, the claim for benefits may genuinely conflict with the ADA claim, and that the plaintiff cannot simply submit a new sworn statement to the trial court contradicting an earlier sworn statement to the Social Security Administration. An explanation must be offered that is "sufficient to warrant a reasonable juror's concluding that, assuming the truth of, or the plaintiff's good faith belief in, the earlier statement, the plaintiff could nonetheless 'perform the essential functions' of her job, 'with or without reasonable accommodation.' "[53] In the years following the *Cleveland* case, plaintiffs have successfully relied on explanations such as the fact that Social Security does not consider a reasonable accommodation that plaintiff believed could permit her to perform the essential

---

[51] 526 U.S. 795 (1999).

[52] *Id.* at 798.

[53] *Id.* at 807. The Court said it was not discussing purely factual contradictions in statements to Social Security and to the trial court. The Court noted that lower courts had nearly always found simple contradiction of previous sworn statements, without explanation, to be insufficient to withstand summary judgment. It said "we do not necessarily endorse these cases, but leave the law as we found it." *Id.* Nevertheless, the Court's requirement of an explanation for what it called a conflict involving a legal conclusion would appear to be equally applicable to conflicts between factual statements.

functions of the job,[54] and the difference between a state disability program's technical definition of permanent and total disability and the ADA's practical definition of qualified individual.[55] Several decisions construing state disability discrimination laws appear to be in harmony with the *Cleveland* approach to judicial estoppel under the ADA.[56]

A corollary of *Cleveland's* holding is that if the claimant fails in obtaining disability benefits, application of judicial estoppel is not appropriate.[57] The plaintiff might still fail on the issue of being qualified, however, if particular sworn statements used in applying for benefits undermine the claim of being able to perform the essential functions of the job with or without reasonable accommodations, when no explanation is offered for the discrepancy.[58]

§ 3.03 DISPARATE TREATMENT AND LIMITING, SEGREGATING, AND CLASSIFYING

An employee or job applicant may establish a violation of ADA by showing unfavorable treatment on the basis of disability through direct evidence or the proof-of-intent-by-inference approach of the race discrimination case *McDonnell Douglas Corp. v. Green.*[59] *Hoffman v. Caterpillar, Inc.*, illustrates both approaches.[60] Hoffman was missing part of her left arm. She received several accommodations and successfully performed her job, which included operating a low-speed scanning machine for the document filing and indexing operation of a large business. Caterpillar refused to train her on a high speed scanner because of its supervisor's belief she could not operate it with one hand; Hoffman believed that her lack of training in operating the machine diminished her chances for promotion and constituted unequal treatment when other employees who asked for training on the machine received it. She was also denied training to operate a console computer used to check accuracy of data entered for scanned documents. Caterpillar contended that it denied that training because Hoffman lacked the needed communication skills to be in a reviewer position, the job of the person operating that machine. The district court granted summary judgment to Caterpillar. The court of appeals vacated and remanded in part and affirmed in part.

The court of appeals noted that with regard to the denial of training on the high-speed scanner, Hoffman had direct evidence of discrimination: the supervisor

---

[54] EEOC v. Stowe-Pharr Mills, Inc., 216 F.3d 373 (4th Cir. 2000).

[55] Murphey v. City of Minneapolis, 358 F.3d 1074 (8th Cir. 2004).

[56] Grant v. Anchorage Police Dep't, 20 P.3d 553 (Alaska 2001) (not finding estoppel); Russell v. Cooley Dickinson Hosp., Inc., 772 N.E.2d 1054 (Mass. 2002) (not finding estoppel).

[57] *See Cleveland*, 526 U.S. at 805 ("[I]f an individual has merely applied for, but has not been awarded, SSDI benefits, any inconsistency in the theory of the claims is of the sort normally tolerated by our legal system."); Giles v. General Elec. Co., 245 F.3d 474, 483 (5th Cir. 2001) ("Without an award of SSDI benefits, the inconsistency between Giles's prior statements and his assertions in this litigation does not give rise to judicial estoppel.").

[58] *Giles*, 245 F.3d at 484.

[59] 411 U.S. 792 (1973).

[60] 256 F.3d 568 (7th Cir. 2001).

admitted that he refused the training request because of Hoffman's disability. Although the district court had ruled that the denial needed to constitute a materially adverse employment action, affecting her compensation, benefits, hours, job title, or ability to advance within the company and that Hoffman had no evidence of that, the court of appeals ruled that when making a direct evidence claim under the ADA, she did not need to show materially adverse employment action. The statute itself specifies discrimination in regard to job training, and if the employee relies on direct evidence, as opposed to an inference such as that under *McDonnell Douglas*, which has adverse employment action as one of its elements, there is no need to show an adverse employment action.[61]

The court of appeals ruled that because Hoffman lacked direct evidence of discrimination on the basis of disability on her claim regarding denial of training for the console computer, she had to rely on the *McDonnell Douglas* inference to sustain that claim. According to the court, in an ADA case, that inference requires a showing that (1) the plaintiff is disabled within the meaning of the ADA; (2) she was meeting the legitimate employment expectations of her employer; (3) she experienced an adverse employment action; and (4) similarly situated employees received more favorable treatment. The court did not reach the issue whether denial of the training for the computer was adverse employment action, because it found that Caterpillar's explanation that Hoffman lacked the needed communication skills was a legitimate, non-discriminatory reason for its action and that she made no effort to rebut that reason. Hence, on the claim regarding training for the console computer, the court of appeals affirmed the grant of summary judgment.[62] Any neutral policy, even one that may have discriminatory effects, will satisfy the employer's obligation to put forward a legitimate, nondiscriminatory reason in a disparate treatment case, and it is then up to the plaintiff to show that the reason is pretextual.[63]

Other instances of disparate treatment have been raised in litigation. Inequality of fringe benefits is an example. One court ruled that an employer's failure to provide access to group health insurance for an employee with AIDS constitutes an ADA violation.[64] Another court found no violation of the ADA when an employee who requested to work part-time as an accommodation for a disability lost coverage for medical insurance benefits as a result of the change to part-time status, when no part-time employees were eligible for the benefits.[65]

Title I defines discrimination to include limiting, segregating, or classifying job applicants or employees in a way that adversely affects the opportunities or status

---

[61] *Id.* at 574–77. The court affirmed the district court's determination that Hoffman could not make a reasonable accommodation claim if it was true that Hoffman could not operate the high-speed scanner by herself and Caterpillar's chosen accommodation was to have other workers run it. *Id.* at 577. The dissent would have required a showing of adverse employment action even on the claim for which direct evidence was advanced. *Id.* at 578–80 (Manion, J., dissenting).

[62] *Id.* at 577–78.

[63] Raytheon Corp. v. Hernandez, 540 U.S. 44 (2003) (discussed *infra* § 3.04).

[64] Anderson v. Gus Mayer Boston Store, 924 F. Supp. 763, 769 (E.D. Tex. 1996) (noting that liability remained subject to possible defense).

[65] Tenbrick v. Federal Home Loan Bank, 920 F. Supp. 1156, 1164 (D. Kan. 1996).

of the individual because of disability.[66] Full integration of people with disabilities into ordinary life on a plane of equality is an overriding goal of the ADA, so this prohibition is central to the statute's mission.[67] The Supreme Court enforced the parallel title II regulation embodying the integration mandate in the prominent case *Olmstead v. L.C.*, which in general requires deinstitutionalization of persons with mental retardation and mental illness served by state government.[68] Nevertheless, the "segregation" term of title I has received little judicial development. In one case, a court permitted an employer to separate a worker with mental illness from where he had previously worked and place him in a new location, rejecting the argument that the separation segregated him on the basis of his disability. The court believed that there was no violation when the new setting included workers without disabilities.[69] Nevertheless, a worker with mental illness succeeded in stating a claim when he was moved to a location in which he had to work alone and was forbidden from talking to anyone.[70]

Sometimes, cases that might raise questions about segregation present themselves as reasonable accommodations cases. In *Vande Zande v. Wisconsin Department of Administration*,[71] discussed below in connection with the reasonable accommodation duty, a worker who used a wheelchair requested as an accommodation that the kitchenette sink and counter at her workplace be lowered, so that she could wash out her coffee cup and otherwise make use of the facility the same as other employees did. Although the adjustment would cost just $150, the defendant rejected the request and the court affirmed dismissal of the ADA claim, saying that it was enough for the worker to be able to use the sink in the bathroom. The court did not discuss the segregation provision, but instead offered the opinion that the worker's characterization of the denial of the ability to use the kitchenette sink as "stigmatizing" was "merely an epithet."[72]

Courts have ruled that harassment amounting to the creation of a hostile environment constitutes actionable disability discrimination. The two leading cases are *Fox v. General Motors Corp.*[73] and *Flowers v. Southern Regional Physician Services.*[74] The *Fox* case involved an auto worker who sustained several back injuries and returned from disability leave with a medical restriction permitting him

---

[66] 42 U.S.C.S. § 12112(b)(1) (LexisNexis 2011).

[67] For a more detailed discussion of this point, see the aptly titled article published just after passage of the ADA by Timothy M. Cook, *The Americans with Disabilities Act: The Move to Integration*, 64 TEMP. L. REV. 393, 398 (1991) ("[T]he primary evil addressed in the ADA was the segregation that continues to impose an isolated, denigrated existence upon persons with disabilities.").

[68] 527 U.S. 581 (1999). This case is discussed *infra* Chapter 6.

[69] Tyler v. Ispat Island Inc., 245 F.3d 969, 973–74 (7th Cir. 2001).

[70] Duda v. Board of Educ., 133 F.3d 1054, 1059–60 (7th Cir. 1998).

[71] 44 F.3d 538 (7th Cir. 1995) (discussed *infra* § 3.05[A]).

[72] *Id.* at 546. An additional case, one that involved allegations of disparate treatment, failure to accommodate, and disparate impact, also commented on segregation in connection with assignment of employees with disabilities to less desirable positions. Cripe v. City of San Jose, 261 F.3d 877, 893–94 (9th Cir. 2001) (discussed *infra* § 3.04).

[73] 247 F.3d 169 (4th Cir. 2001).

[74] 247 F.3d 229 (5th Cir. 2001).

to do only light duty work. A supervisor and foreman blocked the implementation of this accommodation and humiliated Fox when he refused to work beyond his restrictions. At one point, he was assigned to work at a low table that exacerbated his back injury. He was also prevented from obtaining a promotion. Throughout this time, the supervisor and coworkers subjected Fox and other workers on light duty to streams of profanity and abuse. The supervisor instructed the workers to shun Fox and others like him. Unsurprisingly, Fox developed severe depression, anxiety, and other signs of psychological distress. In his suit for damages against General Motors, he received a verdict of $200,000, which the court upheld on appeal.[75] The court of appeals drew an analogy to hostile race and sex environment cases under title VII, noted that the ADA shares language with title VII, and emphasized that Congress enacted the ADA after the language of title VII had been construed to include hostile environment claims.

In *Flowers*, the supervisor of an employee found out about the plaintiff's HIV infection. The supervisor stopped going to lunch with Flowers and socializing with her, instead mounting an eavesdropping campaign against her. The company president shunned her. Flowers was subjected to four drug tests in a week, written up for disciplinary infractions and placed on probation, called names and subjected to other humiliations; ultimately, the company fired her. A jury found in plaintiff's favor on her hostile environment claim, and the court of appeals affirmed the finding of liability, relying on the comparison to race and sex harassment cases under title VII.[76] Courts in other circuits have agreed that a cause of action exists under title I's prohibition against discrimination for disability harassment in the workplace, although in many cases, courts have found the conduct to be insufficiently severe or pervasive to amount to a hostile environment that violates title I's prohibition on discrimination in the terms and conditions of employment.[77] Other legal grounds on which disability harassment may be challenged are developed in Chapter 7.

§ 3.04 STANDARDS, CRITERIA, AND METHODS OF OPERATION WITH DISPARATE IMPACTS; TESTS AND SELECTION CRITERIA

The ADA forbids covered entities from using standards, criteria, or methods of administration that have the effect of discrimination on the basis of disability.[78] It also bars the use of qualification standards, employment tests, or other selection

---

[75] *Fox*, 247 F.3d at 175–76. The court overturned an award of $4000 for unpaid overtime. *Id.* at 181.

[76] *Flowers*, 247 F.3d at 233–36. The court of appeals, however, vacated the damages award on the ground that Flowers failed to present adequate evidence of specific emotional injury. It remanded for entry of an award of nominal damages. *Id.* at 239.

[77] *See* Mark C. Weber, *Exile and the Kingdom: Integration, Harassment, and the Americans with Disabilities Act*, 63 Md. L. Rev. 162, 183–84 & nn.167–68 (2004) (collecting cases).

[78] 42 U.S.C.S. § 12112(b)(3)(A) (LexisNexis 2011). This ground of discrimination is distinct from that of failure to provide reasonable accommodation, although in various cases the same conduct may constitute discrimination of both types. An individual claiming a failure by the employer to provide reasonable accommodation has no obligation to show that the employer's conduct has a disparate impact on persons with disabilities. Henrietta D. v. Bloomberg, 331 F.3d 261, 275–77 (2d Cir. 2003) (section 504 and ADA title II case regarding access to public assistance services).

criteria that screen out or tend to screen out an individual with a disability or a class of individuals with disabilities unless the standard, test, or other selection criteria, as used, is shown to be job-related for the position at issue and is consistent with business necessity.[79] Another ADA provision imposes a duty to select and administer employment tests in the most effective way so that when the test is given to an applicant or employee who has a sensory, manual, or speaking impairment, the results accurately reflect the skills, aptitude, or other characteristic being tested.[80] One of the listed defenses to ADA liability is that an application of qualification standards, tests, or selection criteria has been shown to be job-related and consistent with business necessity, and that the performance cannot be accomplished by reasonable accommodation.[81]

In practice, there is some overlap between the requirements that an employer avoid standards, criteria, or methods of administration that have discriminatory effects and that the employer not use qualification standards, employment tests, or other selection criteria that screen out individuals with disabilities. An illustrative case regarding disparate impact and the screening effects of qualifications and selection criteria is *Cripe v. City of San Jose*.[82] In that case, six police officers with back, neck, and other injuries alleged that, pursuant to a collective bargaining agreement, the city placed them and others who could not perform the duties of a patrol officer in a modified-duty position. This disadvantaged them because an officer had to work as a patrol officer in the year immediately prior to his or her receiving the more desirable position of specialized assignment officer, and those who were in the specialized assignment slot had to return within three years to the patrol officer position. The plaintiffs alleged that in the modified-duty position, they were given no real work and were forced to serve under degrading conditions, cramped into a space that doubled as a supply room, frequently insulted by other officers, forced to work undesirable shifts, and disadvantaged in choice of days off. In addition, they were ineligible for promotion to sergeant, because all new sergeants had to serve in patrol positions for twelve of the first eighteen months in the sergeant position. The plaintiffs did not contend that they could perform the patrol officer functions of making forcible arrests, controlling combative or escaping persons, and responding immediately to physical threat or widespread emergency crisis, but they alleged that these were not essential functions of all the specialized assignment positions for which they wished to be eligible.

The court reversed a grant of summary judgment to the defendants.[83] The court analyzed the case under the ADA provision that forbids the use of qualification standards that screen out or tend to screen out individuals with disabilities or a class of individuals with disabilities. The court first ruled that an issue of fact existed whether specialized-assignment positions such as fraud investigators, background investigators, internal affairs investigators, and recruiters needed the ability to make forcible arrests. Since the plaintiffs did not propose an expansion of the

---

[79] § 12112(b)(6).

[80] § 12112(b)(7).

[81] § 12113(a).

[82] 261 F.3d 877 (9th Cir. 2001).

[83] *Id.* at 895.

number or proportion of officers on the force with disabling conditions that then restricted them to modified-duty assignments (30 out of more than 1,000), the defendants had not established that all specialized-duty officers had to be able to be called out and make forcible arrests in an emergency. The court then ruled that the policies of the police department screened out a class of individuals with disabilities by creating minimum requirements to compete for specialized-assignment positions that rendered only modified-duty status officers, that is, only disabled officers, categorically ineligible. Finally, the court ruled that an issue of fact existed whether the defendants had met their burden of proving that the qualification standards satisfied the relevant defense, that is, that they were job-related and consistent with business necessity.[84] It rejected the police department's assertion that business necessity required that all specialized-assignment officers be able to rotate back into patrol positions, when the department failed to show any need that the thirty officers be able to do so. It also rejected the contention that rotation back to a patrol officer position aided training and prevention of burn-out, when the department had not shown that allowing thirty officers to be eligible for specialized assignments but not patrol duty would have an adverse effect on the police department. The court further rejected the contention that adhering to the collective bargaining agreement embodying the practice that screened out persons with disabilities was a business necessity, when the relevant contract provisions did not relate to seniority protections. The court also ruled any resentment that the correction of the violation engendered was not a legitimate consideration with regard to the business necessity defense. The court found that an issue of fact existed whether the police department policy requiring newly promoted sergeants to perform patrol duties had the effect of keeping officers with disabilities from being promoted.[85]

Not all employment standards that screen out persons with disabilities face scrutiny as challenging as that applied by the Ninth Circuit in *Cripe*. An instance may be when the standards are imposed on the employer by federal law. In *Albertson's, Inc. v. Kirkingburg*, the United States Supreme Court applied the "qualification standards that . . . screen out" provision and held that an employer could rely on a United States Department of Transportation visual acuity requirement for the plaintiff's truck driver position without needing to justify either the government's legal standard itself or the employer's own unwillingness to obtain a waiver of the requirement, when the waiver program was purely experimental and the government did not claim that existing standards could be lowered consistently with public safety.[86]

Employment tests are specifically covered by subsections (b)(6) and (b)(7) of § 12112. An example of a case alleging disparate impact as well as challenging the selection and administration of employment tests is *Belk v. Southwestern Telephone Co.*, in which the Eighth Circuit Court of Appeals overturned a jury verdict in favor

---

[84] The court contrasted the business necessity defense with the undue hardship standard, noting that the undue hardship "test, while strict, is less stringent than the 'business necessity' standard . . . ." The court explained, "To excuse a generally discriminatory provision, which is what the business necessity defense does, certainly requires more of a showing than is needed to excuse an employer from accommodating a specific employee under the undue hardship standard." *Id.* at 890.

[85] *Id.* at 894–95.

[86] 527 U.S. 555 (1999).

of an applicant for a telephone company customer service technician position who had residual effects of polio that weakened his legs and therefore could not pass the employer's physical performance test without modifications to the test's content.[87] The test included an arm lift, an arm strength endurance test, sit-ups, and a leg lift test. The plaintiff passed all but the leg lift portion, and he requested an accommodation for the leg lift to permit him to show he could climb a ladder while carrying extra weight or use a leg press machine, instead of rising from a squatting position while carrying the weight.[88] The plaintiff's case included contentions that the employer engaged in disparate treatment, failure to accommodate, and use of a test that screened out individuals with disabilities and had a disparate impact. The court ruled that the verdict had to be reversed, because the trial judge refused to give a jury instruction stating that an employer may use standards, tests, or other criteria that screen out individuals with disabilities on the basis of disability if the standard, test, or other criterion, as used by the employer, is job related for the position, is consistent with business necessity, and performance cannot be accomplished by reasonable accommodation. The court noted that business necessity is a valid defense to the disparate impact claim relating to the screening-out effect of a test; moreover, the court pointed out that the plaintiff never argued that the refusal to accommodate him on the test was pretextual, as he would have in presenting a disparate treatment claim. In light of the conflicting evidence at trial concerning the job-relatedness and business necessity of the test, the court held that the failure to give the instruction was reversible error.[89]

Cases based on disparate impact-related theories contrast with those that are based on a theory of disparate treatment. In a disparate treatment case, the plaintiff may rely on direct evidence or on an inference that, because the employer has treated the plaintiff differently from persons who do not have the same characteristics as to race, sex, or disability, and the employer was not acting on the basis of a legitimate, nondiscriminatory reason in treating the plaintiff that way, the employer violated the law. *Raytheon Corp. v. Hernandez* clarifies the distinction between ADA disparate treatment cases based on inferential proof and those brought under a disparate impact theory.[90] In that case, a worker had resigned to avoid being discharged after failing a drug test. Two years later, claiming to be rehabilitated, he reapplied to the same employer. He was rejected pursuant to a policy against rehiring employees who had been terminated for workplace misconduct. The person who made the decision said that she did so pursuant to that policy, based on the plaintiff's record of violating workplace conduct rules, and without knowledge that the plaintiff had been a drug addict. The plaintiff put forward a disparate treatment claim, alleging that the employer violated the ADA by rejecting his application on the basis that he had a record of drug addiction or because it

---

[87] 194 F.3d 946 (8th Cir. 1999). The judgment included injunctive relief and attorneys' fees and costs, but no additional relief because of a finding that the employer would have made the same decision to reject the plaintiff for the position regardless of his disability. *Id.* at 949.

[88] The employer modified the test by changing the required angles for the squat, but the plaintiff failed the modified test, being able to perform it carrying 112.3 pounds but not the minimum 148. He also requested a modification of the sit up test, which was denied. *Id.* at 949.

[89] *Id.* at 953.

[90] 540 U.S. 44 (2003).

regarded him as still being a drug addict, or both. He also raised a claim that the employer's no-rehire policy had a disparate impact against persons with disabilities, but this claim was dismissed as untimely. The district court granted summary judgment for the employer. The court of appeals affirmed the district court's determination that the disparate impact claim was untimely, but it reversed the dismissal of the disparate treatment claim, holding that the plaintiff raised genuine issues of fact about his allegations of disparate treatment, specifically whether the plaintiff was qualified for the position that he sought and whether the employer rejected him because of his past record of drug addiction. The court of appeals then considered whether the employer had advanced a legitimate, nondiscriminatory reason for the refusal to rehire. The employer argued that the neutral policy against rehiring any employees previously terminated for violating workplace conduct rules constituted the legitimate, nondiscriminatory reason for the action. The court of appeals had ruled that this reason was not a legitimate, nondiscriminatory one, because, when applied to persons terminated for illegal drug use, such a policy has a disparate impact on recovering drug addicts.

The Supreme Court vacated the decision of the court of appeals, holding that "the Court of Appeals erred by conflating the analytical framework for disparate-impact and disparate-treatment claims." According to the Supreme Court:

> Had the Court of Appeals correctly applied the disparate-treatment framework, it would have been obliged to conclude that a neutral no-rehire policy is, by definition, a legitimate, nondiscriminatory reason under the ADA. And thus the only remaining question would be whether [the plaintiff] could produce sufficient evidence from which a jury could conclude that "[the employer's] stated reason for [the plaintiff's] rejection was in fact pretext."[91]

The Court thus clarified that the disparate impact of a neutral policy on a class of workers with disabilities will not be considered at the phase of a disparate treatment case in which the trier of fact determines whether the employer has advanced a legitimate, nondiscriminatory reason for treating a worker with disabilities in a way different from that in which a worker who does not have disabilities would be treated. A plaintiff wishing to rely on the argument that a neutral rule has discriminatory effects must label the claim as one based on a disparate impact theory.

Compensatory and punitive damages are available against defendants who engage in intentional discrimination in employment, but there is a proviso in the Civil Rights Act of 1991 that its damages provision does not apply to actions against defendants who have engaged in "an employment practice that is unlawful because of its disparate impact."[92] The remedies provisions applicable to title I of the ADA are discussed in greater depth below.[93]

---

[91] *Id.* at 51–52 (quoting McDonnell Douglas Corp. v. Green, 411 U.S. 792, 804 (1973)).

[92] 42 U.S.C. § 1981a(a)(2) (2006).

[93] *See infra* § 3.10.

§ 3.05 FAILING TO PROVIDE REASONABLE ACCOMMODATIONS

The ADA defines discrimination to include the failure to make reasonable accommodations to the known physical or mental limitations of an otherwise qualified individual with a disability, unless the employer or other covered entity can demonstrate that the accommodation would cause an undue hardship on the operation of the business or other entity.[94] It is also a violation of the ADA to deny employment opportunities to an otherwise qualified individual with a disability who is an employee or job applicant, if the denial is based on the need of the employer or other covered entity to make reasonable accommodation to the impairments of the employee or applicant.[95] Reasonable accommodation includes making existing facilities used by employees readily accessible to and usable by individuals with disabilities,[96] and it also includes job restructuring, part-time or modified work schedules, reassignment to a vacant position, acquisition or modification of equipment or devices, appropriate adjustment or modifications of examinations, training materials, or policies, the provision of qualified readers and interpreters, and other similar accommodations.[97]

Undue hardship is an action that requires significant difficulty or expense, when considered in light of (1) the nature and cost of the accommodation needed;[98] (2) the overall financial resources of the facility or facilities involved in the provision of the accommodation, the number of persons employed at the relevant facility, the effect on expenses and resources, or other impact on operation of the facility;[99] (3) the overall financial resources of the covered entity, the number of its employees, the number, type, and location of its facilities;[100] and (4) the type of operation or operations of the covered entity, including the composition, structure and functions of the work force, and the geographic separateness, administrative relationship, or fiscal relationship of the facility or facilities in issue to the covered entity itself.[101]

The requirement that employers provide reasonable accommodations to applicants and employees with disabilities is central to disability discrimination law. From the point of view of the employer, reasonable accommodations might look like preferences.[102] The Supreme Court agreed with that position in *US Airways, Inc.*

---

[94] 42 U.S.C.S. § 12112(b)(5)(A) (LexisNexis 2011).

[95] § 12112(b)(5)(B).

[96] § 12111(9)(A).

[97] § 12111(9)(B).

[98] § 12111(10)(B)(i).

[99] § 12111(10)(B)(ii).

[100] § 12111(10)(B)(iii). The ADA title II legislative history regarding reasonable accommodation in employment specifically mentions the obligation of a large state public welfare agency to employ readers for its blind caseworkers, an accommodation that was required in an employment case decided under section 504. H.R. Rep. No. 101-485, pt. 3, at 51 (1990) (citing Nelson v. Thornburgh, 567 F. Supp. 369 (E.D. Pa. 1983) (Louis H. Pollak, J.), *aff'd*, 732 F.2d 146 (3d Cir. 1984)). Less might be expected of enterprises with smaller budgets.

[101] 42 U.S.C.S. § 12111(10)(B)(iv) (LexisNexis 2011).

[102] Various prominent writers discussed whether reasonable accommodation should be thought of as

v. Barnett:

> The Act requires preferences in the form of "reasonable accommodations" that are needed for those with disabilities to obtain the *same* workplace opportunities that those without disabilities automatically enjoy. By definition any special accommodation requires the employer to treat an employee with a disability differently, *i.e.*, preferentially. And the fact that the difference in treatment violates an employer's disability-neutral rule cannot by itself place the accommodation beyond the Act's potential reach.[103]

Issues have arisen regarding the burdens that apply when a plaintiff claims a violation of the reasonable accommodation duty. The standards for reasonable accommodation and its converse, undue hardship, have also provided fodder for litigation. The particular accommodation of assignment of a worker to a vacant job that worker can perform has been the subject of controversy, as has the process for agreeing on accommodations. Finally, case law standards have begun to emerge regarding the entitlement to reasonable accommodations of specific categories of claimants, specifically alcoholics and drug users and persons not actually disabled but regarded as being disabled.

Compensatory and punitive damages are available against defendants who engage in intentional discrimination in employment, including the failure to provide reasonable accommodations, but there is a proviso in the Civil Rights Act of 1991 that damages may not be awarded under the Act when "the covered entity demonstrates good faith efforts, in consultation with the person with the disability . . . to identify and make a reasonable accommodation that would provide such individual with an equally effective opportunity and would not cause an undue hardship on the operation of the business."[104] The remedies provisions applicable to title I of the ADA are discussed in greater detail below.[105]

[A]   Burdens

Ordinarily, the plaintiff is expected to put forward evidence in support of his or her claims and to bear the risk of losing if the finder of fact is not persuaded. The exception is when an affirmative defense comes into play, in which instance the defendant has the obligation to put forward evidence in support of the defense and, in some instances, to bear the risk of nonpersuasion with regard to the defense. The employee-plaintiff in an ADA case must show that he or she is a qualified individual with a disability, that is, a person with a disability who, with or without reasonable accommodations, can perform the essential functions of the job. The

---

a preference. *See, e.g.,* Carlos A. Ball, *Preferential Treatment and Reasonable Accommodation Under the Americans with Disabilities Act,* 55 ALA. L. REV. 951 (2004); Mary Crossley, *Reasonable Accommodation as Part and Parcel of the Antidiscrimination Project,* 35 RUTGERS L.J. 861 (2004); Michael Ashley Stein, *Same Struggle, Different Difference: ADA Accommodations as Antidiscrimination,* 153 U. PA. L. REV. 579 (2004).

[103]   535 U.S. 391, 397 (2002). The case is also discussed *infra* § 3.07.

[104]   42 U.S.C. § 1981a(a)(3) (2006).

[105]   *See infra* § 3.10.

plaintiff must also show that the defendant has violated the reasonable accommodation provision. On the other hand, the reasonable accommodation provision of the statute states that there is a violation unless the employer "can demonstrate that the accommodation would impose undue hardship" on it. This language suggests that reasonable accommodation and undue hardship are two sides of the same coin,[106] and places the burden of undue hardship firmly on the employer.

In *US Airways, Inc. v. Barnett*, the Supreme Court rejected the contention that the ADA created a " 'burden of proof' dilemma," and endorsed the position of various lower courts that had reconciled the ADA's reasonable accommodation and undue hardship terms by lowering the threshold of proof the plaintiff must meet with regard to the reasonableness of proposed accommodations.[107] For the plaintiff to defeat a motion for summary judgment, he or she needs merely to show that an accommodation "seems reasonable on its face, *i.e.*, ordinarily or in the run of cases."[108] If the plaintiff makes this showing, the defendant "must show special (typically case-specific) circumstances that demonstrate undue hardship in the particular circumstances."[109] The Court applied the approach to a case in which an employee requested as an accommodation that a vacant job be assigned to him despite the fact that the assignment would violate the rules of a bona fide, but not contractually required, seniority system. The Court held that ordinarily, that is, in the run of cases, the accommodation would not be reasonable, but it permitted the employee to show that special circumstances would permit a finding that the assignment constituted a reasonable accommodation on the particular facts of his case.[110]

In its analysis of the issue of burdens, the Court relied on decisions such as *Borkowski v. Valley Central School District*, a case that interpreted section 504 regulations that parallel the relevant ADA provisions.[111] In *Borkowski*, Judge Calabresi of the Second Circuit Court of Appeals considered whether section 504 required a school system to provide a teacher an aide as an accommodation for the teacher's disability.[112] The plaintiff had a neurological impairment that caused her

---

[106] *See* Mark C. Weber, *Unreasonable Accommodation and Due Hardship*, 62 FLA. L. REV. 1119, 1166–71 (2010) (arguing that reasonable accommodation and undue hardship should be considered two sides of the same coin). As indicated by the discussion in the remainder of this section, however, courts in employment cases have tended to view the terms as either slightly or very distinct. *See, e.g.*, Barth v. Gelb, 2 F.3d 1180, 1187 (D.C. Cir. 1993) (federal employment case decided under sections 501 and 504) ("As a general matter, a reasonable accommodation is one employing a *method of accommodation* that is reasonable in the run of cases, whereas the undue hardship inquiry focuses on the hardships imposed by the plaintiff's preferred accommodation in the context of the particular agency's operations.").

[107] 535 U.S. 391, 401 (2002).

[108] *Id.*

[109] *Id.* at 402.

[110] *Id.* at 405. In a concurrence, Justice O'Connor agreed with the two-step approach, but criticized the Court for failing to keep the inquiries regarding reasonable accommodation and undue hardship sufficiently distinct when applying the approach to the seniority system issue. *Id.* at 410–11 (O'Connor, J., concurring).

[111] *Id.* at 402, 405 (citing, inter alia, Borkowski v. Valley Cent. Sch. Dist., 63 F.3d 131 (2d Cir. 1995)).

[112] Borkowski v. Valley Cent. Sch. Dist., 63 F.3d 131 (2d Cir. 1995).

difficulties with concentration, memory, balance, coordination, and mobility; she served as librarian and teacher of library skills in two elementary schools for a three year probationary period. The school district denied her tenure on the basis of observations alleging poor classroom management and suggesting that it was inappropriate to stay seated throughout class. Plaintiff alleged that she was qualified for the job and had been discriminated against on the ground of her disability. The court vacated a grant of summary judgment in favor of the school district, ruling that although a plaintiff bears the burden of production and persuasion on the issue of whether she is qualified for the job, that burden extends only to showing that she can do the job without accommodations or that an accommodation exists that would permit her to perform the job's essential functions. Regarding the requirement that the accommodation be reasonable, the plaintiff bears only a burden of production, and the burden "is not a heavy one," but merely the obligation to "suggest the existence of a plausible accommodation, the costs of which, facially, do not clearly exceed its benefits."[113] If that showing is made, the risk of nonpersuasion is borne by the defendant. Thus, "the defendant's burden of persuading the factfinder that the plaintiff's proposed accommodation is unreasonable merges, in effect, with its burden of showing, as an affirmative defense, that the proposed accommodation would cause it to suffer an undue hardship."[114] The court said that requiring the school district to provide the aide might be viewed as forcing it to eliminate an essential function of the job. Nevertheless, the facts might demonstrate that what the aide would do would instead allow the plaintiff to perform the essential functions. The plaintiff introduced evidence to show that the accommodation of an aide would be available and would allow her to perform the essential functions of the job, so the case should not have been thrown out.[115]

Not all courts have adopted a position identical to that of the court in *Borkowski*. One prominent decision, *Vande Zande v. Wisconsin Department of Administration*,[116] an ADA case, described the plaintiff's burden as "to show that an accommodation is reasonable in the sense both of efficacious and of proportional to costs," and declared that "[e]ven if this prima facie showing is made, the employer has an opportunity to prove that upon more careful consideration the costs are excessive in relation either to the benefits of the accommodation or to the employer's financial survival or health."[117] *Borkowski's* position that the plaintiff need not show proportionality in relation to cost to get to the jury, and that the defendant bears the risk of nonpersuasion on reasonableness appears closer to the approach used by the Supreme Court in *Barnett*. Perhaps that conclusion is best demonstrated by *Barnett's* citation with approval of *Borkowski* and other cases taking a similar tack.

---

[113] *Id.* at 138.

[114] *Id.*

[115] *See id.* at 142. The court found that the school district did not establish undue hardship as a matter of law, so as to permit it to defeat the plaintiff on summary judgment. *Id.* at 142–43.

[116] 44 F.3d 538 (7th Cir. 1995).

[117] *Id.* at 543.

[B] Reasonable Accommodation and Undue Hardship Standards

Irrespective of who bears what burden, there remains the question of precisely what constitutes reasonable accommodation or, conversely, when does a requested accommodation impose undue hardship. The Supreme Court decision regarding reassignment of a worker to a vacant job when that conflicts with the employer's seniority system, *US Airways v. Barnett*,[118] sheds some light on what constitutes reasonable accommodation and what amounts to undue hardship. In holding that an assignment to a vacant position in violation of an established seniority system will not be reasonable in the run of cases, the Court stressed the importance it had given collectively bargained seniority systems in title VII litigation, and the refusal of lower courts to compel reassignment in violation of these seniority systems in cases brought under section 504 and the ADA. Extending the reasoning to cover a non-collectively bargained system, the Court said that providing the accommodation "might well undermine the employees' expectations of consistent, uniform treatment."[119] Particular circumstances could make the accommodation reasonable, however, and the employee remained free to show, for example, that the employer frequently changed the system, diminishing expectations that the system would be followed, or that there are other exceptions and this additional one would not matter.[120]

In the *Vande Zande* case, the Seventh Circuit upheld a grant of summary judgment against an employee with paraplegia who sought to have her employer provide computer equipment to permit her to work at home during a bout of pressure ulcers related to her use of a wheelchair, or, alternatively, to have the employer give her full pay for the period she was home without making her use her limited sick leave days.[121] The court viewed this as a request to work at home, and declared that the majority view was that an employer is generally not required to provide that accommodation. The court declared that what the employer did, that is, allow the plaintiff to work at home at full pay, subject only to a loss of 16.5 hours of sick leave "that might never be needed," met the reasonable accommodation standard as a matter of law.[122] The court also rejected as a matter of law the plaintiff's request that the kitchenette sink and counter on the floor on which her office was located be lowered from 36 inches to 34 inches, so that she could use facility from her wheelchair. Although the proposed adjustment cost just $150, the court said it was enough for the worker to be able to use an accessible sink in the bathroom. The court appeared to have been influenced by the fact that the employer had made various other accommodations, such as modification of the bathrooms, ramping of a step, purchase of adjustable furniture and paying one-half the cost of a cot, adjustment of the plaintiff's schedule of some duties to accommodate medical appointments, and altering the plans for a locker room in a

---

[118] 535 U.S. 391 (2002).

[119] *Id.* at 404.

[120] *Id.* at 405.

[121] 44 F.3d 538 (7th Cir. 1995).

[122] *Id.* at 545.

new building. It asserted that "we do not think an employer has a duty to expend even modest amounts of money to bring about an absolute identity in working conditions between disabled and nondisabled workers."[123]

An approach to reasonable accommodation and undue hardship that differs from that of the *Vande Zande* court is found in the EEOC Interpretive Guidance to title I. The Guidance states that reasonable accommodation should provide the individual with a disability an equal employment opportunity and, "[e]qual employment opportunity means an opportunity to attain the same level of performance, or to enjoy the same level of benefits and privileges of employment as are available to the average similarly situated employee without a disability."[124] The Guidance's provision on undue hardship states that an employer has to "present evidence and demonstrate that the accommodation will, in fact, cause it undue hardship . . . . [T]o demonstrate that the cost of an accommodation poses an undue hardship, an employer would have to show that the cost is undue as compared to the employer's budget."[125] It continues, "Simply comparing the cost of the accommodation to the salary of the individual with a disability in need of the accommodation will not suffice."[126] Nevertheless, excessive cost is not the only basis on which a proposed accommodation might constitute undue hardship. Anticipating *Barnett*, the Guidance notes that an accommodation is not required if it is unduly disruptive to the other employees or the functioning of the business, as long as the disruption is not the result of employees' fears or prejudices concerning the individual's disability.[127]

A number of courts have addressed whether telecommuting and other options permitting employees to work at home are a reasonable accommodation, or whether, on the contrary, imposing the obligation to allow the employee to work at home would constitute undue hardship. As noted in the discussion of who is a

---

[123] *Id.* at 546.

[124] ADA Title I EEOC Interpretive Guidance, 29 C.F.R. § 1630, App. § 1630.9 (2011); *see also* US Airways v. Barnett, 535 U.S. 391, 397 (2002) ("The Act requires . . . 'reasonable accommodations' that are needed for those with disabilities to obtain the *same* workplace opportunities that those without disabilities automatically enjoy.").

[125] ADA Title I EEOC Interpretive Guidance, 29 C.F.R. § 1630, App. § 1630.15(d) (2011). The comparison under the statute is thus one of costs-resources, not cost-benefits. *See* Weber, *supra* note 106 [Unreasonable Accommodations], at 1136 (collecting additional authorities)

[126] ADA Title I EEOC Interpretive Guidance, 29 C.F.R. § 1630, App. § 1630.15(d) (2011). The passage continues: "Moreover, even if it is determined that the cost of an accommodation would unduly burden an employer, the employer cannot avoid making the accommodation if the individual with a disability can arrange to cover that portion of the cost that rises to the undue hardship level, or can otherwise arrange to provide the accommodation." *Id.*

[127] *Id.* The Guidance gives the example of the employer showing that a requested accommodation of raising the temperature in the workplace would make the location unduly hot for the other workers or the customers. *Id.* Employers voluntarily complying with ADA requirements have found that the monetary costs of accommodations are generally low and that the accommodations produce unexpected benefits, according to the studies undertaken by the leading authority on the topic. *See, e.g.*, Peter David Blanck, *The Economics of the Employment Provisions of the Americans with Disabilities Act: Part I — Workplace Accommodations*, 46 DePaul L. Rev. 877, 902–06 (1997) (discussing empirical research on accommodations); *see also* Helen A. Schartz, Kevin M. Schartz, D.J. Hendricks & Peter Blanck, *Workplace Accommodations: Empirical Study of Current Employees*, 75 Miss. L.J. 917 (2006) (reporting on recent study of accommodations and collecting additional research).

qualified individual, courts generally are sympathetic to the argument that most jobs require teamwork, personal interaction, and opportunity to provide or receive direct supervision.[128] Some authorities have taken the position that the ADA requires only "job-related" accommodations to be provided, but the distinction between job-related and personal accommodations is not an obvious one and lacks a clear anchor in the statute.[129]

[C] Job Restructuring and Reassignment to a Vacant Position

The ADA specifies "job restructuring" and "assignment to a vacant position" as examples of a reasonable accommodation.[130] The EEOC's Interpretive Guidance clarifies that an employer may restructure jobs by reallocating nonessential job functions among two positions, moving nonessential functions that the individual with a disability can do into the job for which the individual with a disability is selected, and moving the nonessential functions that the individual cannot do into another job that another person will hold.[131] Reassignment to a vacant position is a response undertaken when an individual cannot be provided accommodation in his or her current position without undue hardship. Reassignment is not available to applicants, and the person seeking reassignment must be able to perform the essential functions of the position sought, with or without reasonable accommodations. The reassignment should be undertaken if the position becomes vacant in a reasonable period of time, even if not vacant at the moment an individual requests reassignment. The salary of the reassigned employee need not remain the same if the new position is at a lower grade; an individual not otherwise entitled to a promotion need not be promoted as an accommodation.

US Airways v. Barnett, described in detail above, entailed a request by a worker who could no longer do his job for a permanent reassignment to a job he could perform.[132] The Court noted that a reasonable accommodation of the type requested is a request for variance from a disability-neutral rule, but stressed that preferential treatment of that type will sometimes be needed to accomplish the ADA's basic goal of equal opportunity.[133] The Court also rejected the contention that because the company's seniority system automatically assigned any open

---

[128] *See, e.g.*, Rauen v. U.S. Tobacco Mfg. Ltd. P'ship, 319 F.3d 891 (7th Cir. 2003); Smith v. Ameritech, 129 F.3d 857 (6th Cir. 1997); Tyndall v. National Educ. Centers, Inc., 31 F.3d 209 (4th Cir. 1994); *see also* Carr v. Reno, 23 F.3d 525 (D.C. Cir. 1994) (section 501–504 case involving federal employment). *But see* Humphrey v. Memorial Hosps. Assn., 239 F.3d 1128 (9th Cir. 2001) (finding issue of fact whether working at home constituted reasonable accommodation); *see also* Langon v. Department of Health & Human Servs., 959 F.2d 1053, 1060–61 (D.C. Cir. 1992) (in federal employment case under Rehabilitation Act, finding issue of fact whether permitting working at home constituted undue hardship).

[129] *See* Samuel R. Bagenstos, *The Future of Disability Law*, 114 YALE L.J. 1, 42–43 (2004); *see also* Lyons v. Legal Aid Soc'y, 68 F.3d 1512 (2d Cir. 1995) (vacating dismissal of claim of employee with limits on ability to walk for assistance from employer with costs of parking close to office).

[130] 42 U.S.C.S. § 12111(9)(B) (LexisNexis 2011).

[131] ADA Title I EEOC Interpretive Guidance, 29 C.F.R. § 1630, App. § 1630.2(o) (2011).

[132] 535 U.S. 391 (2002).

[133] *Id.* at 397.

position to a worker on the seniority list, no position ever was "vacant." The Court said it had no basis to suppose that Congress intended that sort of technical meaning to the term "vacant position."[134] The Court, however, also stressed the importance of seniority systems in creating and fulfilling employee expectations of fair and uniform treatment, and declared that a request for accommodation that entails assignment to a vacant position in violation of the rules of a seniority system will, in the general run of cases, not be a reasonable accommodation.[135] The accommodation might be reasonable, however, if the employer frequently exercised the right to change the seniority system unilaterally, or if there were many exceptions to the seniority rules.[136]

The nuanced analysis of the Supreme Court in *Barnett* is itself somewhat exceptional. The leading cases from the lower courts on reassignment and job restructuring display some reluctance on the part of courts to require fact-specific determinations that might more readily allow the accommodation to be deemed reasonable. *Fedro v. Reno* involved a United States marshal who contracted hepatitis-B while on duty and retired with workers' compensation benefits.[137] After his condition improved, he requested restoration to his original position or reassignment to another position. The Seventh Circuit affirmed entry of judgment against the plaintiff on his claims under the Rehabilitation Act.[138] The court interpreted the plaintiff's request for reassignment to the position of general investigator as a request that two or more part-time general investigator positions in another location be combined into a full-time position and offered to him. Although at the time of the district court decision, the applicable law did not specifically require reassignment to a vacant position, the court determined that the later imposition of that requirement did not change the result in the case. It said that even the amended provision did not require assignment to a position that did not exist, and would exist only if existing positions were combined.[139] It viewed the restructuring of the part-time positions into a full-time job as a mechanism to provide the plaintiff greater earning potential, rather than an accommodation for his disability, though at the same time it conceded that the restructuring was feasible and might have been less expensive to the government than continuing to provide disability compensation benefits.[140] A dissenting judge complained that, on the job restructuring issue, the majority failed to apply the elevated standard of accommodation that binds federal employers,[141] and that the distinction the court

---

[134] *Id.* at 399.

[135] *Id.* at 403.

[136] *Id.* at 405–06.

[137] 21 F.3d 1391 (7th Cir. 1994).

[138] The description of the history of the case is not complete, but it appears that a jury decision was rendered against the plaintiff at least on the claim for restoration of the job of criminal investigator. The Seventh Circuit ruled that on the evidence at trial, the jury could have concluded that he was not able to perform the essential functions of criminal investigator without endangering the health and safety of himself or others, and further ruled that the trial judge's evidentiary rulings on the issue were not manifestly erroneous. *Id.* at 1396–97.

[139] *Id.* at 1395 n.5.

[140] *Id.* at 1396.

[141] *Id.* at 1398–99 (Rovner, J., concurring in part and dissenting in part). Under 29 C.F.R. § 791(b),

drew between accommodations necessitated by the individual's disability and those due to personal needs was invalid in a case such as this one because, "[i]n the real world, few of us can afford to work part-time; fewer still can afford to move half way across the country for a part-time position."[142]

A similar reluctance to require job reassignment or restructuring is found in other cases, although many of them were decided before *Barnett*. In *Hankins v. The Gap, Inc.*, the court ruled that an employee who experienced severe migraine headaches while working as a merchandise picker was not entitled to a transfer to another picking position when the employer made other reasonable and effective accommodations available to her as an alternative, specifically "paid sick leave, paid personal days, a voluntary time-off program," "ample and flexible vacation time," and "treatment for her migraines — including resting time — at the company medical center."[143] *EEOC v. Humiston-Keeling* affirmed a grant of summary judgment against a worker whose arm impairment made it difficult to do her current job and who sought transfer to a clerical position.[144] The court said that the employer could choose better-qualified competing applicants, and that "[t]he contrary rule would convert a nondiscrimination statute into a mandatory preference statute, a result which would be both inconsistent with the nondiscriminatory aims of the ADA and an unreasonable imposition on the employers and coworkers of disabled employees."[145] In *Daugherty v. City of El Paso*, the court reversed a verdict in favor of an insulin-dependent diabetic bus driver who could no longer do his job and who was not reassigned to another position.[146] Although the court at one point suggested that the reassignment would have required creation of a new position or other fundamental alteration of the city's program, it also said that the city escaped liability because, "[t]here was no proof that the city treated him worse than it treated any other displaced employee."[147] These readings of the law seem inconsistent with the concept of reasonable accommodation as what Justice Breyer in *Barnett* described as "preferences,"[148] even if it remains uncertain just how much of a preference the *Barnett* decision demands. Effectively, the more fact-specific analysis employed by *Barnett* should limit the reach of *Daugherty* and the other pre-2002 cases. Despite *Barnett's* holding that the ADA establishes a preference for workers with

---

federal agencies must devise affirmative plans to insure that the special needs of persons with disabilities are met. This standard exceeds the obligations imposed on other employers by section 504. *See* Southeastern Cmty. Coll. v. Davis, 442 U.S. 397, 410–11 (1979) (explaining distinction). *See generally* Weber, supra note 28, at 147–66 (discussing elevated accommodation obligations of federal government).

[142] *Fedro*, 21 F.3d at 1400–01 (Rovner, J., concurring in part and dissenting in part).

[143] 84 F.3d 797, 801 (6th Cir. 1996).

[144] 227 F.3d 1024 (7th Cir. 2000).

[145] Id. at 1028 (quoting Dalton v,. Subaru-Isuzu Auto., Inc., 141 F.3d 667, 679 (7th Cir. 1998)). The *Humiston-Keeling* court went on to declare: "There is a difference, one of principle and not merely of cost, between requiring employers to clear away obstacles to hiring the best applicant for a job, who might be a disabled person or a member of some other statutorily protected group, and requiring employers to hire inferior (albeit minimally qualified) applicants merely because they are members of such a group. That is affirmative action with a vengeance." 227 F.3d at 1028–29.

[146] 56 F.3d 695 (5th Cir. 1995).

[147] *Id.* at 700.

[148] US Airways v. Barnett, 535 U.S. 391, 397 (2002).

disabilities, however, some post-2002 decisions rely on the older cases for the proposition that the ADA does not require preferential treatment, and continue to uphold denials of job reassignment of employees with disabilities on that ground.[149]

[D]   Interactive Process

The EEOC's title I regulations state that an employer may need to undertake an informal, interactive process with a person with a disability who needs an accommodation. The "process should identify the precise limitations resulting from the disability and potential reasonable accommodations that would overcome those limitations."[150] The EEOC Interpretive Guidance states that when an individual with a disability requests an accommodation, the employer, "using a problem solving approach" is to:

(1)   Analyze the particular job involved and determine its purpose and essential functions;

(2)   Consult with the individual with a disability to ascertain the precise job-related limitations imposed by the individual's disability and how those limitations could be overcome with a reasonable accommodation;

(3)   In consultation with the individual to be accommodated, identify potential accommodations and assess the effectiveness each would have in enabling the individual to perform the essential functions of the position; and

(4)   Consider the preference of the individual to be accommodated and select and implement the accommodation that is the most appropriate for both the employee and the employer.[151]

The Guidance continues by noting that when the needed accommodation is obvious, the process may be abbreviated, and that when neither employer nor employee can readily identify the appropriate accommodation, the process may include obtaining technical assistance from the EEOC, state or local rehabilitation agencies, or disability organizations. Employers have the ultimate discretion to choose between effective accommodations.[152] Typical cases upholding liability are those in which the employer refuses to discuss accommodations with the employee or short-circuits the discussions at some point.[153] Typical cases denying liability are those in which the plaintiff fails to provide needed information about physical

---

[149] *E.g.*, Huber v. Wal-Mart Stores, Inc., 486 F.3d 480, 483–84 (8th Cir. 2007). The best-known lower-court case supporting a preference view of job reassignment for employees with disabilities is *Aka v. Washington Hospital Center*, 156 F.3d 1284, 1304 (D.C. Cir. 1998) (en banc). *See generally* Weber, supra note 106, at 1156 (discussing *Aka* and collecting similar cases).

[150] 29 C.F.R. § 1630.2(o)(3) (2011).

[151] ADA Title I EEOC Interpretive Guidance, 29 C.F.R. § 1630, App. § 1630.9 (2011).

[152] *Id.*

[153] *E.g.*, Canny v. Dr. Pepper/Seven-Up Bottling Co., 439 F.3d 894 (7th Cir. 2004) (cutoff of discussion of accommodations); Cutrera v. Board of Supervisors, 429 F.3d 108 (5th Cir. 2005) (termination of employee before proposed meeting with rehabilitation counselor).

restrictions or capabilities.[154]

Courts have debated whether liability may exist when the employee or applicant plaintiff shows that the employer has failed to engage in the interactive process without also showing that the employer denied a reasonable accommodation.[155] Even if the view is adopted that the employer does not violate the statute unless the employer failed to offer a reasonable accommodation that would have enabled the plaintiff to perform the essential functions of the job,[156] the employer's failure to engage in the interactive process may be useful evidence that the employer denied a reasonable accommodation: Its unwillingness even to discuss accommodations with the applicant or employee, much less to experiment with them, undermines a later claim that requested accommodations would have been ineffective or too burdensome.[157] Moreover, failure to engage in the interactive process forfeits the defense to compensatory and punitive damages that applies when the employer demonstrates good faith efforts, in consultation with the person with the disability, to identify and make a reasonable accommodation.[158] Of course, an employer may satisfy the duty to engage in the interactive process, but still be liable for failure to provide reasonable accommodation if it ultimately denies an accommodation that would not impose undue hardship.[159]

ADA Title I bans failure to make reasonable accommodation to the "known" physical or mental limitations of an applicant or employee with a disability. Courts have placed the onus on the individual to make the employer aware of the disability

---

[154] *E.g.*, Kratzer v. Rockwell Collins, Inc., 429 F.3d 108 (8th Cir. 2005) (failure to appear for doctor's appointment and to provide updated evaluation): Allen v. Pacific Bell, 348 F.3d 1113 (9th Cir. 2003) (failure to provide medical documentation).

[155] *See* John R. Autry, Note, *Reasonable Accommodation Under the ADA: Are Employers Required to Participate in the Interactive Process?*, 79 CHI.-KENT L. REV. 665 (2004) (collecting cases).

[156] *E.g.*, McBride v. BIC Consumer Prods. Mfg. Co., 583 F.3d 92, 101 (2d Cir. 2009) ("[A]n employer's failure to engage in a sufficient interactive process does not form the basis of a claim under the ADA and evidence thereof does not allow a plaintiff to avoid summary judgment unless she also establishes that, at least with the aid of some identified accommodation, she was qualified for the position at issue."); Mobley v. Allstate Ins. Co., 531 F.3d 539, 546 (7th Cir. 2008) ("Although it was an admittedly laborious process for Mobley to obtain the accommodation she finally received . . . , the fact that Allstate may have failed to engage in an interactive process . . . is by itself insufficient to establish a failure to accommodate claim when, in the end, Mobley was provided with a reasonable accommodation."); Lucas v. W.W. Grainger, Inc., 257 F.3d 1249, 1256 n.2 (11th Cir. 2001) ("In other words, regardless of whether the ADA required Grainger to engage Lucas in an interactive process, Lucas' discrimination claims fail unless he can show that an accommodation reasonably could have been made."); Smith v. Midland Brake, Inc., 180 F.3d 1154, 1175 (10th Cir. 1999) ("Even if Midland Brake failed to fulfill its interactive obligations to help secure a reassignment position, Smith will not be entitled to recovery unless he can also show that a reasonable accommodation was possible and would have led to a reassignment position.").

[157] *See* Fjellstad v. Pizza Hut of Am., Inc., 188 F.3d 944, 952 (8th Cir. 1999); *see also* Mengine v. Runyon, 114 F.3d 415, 420–21 (3d Cir. 1997) ("Nonetheless, if an employer fails to engage in the interactive process, it may not discover a way in which the employee's disability could have been reasonably accommodated, thereby risking violation of the Rehabilitation Act.").

[158] *Cf.* 42 U.S.C. § 1981a(a)(3) (2006) (establishing good-faith-effort defense to damages awards in accommodations cases).

[159] Tobin v. Liberty Mut. Ins. Co., 433 F.3d 100, 108 (1st Cir. 2005).

when requesting an accommodation.[160]

[E]   Alcoholism and Use of Illegal Drugs

The ADA excludes current users of illegal drugs from the protections of title I when an employer or other covered entity acts on the basis of the employee or applicant's use of the drugs.[161] However, the statute provides that a person will be protected by title I if he or she has successfully completed a supervised drug rehabilitation program and is no longer illegally using drugs or has otherwise been successfully rehabilitated and is no longer illegally using drugs. Someone who is participating in a supervised rehabilitation program who is not engaging in illegal drug use also is protected by the law, as is a person erroneously regarded as engaging in illegal drug use who in fact is not doing so. A person who is in rehabilitation or has completed rehabilitation may be subject to reasonable drug testing policies or procedures.[162] A person who is an alcoholic may be covered by the ADA, if the person meets the definition of a qualified individual.[163]

Employers have a number of prerogatives regarding employees who use alcohol or illegal drugs, and these operate irrespective of whether the employee is covered by title I. Employers may forbid the illegal use of drugs, as well as the use of alcohol at the workplace by all employees; they may require that employees not be under the influence of alcohol or engaged in the use of illegal drugs at the workplace.[164] Moreover, employers may hold an employee who engages in illegal use of drugs or who is an alcoholic to the same qualification standards for employment or for job performance and behavior that the employer holds other employees to. The wording of the statute may cause some confusion, because "qualification standards" is a term normally associated with decisions to hire but in this instance the statute also applies it to job performance and behavior. The underlying message is that uniform rules for hiring and workplace conduct are permissible even if they disadvantage persons who are alcoholics or use illegal drugs.

A more difficult question is whether, in light of that language, a person who is an alcoholic is entitled to reasonable accommodations so that he or she can meet the standards for hiring or performance and behavior. For example, a person with alcoholism may request a leave to participate in a treatment program, or ask for a modified schedule in order to attend meetings of Alcoholics Anonymous. The Title I EEOC Technical Assistance Manual states that the ADA may "require

---

[160] *See, e.g.*, Reed v. LePage Bakeries, Inc., 244 F.3d 254, 260–61 (1st Cir. 2001) (stating that because employee's disability and need for accommodation often are not known to employer until accommodation request is made, ADA's reasonable accommodation requirement usually must be triggered by employee request).

[161] 42 U.S.C.S. § 12114(a) (LexisNexis 2011).

[162] § 12114(b).

[163] *See* Office of Senate Sergeant at Arms v. Office of Senate Fair Employment Practices, 95 F.3d 1102, 1105 (Fed. Cir. 1996).

[164] 42 U.S.C. § 12114(c) (2000). Some additional restrictions regarding alcohol and drugs are permitted under the Drug-Free Workforce Act and federal regulations applicable to specified industries. § 12114(c)(3), (5).

consideration of reasonable accommodation for a drug addict who is rehabilitated and not using drugs or an alcoholic who remains a 'qualified individual with a disability.' " The Manual continues: "For example, a modified work schedule, to permit the individual to attend an ongoing self-help program, might be a reasonable accommodation for such an employee." Various courts have also affirmed that persons who are disabled because of alcoholism are entitled to reasonable accommodations.[165]

Raytheon Corp. v. Hernandez, discussed above in connection with the ban on disparate impact discrimination, gave the Supreme Court the opportunity to determine whether the ADA gave preferential rights for rehiring to an employee lawfully terminated for violating workplace rules concerning drug use.[166] The Supreme Court, however, refused to reach that question because the lower court did not apply the proper analysis in determining whether the failure to rehire the employee was based on his disability.

[F] Accommodations for Persons Regarded as Disabled

As noted in Chapter Two, the ADA Amendments Act codified caselaw establishing that persons protected under the statute solely by virtue of being regarded as having a disability are not entitled to reasonable accommodations.[167] Although many courts took this position, it is not entirely logical, even taking into account the liberalization of the definition of disability in the Amendments.[168] Consider the example of the person with skin graft scars or other disfigurements. It would strike many as form of disability discrimination if an employer refused to make an exception to a requirement that all workers wear a uniform that left affected parts of the worker's body uncovered when the individual would prefer them to be covered, as with long sleeves rather than short, or a higher neckline, or trousers rather than a skirt. If the person claims statutory coverage solely on the

---

[165] *See* Corbett v. National Prods. Co., 1995 U.S. Dist. LEXIS 3949 (E.D. Pa. Mar 27, 1995) (upholding jury verdict when employer failed to provide accommodation of leave to attend alcoholism treatment program); *see also* Brown v. Lucky Stores, Inc., 246 F.3d 1182 (9th Cir. 2001) (rejecting claim on ground that plaintiff never requested accommodation); Office of Senate Sergeant at Arms v. Office of Senate Fair Employment Practices, 95 F.3d 1102, 1107 (Fed. Cir. 1996) (stating that "[t]reatment would seem to be essential to any accommodation for alcoholism" and refusing to require accommodation characterized as retrospective in sense of providing fresh start); Maull v. Division of State Police, 141 F. Supp. 2d 463, 474 (D.D.C. 2001) (quoting language from Manual but further noting "the ADA does not require an employer to lower his job performance expectations in order to accommodate an employee with alcoholism").

[166] 540 U.S. 44 (2003). The case is discussed *supra* § 3.04.

[167] 42 U.S.C.S. § 12201(h) (LexisNexis 2011); *see* 29 C.F.R. § 1630, 2(o)(4) (2011) (employment regulation). Cases on the issue were in conflict, though the no-accommodations cases appeared to predominate. *Compare* Kaplan v. City of N. Las Vegas, 323 F.3d 1226 (9th Cir. 2003); Weber v. Strippit, Inc., 186 F.3d 907 (8th Cir. 1999); *and* Newberry v. East Tex. State Univ., 161 F.3d 276 (5th Cir. 1998) (no accommodations) *with* D'Angelo v. ConAgra Foods, Inc., 422 F.3d 1220 (11th Cir. 2005); Kelly v. Metallics West, Inc., 410 F.3d 670 (10th Cir. 2005); *and* Williams v. Philadelphia Hous. Auth. Police Dep't, 380 F.3d 751 (3d Cir. 2004) (accommodations required).

[168] *See* Lawrence D. Rosenthal, *Reasonable Accommodations for Individuals Regarded as Having Disabilities Under the Americans with Disabilities Act? Why "No" Should Not Be the Answer*, 36 Seton Hall L. Rev. 895 (2006).

basis of the regarded-as part of the definition, however, he or she not be able to demand the accommodation. Nonetheless, many such individuals will be protected as well under the actual impairment or record of impairment parts of the definition, and in that case they may demand reasonable accommodations.

§ 3.06   MEDICAL EXAMINATIONS AND INQUIRIES

The ADA's provisions on medical examinations and inquiries are remarkably complex. They may be broken down by their timing: (1) pre-employment, or more precisely, pre-conditional offer of employment; (2) post-conditional offer, but before beginning employment; and (3) during the course of employment. Even when a clear violation of the statute is shown, there sometimes are difficult issues with regard to proof of damages and other remedies issues. The ADA covers drug tests separately from other medical examinations, and different rules apply with regard to that topic.

[A]   Pre-Employment Inquiries

Before making a conditional offer of employment to a job applicant, the employer is not permitted to conduct a medical examination or make inquiries of the applicant about whether the applicant has a disability or the nature or severity of the disability.[169] Before the conditional offer, however, the employer may make inquiries about the applicant's ability to perform job-related functions.[170] The applicable regulation says that an employer may ask the applicant to describe or demonstrate how, with or without reasonable accommodation, the applicant will be able to perform job-related functions.[171] According to the EEOC Interpretive Guidance, questions that relate to the applicant's ability to perform job-related functions "should not be phrased in terms of disability."[172] For example, an employer may ask whether an applicant has a driver's license if driving is a job function, but may not ask if the applicant has a visual disability.

. If, however, the applicant has a known disability and is requesting a reasonable accommodation, at least one leading case would permit the employer to require the applicant to produce a medical certification of ability to perform the job without restrictions or with specified accommodations. *Grenier v. Cyanamid Plastics, Inc.*, considered the case of Andre Grenier, electrician who was placed on disability leave after displaying irrational behavior on the job.[173] He was terminated after his continuous service credits expired, but later reapplied for his old job, stating that he could do the essential functions with reasonable accommodations. The employer initially denied that it was accepting applications for the position, but said that in any instance it would require a notice from Grenier's physician either stating that he was prepared to return to work without restrictions or identifying the

---

[169]   42 U.S.C.S. § 12112(d)(2)(A) (LexisNexis 2011).

[170]   § 12112(d)(2)(B).

[171]   29 C.F.R. § 1630.14(a) (2011).

[172]   ADA Title I EEOC Interpretive Guidance, 29 C.F.R. § 1630, App. § 1630.13(a) (2011).

[173]   70 F.3d 667 (1st Cir. 1995).

reasonable accommodations that would be needed. Eventually, the employer provided an application, Grenier applied, and the employer rejected him. In Grenier's suit alleging a violation of 42 U.S.C. § 12112(d)(2), the court of appeals affirmed the district court's grant of summary judgment to the employer. The court reasoned that a permissible inquiry could go beyond technical ability and experience, which are not the only essential requirements of a given job. Moreover, under the circumstances, where the employer knows of the applicant's disability, the employer may ask the applicant to describe or demonstrate how, with or without reasonable accommodations, the applicant will be able to do the job.[174] The court went on to reason that in this case the medical certification was an inquiry rather than an examination,[175] and, following an interpretation advanced by the EEOC, held that some inquiries of third parties are permissible under the statute even before a conditional offer of employment. The court said the case should be treated similarly to one in which an employee is returning from disability leave, and that in such a situation, the employer may demand medical certification of the ability to return to work. According to the court, it would interfere with the interactive process of identifying accommodations if the employer could not ask an applicant with a known disability about accommodations even though the EEOC's interpretations prohibit an applicant who voluntarily discloses a disability from being asked at the pre-offer stage about the type of accommodations needed. The court said the reason for that rule is that the inquiry would be likely to elicit information about the nature and severity of the disability, something the court considered irrelevant when the disability is already known to the employer from previous work experience with the applicant.[176]

Providing something of a contrast to Grenier is *Leonel v. American Airlines.*[177] There the court held that a medical examination that revealed the plaintiffs' HIV-positive status was prohibited when it was not the final step in the employee selection process, but instead was to precede a background check that would include employment verification and a criminal history investigation. Referring to state law as well as the ADA, the court declared that "Both the ADA and [California] FEHA deliberately allow job applicants to shield their private medical information until they know that, absent an inability to meet the medical requirements, they will be hired, and that if they are not hired, the true reason for the employer's decision will be transparent."[178]

---

[174] The court said the inquiry would not necessarily be permissible where the employer was less familiar with the nature or extant of the disability or its effect on the applicant's job performance. *Id.* at 675 n.4. Nevertheless, the court declared, "The ADA does not require an employer to wear blinders to a known disability at the pre-offer stage . . . ." *Id.* at 675. In this case, the employee was the recipient of disability benefits, a fact the court stressed at various points in the opinion.

[175] The court noted that the certification did not "necessitate new tests or procedures . . . ." *Id.* at 676.

[176] *See also* Harris v. Harris & Hart, Inc., 206 F.3d 838 (9th Cir. 2000).

[177] 400 F.3d 702 (9th Cir. 2005).

[178] *Id.* at 711. The court allowed a possible out to the employer, however, saying that "American cannot penalize the appellants for failing to disclose their HIV-positive status — unless the company can establish that it could not reasonably have completed the background checks before subjecting the appellants to medical examinations and questioning." *Id.* at 709–10.

The title I provision on pre-employment inquiries is not limited to individuals with disabilities. In *Griffin v. Steeltek, Inc., (Griffin I)*, a person who did not claim he had a disability applied for a position as a grinder but was not hired, he alleged, because of improper medical inquiries.[179] The employer asked whether the applicant had received workers' compensation or disability income payments and whether the applicant had "physical defects which preclude you from performing certain jobs," and asked for a description if the answer to either inquiry was yes. Reversing a grant of summary judgment against the applicant, the court of appeals held that there was no requirement that a plaintiff had to have a disability or be regarded as having a disability in order to recover damages proximately caused by a violation of the medical inquiries provision. It stressed that the underlying policy of preventing disability discrimination is best served by "allowing all job applicants who are subjected to illegal medical questioning and who are in fact injured thereby to bring a cause of action against offending employers, rather than to limit that right to a narrower subset of applicants who are in fact disabled."[180]

Proving a violation of this provision does not guarantee a recovery, however. After the *Griffin I* decision, the case went to trial and the jury rendered a verdict in favor of the employer, declaring in answer to a special interrogatory that the plaintiff had not suffered any injury as a result of being asked the questions.[181] On appeal (*Griffin II*), the court noted that ample evidence supported the conclusion that the plaintiff was not hired because he lacked the requisite experience as a grinder and that the job went instead to a former employee whom the company had tried to locate and rehire before seeking new applicants for the job.[182] Seeing no showing of intentional injury, the court rejected claims for nominal and punitive damages and for attorneys' fees. Other cases support *Griffin II*'s approach.[183]

[B] Medical Examinations After Conditional Offer

Once a conditional offer of employment has been made to an applicant, the employer may require a medical examination before employment begins. The offer may be conditioned on the examination results as long as all entering employees are subjected to such an examination regardless of disability, information obtained is collected and maintained separately and treated confidentially, and the examination results are used consistently with the nondiscrimination requirements of the ADA.[184] The language of this section does not require a medical examination

---

[179] 160 F.3d 591 (10th Cir. 1998).

[180] *Id.* at 594; *see also* Conroy v. New York State Dep't of Corr. Servs., 333 F.3d 88, 94–94 (2d Cir. 2003) (collecting authorities).

[181] Griffin v. Steeltek, Inc., 261 F.3d 1026, 1028 (10th Cir. 2001).

[182] *Id.*

[183] *See, e.g.,* Armstrong v. Turner Indus., Inc., 141 F.3d 554 (5th Cir. 1998).

[184] 42 U.S.C.S. § 12112(d)(3) (LexisNexis 2011). Confidentiality is not absolute. Supervisors and managers may be informed of necessary work restrictions and accommodations; first aid and safety personnel may be informed, when appropriate, if the disability may require emergency treatment; and government officials investigating ADA compliance must be provided relevant information if they request it. § 12112(d)(3)(B).

to be restricted to job functions or be otherwise job-related.[185] Of course, if the information obtained in the medical examination is used to screen out a prospective employee with a disability, the criteria on which that is done must be job-related and consistent with business necessity.[186] The regulations applicable to section 504 on the topic of pre-employment inquiries and medical examinations are generally consistent with the title I requirements, but feature somewhat greater flexibility on when medical examinations can be required and more specificity on how they are to be conducted and used.[187]

[C] Inquiries and Examinations of Current Employees

Current employees are protected under 42 U.S.C. § 12112(d)(4), which forbids medical examinations and inquiries as to whether the employee is an individual with a disability or what the nature and severity of the disability is, unless the examination or inquiry is shown to be job related and consistent with business necessity. Employers are permitted to conduct voluntary medical examinations and take voluntary medical histories that are part of employee health programs at the work site. In addition, employers and other entities covered under title I are explicitly permitted to make inquiries into the ability of the employee to perform job-related functions.[188]

The leading case on this subsection of the law is *Roe v. Cheyenne Mountain Conference Resort, Inc.*[189] In that case, the defendant employer adopted a policy requiring all employees to report all drugs they used, including prescription and other legal medications. The court of appeals affirmed a grant of summary judgment against the defendant on the claim that it violated § 12112(d)(4). The court also overturned denial of injunctive relief and remanded various state law

---

[185] 29 C.F.R. § 1630.14(b)(3) (2011); *see* Norman-Bloodsaw v. Lawrence Berkeley Lab., 135 F.3d 1260 (9th Cir. 1998) ("[T]he ADA imposes no restriction on the scope of entrance examinations; it only guarantees the confidentiality of the information gathered, . . . and restricts the use to which an employer may put the information.").

[186] 42 U.S.C.S. § 12112(b)(6) (LexisNexis 2011); *see* §§ 12112(b)(3) (banning standards, criteria, and methods of discrimination that have discriminatory effect or perpetuate discrimination), 12113(a) (job-related and consistent with business necessity); *see also* 29 C.F.R. § 1630.14(b)(3) (2011) ("Medical examinations conducted in accordance with this section do not have to be job-related and consistent with business necessity. However, if certain criteria are used to screen out an employee or employees with disabilities as a result of such an examination or inquiry, the exclusionary criteria must be job-related and consistent with business necessity, and performance of the essential job functions cannot be accomplished with reasonable accommodation as required in this part."). At least one court has ruled that only persons with disabilities or regarded as having disabilities within the meaning of the ADA may recover for violations of § 12112(d)(3). O'Neal v. City of New Albany, 293 F.3d 998, 1010 & n.2 (7th Cir. 2002). *But see* Garrison v. Baker Hughes Oilfield Operations, Inc., 287 F.3d 955 (10th Cir. 2002) (affirming jury verdict in favor of worker who presented evidence employer used results of medical examination to discriminate against him on basis of perceived disability without reaching conclusion on perceived or actual disability status of plaintiff); *see also* Leonel v. American Airlines, Inc., 400 F.3d 702 (9th Cir. 2005) (permitting case to proceed on basis of showing that employer's conditional offer failed to meet standards of genuine offer, without discussing actual or regarded-as disability status of plaintiffs).

[187] *See* 29 C.F.R. § 32.15 (2011).

[188] 42 U.S.C.S. § 12112(d)(4)(B) (LexisNexis 2011). The information gained must be treated confidentially, maintained separately, and used in a manner consistent with title I. § 12112(d)(4)(C).

[189] 124 F.3d 1221 (10th Cir. 1997).

claims to state court. The defendant waived all but its jurisdictional arguments on appeal, but the court ruled that no jurisdictional obstacle to suit was presented by the fact that the EEOC issued its right-to-sue letter immediately after the plaintiff filed her charge with the agency, the fact that the plaintiff did not allege she was a person with a disability, or the fact that because the employer suspended the policy the injury she experienced was threatened, rather than actual. The court of appeals agreed with the district court that the policy violated § 12112(d)(4).[190] The defendant did not appeal the district court's determination that the inquiries made were not job-related and consistent with business necessity.[191]

Roe established that an employee need not have a disability to assert a claim that the employer violated § 12112(d)(4). The court said:

> [P]laintiff's ability to maintain the particular ADA claim she has alleged does not require her to prove that she is an individual with a disability. As the district judge aptly observed, adopting defendant's position would defeat the very purpose of prohibiting disability related inquiries: "It makes little sense to require an employee to demonstrate that he has a disability to prevent his employer from inquiring as to whether or not he has a disability." . . . We also agree with the district court's reasoning that this common sense rejection of defendant's argument is consistent with the statutory language: "The ADA explicitly prohibits employers from making disability-related inquiries of employees, unless the inquiry is job-related or consistent with business necessity. . . . This provision applies to all employees. Unlike suits based on a failure to provide a reasonable accommodation, this provision is not limited to qualified individuals with disabilities."[192]

Other courts reach the same conclusion.[193] However, courts have suggested that a tangible injury will need to be shown to make out a claim for disability discrimination based on a violation of the inquiry provision.[194] Courts are in conflict as to whether the relevant ADA provision bars an employer from requiring employees returning from sick leave to submit a physician's note stating the nature of the illness.[195]

---

[190] *Id.* at 1230.

[191] On the topic of the consistency of medical inquiries with business necessity, see Brownfield v. City of Yakima, 612 F.3d 1140 (9th Cir. 2010) (upholding requirement of fitness for duty exam of police officer who manifested emotionally volatile behavior as job-related and consistent with business necessity; stating that business necessity is "quite high" but that "standard may be met even before an employee's work performance declines . . . ."); Conroy v. New York State Dep't of Corr. Servs., 333 F.3d 88 (2d Cir. 2003) (reversing grant of summary judgment for employee).

[192] *Id.* at 1229.

[193] *E.g.*, Cossette v. Minnesota Power & Light, 188 F.3d 964, 969 (8th Cir. 1999); Griffin v. Steeltek, Inc., 160 F.3d 591, 595 (10th Cir. 1998).

[194] Cossette v. Minnesota Power & Light, 188 F.3d 964, 970 (8th Cir. 1999) (noting possibility of claims based on disclosure causing inability to obtain other job and illegal disclosure of medical information); *see* Armstrong v. Turner Indus., 141 F.3d 554, 559 (5th Cir. 1998) (affirming summary judgment against applicant alleging violation of pre-offer inquiry provision).

[195] *Compare* Lee v. City of Columbus, Ohio, 636 F.3d 245 (6th Cir. 2011) (policy permitted), *with* Conroy v. New York State Dep't of Corr. Servs., 333 F.3d 88 (2d Cir. 2003) (policy forbidden).

[D] Drug Testing and Related Issues

Title I of the ADA provides explicitly that tests to determine the illegal use of drugs are not considered medical examinations for purposes of the rules outlined above.[196] An employer may ask follow-up questions in response to a positive drug test, asking, for example, about lawful prescription drug use. The employer may be liable under the ADA, however, for making disability-related inquiries before a conditional offer of employment has been made.[197]

§ 3.07 DISCRIMINATION BY CONTRACTUAL ARRANGEMENT

The basic requirement of 42 U.S.C. § 12112(b)(2) is that an employer is barred from participating in contractual or other relationships that have the effect of subjecting a qualified applicant or employee with a disability to discrimination that would otherwise be illegal. The Sixth Circuit Court of Appeals relied on this provision in holding that a city could not lawfully delegate to a doctor the task of determining whether an individual met the medical standards for being a police-man, when the doctor had acted on the unsubstantiated opinion that merely being positive for HIV necessarily disqualifies a job candidate with HIV seropositivity from the position.[198] Although the statutory language specifically refers to contrac-tual arrangements with labor unions as relationships that must not be permitted to have the effect of discrimination, courts have been reluctant to overturn seniority systems embodied in collective bargaining agreements when the systems present obstacles to reassignment of jobs in order to accommodate employees with disabilities.[199] The Supreme Court has lent such holdings a degree of support by stating in *US Airways, Inc. v. Barnett* that if an employer shows that a requested accommodation conflicts with seniority rules, that will ordinarily be sufficient to show that accommodation is not reasonable.[200] The seniority system in *Barnett* was voluntary on the part of the employer, rather than adopted as part of negotiations with a union, so the contractual arrangements provision of the ADA did not come into play. But if it is ordinarily not a reasonable accommodation to modify a voluntarily adopted seniority system to accommodate an employee with a disability, the inference might be drawn that an employer bound by a collective bargaining

---

[196] 42 U.S.C.S. § 12114(d)(1) (LexisNexis 2011).

[197] Harrison v. Benchmark Elecs. Huntsville, Inc., 593 F.3d 1206, 1215–16 (11th Cir. 2010).

[198] Holiday v. City of Chattanooga, 206 F.3d 637 (6th Cir. 2000).

[199] Willis v. Pacific Mar. Ass'n, 236 F.3d 1160, 1165 (9th Cir. 2001); Davis v. Florida Power & Light Co., 205 F.3d 1301, 1307 (11th Cir. 2000); Feliciano v. Rhode Island, 160 F.3d 780, 787 (1st Cir. 1998); Cassidy v. Detroit Edison Co., 138 F.3d 629 634 (6th Cir. 1998); Kralik v. Durbin, 130 F.3d 76, 81–83 (3d Cir. 1997); Foreman v. Babcock & Wilcox Co., 117 F.3d 800, 810 (5th Cir. 1997); Eckles v. Consolidated Rail Corp., 94 F.3d 1041, 1051 (7th Cir. 1996); Benson v. Northwest Airlines, Inc., 62 F.3d 1108, 1114 (8th Cir. 1995); Milton v. Scrivner, Inc., 53 F.3d 1118, 1125 (10th Cir. 1995). These cases preceded *US Airways v. Barnett*, 535 U.S. 391 (2002), and so the continuing validity of their approach to the reasonable accommodations issue needs to be re-evaluated in light of that decision. *See supra* § 3.05 (discussing reasonable accommodation).

[200] 535 U.S. 391 (2002). An employee may present evidence of special circumstances that makes exception to a seniority rule reasonable under particular facts. *Id.* at 394.

agreement ordinarily need not try to force modification of a seniority provision in the contract to provide an accommodation for a worker with a disability.

§ 3.08   ASSOCIATIONAL DISCRIMINATION

Title I of the ADA bars "excluding or otherwise denying equal jobs or benefits to a qualified individual because of the known disability of an individual with whom the qualified individual is known to have a relationship or association."[201] A noteworthy case on this provision is *Den Hartog v. Wasatch Academy*, in which an employee of a boarding school sued after he was fired, allegedly as a consequence of threatening behavior by the employee's mentally ill son with respect to the school's headmaster and his family.[202] The Tenth Circuit Court of Appeals affirmed a grant of summary judgment against the employee. The court noted that no sharp dichotomy can be drawn between disability itself and disability-caused misconduct, so the summary judgment could not be affirmed on the ground that the employee failed to adhere to the standards of conduct imposed on other employees.[203] Unlike some other associational discrimination cases decided against the plaintiffs, in this case the association with the person with a disability did not impair the employee's own job performance.[204] Nevertheless, the court affirmed the summary judgment against the employee, ruling that the defense that an employee constitutes a direct threat to the health or safety of others applies not just to threats posed by employees, as its language suggests, but also to threats posed by associates or relatives of employees. The court thought that any other construction of the defense would be "odd," and would undermine the general legislative policy embodied in the ADA permitting denial of equal treatment when a person with a disability poses a real and objective direct threat.[205] The court felt that the absence of any statutory entitlement to reasonable accommodation of an employee on account of being associated with a person with a disability fortified its decision to extend the applicability of the defense beyond its language.[206]

Courts have tried to determine what a plaintiff must show to establish associational discrimination in the absence of direct evidence that a person was terminated or denied a job on the basis of that person's association with someone with a disability. The *Den Hartog* court advanced a test requiring the plaintiff to show that the plaintiff was qualified for the job at the time of the adverse action; that the plaintiff was subjected to the adverse action; that the plaintiff was known by the employer at the time to have a relative or associate with a disability; and the adverse employment action occurred under circumstances raising a reasonable inference that the disability of the associate or relative was a determining factor in the employer's decision to take the action.[207] The court adapted this test from the

---

[201]   42 U.S.C.S. § 12112(b)(4) (LexisNexis 2011).

[202]   129 F.3d 1076 (10th Cir. 1997).

[203]   *Id.* at 1088.

[204]   *Id.* at 1084.

[205]   *Id.* at 1090–92.

[206]   *Id.* at 1091.

[207]   *Id.* at 1085.

method the Supreme Court adopted in *McDonnell Douglas Corp. v. Green*[208] for evaluating title VII cases where there is no direct evidence of discrimination.[209]

In *Larimer v. International Business Machines, Inc.*, the Seventh Circuit criticized *Den Hartog*'s approach, saying that requiring circumstances that raise a reasonable inference that the disability of the associate caused the action was effectively requiring proof of discrimination, which is what the *McDonnell Douglas* test was designed to keep the plaintiff from having to do.[210] The *Larimer* court, however, also said that a closer adaptation of *McDonnell Douglas*, one that would lead to a finding of discrimination if the plaintiff is meeting the employer's expectations, that the employer knew of the association, that the employer fired the plaintiff and hired someone without such an association, would not be appropriate, because the inference of discriminatory conduct is, in the opinion of the Seventh Circuit, not strong enough.[211]

Larimer, instead, proposed that the plaintiff might raise an inference of discrimination if the action against the plaintiff falls into one of three categories in which the employer has a motive to discriminate on the basis of the plaintiff's association with someone with a disability: (1) "expense" — when the association is likely to cause expense to the employer, as with a spouse who is costly to a company's group health plan; (2) "disability by association" — when the employer fears that the employee will transmit a disabling condition from the person with a disability to the employee him- or herself or to others in the workplace; or (3) "distraction" — when the employer expects that the employee's performance will suffer because of the needs of the person with a disability.[212] The court gave no basis for the origin of these categories nor any explanation of why they ought to be considered exclusive.

Applying its approach to the situation of a computer software salesman who was fired shortly after his wife gave birth to twin daughters who had disabling conditions, incurring large expenses for the company's medical plan, the court upheld a grant of summary judgment. It said that category number one did not apply because there was no evidence that health benefits paid out affected the budget of the unit that employed and discharged the plaintiff; category two did not apply because there was no evidence of communicable disease or increased likelihood of the plaintiff's own future disability; and category three failed because there was no evidence that the plaintiff was absent or distracted at work due to the daughters' disability.[213] By contrast, in *Dewitt v. Proctor Hospital*, a later case in which a hospital fired a nurse whose husband was undergoing expensive cancer treatment, the Seventh Circuit overturned a grant of summary judgment to the hospital, relying on evidence suggesting that the hospital faced financial trouble, was very cost-conscious, bore many of the medical expenses directly, and had

---

[208] 411 U.S. 792, 802 (1973).

[209] *Den Hartog*, 129 F.3d at 1085.

[210] 370 F.3d 698, 701–02 (7th Cir. 2004).

[211] *Id.* at 702.

[212] *Id.* at 700.

[213] *Id.* at 701.

informed managers to be "creative" in cutting costs.[214] Moreover, the employee's supervisor asked her about her husband's condition and lower-cost treatment options, and the timing of the termination was suspicious. The court analyzed the case without relying on the *McDonnell-Douglas* framework.[215]

Relying on the ADA's legislative history, the EEOC's Interpretive Guidance states that persons who are associated with individuals with disabilities are not entitled to reasonable accommodations on account of the association.[216] A person associated with a person who has a disability does not fit within the ADA's definition of "individual with a disability," unlike persons who themselves have a record of an impairment or are regarded as having an impairment.[217] A number of cases state that a person who merely has a casual association with someone with a disability cannot prevail under the association provision.[218]

§ 3.09   ADDITIONAL DEFENSES

Title I lists a number of defenses to employment-related ADA actions. The first, that a qualification, test, or selection criterion that screens out persons with disabilities is shown to be job-related and consistent with business necessity, is discussed above. Another, that religious organizations may prefer their members for employment, is also discussed briefly above. Still another relates to persons with infectious and communicable diseases and food handling, and is discussed briefly in Chapter 2. Additional defenses that are relevant to title I cases are limitations, exhaustion of administrative remedies, that the worker constitutes a direct threat to safety, and that the employment claim is subject to mandatory arbitration.[219] These will be discussed below.

[A]   Limitations

There are two relevant limitations for ADA claims under title I.[220] The first begins to run when the unlawful conduct took place and tolls when the claimant files a charge with the EEOC. The limitations period is 180 days, but if the claimant institutes proceedings with a state or local agency with authority to seek relief from the unlawful practice or begin criminal proceedings with respect to it, the claimant may file the EEOC charge within 300 days of the unlawful conduct or

---

[214] 517 F.3d 944 (7th Cir. 2008).

[215] *Id.* at 948; *see also* Trujillo v. PacifiCorp, 524 F.3d 1149 (10th Cir. 2008) (overturning grant of summary judgment to employer in case involving employees terminated after son ran up large medical expenses for self-insured company).

[216] ADA Title I EEOC Interpretive Guidance, 29 C.F.R. § 1630, App. § 1630.8 (2011).

[217] *See generally supra* § 3.05[F] (discussing accommodations for persons regarded as having disabilities).

[218] *E.g.*, Freilich v. Upper Chesapeake Health, Inc., 313 F.3d 205, 215–16 (4th Cir. 2002); Oliveras-Sifre v. Puerto Rico Dep't of Health, 214 F.3d 23, 26 (1st Cir. 2000).

[219] Of these, only the direct threat provision is listed under the "Defenses" section of the statute. *See* 42 U.S.C.S. § 12113(b) (LexisNexis 2011).

[220] Employment discrimination claims subject to title II of the ADA or section 504 may be subject to different limitations, which are discussed *infra* Chapter 6.

30 days after receiving notice that the state or local agency has terminated proceedings, whichever is earlier.[221] If the state has such an agency and the EEOC gives that agency the first opportunity to look into discrimination complaints, the state is called a deferral state. In deferral states with work sharing agreements that so provide, filing with the EEOC constitutes proper filing with the state or local agency. The deferral state and work sharing concepts are further explained below in the discussion of the exhaustion requirement.

Accrual rules affect the operation of the deadline to file with the EEOC. The traditional approach with respect to federal statutory violations is that the action accrues and the limitations period begins to run when the plaintiff has a complete and present cause of action.[222] Under the familiar "discovery rule," the period's beginning is further delayed when the plaintiff is unaware of the facts about the cause and existence of the injury and by exercise of reasonable diligence should not have discovered the cause and existence of the injury.[223]

Just when it is that the injury takes place has been a source of continuing dispute in the case law under the title VII provisions applicable to title I of the ADA. In *National Railroad Passenger Corp. v. Morgan*, the Supreme Court distinguished between discrete acts of discrimination and conduct which, cumulatively, amounts to a hostile environment.[224] In the former cases, the plaintiff may recover only for discriminatory acts that occur in the 180 or 300 days. In the latter cases, activities stretching back before the limitations period may form part of a continuing violation that goes forward into the period if any relevant activity is within the 180 or 300 days before the filing of the charge.[225]

The second limitations applies if the EEOC dismisses the charge, or if, within 180 days after the filing of the charge or after the conclusion of a period during which the EEOC defers action while the charge is handled by a state or local agency, whichever is later, neither the EEOC nor the Attorney General has filed a civil action against the defendant or has entered into a conciliation agreement to

---

[221] ADA title I incorporates the relevant provisions of title VII of the Civil Rights Act. 42 U.S.C. § 12117(a) (2006). The 180 and 300 days limitations are found at 42 U.S.C.S. § 2000e-5(e) (LexisNexis 2011).

[222] *See, e.g.,* Bay Area Laundry & Dry Cleaning Pension Trust Fund v. Ferber Corp., 522 U.S. 192, 195 (1997).

[223] National R.R. Passenger Corp. v. Morgan, 536 U.S. 101, 114 n.7 (2002) (discussing possible application of discovery rule in title VII case). Congress codified a form of this rule with respect to discrimination in compensation in the Lilly Ledbetter Fair Pay Act, Pub. L. No. 111-2, 123 Stat. 5 (2009) (codified at 42 U.S.C.S. § 2000e-5(e)(3) (LexisNexis 2011)).

[224] 536 U.S. 101 (2002).

[225] *Id.* at 117–18 ("[W]e do not hold, as have some of the Circuits, that the plaintiff may not base a suit on individual acts that occurred outside the statute of limitations unless it would have been unreasonable to expect the plaintiff to sue before the statute ran on such conduct. The statute does not separate individual acts that are part of the hostile environment claim from the whole for the purposes of timely filing and liability. And the statute does not contain a requirement that the employee file a charge prior to 180 or 300 days 'after' the single unlawful practice 'occurred.' Given, therefore, that the incidents constituting a hostile work environment are part of one unlawful employment practice, the employer may be liable for all acts that are part of this single claim. In order for the charge to be timely, the employee need only file a charge within 180 or 300 days of any act that is part of the hostile work environment.").

which the claimant is a party. In that instance, the EEOC will issue a notice of dismissal advising the claimant of the right to sue or will upon request issue a right to sue letter following expiration of the time period. The claimant's civil action must be filed in court within 90 days of receipt of the right to sue letter.[226] Equitable tolling may extend the limitations period,[227] but failings of diligence on the part of the plaintiff will not support tolling, and the tolling doctrine is to be used "sparingly."[228]

Related to the topic of limitations is the affirmative defense of laches, which applies when a person unreasonably delays in asserting rights and the defending party is prejudiced because of the delay. The defending party bears the burden of establishing the defense, and frequently the defense fails because prejudice is not shown or not shown to be the consequence of delays caused by the plaintiff.[229]

[B] Exhaustion of Administrative Remedies

Title I of the ADA requires claimants to file their charges administratively before they may bring suit, and suit is subject to dismissal if the plaintiff has failed to pursue administrative remedies.[230] If there is a state or local agency with authority to seek relief from the unlawful practice or begin criminal proceedings with respect to it, the claimant must institute proceedings in that agency, and may not file a charge with the EEOC until 60 days after filing with the state or local agency, unless the agency has terminated the proceedings first.[231] The charge must allege what the basis is for the claim of discrimination, and courts have refused to consider allegations of discrimination that are insufficiently related to the allegations of the charge and thus fall outside its scope.[232]

States with state or local agencies that can grant relief from conduct that violates the ADA are deemed deferral states. In those states, the EEOC defers action for up to 60 days for the state or local agency to act on the claimant's case.[233] Deferral states may enter into work sharing agreements with the EEOC, which typically provide that filing with the EEOC constitutes filing with the state or local agency as well. Thus in those states a claimant may file the charge initially with the

---

[226] 42 U.S.C.S. § 2000e-5(f)(1) (LexisNexis 2011).

[227] Baldwin County Welcome Ctr. v. Brown, 466 U.S. 147, 152 (1984) (denying tolling in title VII case when plaintiff mailed right-to-sue letter to court rather than filing complaint).

[228] Irwin v. Department of Veterans Affairs, 498 U.S. 89, 96 (1990) (finding no tolling of 30-day period to bring title VII suit against federal government under facts of case).

[229] See, e.g., EEOC v. Watkins Motor Lines, 463 F.3d 436 (6th Cir. 2006) (rejecting defense in ADA title I case).

[230] See 42 U.S.C.S. § 2000e-5 (LexisNexis 2011) (incorporated into ADA title I by reference in 42 U.S.C. § 12117(a)).

[231] § 2000e-5(c). Regarding exhaustion requirements, like limitations, ADA title I incorporates the relevant provisions of title VII of the Civil Rights Act. 42 U.S.C. § 12117(a) (2006).

[232] See, e.g., Kersting v. Wal-Mart Stores, Inc., 250 F.3d 1109, 1118 (7th Cir. 2001) (including incident of retaliatory conduct similar to that listed in charge and committed by same individual, but excluding other incidents dissimilar in nature and committed by others).

[233] 42 U.S.C.S. § 2000e-5(c) (LexisNexis 2011).

EEOC and meet the requirement to institute state or local proceedings by the EEOC filing.

Under its procedures, the EEOC investigates each charge and if it finds reasonable cause for the charge, it attempts to obtain a conciliation agreement from the employer. If the agreement is reached, the EEOC dismisses the charge. The EEOC has up to 30 days after the filing of the charge or the end of the period in which it defers to the state or local agency to obtain the conciliation agreement. The EEOC may file suit if it does not obtain conciliation.[234] If it does not pursue the claim, the EEOC will issue a right to sue letter. If more than 180 days has elapsed from the filing of the charge or the end of the deferral period, whichever is later, the EEOC must issue the letter on the request of the charging party.[235]

Although title II and section 504 share the same requirements of nondiscrimination with title I, title II and section 504 do not include any obligation on aggrieved applicants or employees to file charges of employment discrimination with the EEOC or exhaust other administrative remedies. In the years before passage of the ADA, the rule emerged that section 504 does not require exhaustion prior to bringing a claim; title II incorporates section 504's remedies. Thus the courts generally hold that employment discrimination claims under title II and section 504 do not need to be exhausted.[236]

[C] Direct Threat

One of the defenses listed in the ADA is that " 'qualification standards' may include a requirement that the individual shall not pose a direct threat to the health or safety of other individuals in the workplace."[237] The ADA's § 12111(3) further defines a direct threat as a "significant risk to the health and safety of others that cannot be eliminated by reasonable accommodation."[238] The applicable EEOC regulation defines direct threat as "as significant risk of substantial harm to the health or safety of the individual or others that cannot be eliminated or reduced by reasonable accommodation . . . ."[239] The discrepancy in these definitions of direct threat and the difference between the statute and the regulation involves the risk to the employee him- or herself. The absence of "self or" in front of "others" hardly seems inadvert. The drafters of the statute appear to have made a conscious choice to have danger to the individual taking on the job not constitute a defense to

---

[234] If the respondent is a government, governmental agency, or political subdivision, the EEOC is to refer the matter to the Attorney General instead of filing suit itself. 29 C.F.R. § 1601.27 (2011).

[235] The relevant EEOC procedures are found at 29 C.F.R. §§ 1601.1–.34 (2011).

[236] *E.g.,* Peterson v. University of Wis., Bd. of Regents, 818 F. Supp. 1276 (W.D. Wis. 1993); *see* Bledsoe v. Palm Beach Soil & Water Conservation Dist., 133 F.3d 816, 824 (11th Cir. 1998). As noted *supra* §, 3.01[A], however, a minority position contends that title II does not apply to employment at all.

[237] 42 U.S.C.S. § 12113(b) (LexisNexis 2011).

[238] Courts have stressed the importance of considering reasonable accommodations before concluding a direct threat exists. *See, e.g.,* EEOC v. Wal-Mart Stores, 477 F.3d 561, 572 (8th Cir. 2007) (possible accommodation of wheelchair for greeter prone to falling due to mobility impairment).

[239] 29 C.F.R. § 1630.2(r) (2011).

failure to hire that person for the job.[240] This fits in with the general goal of the ADA to end the paternalism that has historically characterized governmental and social attitudes towards persons with disabilities. The drafters of the regulation inserted the danger to self provision despite its absence in the legislation they were interpreting.

In *Chevron U.S.A., Inc. v. Echazabal*, however, the Supreme Court held unanimously that the regulation including the "or others" language was a permissible regulatory interpretation of the statute.[241] Mario Echazabal had worked for independent contractors at a refinery owned by the defendant. He twice applied for jobs with the defendant and received offers conditioned on passing physical examinations, but the physicals disclosed that he had liver abnormalities associated with hepatitis C. Chevron's doctors said continued exposure to toxins at the refinery would aggravate the disease, and after withdrawing the second employment offer, Chevron asked the independent contractor to reassign the plaintiff to a job not entailing exposure to the chemicals or to remove him from the refinery altogether. Ultimately, the contractor laid him off. When he sued under the ADA, Chevron relied on the medical report saying that plaintiff's employment at the refinery would endanger him and cited the regulation listing the presence of a direct threat to the safety of the individual as justification for failing to hire him and causing him to be discharged. Chevron won on summary judgment in the district court, but the Ninth Circuit Court of Appeals ruled that the threat-to-self regulation exceeded permissible rulemaking under the ADA.

The Supreme Court reversed, responding to the argument that specification of the danger to others excludes danger to self with three points it described as "strike[s] against" application of the expression-exclusion rule.[242] First, the danger to others language appears in a definition of qualification standards as something that may be included, not as part of an exclusive list or meaningful series. Second, Congress used the same language in the ADA that is found in the Rehabilitation Act and that the EEOC had interpreted as including danger to others in its Rehabilitation Act regulations. That three other agencies had not adopted this interpretation only underscored the uncertainty about congressional intentions. Third, a sensible application of rules about dangers could not begin and end with danger to "other individuals in the workplace," for an employer should be able to consider danger to customers or others.[243] Since Congress did not speak exhaustively on threats to the worker's own health, the danger-to-self interpretation gained the advantage of the rule in *Chevron U.S.A. Inc. v. Natural Resources Defense Council*,[244] which requires deference to any reasonable

---

[240] *See* 136 Cong. Rec. S9,697 (daily ed. July 13, 1990) (remarks of Sen. Kennedy) ("It is important, however, that the ADA specifically refers to health and safety threats to others. Under the ADA, employers may not deny a person an employment opportunity based on paternalistic concerns regarding the person's health.").

[241] 536 U.S. 73 (2002).

[242] *Id.* at 80.

[243] *Id.* at 84.

[244] 467 U.S. 837, 843 (1984).

interpretative regulation by the agency charged with making such regulations. The Court supported the conclusion that the regulation was reasonable by noting that an approach contrary to that of the regulation created the possibility of conflict with employer obligations to keep workers safe imposed by the Occupational Safety and Health Act.[245]

The Court's interpretation of the ADA contrasts with its interpretation of title VII's sex discrimination provision in *Automobile Workers v. Johnson Controls, Inc.*[246] There, the Court found facially discriminatory a policy adopted by a battery manufacturer that excluded all women, except those whose infertility was medically documented, from jobs involving actual or potential lead exposure exceeding a standard set by OSHA. The company defended the policy on the basis of the danger to the women workers and their fetuses should the women become pregnant and its own exposure to liability, but the Court said that title VII, as amended by the Pregnancy Discrimination Act, forbade the exclusion.[247] In *Echazabal*, the Court distinguished *Johnson Controls* by stating that it was concerned with a paternalistic judgment based on a broad category of gender, whereas the EEOC's ADA title I regulations require that applications of the direct threat provision have to be made on individualized assessments of risk.[248]

A common use of the direct-threat defense is when the employee is said to pose dangers of inflicting injury or communicating a contagious disease. In *Mauro v. Borgess Medical Center*, the Sixth Circuit Court of Appeals upheld a grant of summary judgment against an operating room technician who had been excluded from his job because he had AIDS.[249] The technician sued the hospital under section 504 and the ADA. The court applied the approach outlined in *Arline v. School Board*,[250] which looks to the nature of the risk, the duration of the risk, the severity of the risk, and the probabilities the disease will be transmitted and will cause varying risks of harm. The risk must be significant for the defense to apply; reasonable medical judgments of public health officials are to be deferred to in making the assessment. In *Mauro*, the court looked to a report of the Centers for Disease Control, which recommended that HIV-infected health workers not perform exposure-prone procedures, such as those involving simultaneous presence of the worker's fingers and a sharp instrument in a poorly visible or highly confined site in a patient's body, unless an expert review panel has been consulted and provides advice on when the workers may continue to perform the

---

[245] *Echazabal*, 536 U.S. at 84–85 (also noting potential concerns of time lost to sickness, turnover costs, and potential state tort liability). The Court found unpersuasive the evidence from the legislative history of congressional intent to exclude danger to self from the direct-threat provision, interpreting the materials as more a general condemnation of paternalism and pretextual safety justifications. *Id.* at 85 n.5.

[246] 499 U.S. 187 (1991).

[247] *Id.* at 199. The Court rejected an argument that sex constituted a bona fide occupational qualification in light of the safety concern. *Id.* at 205. It thought the danger of liability remote, and noted that the common law liability might be considered preempted by the federal sex discrimination statutes. *Id.* at 208–10.

[248] *Echazabal*, 536 U.S. at 85 n.5.

[249] 137 F.3d 398 (6th Cir. 1998).

[250] 480 U.S. 273 (1987). *Arline* is discussed *supra* Chapter 2.

procedures.[251] The evidence in the case demonstrated that cuts and needle sticks were always a possibility for a surgical technician, and that a surgical technician, albeit very rarely, might have to place fingers in a surgical incision when sharp instruments were being used and visibility poor.[252] An expert review panel of the hospital task force found risk present and supported the description of the surgical technician's job duties that included the placing of fingers in incisions on rare occasions.[253] The director of operating rooms at the hospital said the job duties could not be restructured because the need to place fingers in incisions would arise on an emergency basis when other personnel would not be available.[254] The court's reasoning reinforces the need for close review of the facts and individualized decision making when evaluating a direct-threat defense. In infectious disease cases, *Arline* is the key precedent.

An additional area in which courts have applied the direct-threat provision is associational discrimination. *Den Hartog v. Wasatch Academy* upheld a discharge of an employee on the basis of the direct threat defense when the mentally disabled son of an employee constituted a direct threat to others at the boarding school where his father worked.[255] The court used the general legislative policy behind the direct threat provision to extend the defense beyond its terms, which would appear to apply only to employees who themselves pose a direct threat to safety or health.[256]

The placement of the direct-threat provision in the "defenses" section of title I implies that it is to be treated as an affirmative defense. Traditionally, the defendant has the burden to plead, put forward evidence regarding, and bear the risk of nonpersuasion with respect to affirmative defenses. The EEOC Interpretive Guidance confirms the placement of the burden on the defendant as to the direct-threat defense by stating that with regard to safety requirements that screen out a person or persons with disabilities, the employer "must demonstrate that the requirement, as applied to the individual, satisfies the 'direct threat' standard . . . ."[257] Following these statutory and regulatory indications, courts have generally concluded that defendants have the burden of proof on whether the employee is a direct threat.[258] Some authorities, however, argue that the direct-threat issue is in fact embedded in the larger issue of whether the plaintiff is a qualified individual with a disability, a threshold burden that they would impose on

---

[251] *Mauro*, 137 F.3d at 403–04.

[252] *Id.* at 404–06.

[253] *Id.* at 406–07.

[254] *Id.* at 405.

[255] 129 F.3d 1076 (10th Cir. 1997).

[256] *Id.* at 1090–92. *See generally supra* § 3.08 (discussing *Den Hartog* in context of associational discrimination).

[257] ADA Title I EEOC Interpretive Guidance, 29 C.F.R. § 1630, App. § 1630.15(b)–(c) (2011).

[258] *E.g.*, EEOC v. Wal-Mart Stores, 477 F.3d 561, 571 (8th Cir. 2007) ("[W]e now hold that the employer bears the burden of proof, as the direct threat defense is an affirmative defense."); Rizzo v. Children's World Learning Ctrs., Inc., 84 F.3d 758, 764 (5th Cir. 1996) ("An employee who is a direct threat is not a qualified individual with a disability. As with all affirmative defenses, the employer bears the burden of proving that the employee is a direct threat.").

the plaintiff.[259] This approach, however, renders meaningless the direct-threat issue's statutory label as a defense and ignores the EEOC's interpretation.[260]

[D] Mandatory Arbitration

The Supreme Court has retreated from early caselaw that disfavored defenses to civil rights claims based on agreements to arbitrate disputes. In 1974, the Court stated in *Alexander v. Gardner-Denver Co.* that "we think it clear that there can be no prospective waiver of an employee's rights under Title VII;" it went on to rule that the employee's race discrimination suit was not barred even by the completion of the arbitration process pursuant to a collective bargaining agreement that forbade discrimination and provided for mandatory arbitration.[261] Seventeen years later, in *Gilmer v. Interstate/Johnson Lane Corp.*, the Court held that a court should have compelled arbitration rather than proceeding with a suit filed under the Age Discrimination in Employment Act (ADEA), when the plaintiff had executed a standard securities industry form agreeing to subject all disputes with his employer to arbitration.[262] *Gilmer* can be distinguished on its facts from *Alexander* — the *Gilmer* agreement more clearly embraced statutory claims than did that in *Alexander*, the *Gilmer* agreement was individual rather than one made by a union on the employees' behalf, and *Gilmer*, unlike *Alexander*, was decided under the Federal Arbitration Act, which embodies a strong policy in favor of arbitration.[263] But the Court's enforcement of the *Gilmer* agreement signaled the Court's more positive view of arbitration defenses in civil rights actions. In 2009, the other shoe dropped. The Court in *14 Penn Plaza LLC v. Pyett* ruled that a term in a collective bargaining agreement that "clearly and unmistakably" required union members to arbitrate claims arising under ADEA should be enforced, and overturned the lower courts' refusal to compel arbitration.[264] The Court did not overrule *Alexander*, but distinguished it on the ground that arbitration in that case had not been mandatory under the collective bargaining agreement, and all that was essential to *Alexander*'s holding was that the arbitrator's decision did not have a preclusive effect.in the subsequent title VII suit.[265] The Court disapproved the

---

[259] *See, e.g.*, Rizzo v. Children's World Learning Ctrs., Inc., 213 F.3d 209, 217–21 (5th Cir. 2000) (en banc) (Jones, J., dissenting) (arguing that defendant's burden on direct-threat issue should apply only with regard to non-essential functions of job); Borgialli v. Thunder Basin Coal Co., 235 F.3d 1284, 1292 (10th Cir. 2000) (placing burden of direct-threat issue on employer only when direct threat is not tied to issue of essential job functions).

[260] A more plausible basis on which to avoid dealing with the burdens issue is for a court to find that a specific threat or other act of misconduct is a legitimate, nondiscriminatory ground on which to discipline or fire the worker, undermining the plaintiff's inference-based claim of discrimination on the ground of disability. *See, e.g.*, Bodenstab v. County of Cook, 569 F.3d 651, 658–59 (7th Cir. 2009). For a criticism of some courts' failure to be sufficiently rigorous in evaluating supposed threats, see Ann Hubbard, *Understanding and Implementing the ADA's Direct Threat Defense*, 95 Nw. U. L. Rev. 1279 (2001).

[261] 415 U.S. 36, 51 (1974).

[262] 500 U.S. 20 (1991).

[263] *See id.* at 35.

[264] 129 S. Ct. 1456, 1461 (2009).

[265] *Id.* at 1466–67. The Court said, though, that Alexander "would be a strong candidate for

statements in *Alexander* that were critical of arbitration as a mechanism for vindicating civil rights claims. It conceded that *Alexander* "was correct in concluding that federal antidiscrimination rights may not be prospectively waived," but said that an agreement to arbitrate is merely the waiver of "the right to seek relief from a court in the first instance" rather than a waiver of the underlying right.[266]

There seems little doubt that courts will apply *14 Penn Plaza* to ADA cases, despite the presence of a strong dissent criticizing further abandonment of the policy against arbitration of civil rights disputes, a policy that Congress was likely to have relied upon when it passed the ADA.[267] The *14 Penn Plaza* dissent argued that considerations of stare decisis called for maintaining a broad reading of *Alexander* and adhering to the skeptical view of arbitration of civil rights claims that the Court had relied on in reaching the result in that case.[268]

Previous Supreme Court ADA caselaw did not reach the issue whether arbitration agreements would be given effect. In *Wright v. Universal Maritime Service Corp.*, the Court ruled that the collective bargaining agreement did not contain a clear and unmistakable waiver of the right to file suit under the ADA.[269] Although the arbitration clause was broadly worded to cover all matters under dispute, including terms and conditions of employment, the collective bargaining agreement did not contain any antidiscrimination provision. Although the Court noted that the ADA says that "[w]here appropriate and to the extent authorized by law, the use of alternative means of dispute resolution, including . . . arbitration, is encouraged to resolve disputes arising under this chapter," it held that if the waiver of rights to a judicial forum is not clear and unmistakable, then "it is not 'appropriate,' within the meaning of the ADA, to find an agreement to arbitrate."[270] The Court did not reach the question whether the waiver would have been enforceable if it had been clear and unmistakable.[271]

In another case, the Supreme Court held that an employee's arbitration agreement does not bar the EEOC's pursuit of an ADA claim for backpay,

---

overruling" if a broad view of its holding were accepted. *Id.* at 1469 n.8.

[266] *Id.* at 1469.

[267] The ADA, of course, predates *Gilmer* and *14 Penn Plaza*, and the Judiciary Committee Report on the ADA bill states that "the Committee believes that any agreement to submit disputed issues to arbitration, whether in the context of a collective bargaining agreement or in an employment contract, does not preclude the affected person from seeking relief under the enforcement provisions of this Act. This view is consistent with the Supreme Court's interpretation of title VII of the Civil Rights Act of 1964, whose remedial provisions are incorporated by reference in title I. The Committee believes that the approach articulated by the Supreme Court in *Alexander v. Gardner-Denver Co.* applies equally to the ADA and does not intend that the inclusion of Section [12212] be used to preclude rights and remedies that would otherwise be available to persons with disabilities." H.R. REP. No. 101-485, pt. 3, at 77 (1990) (Conference Committee Report incorporating Judiciary Committee Report). The Court in *14 Penn Plaza* refused to find that similar legislative history barred mandatory arbitration. 129 S. Ct. at 1465 n.6.

[268] *14 Penn Plaza* at 1475–76 (Souter, J., dissenting, joined by Justices Stevens, Ginsburg, and Breyer).

[269] 525 U.S. 70 (1998).

[270] *Id.* at 82 n.2 (quoting 42 U.S.C. § 12212).

[271] *Id.* at 82.

reinstatement, and damages on the employee's behalf.[272] Some lower courts have enforced arbitration agreements in ADA cases,[273] though one case refused to give effect to an agreement imposed on current employees on the ground that the agreement lacked consideration and so did not constitute an enforceable contract.[274]

§ 3.10 REMEDIES

The remedies provision of title I borrows the "powers, remedies and procedures" of title VII of the Civil Rights Act of 1964.[275] These remedies are supplemented by the damages provisions of the Civil Rights Act of 1991.[276] Applicable remedies in employment cases include compensatory and punitive damages; backpay, injunctions and other equitable relief; and attorneys fees.

[A] Compensatory and Punitive Damages

In cases against private employers, federal agencies or other covered entities under title I, plaintiffs may receive compensatory and punitive damages pursuant to 42 U.S.C. § 1981a, part of the Civil Rights Act of 1991.[277] Damages may be obtained from a defendant that engaged in unlawful intentional discrimination, but not against a defendant that engaged in an employment practice that is illegal because of its disparate impact.[278] If the complaining party seeks compensatory or punitive damages under § 1981a, any party to the case may demand a trial by jury.[279]

The right to damages is subject to a possible exception in cases that rest on the failure to provide reasonable accommodations. When the alleged discriminatory practice involves failure to provide a reasonable accommodation, damages may not be awarded if the defendant demonstrates that it made good faith efforts, "in consultation with the person with the disability . . . to identify and make a reasonable accommodation that would provide such individual with an equally effective opportunity and would not cause an undue hardship on the operation of

---

[272] EEOC v. Waffle House, Inc., 534 U.S. 279 (2002).

[273] Miller v. Public Storage Mgmt., Inc., 121 F.3d 215 (5th Cir. 1997); Austin v. Owens-Brockway Glass Container, Inc., 78 F.3d 875 (4th Cir. 1996); see also Bercovitch v. Baldwin Sch., Inc., 133 F.3d 141 (1st Cir. 1998) (non-employment case). But see Brisentine v. Stone & Webster Eng'ing Corp., 117 F.3d 519 (1997) (finding waiver in collective bargaining agreement ineffective to bar individual's ADA action).

[274] Gibson v. Neighborhood Health Clinics, Inc., 121 F.3d 1126 (7th Cir. 1997).

[275] 42 U.S.C. § 12117(a) (2006).

[276] 42 U.S.C. § 1981a (2006).

[277] Damages relief is available against federal defendants in employment cases brought under section 501 of the Rehabilitation Act. 29 U.S.C.S. § 791 (LexisNexis 2011). Section 1981a constitutes a waiver of the federal government's sovereign immunity from damages actions. See Lane v. Pena, 518 U.S. 187, 194 (1996) (contrasting section 501 claims with non-employment claims against the federal government brought under section 504).

[278] 42 U.S.C. § 1981a(a)(2) (2006).

[279] § 1981a(c).

the business."[280] This safe harbor is not applicable to cases brought under section 504.[281]

There are limits on the compensatory and punitive damage awards authorized under § 1981a. The size of the award is keyed to that of the defendant. Defendants with more than 14 but fewer than 101 employees in each of 20 or more calendar weeks are liable for a maximum of $50,000 for each complaining party; those with more than 100 and fewer than 201 for $100,000; those with more than 200 and fewer than 501 for $200,000; and those with more than 500 for $300,000.[282] These damages amounts are to include compensatory awards for future monetary losses, emotional pain, suffering, inconvenience, mental anguish, loss of enjoyment of life, and other nonpecuniary losses, as well as all punitive damages. They do not include any award of backpay, interest on backpay, or other relief made available under the equitable remedies provision of title VII and accordingly available under ADA title I.[283]

If an employment discrimination action is brought under title II of the ADA, the title applying to state and local government activities, the remedies are those applicable to section 504 claims.[284] For section 504, § 794a(a)(1) incorporates the remedies of title VII; in § 1981a(a)(2), a reference to § 794a(a)(1) also confirms that the damages remedy made available by § 1981a applies to section 504 plaintiffs. Nevertheless, § 794a(a) goes on to incorporate the remedies of title VI of the Civil Rights Act of 1964 in its subsection (2). Title VI of the Civil Rights Act permits damages relief for intentional conduct,[285] and there is no cap on compensatory damages, although Supreme Court has ruled out punitive damages against federal grantees subject to section 504 and state and local governmental entities subject to title II.[286] The apparent upshot is that a section 504 or title II employment plaintiff may, by citing § 794a(a)(2), bypass § 1981a and escape the limit on damages that it

---

[280] § 1981a(a)(3). *See generally* Rascon v. US West Communications., Inc., 143 F.3d 1324 (10th Cir. 1998) (discussing provision and upholding district court determination that employer failed to sustain defense). The good-faith-efforts provision applies to title I cases and to cases against federal government entities brought pursuant to section 501 of the Rehabilitation Act, 42 U.S.C.S. § 791 (LexisNexis 2011) and its regulations.

[281] Roberts v. Progressive Independence, Inc., 183 F.3d 1215 (10th Cir. 1999).

[282] 42 U.S.C. § 1981a(b)(3) (2006). In each instance, the number of employees is for each of 20 calendar weeks in the current or preceding calendar year and the damages maximum is for each complaining party.

[283] 42 U.S.C. § 1981a(b)(2) (2006) (referring to 42 U.S.C. § 2000e-5(g)).

[284] 42 U.S.C. § 12133 (2000) (incorporating by reference 29 U.S.C. § 794a).

[285] But only for intentional conduct. Alexander v. Sandoval, 532 U.S. 275, 282–83 (2001) ("In *Guardians* [*Assn. v. Civil Service Commission of New York City*, 463 U.S. 582 (1983)], the Court held that private individuals could not recover compensatory damages under Title VI except for intentional discrimination.").

[286] In *Barnes v. Gorman*, 536 U.S. 181, 189 (2002), the Supreme Court interpreted title II and section 504 to exclude the possibility of awards of punitive damages. Generally, the only defendants subject to damages are the public entity in II and federal grantee in 504, *see, e.g.,* Alsbrook v. City of Maumelle, 184 F.3d 999, 1005 n.8 (1999) (en banc), though an argument may be made that damages claims against individuals for violations of these statutes should be found either on the basis of an implied cause of action or by making use of the civil rights cause of action provided by 42 U.S.C. § 1983, *see* Gary S. Gilden, *Dis-Qualified Immunity for Discrimination Against the Disabled*, 1999 U. Ill. L. Rev. 897.

contains. This conclusion may seem anomalous at first, but it has some justification. Not only is it the reading of § 794a(a)(2) that is most logical given the language and context of that statutory term, but it is also the reading that is consistent with the congressional intent to harmonize title II with section 504 and to have the passage of title II not diminish the rights and remedies that previously existed under section 504. After all, the entities subject to title II — state and local governments — nearly all receive federal aid and so have always been subject to section 504 and its uncapped damages remedies for intentional discriminatory conduct. Moreover, this reading of the law treats those entities subject title II but not title I, *i.e.*, local governments with fewer than 15 employees, consistently with all other entities subject to title II. State government employers may argue that Eleventh Amendment principles shield them from liability, however. This defense is discussed at length in Chapter 6.[287]

[B] Backpay, Reinstatement, Injunctions, and Other Equitable Relief

Another one of the remedies title I incorporates from title VII of the Civil Rights Act is the power to enjoin covered entities "from engaging in . . . unlawful employment practice[s] . . . or [to provide] any other equitable relief as the court deems appropriate."[288] Typical equitable relief includes backpay, orders for initial hiring or reinstatement in a job (or front pay if hiring relief is not practical), and prejudgment interest. A range of judicial discretion exists, but all these remedies are routinely awarded.[289] Courts routinely provide permanent injunctive relief against employers' discriminatory practices once the plaintiff has established a violation of the law.[290] Nevertheless, in some instances, even in cases addressing systemic conduct, courts have ruled that the prospects for a recurrence of discriminatory conduct are so low that injunctive relief is not warranted.[291]

Injunctive relief may be temporary, as when a temporary restraining order is issued before a decision on a preliminary injunction or a preliminary injunction is issued pending the final decision on a case. A noteworthy case concerning

---

[287] *See* Board of Trustees v. Garrett, 531 U.S. 356 (2001) (upholding Eleventh Amendment defense against monetary remedy in ADA title I claim for monetary relief against arm of state government). *But see* Tennessee v. Lane, 541 U.S. 509 (2004) (rejecting Eleventh Amendment defense in title II claim for monetary relief for denial of access to courts).

[288] 42 U.S.C.S. § 2000e-5(g)(1) (LexisNexis 2011) (incorporated by reference into 42 U.S.C. § 12117(a)).

[289] Many cases consider equitable remedies for employment discrimination that violates the ADA. Among those with useful discussions are: Dilley v. Supervalu, Inc., 296 F.3d 958 (10th Cir. 2002) (approving reduction of backpay award but overturning denial of reinstatement); Moysis v. DTG Datanet, 278 F.3d 819 (8th Cir. 2002) (granting backpay without deduction for workers' compensation award; denying front pay).

[290] *See, e.g.*, Roe v. Cheyenne Mountain House Retreat, Inc., 124 F.3d 1221 (10th Cir. 1997) (overturning denial of post-judgment request for injunction against practice of employer that violated ADA); Bombrys v. City of Toledo, 849 F. Supp. 1210 (N.D. Ohio 1993) (granting injunction against exclusion of insulin-dependent persons with diabetes from police force).

[291] *E.g.*, EEOC v. Wal-Mart Stores, Inc., 187 F.3d 1241 (10th Cir 1999) (denying injunctive relief in case involving failure to provide accommodations for employee with hearing impairment).

preliminary injunctive relief against employment discrimination based on disability is the aptly titled case of a schoolteacher, *Chalk v. United States District Court*.[292] In *Chalk*, the Ninth Circuit overturned the denial of a preliminary injunction under section 504 to a teacher who lost his instructional position because he had an HIV infection. In remanding for entry of an order that he be reinstated, the court stressed that all the traditional requirements for preliminary injunctive relief were met: There was a high probability of success on the merits, because the school district had no reason for its action except the teacher's disease, and the evidence established that no significant risk of contagion existed; removal from the classroom and assignment to an administrative position constituted irreparable injury for an individual who derived intense personal satisfaction from his job teaching a small class of children with hearing impairments; the balance of hardships weighed in the plaintiff's favor, given the low risks of communication of the disease and the reality of harm to him; and the public interest was not adverse, even if some apprehensions might surface in the school community once news of the reinstatement surfaced.[293]

The prominence of the *Chalk* decision may obscure the fact that courts are generally reluctant to grant preliminary injunctive relief in employee discharge actions brought under the ADA, section 504, and other civil rights statutes.[294]

[C] Attorneys' Fees

The ADA provides a general grant of attorneys' fees and litigation expenses to the prevailing party other than the United States in actions and administrative proceedings under the statute.[295] Moreover, 42 U.S.C. § 2000e-5(k), which is incorporated by reference into the remedies section of title I of the ADA, states that in any action or proceeding, the court may allow the prevailing party, other than the EEOC or the United States, reasonable attorneys' fees, which may include expert costs. In non-title I employment cases in which the provisions of section 504 are applicable directly or by reference, the Rehabilitation Act provides for courts to award reasonable attorneys' fees to any prevailing party other than the United States.[296] In disability discrimination cases, as in civil rights proceedings in general, the term prevailing party includes defendants who win, but the standards for entitlement to fees are asymmetrical. If the claimant prevails in receiving some relief on the merits of the claim, fees are to be awarded as a matter of course; defendants that prevail receive fees only when the underlying proceeding is frivolous.[297]

---

[292] 840 F.2d 701 (9th Cir. 1988).

[293] *Id.* at 712. On the last point, the opinion noted that the public reaction to the teacher's reinstatement turned out to be positive. *Id.* at 711 n.14.

[294] *See, e.g.*, Roth v. Lutheran Gen. Hosp., 57 F.3d 1446 (7th Cir. 1995) (denying preliminary injunctive relief); Remlinger v. Nevada, 896 F. Supp. 1012 (D. Nev. 1995) (same); *cf.* Sampson v. Murray, 415 U.S. 61, 90 (1974) ("[I]t seems clear that the temporary loss of income, ultimately to be recovered, does not usually constitute irreparable injury.").

[295] 42 U.S.C. § 12205 (2006).

[296] 29 U.S.C.S. § 794a(b) (LexisNexis 2011).

[297] *See* Christiansburg Garment Co. v. EEOC, 434 U.S. 412 (1978). The topic of entitlement to

attorneys' fees is an enormous one. Significant cases describing the contours of the right include Buckhannon Bd. and Care Home, Inc. v. West Virginia Dept. of Health and Human Servs., 532 U.S. 598 (2001), and Farrar v. Hobby, 506 U.S. 103 (1992).

Chapter 4

EDUCATIONAL DISCRIMINATION

§ 4.01 PRIMARY AND SECONDARY EDUCATION

When it comes to education, disability law includes both matters having to do with elementary and secondary education in the public schools and matters relating to college and university education. The federal special education statute — the Individuals with Disabilities Education Act[1] ("IDEA") — is the principal source of law regarding education of children with disabilities in public primary and secondary schools. Other provisions, including section 504 of the Rehabilitation Act and title II of the ADA, are of dominant importance in college and university matters, although those provisions have a role to play in elementary and secondary school as well. In some cases, the United States Constitution, ADA title III, and state law also affect the topic of disability and education, both for elementary and secondary students and for students in higher education. This section will focus on public primary and secondary education, discussing IDEA in general, then take up issues of eligibility for special education, the concept of appropriate education, the requirement of education in the least restrictive environment, student discipline issues, entitlement to testing accommodations, and IDEA procedures and remedies.[2]

[A] Overview of the Individuals with Disabilities Education Act

From early in the history of public schooling in the United States, efforts at adapting education to meet the needs of students with disabilities coexisted with efforts to exclude students with disabilities from ordinary educational opportunities. In the wake of *Brown v. Board of Education*[3] and the struggle for equality of education by African-Americans, parents of children with disabilities campaigned for equal rights to education for their children. Congress became involved by subsidizing local efforts to provide education to children with disabilities, but did not create any enforceable statutory right to education until parents began filing suits claiming that their children had an entitlement to an education equal to that of children without disabilities under the Due Process and Equal Protection Clauses of the United States Constitution. In *Pennsylvania*

---

[1] 20 U.S.C. §§ 1400–1487 (2006).

[2] More guidance on special education law in general may be found in the following works: MARK C. WEBER, RALPH MAWDSLEY & SARAH REDFIELD, SPECIAL EDUCATION LAW: CASES AND MATERIALS (Lexis-Nexis 3d ed. 2010); MARK C. WEBER, SPECIAL EDUCATION LAW AND LITIGATION TREATISE (3d ed. 2008 & supps).

[3] 347 U.S. 483 (1954).

Association for Retarded Citizens ("PARC") v. Pennsylvania, a federal district court resolved an education rights suit by entering a consent decree requiring "access to a free public program of education and training appropriate to [the] capacities" of every child with mental retardation in the state, as well as participation rights and dispute resolution processes for parents.[4] In *Mills v. Board of Education,* the court compelled the District of Columbia to provide a similar set of educational rights to a class of children with various disabilities, many of whom had been excluded from school by the operation of disciplinary measures.[5] Despite the litigation campaign, however, as of 1975 about 1.75 million children with disabilities were excluded from public school, and 2.5 million were in programs that did not meet their educational needs.[6]

In the Education for All Handicapped Children Act of 1975 ("EAHCA"), Congress provided money to states that guaranteed they would provide a free, appropriate public education to every child identified as having a disability and being in need of special education.[7] The education was to be provided to the maximum extent appropriate with children without disabilities, and related services were to be provided to the children to enable them to learn in those settings. The law set out participation rights for parents of children with disabilities, including notice and the ability to meet with school personnel to develop an Individualized Education Program ("IEP") that would specify the education and related services to be offered the child. Disputes between parents and school districts[8] over programs, placements, and other issues were to be resolved by an independent hearing officer in a "due process hearing." The federal funding for the services originated in a recognition that, on the whole, education for children with disabilities tends to be more costly than that for children without disabilities. The federal government was originally to provide 40% of the cost of educating children with disabilities, but with the amounts actually appropriated, the federal share has been more in the neighborhood of 20%. Nevertheless, soon every state applied for the funding and undertook to guarantee the educational rights provided by the statute.[9] The Education for All Handicapped Children Act has been amended over the years, and is now titled the Individuals with Disabilities Education Act, usually abbreviated into the acronym IDEA.

---

[4] 343 F. Supp. 279, 313 (E.D. Pa. 1972).

[5] 348 F. Supp. 866 (D.D.C. 1972).

[6] H.R. REP. No. 94-332, at 10 (1975).

[7] Pub. L. No. 94-142, 89 Stat. 775 (1975).

[8] Like other federal education statutes, the federal special education law refers to local school districts and other governmental entities with that role as "local educational agencies," a term frequently abbreviated as "LEA." At times, the statute also uses the term "public agencies" to embrace both local school districts and other entities, such as state schools, that might be educating some children with disabilities. To simplify the discussion, this chapter will generally use the term "school district" for all entities covered by the law that owe obligations to educate individual students.

[9] New Mexico held out at first, but then applied for funding when a court applied section 504 of the Rehabilitation Act to impose similar rights to education for children meeting that statute's definition. *See* New Mexico Ass'n for Retarded Citizens v. New Mexico, 678 F.2d 847, 853 n.6 (10th Cir. 1982) (describing nonparticipation).

IDEA does not operate in a vacuum. Two years before passage of the law, Congress enacted the Rehabilitation Act of 1973, which contained section 504 forbidding disability discrimination in federally funded activities. These activities, of course, include public education, and so duties apply to elementary and secondary schools under that statute. Moreover, when Congress passed the ADA in 1990, it included a title addressed to state and local government activities, and so that law too covers public schooling. The constitutional obligations of equal protection and due process that formed the basis for *PARC*, *Mills*, and similar lawsuits continue to operate as well. IDEA does not have a preemptive effect on these other federal remedies. Although in the 1984 case *Smith v. Robinson*, the Supreme Court ruled that the EAHCA was meant to be the exclusive avenue for claims of disability discrimination in public education in cases in which it applied, Congress overruled that decision by passing the Handicapped Children Protection Act of 1986. *Smith* had ruled that because the EAHCA had no attorneys' fees provision, parents could not make supplemental claims for the same relief under section 504 or 42 U.S.C. § 1983 to enforce the Equal Protection Clause and then obtain attorneys' fees through the fees provisions applicable to those laws. The Handicapped Children's Protection Act established an explicit entitlement to attorneys' fees in EAHCA cases (an entitlement that continues in IDEA). It also provided that subject to an exhaustion requirement, the rights, procedures, and remedies available under the Constitution, section 504, and other federal laws protecting the rights of children with disabilities are not restricted or limited by passage of the EAHCA. This provision also continues in IDEA, and currently includes a reference to the ADA as well.[10] Section 504 and title II of the ADA have particular importance with regard to services for children who may not meet IDEA's eligibility standards and with regard to claims for compensatory damages.[11]

The latest changes in IDEA came in the form of the Individuals with Disabilities Education Improvement Act ("Improvement Act"), passed in December, 2004. The Improvement Act continued the basic structures and entitlements of IDEA, but made a number of changes to promote coordination with the No Child Left Behind initiative; to permit the allocation of some funding to services for children not yet determined to be eligible for services as children with disabilities and to children in need of special education in private schools; to allow for alternate mechanisms for determining whether a child has a learning disability; to promote settlement of due

---

[10] 20 U.S.C. § 1415(*l*) (2006). There remains a controversy in the case law and the academic commentary whether IDEA preempts at least some § 1983 claims for violations of IDEA itself. *See infra* § 4.01[E].

[11] Private elementary and secondary schools are not covered by IDEA or title II, but they are covered by ADA title III, unless they are controlled by religious organizations. *See* 42 U.S.C. § 12187 (2006) (title III exemption). Section 504 covers a private school, even a religious one, if it receives federal funding; federal funding is unusual except for post-secondary institutions, however. Private school students may receive federally funded special education services, but the law does not provide an enforceable individual entitlement to appropriate services. *See generally* Mark C. Weber, *Services for Private School Students Under the Individuals with Disabilities Education Improvement Act: Issues of Statutory Entitlement, Religious Liberty, and Procedural Regularity,* 36 J.L. & EDUC. 163 (2007) (discussing publicly funded special education services for private school students).

process hearing decisions; and to adjust rights and responsibilities in disciplinary matters.[12]

Congress been accused of over-legalizing the field of special education by passing the EAHCA and IDEA. In particular, the 2002 report of the President's Commission on Excellence in Special Education charged that "the current system often places process above results, and bureaucratic compliance above student achievement, excellence, and outcomes. The system is driven by complex regulations, excessive paperwork and ever-increasing administrative demands at all levels . . . ."[13] Supporters of the present law point out that before the 1975 statute began the regime of legal control, millions of children languished at home or in classes that amounted to little more than warehousing. They contend that the current laws are needed to keep children in school and give parents the tools to obtain services that will educate their children effectively. They see IDEA as a mechanism to provide rights to education that children without disabilities take for granted, but that children with disabilities and their parents continually have to struggle to obtain.[14] Although some observers expected that the Improvement Act would represent a significant deregulation of special education, the changes the law made in that regard were exceedingly modest, primarily altering a limited number of documentation requirements and permitting waivers of attendance of non-essential personnel at meetings.[15]

[B] Eligibility and Evaluation

To be eligible for services under IDEA, a child must have one of the disabling conditions specified in 20 U.S.C. § 1401(3)(A)(i)[16] and, "by reason thereof," need special education and related services.[17] The specification of disability categories risks treating children as manifestations of medical conditions rather than individuals. On the other hand, eligibility restrictions of this type allay the concern that large amounts of federal special education funding might simply be absorbed by general education rather than serving the children Congress intended to benefit. Nevertheless, worries persist regarding overrepresentation of African-American children in some disability categories and the negative effect

---

[12] These and other changes made by the Improvement Act are discussed in Mark C. Weber, *Reflections on the New Individuals with Disabilities Education Improvement Act*, 58 FLA. L. REV. 7 (2006).

[13] PRESIDENT'S COMMISSION ON EXCELLENCE IN SPECIAL EDUCATION, A NEW ERA: REVITALIZING SPECIAL EDUCATION FOR CHILDREN AND THEIR FAMILIES 7 (2002), *available at* http://www.ed.gov/inits/commissionsboards/whspecialeducation/.

[14] For an overview of opinions on the role of IDEA, see Special Report, *IDEA 25: Progress and Problems*, EDUCATION WEEK, November/December 2000.

[15] *See* Weber, *supra* note 12 at 39–40 (describing changes in paperwork requirements).

[16] The list currently includes the following: mental retardation (now known as intellectual disability), hearing impairments (including deafness), speech or language impairments, visual impairments (including blindness), serious emotional disturbance (referred to in this chapter as "emotional disturbance"), orthopedic impairments, autism, traumatic brain injury, other health impairments, or specific learning disabilities.

[17] 20 U.S.C. § 1401(3)(A)(ii) (2006). On the general topic of eligibility under IDEA, see Mark C. Weber, *The IDEA Eligibility Mess*, 57 BUFF. L. REV. 83 (2009).

classification in general has on teachers' and others' expectations for the educational achievement of children given disability labels.[18] In recent years, Congress has responded to the problems of labeling, first by permitting states and school districts to identify children aged three through nine simply as being developmentally delayed,[19] and second, in the Improvement Act, by permitting school districts to use up to 15% of their federal special education funding for "early intervening services" for children not identified as IDEA-eligible who need extra academic and behavioral support to succeed in the general education environment.[20]

Of the categories of disability in the eligibility provision, a source of continuing controversy is "specific learning disabilities." IDEA further defines that term as "a disorder in 1 or more of the basic psychological processes involved in understanding or in using language, spoken or written, which disorder may manifest itself in the imperfect ability to listen, think, speak, read, write, spell, or do mathematical calculations."[21] The term includes "perceptual disabilities, brain injury, minimal brain dysfunction, dyslexia, and developmental aphasia," but does not include learning problems that are "primarily the result of visual, hearing, or motor disabilities, of mental retardation, of emotional disturbance, or of environmental, cultural, or economic disadvantage."[22] Critics have voiced dissatisfaction over conventional methods for determining learning disabilities, such as relying on severe discrepancies in subparts of a child's IQ test score relating to ability and achievement.[23] The Improvement Act responded to this criticism by permitting school districts not to use the discrepancy between ability and achievement to determine the presence of a specific learning disability.[24]

The question remains which method to use for identifying children with learning disabilities if a school district abandons the conventional ones. The Improvement Act permits "a process that determines if the child responds to scientific, research

---

[18] See § 1400(12) (2006) (congressional findings concerning African-American overrepresentation in mental retardation and emotional disturbance identification categories). One source critical of current approaches to eligibility for services links the operation of those approaches to over-representation of African Americans in special education and other ills. Robert A. Garda, Jr., *Untangling Eligibility Requirements Under the Individuals with Disabilities Education Act*, 69 Mo. L. Rev. 441 (2004); Robert A. Garda, *The New IDEA: Shifting Educational Paradigms to Achieve Racial Equality in Special Education*, 56 ALA. L. Rev. 1071 (2005); Robert A. Garda, Jr., *Who Is Eligible Under the Individuals with Disabilities Education Improvement Act?*, 35 J.L. & EDUC. 291 (2006). *But see* Weber, *supra* previous note at 143–51 (attributing problems to removal of children to separate special educational settings rather than determination of special education eligibility).

[19] 20 U.S.C. § 1401(3)(B) (2006).

[20] § 1413(f) (2006).

[21] § 1401(30) (2006).

[22] § 1401(30)(B)–(C) (2006).

[23] See, e.g., Ford v. Long Beach Unified Sch. Dist., 291 F.3d 1086 (9th Cir. 2002) (refusing to require use of IQ testing to determine discrepancy and affirming finding that child lacked eligibility for special education on ground of learning disability). There is a larger controversy over the appropriate response of the educational system to individuals with learning disabilities. *See, e.g.*, MARK KELMAN & GILLIAN LESTER, JUMPING THE QUEUE: AN INQUIRY INTO THE LEGAL TREATMENT OF STUDENTS WITH LEARNING DISABILITIES (1997); Anne Proffitt Dupre, Book Review, 49 J. LEGAL EDUC. 301 (1999) (reviewing JUMPING THE QUEUE).

[24] 20 U.S.C. § 1414(b)(6)(A) (2006).

based-intervention as a part of evaluation."[25] The Notice of Proposed Rulemaking[26] and Explanation of Major Changes in the Regulations accompanying the final administrative regulations[27] for the Improvement Act criticize discrepancy methods and provide extensive discussion of the response-to-intervention ("RTI") and similar models, suggesting that they can satisfactorily identify students with specific learning disabilities. Nevertheless, the Explanation of Major Changes acknowledges that many sources are critical of the efficacy of RTI and other non-discrepancy models, particularly in distinguishing specific learning disabilities from mental retardation and discovering learning disabilities in children who are gifted.[28] Authorities may be found to challenge any method of determining the presence of learning disabilities, including discrepancy testing, RTI, and other approaches. Perhaps as a response to that reality and the general difficulties of evaluating children for disabling conditions, the Improvement Act retains the provision from previous law that bars school districts from using any single measure or assessment as the sole criterion for determining whether a child is a child with a disability or determining an appropriate educational program for the child.[29]

Eligibility and evaluation of children with attention deficit disorder ("ADD") and attention deficit hyperactivity disorder ("ADHD") have also led to conflict. Although Congress has resisted efforts to list ADD and ADHD in the set of conditions specified in the statute, children with these conditions have frequently obtained eligibility under the "other health impairments" or the "specific learning disabilities" categories. After a period in which coverage was uncertain, the Department of Education issued a regulation, currently in force, that lists ADD and ADHD as examples of chronic or acute conditions that might cause other health impairment. Other health impairment suffices for eligibility if it adversely affects a child's educational performance and the child has "limited strength, vitality, or alertness, including a heightened alertness to environmental stimuli, that results in limited alertness with respect to the educational environment."[30] Additional chronic or acute health conditions are also specified in the regulation. In considering a child's eligibility under IDEA, it is important to keep in mind that a child who does not have a condition that satisfies the IDEA definition may be entitled to services and modifications of policies under section 504. Issues in connection with eligibility under that statute are discussed later in this section.

The term of the IDEA eligibility definition regarding the need for special education has also led to some controversies. Although some of the case law regarding the entitlement to appropriate education stresses that a child is entitled not to the ideal education, but rather one that provides meaningful access to

---

[25] § 1414(b)(6)(B).

[26] See 70 Fed. Reg. 35,802–03 (June 21, 2005).

[27] See 71 Fed. Reg. 46,646–59 (Aug. 14, 2006).

[28] See id. at 46,651–52.

[29] 20 U.S.C. § 1414(b)(2)(B) (2006).

[30] 34 C.F.R. § 300.8(c)(9) (2011). To be eligible, the child must also need special education and related services by reason of the impairment. See § 300.8(b)(2) (2006).

education, "some educational benefit," these decisions do not relate to eligibility.[31] Both the United States Department of Education[32] and the courts[33] have taken the position that a child may be eligible for special education even if the child is performing adequately in the classroom and passing from grade to grade. Some courts have upheld the eligibility of children performing at levels far above average, as long as the children have needs that fall into categories deemed to be within the scope of special education and related services.[34] Giftedness, however, is not itself a disabling condition under the federal law's definition.[35]

At times, school authorities have tried to exclude children from eligibility on the ground that they are too disabled to benefit from educational services. In *Timothy W. v. Rochester, New Hampshire School District*, the First Circuit Court of Appeals ruled that a school district had to serve a child with multiple disabilities, including profound mental retardation, spastic quadriplegia, cerebral palsy, seizure disorder, and cortical blindness.[36] The district court agreed with the school district that the child was not capable of benefiting from special education and excused it from serving him, but the court of appeals reversed, emphasizing that the "all" term in the title and body of the Education for All Handicapped Children Act meant what it said. The court supported its conclusion by stressing that special education includes instruction in hospitals and institutions, and embraces basic functional skills as well as cognitive skills. The record demonstrated that the child could respond to tactile stimulation, his mother's voice and touch, and the sound of other familiar voices. He parted his lips when spoon fed. The services the child needed, such as sensory stimulation, physical therapy, socialization, physical therapy to promote consistency in responding to sounds and partial participation in eating, and training related to head control, fit within the definition of services covered under the Act. The court determined that the legislative history of the EAHCA, the Act's explicit requirement priority for serving the children with most severe disabilities, and the case law involving children with profound disabilities supported its position. Although the school district tried to use the Supreme Court's decision in *Board of Education v. Rowley*[37] to support a conclusion that the child had to be able to benefit from a public education, the court of appeals distinguished that case as one involving methods of serving a deaf child performing at above an average level, not a case concerning eligibility for services. Other

---

[31] *See* Board of Educ. v. Rowley, 458 U.S. 176, 200 (1982) ("some educational benefit" standard). *Rowley* went on to note that not every child passing from grade to grade will necessarily be deemed to be receiving appropriate education under the Act, however. *Id.* at 203 n.25.

[32] Letter to Anonymous, 41 Individuals with Disabilities Educ. L. Rep. 212 (U.S. Dep't of Educ., Off. Of Special Educ. & Rehabilitative Servs. 2004) (forbidding use of eligibility requirement that a child fail to progress from grade to grade).

[33] *See, e.g.,* Westchester Area Sch. Dist. v. Bruce C., 194 F. Supp. 2d 417 (E.D. Pa. 2002) (upholding eligibility of child with attention deficit disorder despite child's satisfactory grades).

[34] *See, e.g.,* Mr. & Mrs. I. v. Maine Sch. Admin. Dist. 55, 2007 U.S. App. LEXIS 5128 (1st Cir. Mar. 5, 2007) (finding child with Asperger's Syndrome eligible for special education).

[35] Roane County Sch. Sys. v. Ned A., 22 Individuals with Disabilities Educ. L. Rep. 574 (E.D. Tenn. 1995).

[36] 875 F.2d 954 (1st Cir. 1989).

[37] 458 U.S. 176 (1982) (discussed *infra* § 4.01[C]).

Supreme Court case law supported broad standards of eligibility.[38] The *Timothy W.* case stands for a "zero-reject" principle that permits no child to be rejected as too disabled.[39]

Age is another IDEA qualification standard. Generally speaking, the eligible age range is 3 through 21.[40] In the 1980s, Congress added what is now Part C of IDEA, providing federal funding for services for children with disabilities from birth to the age three, and states have joined this program as a complement to their participation in Part B, the basic program serving school-aged children.[41]

Some children clearly have disabilities but do not need special education or related services, for example, a child with paraplegia but no other impairment who has completed her physical education requirement. As noted above, such a child does not meet the eligibility standards for IDEA. Nevertheless, public schools owe that child duties of nondiscrimination, including reasonable accommodation, under title II of the ADA and section 504. Thus the child would be entitled to have the school remove architectural barriers and waive rules that operate unfairly, for example, allowing the child to use a building elevator even though the elevator is off limits to other students. In other instances, a child — say a child with ADHD to a degree that substantially limits the child's major life activity of learning but does not meet the standards of the federal regulation[42] — may need extensive services that might be characterized as special education and related services, but the child does not have an impairment that fits into the list in the definitions section of IDEA. If the child meets the definition of individual with a disability for the ADA or section 504, the school would be obliged not to discriminate, and would have to afford reasonable accommodation. In fact, the section 504 educational regulations state that all qualified children who meet the section 504 disability definition are entitled to a free, appropriate public education, defined as "regular or special education and related services that . . . are designed to meet the individual educational needs of handicapped persons as adequately as the needs of nonhandicapped persons are met."[43] Courts have frequently interpreted this

---

[38] The court relied on Honig v. Doe, 484 U.S. 305 (1988) (discussed *infra* § 4.01[F]).

[39] *Timothy W.*, 875 F.2d at 960.

[40] 20 U.S.C. § 1412(a)(1) (2006). If state law is not consistent with providing public education to children 3 through 5 or 18 through 21, the obligation to provide free, appropriate public education does not apply with regard to children with disabilities of those ages. § 1412(a)(1)(B)(i). There is also a state option to exclude children aged 18 through 21 incarcerated in an adult correctional facility who were not previously identified as children with disabilities or lacked an individualized education program. § 1412(a)(1)(B)(ii).

[41] *See* 20 U.S.C. §§ 1431–44 (2006) (Part C Program).

[42] *See* 34 C.F.R. § 300.8(c)(9) (2011) (discussed *supra* this section). The ADA Amendments Act of 2008, Pub. L. No. 110-325, 122 Stat. 3553, greatly expands coverage of the ADA and section 504, and so it is likely there will be many more children who are protected by section 504 and the ADA who are not deemed eligible for services under IDEA. *See* Mark C. Weber, *A New Look at Section 504 and the ADA in Special Education Cases*, 16 TEX. J. C.L. & C.R. 1, 5–9 (2010) (discussing expanded coverage); *see also supra* Chapter 2 (discussing coverage of Amendments Act).

[43] 34 C.F.R. § 104.33(b)(1) (2011). The "as adequately" language has received little development since *Board of Education v. Rowley*, 458 U.S. 176 (1982), despite the position of some commentators that if it were applied in a section 504 action joined to an IDEA action (as permitted by the Handicapped Children's Protection Act) it could serve to elevate standards of appropriate education for the large

provision to require children who do not meet the IDEA eligibility standards but who do meet the section 504-ADA definition to be entitled to no different set of services than a child who meets the IDEA standards would be.[44]

[C]   Appropriate Education

Under IDEA, each child with a disability is entitled to free, appropriate public education, a term sometimes abbreviated as "FAPE." A number of early cases focused on the "free education" term as parents challenged various fees that states and school districts charged parents of children with disabilities.[45] In recent years, however, the focus has more often been on what constitutes "appropriate education." The Supreme Court weighed in on the issue of appropriate education in *Board of Education v. Rowley*, its first decision interpreting the law that is now IDEA.[46]

In *Rowley*, the parents of a deaf first-grader challenged her individualized education program because it did not include the services of a sign language interpreter. The program provided for a wireless hearing aid, an hour of tutoring a day, and three hours of speech therapy each week, and the child was performing better than the average student in her class and advancing easily from grade to grade. Nevertheless, she understood less than 60% of what was being said in class, even under the best of conditions.[47] The district court looked at, among other things, section 504 regulations requiring an opportunity to achieve commensurate with the opportunities provided other children, and concluded that services should be provided so that the shortfall between the child's ability and her achievement would be no greater than that of children without disabilities.[48] The court of appeals affirmed over a strenuous dissent.[49]

The Supreme Court reversed. Writing for the Court, Justice Rehnquist looked first to the statutory definition of free, appropriate public education. Although he

---

numbers of children who are covered by both IDEA and section 504. *See* Thomas F. Guernsey, *The Education for All Handicapped Children Act, 42 U.S.C. § 1983, and Section 504 of the Rehabilitation Act of 1973: Interaction Following the Handicapped Children's Protection Act of 1986*, 68 NEB. L. REV. 564, 591 (1989) ("Unless a school system is willing to publicly assert the proposition that it is providing a minimal educational experience to its nonhandicapped students, it seems that congressional action [overruling *Smith* and restoring a section 504 remedy] has circumvented *Rowley's* minimal standard in those areas where the EAHCA and section 504 overlap."); Mark C. Weber, *The Transformation of the Education of the Handicapped Act: A Study in the Interpretation of Radical Statutes*, 24 U.C. DAVIS L. REV. 349, 417–18 (1990) [herinafter *"Transformation"*] ("The Handicapped Children's Protection Act thus restored the force of regulations promulgated under section 504, which define appropriate education as that which both satisfies the Education of the Handicapped Act and meets an equality standard. . . ."); *see also* Weber, *supra* previous note, at 11–21 (applying as-adequately standard to children eligible under section 504 and ADA alone and to dually IDEA eligible children).

[44] *See* Brett v. Goshen Cmty. Sch. Corp., 161 F. Supp. 2d 930, 939–40 (N.D. Ind. 2001) (collecting cases).

[45] *E.g.*, Parks v. Pavkovic, 753 F.2d 1397 (7th Cir. 1985).

[46] 458 U.S. 176 (1982).

[47] Rowley v. Board of Educ., 483 F. Supp. 528, 532 (S.D.N.Y. 1980).

[48] *Id.* at 533–35.

[49] Rowley v. Board of Educ., 632 F.2d 945 (2d Cir. 1980); *see id.* at 948–55 (Mansfield, J., dissenting).

labeled the language "cryptic," he said that it did not support a proportionate maximization standard.[50] In examining the legislative history, the opinion declared that the *PARC* and *Mills* cases had strongly influenced Congress, and that these decisions focused on access, as had members of Congress who, when describing unserved children, equated receipt of any form of special education with receipt of appropriate education. Moreover, the comparisons involved in determining commensurate opportunity would entail "impossible measurements."[51] Providing precisely the same services as those given to children without disabilities would not be an appropriate education for children with disabilities, but trying to maximize the potential of every child with a disability would be "further than Congress intended to go."[52] Furthermore, Congress had stressed the equal protection rights of the children with disabilities, and equal protection had been a principal basis for the *PARC* and *Mills* cases. In the period before Congress passed the special education law, the Court, in cases challenging educational financing on grounds of equal protection, had determined that equal protection does not require states to spend equal amounts on the education of each child.[53] The Court said the need identified by Congress was to provide a "basic floor of opportunity" consistent with equal protection, which the Court equated with "equal access."[54] The Court suggested that the special education law embodied the same equal protection principle. Nevertheless, the opinion acknowledged that the Congress was requiring an education "sufficient to confer some educational benefit" in return for the money it was providing the states.[55] Moreover, the congressional goal of self-sufficiency for persons with disabilities supported a requirement of at least some educational benefit. Warning that the law covers a vast range of children with disabilities, the Court said it did not attempt to establish a single test for determining the adequacy of educational benefits due all children the law covers. For a child mainstreamed into a regular classroom setting, however, the services "should be reasonably calculated to enable the child to achieve passing marks and advance from grade to grade."[56]

Turning then to the procedural requirements of the law, the Court agreed that courts have power to review the substance of programs devised for children with disabilities, but said that the existence of layers of procedural protection and the requirement that the courts on review receive the record of the state administrative proceedings imply that "due weight" be given the proceedings.[57] Furthermore, questions of educational theory are for resolution by the states, which can make choices regarding methodology. Applying all these principles, the Court concluded that the child who was receiving an adequate education, performing better than average, and advancing easily from grade to grade while

---

[50] Board of Educ. v. Rowley, 458 U.S. 176, 188(1982).

[51] *Id.* at 198.

[52] *Id.* at 198–99.

[53] *Id.* at 199–200 (citing, inter alia, San Antonio Indep. Sch. Dist. v. Rodriguez, 411 U.S. 1 (1973)).

[54] *Id.* at 200.

[55] *Id.* at 200–01.

[56] *Id.* at 204.

[57] *Id.* at 206.

receiving personalized instruction calculated by the local administrators to meet her needs, was not also entitled to the services of a sign language interpreter.

Justice Blackmun's concurrence found an equality standard in the legislative history and goals of the statute. Therefore, "the question is whether Amy's program, viewed as a whole, offered her an opportunity to understand and participate in the classroom that was substantially equal to that given her non-handicapped classmates."[58] The standard should be based on equal educational opportunity and equal access, rather than a child's achievement of a particular educational outcome. Blackmun believed the standard met in this case. Justice White, whose dissent was joined by Justices Brennan and Marshall, stressed the many statements in the legislative history about full educational opportunity, equality of educational opportunity, equivalent education of children with disabilities and those without, and the maximization of each child's potential.[59] White also found equal opportunity language in the *Mills* case. Endorsing the approach taken by the lower courts, the dissent said the majority's approach would have the law require nothing more than that the child "receive a teacher with a loud voice."[60]

Rowley has received much criticism from academics and other sources, but despite the disclaimer that confined its analysis to the facts of the case, it has been applied to uphold denial of services in a wide range of instances. Acceptance of *Rowley* has not, however, kept courts and administrative decision makers from ordering very extensive educational services for many children with disabilities. In some cases, courts have stressed that the child's impairment has far more severe effects on the child's progress than was the case in *Rowley*.[61] In others, courts appear to have taken to heart *Rowley*'s idea about success in the mainstream and ordered enough supplementary support to enable children, both those with milder and often those with quite severe conditions, to hold their own in a general education classroom.[62] In still other cases, courts have developed the concepts of least restrictive environment, individualized decision making, state educational standards, and deference to administrative decision making to require far more of school districts than a casual reader of *Rowley* might predict.[63] Autism cases are a current example. Recently, a number of courts have demanded that schools provide extensive services, including many hours of applied behavioral analysis

---

[58] *Id.* at 211 (Blackmun, J., concurring).

[59] *Id.* at 212–14 (White, J., dissenting).

[60] *Id.* at 215. White further challenged the majority on the topic of affording due weight to administrative determinations on judicial review. *Id.* at 216–18. For current commentary on *Rowley*, see Symposium, Rowley *After Thirty Years*, J. L. & Educ. (forthcoming Feb. 2012).

[61] Among the most prominent of these cases is *Polk v. Central Susquehanna Intermediate Unit 16*, 853 F.2d 171 (3d Cir. 1988), which required that a child with encephalopathy be provided physical therapy.

[62] *See, e.g.*, Woolcott v. State Bd. of Educ., 351 N.W.2d 601 (Mich. App. 1984) (ordering provision of cued speech interpreter for child with hearing impairment).

[63] *See* Weber, *Transformation, supra* note 43 at 388–403 (collecting cases as of 1990); *see also* Scott F. Johnson, *Reexamining* Rowley: *A New Focus in Special Education Law*, 2003 BYU Educ. & L.J. 561, 561 (stating that in light of succeeding developments the "some educational benefit" standard "no longer accurately reflects the requirements of the IDEA.").

programming, for students with autism. For support, the courts have relied on procedural failings by school districts;[64] the meaningful access standard itself and the requirement of individualized determination of educational needs;[65] and least restrictive environment concepts.[66]

Appropriate education includes both instruction and related services.[67] The Supreme Court has developed legal requirements regarding related services by upholding demands for extensive services for children with severe physical impairments despite arguments that the services are medical in nature, and hence excluded by the definition of related services, which covers medical services "for diagnostic and evaluation purposes only."[68]

In *Irving Independent School District v. Tatro*, the Court ruled that a child who could not urinate normally was entitled to have the school district provide clean, intermittent catheterization services.[69] The Court relied on regulations defining covered school health services as those provided by a qualified school nurse or other qualified person and medical services as those provided by a physician. Although a physician might prescribe and supervise catheterization, state law permitted nurses and others to perform it, so the medical exception did not apply.

In *Cedar Rapids Community School District v. Garret F.*, the Court extended *Tatro* and upheld an order that a school district give a child with quadriplegia who could not breathe on his own a wide array of services, including catheterization, tracheotomy suctioning, ventilator maintenance, administration of airbag breathing during maintenance, monitoring and observation of equipment, and other procedures.[70] Since none of the procedures needed to be performed by a licensed physician, the approach developed in *Tatro* led to the conclusion that the services had to be provided regardless of cost or other burdens to the school district.

Appropriate education under IDEA might embrace extracurricular activities, but cases on the topic are infrequent.[71] The bulk of litigation about extracurriculars has dealt with claims that age or other eligibility requirements for sports participation violate ADA and section 504 nondiscrimination requirements when, for example, a student with a disability is over the applicable age limits because of

---

[64] *See* Terry Jean Seligmann, Rowley *Comes Home to Roost: Judicial Review of Autism Special Education Disputes,* 9 U.C. Davis J. Juv. L. & Pol'y 217, 267–70 (2005) (collecting cases).

[65] *See* Deal v. Hamilton County Bd. of Educ., 392 F.3d 840, 858–59 (6th Cir. 2004); G. v. Fort Bragg Dependent Schs., 343 F.3d 295, 307–08 (4th Cir. 2003).

[66] L.B. v. Nebo Sch. Dist., 379 F.3d 966 (10th Cir. 2004). The results in these cases are not uniformly in favor of parents' claims for extensive services, however. *See* Seligmann, *supra* note 64, at 272 n.229 (citing studies of case outcomes).

[67] *See* 20 U.S.C. § 1401(26) (2006) (listing examples of related services).

[68] § 1401(26)(A) (2006).

[69] 468 U.S. 883 (1984).

[70] 526 U.S. 66 (1999).

[71] *But see* Dennin v. Connecticut Interscholastic Athletic Ass'n, 913 F. Supp. 663 (D. Conn.), *judgment vacated and app. dismissed as moot,* 94 F.3d 96 (2d Cir. 1996) (noting inclusion of participation on swimming team in child's individualized education program but upholding challenge to eligibility barrier on basis of section 504, ADA, and other authority).

educational needs related to disability. Courts diverge in their response to cases of this type.

For example, in *Pottgen v. Missouri State High School Activities Association*, the Eighth Circuit considered the case of a child who was over the age limit for participation in high school baseball because he repeated two grades in elementary school before his learning disabilities were discovered and specialized services provided to him.[72] The court rejected his claim that the reasonable accommodation duty of section 504 and title II of the ADA required waiver of the age maximum, reasoning that an age limit is an essential eligibility requirement in high school athletics, preventing unfair competitive advantage, protecting younger athletes, and discouraging red-shirting (the practice of spending an additional year or more in school and not competing during that time in hope of growing stronger and becoming more competitive).

By contrast, *Dennin v. Connecticut Interscholastic Athletic Association* required a waiver of an age maximum in the case of a swimmer with Down Syndrome who spent four rather than three years in middle school because of his disability-related educational needs.[73] The court reasoned that under the facts of the case, the goals of the age requirement did not apply: the child had no competitive advantage, was not a safety risk to smaller athletes because swimming is not a contact sport, and did not delay his education in order to compete more effectively. The individualized treatment required by the disability discrimination statutes therefore dictated waiver of the rule.

[D] Least Restrictive Environment

IDEA requires that, to the maximum extent appropriate, children with disabilities be educated with children who are not disabled, and that special classes and other removals from the regular educational environment occur only when the nature or severity of a child's disability prevents satisfactory education in regular classes with supplementary aids and services.[74] Courts have used various approaches in implementing this requirement. In one of the more prominent cases, *Sacramento City Unified School District v. Rachel H.*, the Ninth Circuit ordered the placement of a nine-year-old child with moderate mental retardation in a full-time general education program with the provision of a part-time aide and other related services.[75] The court of appeals affirmed the district court's findings that the child obtained academic and nonacademic benefits from a program that integrated her into general education, that an aide would be needed on only a part-time basis, and that the school district's contention that it would lose needed special education funding for the child ignored a rule allowing the state to waive the requirement that a child has to be in special education 51% of the time to qualify

---

[72] 40 F.3d 926 (8th Cir. 1994). This case appears to represent the majority approach at the present time.

[73] 913 F. Supp. 663 (D. Conn.), *judgment vacated and app. dismissed as moot*, 94 F.3d 96 (2d Cir. 1996).

[74] 20 U.S.C. § 1412(a)(5)(A) (2006).

[75] 14 F.3d 1398 (9th Cir. 1994).

for state funding. The Ninth Circuit adopted a test that looked to (1) the educational benefits of full-time placement in general education, (2) the nonacademic benefits of placement in general education, (3) the effect the child had on the teacher and children in the class, and (4) the costs of the mainstreamed placement. The factors pointed in favor of the mainstreamed placement for the child, even though the child's curriculum was not the same as that of the rest of the class. In another prominent case, *Oberti v. Board of Education,* the Third Circuit required the mainstreaming of an eight-year-old with Down Syndrome, emphasizing that education in the general classroom could work if the school provided supplementary aids and services, specifically assistance of a trained itinerant instructor, special education training for the general education teacher, modification of some of the academic curriculum, parallel instruction to allow learning at a different academic level, and part-time use of a resource room.[76]

Previous cases had adopted multifactor tests for determining challenges to placements outside the mainstream classroom. The *Roncker v. Walter* test ties directly to the language of the statute, which emphasizes the use of supplementary aids and services as a means of keeping a child in general education.[77] The test asks whether a specialized, nonintegrated setting is considered educationally superior, and if so, whether the services that make it superior could feasibly be provided in a general education setting. If they can, the court requires that the less restrictive setting be provided, with the necessary services. Courts using this test (1) compare the benefits the child receives from special education against those from general education; (2) ask if the child would disrupt a general education classroom; and (3) evaluate the relevant costs.

Oberti and a number of other cases follow a test articulated in *Daniel R.R. v. State Board of Education,* which also asks whether education in the general education classroom can be achieved satisfactorily with supplementary aids and services.[78] In asking this question, the court considers (1) what the school district has done to accommodate the child in the general education classroom, (2) the educational benefit to the child from mainstreamed schooling, (3) the child's overall educational experience in general education, and (4) what effect the child's presence has on the general education class. If the answer is that education in the general education class cannot be achieved satisfactorily, the court asks if the school has made efforts to include the child in school programs with nondisabled children whenever possible. Both tests establish a strong presumption in favor of the provision of extra services to make the least restrictive environment succeed for a given child, and the choice of factors may matter less than the underlying attitudes of courts or other decision makers towards accommodation of children with disabilities in the general education environment. Of particular significance is

---

[76] 995 F.2d 1204 (3d Cir. 1993).

[77] 700 F.2d 1058 (6th Cir. 1983) (overturning decision that placed child with severe mental retardation in specialized school); *see* 20 U.S.C. § 1412(a)(5)(A) (2006) ("[S]pecial classes, separate schooling, or other removal of children with disabilities from the regular educational environment [may] occur[] only when the nature or severity of the disability of a child is such that education in regular classes with the use of supplementary aids and services is not satisfactory.").

[78] 874 F.2d 1036 (5th Cir. 1989) (affirming decision that child with developmental disabilities received no educational benefit from mainstreamed placement).

how seriously courts take the language of the statute that insists that removal from the general education environment occur only when related services cannot make that setting a satisfactory one, and thus how much they are willing to cause school districts to provide in the way of supplementary aids and services to children who need the services to succeed in the mainstream.[79]

As the *Rachel H.* case suggests, systemic policies, such as the funding arrangements at issue there, affect school district decisions whether the place children in the least restrictive setting. Parents have in some cases mounted broad-based challenges to these policies, asking courts to require school districts to adopt procedures to keep children from being removed from mainstream classes and to give them adequate support when there.[80]

Despite the general statutory principles requiring placement in the least restrictive environment, and despite language in the regulations saying that the educational placement of a child should be as close as possible to the child's home, and that unless the individualized educational program requires some other arrangement, the child is to be educated in the school that he or she would attend if not disabled,[81] courts generally have not compelled school districts to provide all needed services to children in their neighborhood schools.[82] The regulations' language permits the school district to assert that education in the closest school is not possible; moreover, school districts have the power to write the individualized education program to require placement at another location. Though it might be argued that school districts violate at least the spirit of the statute and regulations by requiring children with disabilities to travel to schools where service delivery is more convenient for the district, courts appear to be sympathetic to the argument that providing all needed services for all children at all locations would be too costly for school districts to afford.

Although the policies behind IDEA and the disability discrimination statutes, as well as the consensus of educational experts, support integration of children with disabilities into the educational mainstream, the topic remains controversial. Some critics contend that positive educational outcomes have not been demonstrated adequately, and they note that teachers are inadequately trained and peers inadequately prepared for responding to students with disabilities.[83] Defenders of integration agree that mainstreaming may be done badly, but contend that if adequate related services are provided to students with disabilities and proper

---

[79] *See generally* Mark C. Weber, *The Least Restrictive Environment Obligation as an Entitlement to Educational Services: A Commentary*, 5 U.C. Davis J. Juv. L. & Pol'y 147 (2001) (interpreting least restrictive environment duty as duty to provide related services).

[80] *See, e.g.*, Corey H. v. Board of Educ., 995 F. Supp. 900 (N.D. Ill. 1998) (requiring state to produce compliance plan to make school district obey least restrictive environment duties); J.G. v. Board of Educ., 26 Individuals with Disabilities Educ. L. Rep. 114 (W.D.N.Y. 1998) (entering consent decree requiring compliance with least restrictive environment duties).

[81] 34 C.F.R. § 300.116(b)(3) & (c) (2011).

[82] *See, e.g.*, Murray v. Montrose County Sch. Dist., 51 F.3d 921 (10th Cir. 1995).

[83] *See, e.g.*, Ruth Colker, *The Disability Integration Presumption: Thirty Years Later*, 154 U. Pa. L. Rev. 789 (2006); Anne Proffitt Dupre, *Disability and the Public Schools: The Case Against "Inclusion"*, 72 Wash. L. Rev. 775 (1997).

training and preparation afforded teachers and nondisabled students, everyone benefits when students with disabilities are integrated into the general education setting.[84] The report of the President's Commission on Excellence in Special Education supports the idea of general education taking ownership of students receiving special education services and calls for schools to recognize that "[c]hildren placed in special education are general education children first" and "qualifying for special education [ought to be] a gateway to more effective instruction and strong intervention."[85]

[E] Procedures and Remedies

IDEA establishes an elaborate set of procedures for parents and guardians to participate in and contest the educational decisions about their children. As the Supreme Court commented in *Rowley*, "When the elaborate and highly specific procedural safeguards embodied in [20 U.S.C.] § 1415 are contrasted with the general and somewhat imprecise substantive admonitions contained in the Act, we think that the importance Congress attached to these procedural safeguards cannot be gainsaid."[86] Justice Rehnquist continued: "It seems . . . no exaggeration to say that Congress placed every bit as much emphasis upon compliance with procedures giving parents and guardians a large measure of participation at every stage of the administrative process . . . as it did upon the measurement of the resulting IEP against a substantive standard."[87] Relevant topics here include identification, evaluation, and IEP-related rights; due process hearing issues; judicial appeals; remedies available in hearings and court actions; attorneys' fees claims; and claims for damages beyond tuition reimbursement.

Procedural rights begin with the identification and evaluation of children thought to have disabilities. Parents are to receive notice of the school district's intention to begin or change the identification, evaluation, or educational placement of their child, or the district's refusing to do so.[88] They have the right to withhold consent to evaluation, subject to hearing rights that the school system can exercise,

---

[84] *See, e.g.*, Wayne Sailor & Blair Roger, *Rethinking Inclusion: Schoolwide Applications*, 86 Phi Delta Kappan 503 (2005) (collecting sources supporting integration and outlining potential improvements in integrated educational programs); Mark C. Weber, *A Nuanced Approach to the Disability Integration Presumption*, 156 U. Pa. L. Rev. Pennumbra 174 (2007) (supporting inclusion with sufficient supporting aids and services); Daniel H. Melvin II, Comment, *The Desegregation of Children with Disabilities*, 44 DePaul L. Rev. 599 (1995) (collecting and analyzing sources); *see also* National Association of School Psychologists, Position Statement on Inclusive Programs for Students with Disabilities, at http://www.nasponline.org/information/pospaper_ipsd.html (Apr. 1, 2000) (position statement calling for inclusive schools and listing potential benefits).

[85] President's Commission on Excellence in Special Education, *supra* note 13, at 7.

[86] 458 U.S. at 205.

[87] *Id.* at 205–06.

[88] 20 U.S.C. § 1415(b)(3), (c)(1), (d) (2006). The rights extend also to initiation or change in the provision of free, appropriate public education of the child. Statutory rights also guarantee access to records, participation in meetings, and independent evaluation, § 1415(b)(1), as well as procedures for appointment of a surrogate parent when the child's parents cannot be found or the child is a ward of the state, § 1415(b)(2).

and they can withhold consent to placement of their child in special education.[89] If the parents believe that the evaluation is not appropriate, they have the right to demand an independent evaluation at public expense, subject to the school district demanding a hearing to show the evaluation was appropriate.[90] The parents have notice and participation rights for the meeting to devise the individualized education program ("IEP"), which itself has specified components designed to keep parents and school personnel informed of what the child's current level of functioning is, what services the child will receive, and what measurable goals the child can be expected to attain.[91] The IEP is to be revised at least once a year.[92]

If parents disagree with the IEP that emerges from the meeting process or if they have any complaint relating to the free, appropriate public education of the child, they may demand a due process hearing.[93] They may also invoke state-provided mediation at any time.[94] At the due process hearing, both parent and school district have the right to obtain documents, to present and cross examine witnesses, and to obtain a written final decision from an independent hearing officer.[95] The state may establish a process for an appeal to an independent review officer, or it may have the due process decision be the final one. The final decision may be appealed to state court or federal district court, and the court is to receive the record of the proceedings below and may receive additional evidence to assist in making its desicion.[96] During the pendency of due process hearing proceedings and court appeals (with the exception of some proceedings having to do with disciplinary matters), the child is to remain in his or her current educational placement.[97] This subsection of the statute is sometimes called the "stay-put" or "maintenance of placement" provision.

In *Schaffer v. Weast*, the Supreme Court considered whether the parents or the school district should have the burden of persuasion in due process hearings.[98] The Court placed the burden on the party seeking relief, which will generally be the parents if the contest is over a proposed IEP. The Court reasoned that the default rule is for plaintiffs to bear the burden of persuasion. The Court noted that the

---

[89] § 1414(a)(1)(D) (2006); *see* 34 C.F.R. § 300.300(a)–(b) (2011). Subsection.300(b)(3) gives parents an absolute right to not consent to services and excuses school district IEP obligations when that occurs.

[90] § 300.502.

[91] *See* 20 U.S.C. § 1414(d) (2006).

[92] § 1414(d)(4). A 2004 amendment to IDEA permits a demonstration project for optional multi-year IEPs in up to 15 states. § 1414(d)(5).

[93] § 1415(f); *see also* § 1415(b)(6)–(8), (c)(2) (specifying additional hearing-related procedures).

[94] § 1415(e) (2006). If mediation does not take place following the filing of a hearing request, the school is to offer a resolution session, a meeting between parent and the decision maker for the school system. § 1415(f)(1)(B). If the parent does not bring an attorney to the session, the school district cannot do so either. § 1415(f)(1)(B)(i)(II).

[95] § 1415(f) (2006).

[96] § 1415(i) (2006). The statute says the court shall receive evidence, but courts have ruled that this duty is not absolute. *See* Town of Burlington v. Department of Educ., 736 F2d 773, 790 (1st Cir. 1984), *aff'd*, 471 U.S. 359 (1985).

[97] 20 U.S.C. § 1415(j) (2006).

[98] 546 U.S. 49 (2005).

parents have ample access to evidence within the control of the school district by virtue of their extensive rights to participate in the educational process. The Court reserved the issue whether states may override this allocation of the burden by placing it always on the school district.[99]

Only in exceptional cases may the parents bypass the exhaustion of administrative remedies and proceed directly to court, and many court cases are dismissed because of failure to exhaust.[100] Some courts dismissed IDEA suits on the ground that they were brought pro se by parents.[101] Although there is ordinarily no obstacle to suing pro se, these courts argued that parents may not proceed pro se with all or some IDEA claims because doing so would entail representing the child, which a non-attorney is not permitted to do.[102] The Supreme Court ultimately rejected this reasoning and ruled that because parents themselves are given rights under IDEA, they may file suit on their own behalf.[103]

Relief in due process proceedings and judicial appeals encompasses orders for future conduct, compensatory education, and reimbursement of tuition and other expenses. In addition, courts may award attorneys' fees to prevailing parents in IDEA administrative or judicial proceedings.[104] The Supreme Court established that the law that is now IDEA furnishes a tuition reimbursement remedy in *Burlington School Committee v. Department of Education*.[105] The reasoning was simply that the remedy just required the district to be paying what it should have been paying all along; unilateral placement by parents could be expected if the parents were to safeguard the interests of their children through the ponderous administrative and judicial review process. In *Florence County School District Four v. Carter*, the Court extended Burlington's reimbursement remedy to placements by parents in schools that are not approved by the state's educational authority.[106] The Court explained that the statutory requirement that education be provided under public supervision and direction could not have been intended to apply to a parent's unilateral placement. It further commented that parents who place unilaterally act at their own financial risk, for they will receive reimbursement only if they prevail both on the issue that the public placement was not appropriate under IDEA and the issue that the private school placement was. Finally, the Court noted that reimbursement could be reduced if the cost of the private education is unreasonable. The current version of IDEA codifies the tuition

---

[99] *Id.* at 61–62.

[100] *E.g.,* Polera v. Board of Educ., 288 F.3d 478 (2d Cir. 2002). Exhaustion may be excused under some circumstances, however. *See, e.g.,* McAdams v. Board of Educ., 216 F. Supp. 2d 86 (E.D.N.Y. 2002).

[101] *E.g.,* Cavanaugh v. Cardinal Loc. Sch. Dist., 409 F.3d 753 (6th Cir. 2005), *abrogated by* Winkelman v. Parma City Sch. Dist, 550 U.S. 516 (2007).

[102] *Compare* Maroni v. Pemi-Baker Reg'l Sch. Dist., 346 F.3d 247 (1st Cir. 2003) (permitting parent to proceed pro se), *with* Collinsgru v. Palmyra Bd. of Educ., 161 F.3d 225 (3d Cir. 1998) (barring parental pro se representation, finding child to be real party in interest, and affirming dismissal of action), *abrogated by* Winkelman v. Parma City Sch. Dist., 550 U.S. 516 (2007).

[103] Winkelman v. Parma City Sch. Dist., 550 U.S. 516 (2007).

[104] 20 U.S.C. § 1415(i)(3)(B)–(G) (2006).

[105] 471 U.S. 359 (1985).

[106] 510 U.S. 7 (1993).

reimbursement remedy, providing that if the parents of a child who previously received special education and related services under the authority of a school district enroll the child in a private school, a hearing officer or court may require the district to reimburse the parents for the cost of the enrollment if it finds that the district had not made a free, appropriate public education available to the child in a timely manner before the private school enrollment.[107] The reimbursement may be reduced or denied, however, if at the most recent IEP meeting that the parents attended before removal of the child from the public school, the parents failed to inform the IEP team that they were rejecting the placement proposed by the public school. The information provided by the parents must include making a statement of their concerns and their intent to enroll the child in a private school at public expense. Alternatively, the parents may meet their obligations if, ten business days before removal of the child from the public school, they give written notice to the school district of their rejection of the placement, their concerns, and their intent to enroll the child in private school at public expense.[108] The parents must or may be excused from giving notice under limited circumstances.[109] Reimbursement may also be reduced or denied if the parents failed to make the child available for evaluation if the school district properly notified them before the removal from the public school of its intent to evaluate the child, or upon a judicial finding of unreasonableness with respect to actions taken by the parents.[110]

In *Forest Grove School District v. T.A.*, the Supreme Court ruled that this codification of the tuition reimbursement remedy does not bar parents whose child has not previously received special education and related services through the public school from obtaining tuition reimbursement from a hearing officer or court.[111] The Court read the codification of the remedy as not altering the reimbursement relief that *Burlington* and *Carter* found could be ordered under the general remedies term of the statute.[112]

Prevailing parents are entitled to attorneys' fees, though typically they must resort to an action in court following success in due process proceedings in order to receive them.[113] The standards applied resemble those applied in other civil rights actions; there is even a statutory version of Federal Rule 68 allowing under some circumstances for denial of fees accrued after an offer of settlement if the parents rejected the settlement offer and the offer was as favorable as the relief finally obtained.[114] Under the 2004 amendment to IDEA, parents and their attorneys may also be liable for fees of the school district or state educational agency; against the

---

[107] 20 U.S.C. § 1412(a)(10)(C)(ii) (2006).

[108] 20 U.S.C. § 1412(a)(10)(C)(iii)(I) (2006).

[109] 20 U.S.C. § 1412(a)(10)(C)(iv) (2006) (including considerations such as harm to child and parental illiteracy).

[110] 20 U.S.C. § 1412(a)(10)(C)(iii)(II)–(III) (2006). The reimbursement and reimbursement denial provisions are codified under the section of IDEA relating to state obligations rather than that relating to procedural protections for parents, making them a potential trap for the unwary.

[111] 129 S. Ct. 2484 (2009).

[112] *Id.* at 2496.

[113] 20 U.S.C. § 1415(i)(3)(B)(i) (2006) (stating that "a court" may award fees).

[114] *See* § 1415(i)(3)(D) (2006); *cf.* FED. R. CIV. P. 68 (offer of judgment rule).

attorney if the due process complaint or appeal was frivolous, unreasonable, or without foundation (or maintained after the litigation clearly met that standard) and against the parent or attorney if the due process complaint or appeal was presented for an improper purpose.[115] The Supreme Court has ruled that the parents' right to attorneys' fees does not encompass non-attorney expert witness fees, and so those costs are not recoverable by prevailing parents.[116]

Courts have been reluctant to permit an action for damages (beyond tuition reimbursement available under IDEA) to be brought under 42 U.S.C. § 1983 for violations of IDEA.[117] However, courts generally have upheld actions for injunctive relief under § 1983, when bypassing the administrative procedures of IDEA is appropriate because the parents were blocked from using the procedures or because of some other reason.[118] Courts have permitted actions for damages for intentional conduct by school districts that constitutes disability discrimination in violation of section 504 and ADA title II,[119] though a number of courts have required administrative exhaustion in many of these cases.[120] In damages cases under section 504 and title II, courts frequently apply a test for intentional discriminatory conduct that entails a showing of bad faith conduct or gross misjudgment.[121] Constitutional claims have also supported damages liability in some cases concerning improper treatment of children in special education settings.[122]

[F]   Student Discipline

Discipline for children with disabilities embraces several matters. First, appropriate education for some children includes positive interventions to achieve behavior-related goals. Second, procedural rights provided to children with disabilities to keep them from being improperly removed from educational settings affect the operation of suspensions, expulsions, and other disciplinary measures when IDEA-eligible children are targeted. Third, debates continue over whether and to what degree rights and procedures regarding student discipline ought to differ for children with disabilities compared to students without disabilities.

Ideally, school discipline is positive, directed to educating children about what constitutes good behavior and how to conform to behavior standards. For a child

---

[115]   20 U.S.C. § 1415(i)(3)(B)(i)(II)–(III) (2006).

[116]   Arlington Cent. Sch. Dist. Bd. of Educ. v. Murphy, 548 U.S. 291 (2006).

[117]   *E.g.*, Padilla v. School Dist. No. 1, 233 F.3d 1268 (10th Cir. 2000).

[118]   *E.g.*, Robinson v. Pinderhughes, 810 F.2d 1270 (4th Cir. 1987) (district's refusal to obey hearing decision); Manecke v. School Bd., 762 F.2d 912 (11th Cir. 1985) (district's failure to act on request for hearing).

[119]   *E.g.*, McCormick v. Waukegan Sch. Dist. No. 60, 374 F.3d 564 (7th Cir. 2004); Baird v. Rose, 192 F.3d 462 (4th Cir. 1999).

[120]   *E.g.*, Frazier v. Fairhaven Sch. Comm., 276 F.3d 52 (1st Cir. 2002); Charlie F. v. Board of Educ., 98 F.3d 989 (7th Cir. 1996).

[121]   *E.g.*, M.P. v. Independent Sch. Dist. No. 721, 326 F.3d 975 (8th Cir. 2003).

[122]   *E.g.*, Sutton v. Utah State Sch. for the Deaf and Blind, 173 F.3d 1226 (10th Cir. 1999) (upholding substantive due process claim against principal for failure to adopt or implement policy to prevent peer sex abuse at state school).

whose disability affects the ability to learn or obey rules, appropriate education and related services include interventions related to behavior. The IDEA regulations state that "in the case of a child whose behavior impedes the child's learning or that of others," the team developing the individualized education program must "consider the use of positive behavioral interventions and supports, and other strategies, to address that behavior."[123] Courts have ruled that failure to include needed behavioral services in a child's program may be a denial of appropriate education.[124]

When schools impose some more traditional forms of student discipline on children with disabilities as a response to their behaviors, the concern arises that the school may be punishing the child for something that is simply a manifestation of the disability.[125] Moreover, since expulsions were a major reason that children with disabilities were out of school in the period before passage of the law that is now IDEA, procedural rights to challenge exclusions from school assume prime importance in when schools impose disciplinary measures that entail taking the child out of his or her regular class.[126] In *Honig v. Doe*, the parents of a child who was expelled for violating school rules demanded pursuant to the law that is now IDEA that no change of placement occur during the pendency of a hearing request and any appeals of the hearing decision.[127] The Court ruled that the removal of the child from school constituted a change of placement and that the child had to remain in the existing placement when the parents made a due process hearing request challenging the discipline. The Court's reasoning stressed the unequivocal language of the statute requiring that the child be kept in the current educational placement. The Court rejected the argument that the stay-put provision did not apply to discipline, pointing out that Congress was well aware that before the passage of the federal law, disciplinary measures had been used to remove children with disabilities from the schools. Although the statute did not provide an emergency exception to the stay-put obligation, the Court stated that school districts could go to court in proper cases, without exhausting administrative remedies, to get injunctions temporarily enjoining a child from attending school.

In subsequent years, Congress has modified the stay-put right in discipline cases so it is no longer as absolute as it was at the time of *Honig*. At the same time, Congress has steadfastly maintained the basic principle that no child with disabilities ever be cut off entirely from receiving a free, appropriate public education.[128] Under the current codification, suspensions of children with

---

[123] 34 C.F.R. § 300.324(a)(2)(i) (2011).

[124] *See, e.g.*, Neosho R-V Sch. Dist. v. Clark, 315 F.3d 1022 (8th Cir. 2003).

[125] *See* S-1 v. Turlington, 635 F.2d 342 (5th Cir. 1981) (affirming preliminary injunction requiring hearings before expulsion regarding whether misconduct constituted manifestation of their disabilities), *abrogated in part not relevant, by* Honig v. Doe, 484 U.S. 305 (1988).

[126] *See* Mills v. Board of Educ., 348 F. Supp. 866, 869–70, 875 (D.D.C. 1972) (describing reasons for exclusion from school of named plaintiffs and others).

[127] 484 U.S. 305 (1988).

[128] 20 U.S.C. § 1412(a)(1)(A) (2006) (stating that free, appropriate public education must be available to all children with disabilities "including children with disabilities who have been suspended or expelled from school").

disabilities for up to ten school days are permitted if nondisabled children are treated the same way for the same behavior.[129] For discipline entailing suspension of more than ten school days, a manifestation determination must be made within ten school days.[130] The IEP team must review all the relevant information in the child's file, any teacher observations, and any relevant information from the parents and determine if the conduct was caused by or had a direct and substantial relationship to the child's disability or was the direct result of the school district's failure to implement the IEP. If the behavior was not a manifestation of the child's disability, the child may be subject to the same discipline as nondisabled children, but the child must continue to receive free, appropriate public education, although it can be provided in an interim, alternative educational setting.[131] If the behavior was a manifestation, the IEP team has to conduct a functional behavioral assessment, and implement a behavioral intervention plan for the child if there was no previous assessment.[132] It must also return the child to the original placement, unless the conduct entailed activity at school, on school premises, or at a school function, that constituted: (1) carrying or possessing a weapon; (2) knowingly possessing or using illegal drugs, or selling or soliciting the sale of a controlled substance; or (3) inflicting serious bodily injury on another person.[133] For one of those three activities, the child may be removed to an interim alternative educational setting for not more than 45 school days even if the behavior is a manifestation of the disability.[134] The interim alternative educational setting must enable the child to continue to participate in the general educational curriculum, although in another setting, and to progress toward the goals in the child's IEP while receiving, as appropriate, behavioral assessment and behavioral intervention services and modifications, to address recurrence of the behavior.[135]

The parent may use the due process hearing procedure to challenge a discipline decision or manifestation determination, and the school district may also use it when it believes that maintaining the child's current educational placement is substantially likely to cause injury to the child or others.[136] The hearing officer may return the child to the original placement, or may order a change of placement to an appropriate interim, alternative educational setting for not more than 45 school days if maintaining the current placement is substantially likely to result in injury to the child or others.[137] During the pendency of the due process hearing, the child is to remain in the interim alternative educational setting pending the decision of the hearing officer or the expiration of the relevant time period

---

[129] § 1415(k)(1)(B). The applicable regulation requires services in the interim, alternative educational setting for any removal that entails more than ten days away from the child's current placement in the same school year, even if the days are not consecutive. 34 C.F.R. § 300.530(b)(2) (2011).

[130] § 1415(k)(1)(E).

[131] § 1415(k)(1)(C).

[132] § 1415(k)(1)(F).

[133] § 1415(k)(1)(F)(iii).

[134] § 1415(k)(1)(G).

[135] § 1415(k)(1)(D).

[136] § 1415(k)(3)(A).

[137] § 1415(k)(3)(B).

applicable to children without disabilities, although an expedited hearing is to be arranged.[138] Protections exist in limited circumstances for children believed by their parents to be children with disabilities but not yet determined by the school district to be eligible for special education.[139]

Some authors have questioned the wisdom of affording students with disabilities the protections in the disciplinary process that IDEA provides, saying that the law undermines school authorities or constitutes an impermissible double standard compared to treatment of nondisabled students.[140] Defenders of the protections stress the long history of the use of disciplinary measures to exclude children with disabilities from school and argue that positive behavioral supports and similar measures, if properly implemented, can supplant the use of discipline that excludes children from school.[141] The current provisions represent a compromise of interests. Though they plainly do not satisfy everyone, they have survived congressional revision since 1997 with only modest changes.

§ 4.02   POST-SECONDARY EDUCATION

Several statutes afford protection against disability discrimination in higher education. Public colleges and universities are covered by title II of the ADA. In addition, because they receive federal funding, they are covered by section 504. The duties imposed by these statutes are essentially the same, so often authorities refer to one or the other law or to the section 504-title II combination. Private colleges and universities are covered by section 504 if they receive federal funding, and nearly all do, so their obligations match those of their public counterparts. In addition, if the school is private and not religious, title III of the ADA applies to it. The protections afforded by the section 504-title II combination are significant. Nevertheless, students with disabilities are badly underrepresented in college and university populations. The President's Commission on Excellence in Special Education reported in 2002 that enrollment rates of students with disabilities in higher education are 50% lower than the rates among the general population.

Because employment discrimination issues are covered elsewhere in this book, the discussion here will focus on services for students, and will give primary attention to the duties imposed by section 504 and title II. An important aside, however, is that title III of the ADA has a specific provision regarding accessibility obligations of entities such as testing services that offer examinations and courses for credentialing and related purposes.[142] That provision will be discussed in this chapter. Issues of Eleventh Amendment immunity relating to state government entities (including universities) are discussed in the Chapter 6, which takes up state and local government discrimination. Because section 504 and title II are the basic

---

[138] § 1415(k)(4).

[139] § 1415(k)(5).

[140] *See, e.g.*, Anne Proffitt Dupre, *A Study in Double Standards, Discipline, and the Disabled Student*, 75 WASH. L. REV. 1 (2000).

[141] *See* H. Rutherford Turnbull, III, et al., *IDEA, Positive Behavioral Supports, and School Safety*, 30 J.L. & EDUC. 445 (2001).

[142] 42 U.S.C. § 12189 (2006).

sources of rights of students in higher education, issues of who is a person with a disability are often of critical importance. Since that issue has already been discussed in Chapter 2, however, it will not be revisited here except with regard to students with learning disabilities.[143]

[A] Overview of Higher Education Discrimination

The fundamental obligations of section 504 and title II are not to exclude qualified individuals with disabilities from participation in the services, programs or activities of the covered entity; not to deny those persons the benefits of the services, programs, or activities; and not to subject them to discrimination, by reason of the disability.[144] When applied to post-secondary education, the nondiscrimination obligation embraces topics such as qualifications and reasonable accommodation, the degree of deference to be afforded academic decisions on those issues, specific issues pertaining to students in higher education who have learning disabilities, and the treatment of entities that provide courses and examinations for credentialing and similar purposes.

[B] Qualifications and Reasonable Accommodation

The Supreme Court's first case on section 504 of the Rehabilitation Act involved higher education. In *Southeastern Community College v. Davis*, a community college denied a student with a severe hearing impairment admission to a registered nurse training program.[145] Hearing aids permitted Davis to hear sounds, but she needed to look directly at the speaker and read lips to understand spoken language; she nevertheless was already credentialed as a licensed practical nurse and had done some private duty work.[146] Davis lost at the trial level, where the court found that she was not "otherwise qualified" under section 504 because nurses and doctors in various settings wear surgical masks or need to communicate instantly with vocal means, so she could not safely perform in her training program and in the profession. The court of appeals reversed, saying that "otherwise qualified" referred to meeting the technical and academic qualification standards of the program without regard to any limits imposed by the disability. The Supreme Court overturned the court of appeals, declaring that the court of appeals' understanding of the "otherwise qualified" term was incorrect in ignoring the effects of the disability: "An otherwise qualified person is one who is able to meet all of a program's requirement in spite of his handicap."[147] The Court also referred to regulations permitting legitimate physical qualifications for participation in particular programs. Asking whether the ability to understand speech without reliance on lipreading was actually necessary for patient safety during the clinical

---

[143] *See generally infra* § 4.02[D] (discussing learning disability issues).

[144] See 42 U.S.C. § 12132 (2006) (title II).

[145] 442 U.S. 397 (1979).

[146] The Court characterized the work as "a little bit of private duty," said that Davis had not done the work for several years before applying for the registered nursing program, and distinguished the jobs of licensed practical nurse and registered nurse on the ground that the registered nurse works with less supervision and does more technically sophisticated work. *Id.* at 401 n.1.

[147] *Id.* at 406.

program, the Court relied on district court findings that it was. The Court considered whether conduct by Southeastern could permit Davis to participate, for example by providing more individual supervision or waiving some course requirements. It cited regulations requiring institutions to make modifications in their programs and provide auxiliary aids to persons with disabilities. But it concluded that the forms of individual attention and curricular changes needed would constitute a fundamental alteration of the program, far more than a modification. A broader interpretation of the regulations would be at odds with the statute. Unlike the statutory provision pertaining to federal employment, which requires affirmative action to hire, place, and advance persons with disabilities, section 504 creates more limited duties. In some situations, an insistence on maintaining the "past requirements and practices might arbitrarily deprive genuinely qualified handicapped persons of the opportunity to participate in a covered program," particularly in light of expected technological advances over time.[148] "Thus situations may arise where a refusal to modify an existing program might become arbitrary and discriminatory."[149] But the Court found that the modifications in this case would substantially lower academic standards, and said the statute did not compel such "substantial modifications of standards."[150]

Other cases reflect a similar approach. In *Ohio Civil Rights Commission v. Case Western Reserve University*, decided under the state law parallel to the ADA, the Ohio Supreme Court upheld the reversal of an order of the commission that had required a blind student to be admitted to medical school.[151] The plaintiff was an honors graduate in chemistry who lost her sight in her junior year and completed her undergraduate degree with the use of accommodations. She planned to become a psychiatrist. The school ultimately denied her admission after faculty members who interviewed her concluded that she would be unable to complete the medical school program. The faculty members reaching that conclusion raised concerns about the a blind person being able to read x-rays, start I.V.s, do microscope work, and do clinical activity. They were aware of a blind person who had graduated from Temple University School of Medicine some years earlier but did not contact that person or Temple. Accommodations that person received included extensive tutoring from professors (permitting less time for tutoring of others) and modification of lectures so that raised line drawings were provided and verbal descriptions made of visual data. During the blind student's clerkships, fellow students or others performed activities that required visual observations and described the observations to him; he spent less time in the surgery rotation than other students did. The Ohio court applied a standard for "otherwise qualified" that echoed that used by the Supreme Court in *Davis*: "able to safely and substantially perform an educational program's essential requirements with reasonable accommodation. An accommodation is not reasonable when it requires fundamental alterations in the essential nature of the program or imposes an undue financial or administrative burden." Relying in part on *Davis*, the court ruled that the needed

---

[148] *Id.* at 412.

[149] *Id.* at 412–13.

[150] *Id.* at 413.

[151] 666 N.E.2d 1376 (Ohio 1996).

accommodations were not reasonable. It deferred to the academic decision making of the school on the point.

In *McGregor v. Louisiana State University Board of Supervisors*, the Fifth Circuit Court of Appeals gave a limited reach to reasonable accommodation in the case of a law student who had impairments resulting from head and spinal injuries.[152] The court affirmed a grant of summary judgment against the law student, who was not retained for second year after receiving low grades. The student had requested a part-time schedule as an accommodation, but the school refused and provided only a special parking permit and additional time on one examination first semester. Although his grades were below those for retention at the end of the semester, the school permitted him to audit Constitutional Law and Legal Writing and Research. The Constitutional Law professor was assigned to provide him individual tutoring, and spent one hour a week with the student outside of class. The student passed both courses. The school then waived the requirement that the student wait a year for readmission and readmitted him as a first year student the next fall, on the condition that he start over, forfeiting his previous credits, that he be placed on academic probation, that he carry a full course load during the year, and that he not engage in outside work that year. The school also adjusted the student's schedule so that his classes would be in locations accessible by wheelchair. In the fall, he was allowed to take three of four examinations at home and allowed double time for the fourth. Rather than agreeing to allow in-home examinations in the spring, the school allowed extra time, modification of location for the tests, use of a typewriter or dictaphone, assistance of a proctor in personal needs and permission to eat and drink to maintain blood sugar levels. The student's spring grades met the ordinary minimum for retention, but not the slightly higher level required of a student on probation. Although the school agreed to readmit the student for the next year, it would again have been as a first year student with permission to audit a course in fall and a spring course load of two courses in which his grades had been below the probationary minimum in the past spring. He would begin to take an elective the next summer and postpone two other first-year courses to the next school year semester as well as one upper-division elective. The exams could be taken at home with a proctor from the school. The student contended that the accommodations did not adequately address the fatigue and pain that inhibited his learning, and asked for a part-time schedule as well as at-home examinations. The school did not normally offer a part-time program, and the court felt that requiring it to do so exceeded the standard for reasonable accommodation articulated in the *Davis* case. It also described the decisions to require a full-time program and in-class examinations as reasonable academic decisions, and affirmed the decision against the student.

Although these and other decisions rely on *Davis*, the bald statement from that case, "[a]n otherwise qualified person is one who is able to meet all of a program's requirement in spite of his handicap,"[153] needs to be read in light of subsequent developments. In *School Board v. Arline*, a 1987 section 504 case concerning

---

[152] 3 F.3d 850 (5th Cir. 1993).

[153] 442 U.S. at 406.

employment, the Supreme Court clarified that an otherwise qualified person is one who can perform the essential functions of the job with reasonable accommodations.[154] In reality, *Davis* itself and the cases described above all consider reasonable accommodations, while nevertheless holding that defendants need not make fundamental alterations in their programs. Moreover, title II of the ADA explicitly adopts the reasonable-accommodation approach to "qualified."[155] Courts have taken seriously the requirement that academic institutions afford reasonable modifications of their ordinary rules. In *Lane v. Pena*, the district court required that the Merchant Marine Academy not disenroll a student who developed diabetes.[156] Although the condition rendered the student ineligible for service as a midshipman or naval reserve officer in the regular navy, and eligibility for that service could have been read as a condition for continued enrollment in the Merchant Marine Academy, the court ruled that continuous eligibility for service in the naval reserve was not an essential requirement of the program, and that the academy should have accommodated the student by permitting his continued enrollment. A large portion of the students never enter the reserve, and the student himself maintained an excellent record in the academy with regard to both academic and physical performance; moreover, the applicable rule was subject to a permissive waiver provision.

The federal regulations applicable to section 504 cover higher education in some detail, listing various rules modifications and auxiliary aids and services that colleges and universities must provide for students with disabilities.[157] Compulsory modifications of academic requirements "may include changes in the length of time permitted for the completion of degree requirements, substitution of specific courses required for the completion of degree requirements, and adaptation of the manner in which specific courses are conducted."[158] Academic rules may not prohibit tape recorders in classrooms or of dog guides in campus buildings if that would have the effect of limiting the participation of students with disabilities.[159] For examinations, the educational institution has to provide students who have a

---

[154] 480 U.S. 273, 287 n.17 (1987).

[155] 42 U.S.C. § 12131(2) (2006) ("The term 'qualified individual with a disability' means an individual with a disability who, with or without reasonable modifications to rules, policies, or practices, the removal of architectural barriers, or the provision or auxiliary aids and services, meets the essential eligibility requirements for the receipt of services or the participation in programs or activities provided by a public entity.").

[156] 867 F. Supp. 1050 (D.D.C. 1994), *vacated in part & aff'd in part*, 1995 U.S. App. LEXIS 20039 (D.C. Cir. June 5, 1995), *aff'd*, 518 U.S. 187 (1996). The partial vacatur regarded the application of federal sovereign immunity from monetary damages awards.

[157] Courts have permitted academic institutions to inquire about students' and prospective students' disabilities if the students request accommodations or admission to a specialized program for individuals with disabilities. *See, e.g.*, Halasz v. University of New England, 816 F. Supp. 37 (D. Me. 1993) (also upholding educational institution's decisions regarding program admissions and accommodations for student with learning disability and Tourette's Syndrome). The section 504 regulations provide in general that colleges and universities may not make pre-admission inquiries about whether an applicant is disabled, but may make inquiries after admission about disabilities that may need accommodations. 34 C.F.R. § 104.42(b)(4) (2011).

[158] 34 C.F.R. § 104.44(a) (2011).

[159] § 104.44(b).

disability impairing sensory, manual, or speaking skills with testing methods that "will best ensure that the results of the evaluation represents the student's achievement in the course, rather than reflecting the student's impaired sensory, manual, or speaking skills (except where such skills are the factors that the test purports to measure)."[160] Auxiliary aids that may need to be provided "may include taped texts, interpreters or other effective methods of making orally delivered materials available to students with hearing impairments, readers in libraries for students with visual impairments, classroom equipment adapted for use by students with manual impairments, and other similar services and actions," although "attendants, individually prescribed devices, readers for personal use or study, or other devices or services of a personal nature" need not be furnished.[161] Other provisions require reasonable accommodations in housing, financial and employment assistance, and nonacademic services.[162]

One possibility for accommodation that remains largely unexplored, however — and one that may make sense in cases such as *Davis* — is having educational institutions issue modified degrees for persons whose disabilities prevent them from completing otherwise essential portions of the program. If courses or activities are omitted, the gap in training would be reflected in the credential, and the college or university would neither have to lower its academic standards nor risk misleading employers or others who might believe that a person with a degree of a given kind is able to perform all tasks customarily performed by the person with that credential. This form of accommodation might be deemed reasonable because it would permit the student to obtain the learning he or she desires while also permitting the educational institution to uphold whatever academic standards might maintain the integrity of its degrees.

[C] Academic Deference

On issues of qualification of students or reasonable accommodations for them, many courts have given academic institutions some measure of deference when evaluating their decisions. *Wynne v. Tufts University School of Medicine* compared section 504 actions against universities with civil rights actions against individual government officials for damages.[163] Under the doctrine of official immunity, courts give government officials immunity from damages awards against them; personal liability exists only when the official's action both violates the plaintiff's civil rights and constitutes objectively unreasonable conduct that violates clearly established rights. The court reasoned that the interests of academic institutions in autonomy supported a similar protection from liability if the institution submitted undisputed facts showing that the appropriate college or university officials considered the alternative means of accommodation, their feasibility, cost, and effect on the academic program, and came to a rationally justifiable conclusion that the available alternatives would result either in lowering academic standards or requiring

---

[160] § 104.44(c).

[161] § 104.44(d).

[162] §§ 104.45–.47. Both private litigation and the administrative activity of the Office for Civil Rights of the Department of Education enforce the requirements of section 504 and title II of the ADA.

[163] 932 F.2d 19 (1st Cir. 1991).

substantial program alteration. The court applied that approach to a medical student with various information processing difficulties suggesting dyslexia. The student did well in some evaluations, but failed a number of multiple choice examinations. The student said the school should have offered an alternative to written multiple choice examinations. The court overturned a grant of summary judgment to the school, finding that on the existing evidence, the school did not appear to have given any consideration to possible alternatives to multiple choice tests, nor discuss the merits of such testing, or even disclose who had decided the accommodation request. On a subsequent appeal following a later grant of summary judgment, however, the court affirmed, saying that the university considered reasonable alternative means of testing and came to a rationally justifiable conclusion that the multiple choice format was the best way to test biochemistry.[164] Although some evidence suggested other means would work, the court resolved the dispute by applying deference to the academic institution.

In *Zukle v. Regents of the University of California*, the Ninth Circuit affirmed a grant of summary judgment against a medical student with learning disabilities who had been dismissed from medical school after receiving poor grades despite various accommodations.[165] The court accorded deference to the decision of the school, stressing that courts have limited abilities, compared with educational professionals, to determine whether students meet academic standards. The court pointed to the accommodations the school provided, including extra time on exams, allowance to retake courses, and deceleration of the usual schedule, and deferred to the decision of the school to refuse to permit rearranging of the schedule of two clerkships as an additional accommodation. The court also deferred to the decision to refuse to allow the student to reduce the time in one clerkship to allow more studying for the written exam, which the school said would compromise the clerkship's purpose of simulating medical practice.

Not all courts give deference to academic decision making. In *Pushkin v. Regents of the University of Colorado*, the court affirmed a grant of injunctive relief to a doctor who had multiple sclerosis, compelling the university to admit him to a psychiatric residency program.[166] The university argued that its conduct should be evaluated in the same manner as an equal protection challenge, by use of a rational basis test that would insulate the decision from challenge if it was reasonable. The court responded, "The inquiry has to be on whether the University has, in fact, discriminated on the basis of handicap. The mere fact that the University acted in a rational manner is no defense to an act of discrimination."[167] Evaluating the record of the district court and giving weight to the findings of fact and credibility determinations of that court, the court of appeals affirmed the decision that the university discriminated against the applicant doctor. As the analysis in *Pushkin* court suggests, doubts may be raised whether academic deference is proper in applying the disability discrimination laws. There is no particular reason to believe that whatever decision making process the institution

---

[164] Wynne v. Tufts Univ. Sch. of Med., 976 F.2d 791 (1st Cir. 1992).

[165] 166 F.3d 1041 (9th Cir. 1999).

[166] 658 F.2d 1372 (10th Cir. 1981).

[167] *Id.* at 1383.

employs is more closely attuned to the purposes of section 504 and title II than the processes employed by businesses or state and local government agencies, but no deference is afforded business or government. Moreover, the *Wynne* court's analogy to qualified immunity for government officials may be subject to question. Qualified immunity doctrine protects individuals, not institutions, and bars only damages liability, not injunctive relief.[168] The doctrine exists largely to avoid deterring persons from engaging in public service because of fear of liability for wrong but reasonable decisions.[169] Courts apply academic deference to protect institutions, some of them exceedingly powerful, well-resourced actors in their communities, and use it to insulate the institutions from not just damages but also from orders to comply with the law in the future.

Courts that give academic deference need to determine how demanding they want to be in finding that the school has a process and that the process fully evaluated the qualifications of the student or the reasonableness of the accommodations. In the original *Wynne* decision, for example, the court refused to defer to the university's decision because the process was incomplete. Another noteworthy case where a court insisted that the academic institution carefully follow reasonable processes in reaching its decision before receiving deference is *Wong v. Regents of the University of California*.[170] *Wong* reversed a grant of summary judgment against a medical student whose disability affected the way he processed verbal information and expressed himself verbally. The student contended that he should have been afforded eight weeks of extra reading time between two of his clerkships. He had been given that modification of the rules for other clerkships, but was denied the modification for the ones in issue. The court acknowledged the academic deference rule, but it said the rule requires a court to defer to an institution's academic decisions only when the institution made itself aware of the nature and extent of the student's disability, explored alternative means for accommodating the student, and exercised professional judgment in determining if the requested accommodations would give the student the opportunity to complete the program without fundamentally or substantially changing the school's standards. The court said deference was not warranted in Wong's case because the university did not show that the dean fully investigated the accommodation Wong proposed to determine if the school could feasibly implement it or some alternative modification without substantially altering the school's standards. The dean did not discuss the proposal with any of the professionals who had worked with the student to identify the disability and recommended accommodations. The dean himself did not have the ability to formulate accommodations, and there was no evidence of that the dean considered the effects of the accommodation on the medical school's program requirements or academic standards. The court held that the issue whether the accommodation might cause disruption was for the jury to decide.

Wong and the 1991 *Wynne* decision are among the cases that are more demanding of academic institutions. Courts in other cases have been less insistent

---

[168] Owen v. City of Independence, 445 U.S. 622 (1980).

[169] *See* Harlow v. Fitzgerald, 457 U.S. 800, 814 (1982).

[170] 192 F.3d 807 (9th Cir. 1999).

that the university's process be thorough and transparent, and have simply accepted decisions of universities with little discussion of the decision making the university employed.[171]

[D] Specific Issues Regarding Learning Disabilities

As the previous subsection may suggest, many of the cases regarding disability discrimination in higher education involve students who have learning disabilities. Two additional noteworthy aspects of higher education litigation concerning students with learning disabilities are, first, the prospect of systemic cases alleging that general policies and conduct regarding students with learning disabilities violate the law, and second, the presence of questions about how to evaluate whether a person with a learning disability has a condition such that he or she is a person with a disability covered by the law.

In one notable case, *Guckenberger v. Boston University*, students with learning disabilities brought a broad challenge against university actions that affected the quality of their educational experience, including new eligibility and documentation requirements for students seeking accommodations for their learning disabilities, refusal to permit course substitutions for mathematics and foreign language, and communications said to have created an unwelcoming educational setting for students with learning disabilities. The federal district court in Massachusetts issued three opinions dealing with various aspects of the systemic complaint.[172]

The first opinion granted class certification on some claims and responded to motions to dismiss.[173] In that decision, the court considered the allegations that the university created a hostile learning environment with speeches by the president referring to students with disabilities as "a plague" and other conduct.[174] The court ruled that an ADA title III and section 504 cause of action exists for the creation of a hostile learning environment, but determined that the conduct alleged was insufficient to support the claim, particularly in light of First Amendment concerns over academic freedom. The court upheld a claim based on breach of contract regarding the availability of course substitutions and learning disability services after the students matriculated, while dismissing without prejudice a claim based on promissory estoppel. It dismissed an intentional infliction of emotional distress claim, and made various orders regarding the capacity of particular parties to the case to remain in the litigation.

In the second opinion in the case, the court after trial issued a comprehensive order determining (1) that the university was subject to federal nondiscrimination obligations; (2) that university requirements adopted in 1995 requiring retesting of students with learning disabilities every three years and refusing to accept evaluations by persons who were not physicians, clinical psychologists, or licensed

---

[171] *E.g.*, Anderson v. University of Wis., 841 F.2d 737 (7th Cir. 1988) (affirming summary judgment against plaintiff in case involving dismissal of law student with alcoholism).

[172] A fourth opinion and order awarded fees and costs. Guckenberger v. Boston Univ., 8 F. Supp. 2d 91 (D. Mass. 1998).

[173] Guckenberger v. Boston Univ., 957 F. Supp. 306 (D. Mass. 1997).

[174] *See id.* at 312.

psychologists violated the law because they screened out persons with disabilities but the university failed to show they were necessary; (3) that newer retesting requirements permitting waiver of the three-year requirement were not shown to screen out persons with disabilities; (4) that even as modified to permit persons with doctorates in education and other appropriate specialties, but not persons with masters' degrees, the qualification-of-evaluator requirement illegally screened out persons with disabilities; (5) that the requirement could permissibly be applied to students with attention deficit disorder or attention deficit hyperactivity disorder; (6) that the university's policy in 1995–96 of having the president and his assistant actively participate in closed-door evaluations of students' cases despite acting on the basis of uninformed stereotypes violated the law; (7) that a new procedure involving a clinical psychologist and restricting the review of the president and assistant did not violate the law; (8) that the plaintiffs lacked a statutory right of action to force the university to create a grievance process; (9) that no general obligation existed to modify degree requirements; (10) that in this case refusal to modify the degree requirements to provide course substitutions, particularly regarding foreign languages, was motivated by uninformed stereotypes by the university president and his staff that many students with learning disabilities are fakers and lazy, and that many evaluators are unprofessional and overdiagnose; (11) that the university failed to show that it met its duty of considering alternative means for accommodating students with learning disabilities who had difficulty learning foreign languages and coming to a rationally justifiable conclusion that a course substitution would lower academic standards or impose a substantial program alteration; (12) that the plaintiffs failed to demonstrate that modification of the mathematics requirement was a reasonable accommodation; and (13) that three plaintiffs prevailed on their contract claims because the university failed to honor express promises regarding documentation requirements and availability of accommodations.[175]

In its third opinion, the court determined that the foreign language requirement as reconsidered by the university did not violate the duty to provide reasonable accommodations.[176] The court determined that the maintenance of the requirement for the College of Arts and Sciences after deliberation by a committee of faculty and administrators who heard students and conducted multiple meetings satisfied the obligations of reasoned decision making imposed by the disability discrimination laws and the court's previous decision.

The full impact of the *Guckenberger* litigation is mixed, with plaintiffs experiencing greater success challenging documentation and general accommodations practices than basic degree requirements. The case holds open the possibility of hostile environment claims while circumscribing them based on statutory interpretation and First Amendment concerns. It shows the operation of academic deference regarding mandatory curricular content.

A further issue that sometimes appears in cases brought by students with learning disabilities is whether the students are individuals with disabilities within

---

[175] Guckenberger v. Boston Univ., 974 F. Supp. 106 (D. Mass. 1997).

[176] Guckenberger v. Boston Univ., 8 F. Supp. 2d 82 (D. Mass. 1998).

the coverage of section 504 and the ADA. Students in higher education should be expected to benefit from the expanded definition of person with a disability in the ADA Amendments Act of 2008,[177] which defines major life activities to include communicating, thinking, learning, reading, and concentrating, and adds to the list operations of major body functions — including neurological and brain — as well.[178] Moreover, the impairment is to be evaluated in its unmitigated state, substantial limits are liberally interpreted, and impairments that are episodic or in remission are covered.[179] Regarded-as coverage is also expanded, though persons solely eligible under the regarded-as prong are not entitled to reasonable accommodations.[180] Under previous law, a number of courts used comparisons of abilities of the students bringing disability discrimination actions under section 504 and titles II or III of the ADA with the abilities of the general public in determining whether the students are substantially limited in the major life activity of learning.[181] Moreover, they sometimes relied on a student's previous academic success to find the absence of a disability that triggers coverage.[182] When revising its regulations in light of the ADA Amendments Act, the Equal Employment Opportunity Commission rejected interpretations of this type. The Commission relied on legislative history generally supporting comparisons with "most people," but said the comparison "requires a careful analysis of the method and manner in which an individual's impairment limits a major life activity."[183] As the Act's legislative history and the Commission pointed out, "For the majority of the population, the basic mechanics of reading and writing do not pose extraordinary lifelong challenges; rather, recognizing and forming letters and words are effortless, unconscious, automatic processes."[184] The Commission quoted part of the legislative history: "[I]t is critical to reject the assumption that an individual who has performed well academically cannot be substantially limited in activities such as learning, reading, writing, thinking, or speaking."[185]

---

[177] Pub. L. No. 110-325, 122 Stat. 3553 (codified in relevant part at 42 U.S.C.S. § 12102(1)–(3)) (LexisNexis 2011). *See generally supra* Chapter 2 (discussing ADA Amendments Act). 42 U.S.C.S. § 12102(2) (LexisNexis 2011).

[178] 42 U.S.C.S. § 12102(2) (LexisNexis 2011).

[179] § 12102(4).

[180] §§ 12102(3), 12201(h).

[181] *Compare* Wong v. Regents of the Univ. of Cal., 410 F.3d 1052 (9th Cir. 2005). (comparing to general population), *and* Gonzalez v. National Bd. of Med. Exam'rs, 60 F. Supp. 2d 703 (E.D. Mich. 1999) (same), *with* Vinson v. Thomas, 288 F.3d 1145 (9th Cir. 2002) (not employing general population comparison).

[182] *See Wong*, 410 F.3d at 1065.

[183] ADA Title I EEOC Interpretive Guidance, 29 C.F.R. pt. 1630, app. § § 1630.2(j)(4) (2011).

[184] *Id.*

[185] *Id.* (quoting 2008 Senate Statement of Managers at 8); *see also id..* at § 1630.2(j)(1)(v) ("Individuals diagnosed with dyslexia or other learning disabilities will typically be substantially limited in performing activities such as learning, reading, and thinking when compared to most people in the general population," particularly when mitigating measures are disregarded.)

[E]   Courses and Examinations

The ADA contains a specific provision addressed to entities that offer examinations or courses relating to applications, licensing, certification, or credentialing for secondary or post-secondary education, professional, or trade purposes.[186] The section of the statute is found at the end of title III, the title that applies to goods, services, facilities, privileges, advantages, or accommodations of privately run places of public accommodation. As noted above, title III governs schools if they are not operated by the government and not religious.[187] Title III contains broad provisions forbidding discrimination and compelling actions such as reasonable modification of policies, practices, and procedures, when the modifications are needed by persons with disabilities,[188] in addition to the "examinations and courses" section. The only specific obligation that the examinations and courses section explicitly imposes on entities covered by it is the duty "to offer such examinations or courses in a place and manner accessible to persons with disabilities or offer alternative accessible arrangements for such individuals."[189] Regulations promulgated by the Department of Justice to enforce the provision expand on the nature of the obligations, putting into place duties that are similar to those applicable to colleges and universities covered by section 504. Revisions effective in 2011 establish that in considering requests for modification, accommodations, or auxiliary aids or services, the relevant entity has to give "considerable weight to documentation of past modifications, accommodations, or auxiliary aids or services received in similar testing situations," and to "such modifications, accommodations, or related aids and services provided in response to an Individualized Education Program (IEP) provided under the Individuals with Disabilities Education Act" or a section 504 services plan.[190]

In *Doe v. National Board of Medical Examiners*, the court overturned a preliminary injunction that had barred the board from flagging the United States Medical Licensing examination score of a fourth-year medical student whose multiple sclerosis required him to take the test under nonstandard conditions.[191] The court of appeals held that the district court erred by analyzing the challenge to the flagging of the score under the general provisions of title III rather than under the specific provision, § 12189. The court of appeals relied on the legal principle that specific provisions of a statute rather than more general provisions should control a case to which the specific provisions might be applied. The court concluded that the duty of accessibility could not be stretched to require the

---

[186] 42 U.S.C. § 12189 (2006). For a comprehensive discussion ultimately upholding the standing of an individual with a learning disability to assert a claim under this provision and refusing to dismiss the claim on grounds of plausibility, see Shaywitz v. American Bd. of Psychiatry & Neurology, 675 F. Supp. 2d 376 (S.D.N.Y. 2009).

[187] *See* § 12181(7)(J).

[188] § 12182(b)(2)(iii).

[189] § 12189.

[190] 28 C.F.R. § 36.309 (2011).

[191] 199 F.3d 146 (3d Cir. 1999). The condition caused the plaintiff muscle spasms, fine motor problems, and the need to use the bathroom frequently and with urgency. He was provided extra time on the test and a separate test room near a men's room.

testing entity to delete the flag from the score when the expert testimony stated that it was impossible to know how scores of exams taken with accommodations should compare to scores of exams taken under standard conditions. The court also said that application of the general provisions to the case would not have produced a different result.

The flagging of test scores would appear to comply with the ADA if the testing entity can show that reporting of an unflagged score constitutes a fundamental alteration of the nature of the services provided or otherwise causes an undue burden.[192] Nevertheless, the *Doe* court's reliance on section 12189 to the exclusion of the rest of title III would appear to exempt an examination or courses entity from having to provide integrated services, fair eligibility criteria, reasonable modifications in other practices, and anything else that title III requires, as long as it merely furnishes "accessible arrangements." An alternative reading might be that Congress viewed § 12189's requirements as additional ones for entities that conduct examinations, rather than substitute obligations. Congress may also have added the examinations and courses provision to title III because it was uncertain whether all testing organizations would qualify as public accommodations, and it wanted to impose at least the minimal requirement of accessibility on entities giving examinations and courses. In that instance, more minimal duties might be appropriate, but only if the testing entity fails to qualify as a public accommodation under title III.[193] One prominent decision applied the general provisions of title II and the specific provisions of § 12189 in tandem in a case involving the failure to provide requested accommodations for the bar examination.[194]

---

[192] *See* 42 U.S.C. § 12182(b)(2)(A)(i)–(iii) (2000).

[193] *See generally infra* Chapter 5 (discussing coverage of title III).

[194] D'Amico v. New York State Bd. of Law Exam'rs, 813 F. Supp. 217 (W.D.N.Y. 1993) (requiring bar examination accommodations for individual with visual disability).

Chapter 5

PUBLIC ACCOMMODATIONS DISCRIMINATION

§ 5.01 OVERVIEW OF PUBLIC ACCOMMODATIONS DISCRIMINATION

Title III of the ADA bars disability discrimination in ordinary consumer activity and requires accessibility of new and newly altered private structures other than housing. The general rule is that no individual shall be discriminated against on the basis of disability in the full and equal enjoyment of goods, services, facilities, privileges, advantages, or accommodations of any place of public accommodation by anyone who owns, leases, leases to, or operates a place of public accommodation.[1] That ban encompasses denials of participation, unequal benefits from participation, and unnecessary separation.[2] An affirmative duty exists to afford goods, services, facilities, privileges, advantages, and accommodations to individuals with disabilities in the most integrated setting appropriate.[3] The law also bans use of standards, criteria, or other methods of administration that have the effect of discriminating on the basis of disability or that perpetuate the discrimination of others who are subject to common administrative control.[4] Associational discrimination is also forbidden.[5]

In further defining the prohibition on discrimination, title III outlaws: (1) the use of eligibility criteria that screen out or tend to screen out individuals with disabilities or any class of them unless the criteria can be show to be necessary for the provision of the goods, services, facilities, etc.;[6] (2) the failure to make reasonable modifications in policies, practices, or procedures, when necessary to afford the goods, services, facilities, etc. to individuals with disabilities, unless the entity can demonstrate that making the modifications would fundamentally alter

---

[1] 42 U.S.C. § 12182(a) (2006).

[2] § 12182(b)(1)(A). Both direct conduct and action by contracting or licensing are forbidden. With regard to separate benefit, the separate arrangement is forbidden "unless such action is necessary to provide the individual or class of individuals with a good, service, facility, privilege, advantage, or accommodation, or other opportunity that is as effective as that provided to others." § 12182(b)(1)(A)(iii).

[3] § 12182(b)(1)(B). If separate or different programs or activities are provided, an individual with a disability is not to be denied the opportunity to participate in programs or activities that are not separate or different. § 12182(b)(1)(C).

[4] § 12182(b)(1)(D).

[5] § 12182(b)(1)(E). *See generally supra* Chapter 3 (discussing associational discrimination in employment).

[6] § 12182(b)(2)(A)(i).

the nature of the goods, services, facilities, etc.;[7] (3) the failure to afford auxiliary aids and services to ensure that no individual with a disability is excluded, denied services, segregated or otherwise treated differently from other individuals, unless the entity can demonstrate that providing the aids and services would fundamentally alter the nature of the good, service, facility, etc. or would result in an undue burden;[8] (4) the failure to remove architectural barriers, and communication barriers that are structural in nature, in existing facilities, where the removal is readily achievable;[9] and (5) if the entity can demonstrate that the removal of a barrier is not readily achievable, the failure to make goods, services, facilities, etc. available through alternative methods, if such methods are readily achievable.[10]

Title III also imposes duties regarding the accessibility of new construction and alteration of buildings.[11] The duties regarding new construction and alteration apply not only to public accommodations, but also to commercial facilities, which are those facilities intended for nonresidential use whose operations will affect commerce, with the exception of railroad-related equipment and property and facilities covered or expressly exempted from coverage under the Fair Housing Act.[12] Thus the full range of nondiscrimination duties applies where retail or other consumer transactions occur (that is, in public accommodations), but a narrower duty related to accessibility of newly constructed or altered space applies in employees-only (that is, in commercial facility) areas. Of course, extensive accessibility duties regarding commercial facility areas might arise because of the need to meet the employment-related obligations of ADA title I.

Facilities constructed for first occupancy after January 26, 1993, have to be readily accessible for persons with disabilities.[13] To do so, they must conform to the Americans with Disabilities Act Accessibility Guidelines ("ADAAG") devised by the Architectural and Transportation Barriers Compliance Board and adopted by the Department of Justice.[14] The ADAAG standards were updated in 2004 and adopted in the 2010 Standards for Public Accommodations and Commercial Facilities. Regulations effective in 2011 establish that new construction and alterations must comply with the 1991 ADAAG standards when the date of the last application for a building permit or permit extension is before September 15, 2010, or if no permit is required, the start of the physical construction or alterations occurs before that

---

[7] § 12182(b)(2)(A)(ii).

[8] The phrasing actually forbids the failure to "take such steps as may be necessary to ensure that no individual with a disability is excluded, denied services, segregated or otherwise treated differently than other individuals because of the absence of auxiliary aids and services. . . ." § 12182(b)(2)(A)(iii).

[9] This duty also applies to transportation barriers in existing vehicles and rail passenger cars used by an establishment for transporting individuals, but not including removal of barriers that would require retrofitting of vehicles or rail passenger cars by the installation of a lift. § 12182(b)(2)(A)(iv).

[10] § 12182(b)(2)(A)(v).

[11] § 12183.

[12] § 12181(2). Title III also covers discrimination regarding privately operated surface transportation. This topic is considered *infra* Chapter 7.

[13] § 12183(a)(1).

[14] 28 C.F.R. § 36.406 (2011). The guidelines are published as Appendix D to 28 C.F.R. § 36.

date.[15] New construction and alterations must comply with either the 1991 ADAAG or 2010 standards if the applicable date is on or after September 15, 2010, and before March 15, 2012.[16] New construction and alterations have to comply with the 2010 standards if the applicable date is on or after March 15, 2012.[17]

Where the entity can demonstrate that it is structurally impracticable to meet the accessibility obligation because of "rare circumstances when the unique characteristics of terrain prevent the incorporation of accessibility features,"[18] the facility need not be made fully accessible, but there remains a duty to make the facility accessible to the extent that it is not structurally impracticable, and portions that can be made accessible have to be made accessible. Similarly, the facility has to be made as accessible as possible. If the facility cannot be made accessible to those in wheelchairs, for example, it must be made accessible to those individuals with disabilities who do not use wheelchairs, such as persons who use crutches.[19]

Alterations also trigger duties to make space accessible, beyond the barrier-removal obligation that always applies. If a place of public accommodation or commercial facility is altered beginning any time after January 26, 1992, the altered portions must be readily accessible by individuals with disabilities, including those who use wheelchairs, in conformance with ADAAG standards.[20] Alterations are defined broadly to include such things as remodeling, renovation, rehabilitation, reconstruction, and historic restoration, but not normal maintenance, reroofing, asbestos removal, or changes in electrical and mechanical systems, unless those activities affect the usability of the building or facility.[21] Alterations to buildings or facilities eligible for inclusion for listing in the National Register of Historic Places or designated as historic under state or local law are covered by special ADAAG rules, and alternative methods of access may need to be provided.[22]

Department of Justice regulations effective in 2011 establish a safe harbor regarding barrier removal for elements in existing facilities that have not been altered on or after March 15, 2012 and that comply with the technical and scoping specifications for those elements in the 1991 AGAAG. The provision states that these elements are not required to modified in order to comply with the 2010 standards; however, it goes on to list a number of elements covered by the 2010 standards that are not eligible for safe-harbor treatment.[23]

Congress did not require installation of elevators, even for new construction, for facilities that are less than three stories or have an area of less than 3,000 square feet per story unless the building is a shopping center or mall, or the professional

---

[15] § 36.406(a)(1).

[16] § 36.406(a)(2).

[17] § 36.406(a)(3).

[18] § 36.401(c)(1).

[19] § 36.401(c)(2)–(3).

[20] § 36.402(a)–(b).

[21] § 36.402(b)(1).

[22] § 36.405.

[23] § 36.304(d)(2). Examples of items not eligible for the safe harbor include amusement rides, exercise machines and equipment, fishing piers and platforms, and various others.

office of a health care provider.[24] Under the federal regulations, terminals and other stations for specified public transportation and airport passenger terminals must also have elevators.[25]

Given all the detail that must be observed in complying with title III, it is easy to forget that some of the most basic public accommodations cases consider instances of outright discrimination against persons with disabilities in ordinary daily activities. In *Anderson v. Little League Baseball*, the court entered a temporary injunction against the Little League's enforcement of a rule that would have kept persons in wheelchairs from coaching from anywhere but the dugout.[26] This rule prevented the plaintiff from participating in games as an on-field base coach. No challenge was made to the applicability of title III, but the league defended the policy by invoking the provision in title III that allows covered entities to deny participation or benefits when the individual poses a direct threat to the health or safety of others.[27] The court stressed that the regulation enforcing that provision requires an individualized assessment of the nature and severity of the risk, which the defendant had not undertaken. In contrast, the plaintiff was able to point to three years of experience he had as a base coach without any incident. The court recognized benefits from allowing the plaintiff to participate as a coach in the game, and so compelled the defendant to permit him to coach on-field.

§ 5.02 DEFINING PUBLIC ACCOMMODATIONS

Title III defines public accommodations as the following private entities whose operations affect commerce:

(A)   an inn, hotel, motel, or other place of lodging, except for an establishment located within a building that contains not more than five rooms for rent or hire and that is actually occupied by the proprietor of such establishment as the residence of such proprietor;

(B)   a restaurant, bar, or other establishment serving food or drink;

(C)   a motion picture house, theater, concert hall, stadium, or other place of exhibition or entertainment;

(D)   an auditorium, convention center, lecture hall, or other place of public gathering;

(E)   a bakery, grocery store, clothing store, hardware store, shopping center, or other sales or rental establishment;

(F)   a laundromat, dry-cleaner, bank, barber shop, beauty shop, travel service, shoe repair service, funeral parlor, gas station, office of an accountant or lawyer, pharmacy, insurance office, professional office of a health care

---

[24] The statute delegates to the Attorney General the power to designate other categories of facilities where elevators are to be required. 42 U.S.C. § 12183(b) (2006).

[25] 28 C.F.R. § 36.404(a) (2011).

[26] 794 F. Supp. 342 (D. Ariz. 1992).

[27] 42 U.S.C. § 12182(b)(3) (2006).

provider, hospital, or other service establishment;

(G) a terminal, depot, or other station used for specified public transportation;

(H) a museum, library, gallery, or other place of public display or collection;

(I) a park, zoo, amusement park, or other place of recreation;

(J) a nursery, elementary, secondary, undergraduate, or postgraduate private school, or other place of education;

(K) a day care center, senior citizen center, homeless shelter, food bank, adoption agency, or other social service center establishment; and

(L) a gymnasium, health spa, bowling alley, golf course, or other place of exercise or recreation.[28]

Although title III of the ADA is to some degree modeled on title II of the Civil Rights Act of 1964, which forbids race discrimination in public accommodations, the definition of a public accommodation in the ADA is actually broader than that of the Civil Rights Act.[29]

The statute's coverage is wide, but disputes have emerged in some instances over whether a given activity is or is not a public accommodation. The leading case is *PGA Tour, Inc. v. Martin*, in which a golfer with a degenerative circulatory disorder requested an accommodation to allow the use of a golf cart in competitions of the PGA Tour and the Nike Tour.[30] When the accommodation was denied for the final stage of the qualifying tournament for the tours (the qualifying tournament is called the "Q-School"), he sued under title III, and the district court and court of appeals granted relief. In the Supreme Court, the defendants argued that title III did not apply to them. The Court noted that golf courses were covered by title III's definition of public accommodations, and that the tours lease and operate golf courses for their activities. The defendants, however, contended that competing golfers are not "clients and customers" seeking "goods and services" from a place

---

[28] 42 U.S.C. § 12181 (2006). The term "commerce" is defined as "travel, trade, traffic, commerce, transportation, or communication (A) among the several States; (B) between any foreign country or any territory or possession and any State; or (C) between points in the same State but through another State or foreign country." § 12181(1). A "private entity" is "any entity other than a public entity (as defined in section 12131(1) [ADA title II] . . .)." § 12181(6).

[29] Title II of the Civil Rights Act has a more restrictive list of establishments it covers. 42 U.S.C. § 2000a(b) (2006) ("Each of the following establishments which serves the public is a place of public accommodation within the meaning of this subchapter if its operations affect commerce, or if discrimination or segregation by it is supported by State action: (1) any inn, hotel, motel, or other establishment which provides lodging to transient guests, other than an establishment located within a building which contains not more than five rooms for rent or hire and which is actually occupied by the proprietor of such establishment as his residence; (2) any restaurant, cafeteria, lunchroom, lunch counter, soda fountain, or other facility principally engaged in selling food for consumption on the premises, including, but not limited to, any such facility located on the premises of any retail establishment; or any gasoline station; (3) any motion picture house, theater, concert hall, sports arena, stadium or other place of exhibition or entertainment; and (4) any establishment (A)(i) which is physically located within the premises of any establishment otherwise covered by this subsection, or (ii) within the premises of which is physically located any such covered establishment, and (B) which holds itself out as serving patrons of such covered establishment.").

[30] 532 U.S. 661 (2001).

of public accommodation.[31] They viewed a competing golfer's position more as that of an employee, except that the golfer is an independent contractor and so not covered by title I of the ADA. The Court concluded that a competitor should be viewed as a customer, for each competitor pays $3,000 to enroll in the Q-School and obtain the privilege of competing. The Court cited authority similarly construing the public accommodations provisions of title II of the Civil Rights Act. In a sharply worded dissent, Justice Scalia said that title III of the ADA should be read to apply only to customers and clients, and that classifying a professional athlete — even an aspiring one — as a customer distorted the meaning of that term and the sense of the statute as a whole.[32] The Court's majority further concluded that permitting the plaintiff to use a cart was a modification of the rules that did not fundamentally alter the relevant competitions. This holding with regard to reasonable modifications and fundamental alteration is discussed below.[33]

Courts have addressed some additional title III coverage issues. In a case subsequent to Martin's, the Supreme Court ruled that title III could be applicable to foreign-flag cruise ships.[34] This case is discussed in § 7.04, *infra*. Authorities conflict about when Internet sites may be covered by title III. This topic is addressed in § 7.03, *infra*.

Some enterprises are exempt from title III's coverage. Private clubs or establishments that are exempt from title II of the Civil Rights Act are also outside the coverage of title III of the ADA.[35] The facilities of a private club that are used by non-exempt entities, however, are covered by title III, according to the Department of Justice Interpretive Guidance.[36] Religious organizations and entities controlled by religious organizations, including places of worship, are also outside title III's coverage.[37] A private residence is not covered by title III, but when a place of public accommodation is located in a private residence, as might be the case with a doctor or lawyer working out of home, the part of the residence used exclusively as a residence is not covered by title III, but parts used exclusively in the operation of the place of public accommodation and parts used both for the public accommoda-

---

[31] The reference to clients and customers is in 42 U.S.C. § 12182(b)(1)(A)(iv) (2006) (current codification).

[32] *PGA Tour, Inc.*, 532 U.S. at 691 (Scalia, J., dissenting). Justice Thomas joined the dissent.

[33] *See generally infra* § 5.03[A] (discussing reasonable modifications and fundamental alterations).

[34] Spector v. Norwegian Cruise Line, Ltd., 545 U.S. 119 (2005).

[35] 42 U.S.C. § 12187 (2006).

[36] ADA Title III Department of Justice Interpretive Guidance, 28 C.F.R. § 36, App. C § 36.201 (2011), which provides:

   [I]f the private club rents to a day care center that is open to the public, then the private club would have the same obligations as any other public accommodation that functions as a landlord with respect to compliance with title III within the day care center. In such a situation, both the private club that "leases to" a public accommodation and the public accommodation lessee (the day care center) would be subject to the ADA. This same principle would apply if the private club were to rent to, for example, a bar association, which is not generally a public accommodation but which . . . becomes a public accommodation when it leases space for a conference.

[37] 42 U.S.C. § 12187 (2006).

tion and for residential purposes are covered.[38] The parts of the residence used to enter the place of public accommodation in the home, including any front sidewalk, door, or entryway and hallways, and all parts of the residence available to or used by customers or clients, including restrooms, are covered.[39]

§ 5.03   REASONABLE MODIFICATIONS AND AUXILIARY AIDS AND SERVICES

The provisions of title III requiring reasonable modifications in policies, practices, and procedures, and requiring auxiliary aids and services have received some development from the courts.

[A]   Reasonable Modifications and Fundamental Alteration

The Supreme Court interpreted the reasonable modifications requirement in *PGA Tour, Inc. v. Martin*, the case concerning the golfer who wished to use a golf cart in professional competitions but under applicable rules was denied that accommodation after the first two rounds of the qualifying Q-School.[40] Martin's medical condition was severe and caused him pain and atrophy of his right leg. Besides being painful, walking created a significant risk of hemorrhaging, developing blood clots, and fracturing the shin bone so badly as possibly to cause amputation. Although the trial court found that the purpose of the rule against carts was to inject fatigue as a factor into the making of golf shots, it also found that fatigue would be minimal under normal circumstances and that even with the use of a cart, Martin typically would walk a mile during a round of golf, which gave him more fatigue than that of an able-bodied competitor walking the course. Martin had received permission to use a cart during the later part of his NCAA career. The defendants did not contest that the modification of the rules was reasonable in the sense of being necessary for Martin to compete, but argued that it would constitute a fundamental alteration of the nature of the competition, and so was not required.

The Court said that a modification of tournament rules could be a fundamental alteration in two ways, either by changing something basic about the game in a way that would be unacceptable even if it affected all competitors equally (the example was increasing the size of the hole), or by changing something with only a minor impact on the game that might give the person with a disability not just access but a competitive advantage over others. The Court rejected the idea that allowing Martin to use a cart would be either sort of fundamental alteration. Carts are in wide use and are widely accepted both in amateur and professional play. "From early on, the essence of the game has been shot-making"; the walking rule is "an optional condition buried in an appendix to the Rules of Golf."[41] Even distinguishing golf at its most competitive level from the ordinary game, total

---

[38] 28 C.F.R. § 36.207(a) (2011).

[39] § 36.207(b).

[40] 532 U.S. 661 (2001).

[41] *Id.* at 683, 685.

uniformity of conditions will be impossible, and the fatigue from walking during a four-day tournament with ample opportunities for rest and refreshment will not be significant, according to the findings of the district court. In fact, even when competitors are permitted to use carts, they frequently opt to walk. And even if the walking rule's purpose was to inject fatigue into the competition, Martin endured greater fatigue riding than his competitors did walking, and so the purpose of the rule was met.

Justice Scalia responded that title III requires only access to goods, services, and privileges, and that if the PGA Tour wished to provide only "walk-around golf," the law did not compel it to furnish something else.[42] He argued that for purposes of the fundamental alteration standard, the PGA Tour could define the game however it chose, and that in games all rules are entirely arbitrary. The dissent said that the question whether someone riding around a golf course from shot to shot is really a golfer is an "incredibly difficult and incredibly silly question" that the Court should not try to answer.[43] Whatever the rhetorical power of the dissent, the majority was unpersuaded, and established an approach that permits courts to consider the question of what is essential for purposes of the fundamental alteration defense to be a question of fact, not a question the defendant has a prerogative to decide.

In other cases, courts have found proposed modifications of policies and practices to cross the line into fundamental alterations. Two examples are drawn from the extremes of the age range of students in private, non-federally-funded education.[44] In *Breece v. Alliance Tractor-Trailer Training II, Inc.*, a court determined after trial that a trainee truck driver with a severe hearing impairment was not entitled to modifications of the truck driving school program consisting of use of a driving simulator, greater direction or instruction before the road driving segment of the course, a sign language interpreter in the truck cab, or a speaker on his shoulder near his better ear to amplify the instructor's voice.[45] The court ruled that the modifications would fundamentally alter the nature of the intensive driver training program. In-class instruction would not be a substitute for actual road driving, which is integral to the program; simulators were not effective, according to the testimony; and having to watch a sign language interpreter while driving would constitute a direct threat to safety. Voice amplification would be ineffective in a noisy truck cab.

Another decision after trial, *Roberts v. Kindercare Learning Centers, Inc.*, determined that having a one-on-one aide for a significant portion of the week at a private day care center constituted a fundamental alteration and so did not need to be afforded a child with traumatic brain injury and other disabilities who needed the modification of the ordinary care program.[46] The court said that the undisputed

---

[42] *Id.* at 699 (Scalia, J., dissenting).

[43] *Id.* at 700 (Scalia, J., dissenting).

[44] Private, non-federally-funded educational institutions are not covered by ADA title II or section 504. *See generally supra* Chapter 4 (discussing statutory coverage of schools).

[45] 824 F. Supp. 576 (E.D. Va. 1993).

[46] 896 F. Supp. 921 (D. Minn. 1995), *aff'd*, 86 F.3d 844 (8th Cir. 1996) (per curiam).

evidence showed that there were two distinct types of child care, group and individual. The day care center was in the group care business, and requiring it to provide substantial levels of one-on-one care "essentially places it into a child care market it did not intend to enter," fundamentally altering the nature of its service.[47] Moreover, the modification would constitute an undue burden because, given the unpredictability of when the child's usual personal care attendant would be absent, the day care center would need to hire a full-time care giver, whose cost would be double that of the tuition the child would generate, and the business operated on a shoestring budget. The child could not safely be cared for without the one-on-one service.

These cases evoke *Southeastern Community College v. Davis*, which interpreted section 504 not to require modifications in an academic program that would undermine the goals of the program, change the program's scope, or create unsafe conditions.[48]

Permitting the use of service animals is a modification of policies and procedures that title III may require. In *Johnson v. Gambrinus Co./Spoetzl Brewery*, the court affirmed the entry of an injunction requiring a brewery to permit persons with disabilities to be accompanied by service animals on tours of the facility, affording "the broadest feasible access to the public tour of the Spoetzl Brewery consistent with the brewery's safe operation."[49] The court compared the reasonable modifications duty of ADA title III to the reasonable accommodation duty of ADA title I, and declared that fundamental alteration is merely a specific type of undue hardship. Applying the analogy, the court said that a plaintiff has a duty of proving that a modification was requested and that it was reasonable in the ordinary run of cases. If the plaintiff meets that burden, the defendant then must make the modification unless it pleads and proves that the requested modification would fundamentally alter the nature of the public accommodation. That requires a showing that focuses on the specifics of the plaintiff's and defendant's circumstances. The court deferred to federal regulations and related commentary favoring modifications to permit service animals except in the rare circumstances that a fundamental alteration would occur or safe operations would be jeopardized.[50] A regulation of the Food and Drug Administration permitting guard and guide dogs in areas of a plant where contamination is unlikely was found not to support the brewery's blanket policy against service animals, and the trial judge made findings of fact that contamination was impossible or unlikely at various points of the tour. The court found that the plaintiff met his burden of showing reasonableness of the modification in the run of cases and that the defendant failed to meet its burden of showing that a fundamental alteration would occur if the blanket policy were changed. Further proceedings would determine precisely what policy would provide maximum access consistent with safe brewery operations.

---

[47] *Id.* at 926.

[48] 442 U.S. 397 (1979) (discussed in *supra* § 4.02).

[49] 116 F.3d 1052, 1056 (5th Cir. 1997). The court also affirmed a monetary award pursuant to state law.

[50] *Id.* at 1060 (citing 28 C.F.R. § 36.302(c)(1) and applicable Department of Justice Interpretive Guidance).

In another instance, a court affirmed a judgment requiring a concert hall to modify its policies and permit the admission of a service animal, even one that had made a disruptive noise on a previous occasion, "if the noise was made and intended to serve as means of communication for the benefit of the disabled owner or if the behavior would otherwise be acceptable to the [concert hall] if engaged by humans."[51] The suit was brought by a patron with quadriplegia whose dog assisted her by retrieving small objects and protecting her, but which had briefly made noise at some previous concerts. The court noted the absence of complaints about the noise and ruled that the defendants did not support their assertions that the required change in policy would be a fundamental alteration.

The Department of Justice issued regulations effective March 15, 2011 that address service animals in places of public accommodations. The regulations define a service animal as "any dog that is individually trained to do work or perform tasks for the benefit of an individual with a disability," including a mental disability.[52] The work or tasks performed by the animal have to be directly related to the disability for the animal to qualify, and include "helping persons with psychiatric and neurological disabilities by preventing or interrupting impulsive or destructive behaviors," but do not include "the provision of emotional support, well-being, comfort or, or companionship."[53] The regulations retain the requirement that a public accommodation has to make reasonable modifications in policies practices, or procedures to permit the use of a service animal by an individual with a disability, although the public accommodation may ask that the animal be removed if it is out of control and its handler does not take effective action to control it, or the animal is not housebroken.[54] Inquiries about the nature or extent of a person's disability are not permitted, but a public accommodation may ask if the animal is required because of a disability and what work or task the animal is trained to perform.[55] The public accommodation is not permitted to demand documentation, and may not make the inquiries about a service animal when it is readily apparent that the animal is trained to do work or perform tasks for the individual with a disability, as with a guide dog for a person with low vision. Surcharges are forbidden, though charges may be made for damage the animal

---

[51] Lentini v. California Center for the Arts, Escondido, 370 F.3d 837, 842 (9th Cir. 2004). The court also affirmed the entry of monetary relief under a state law claim. Not all the caselaw is supportive of claims for access to facilities by individuals accompanied by service animals. *See, e.g.,* Rose v. Springfield-Greene County Health Dep't, 668 F. Supp. 2d 1206 (W.D. Mo. 2009) (rejecting claim regarding access accompanied by monkey), *aff'd,* 377 F. App'x 573 (8th Cir. 2010); Roe v. Providence Health Sys.-Oregon, 655 F. Supp. 2d 1164 (D. Or. 2009) (allowing exclusion of large dog that emitted foul odor and was prone to infections, which in-patient with disability wanted to accompany her in hospital).

[52] 28 C.F.R. § 36.104 (2011). Miniature horses may be covered by the service animal rules under conditions specified in § 36.302(c)(9). The Department rejected proposals to expand the definition of service animal to other species. ADA Title III Department of Justice Guidance on Revisions to ADA Title III Regulation, 28 C.F.R. § 36, App. A § 36.104 (2011).

[53] § 36.104. The Department's Guidance on the regulations further distinguishes trained animals from a pet or support animal that does not have special training. A dog that is trained to provide grounding in time and place for an individual with a dissociative disorder is covered. ADA Title III Department of Justice Guidance on Revisions to ADA Title III Regulation, 28 C.F.R. § 36, App. A § 36.104

[54] § 36.302(c)(1)–(2).

[55] § 36.302(c)(6).

causes if the public accommodation normally charges individuals for damage they cause.[56]

[B]　Auxiliary Aids and Services and Undue Burden

Title III requires auxiliary aids and services when needed to prevent an individual with a disability from being excluded, denied services, segregated, or otherwise treated differently than other individuals, unless the covered entity can demonstrate that taking steps to provide the aids and services would fundamentally alter the nature of the goods, services, facilities, privileges, advantages, or accommodations, or would result in an undue burden. The federal regulation interpreting this provision gives examples of auxiliary aids, focusing on methods of communication. According to the regulation, examples of auxiliary aids and services are qualified interpreters, computer-aided transcription services, written materials, telephone handset amplifiers, assistive listening devices, and various other methods of making communications effective for persons with hearing impairments, as well as qualified readers, taped texts, audio recordings, and various other methods of making communications effective for persons with visual impairments.[57]

An early case on the topic dealt with auxiliary aids and services to permit communication. In *Aikins v. St. Helena Hospital*, the court denied a motion for summary judgment and permitted a claim for violation of section 504 to proceed in the case of a deaf woman whose husband was treated at a hospital following a cardiac arrest.[58] Paramedics treated the victim within four minutes of being called to the scene, but that may have been as long as fifteen minutes after the attack. When they transported him to the hospital, he was treated by an independent contractor emergency room physician who determined to perform an angioplasty while under the impression that the victim had been treated by paramedics within four minutes after the attack. The physician attempted to consult the plaintiff and obtain her consent, but she could not understand him and requested an interpreter. A hospital operator with some knowledge of fingerspelling tried to communicate with her, but gave up within a minute. The couple's neighbors also arrived, but their communication efforts were unsuccessful, and the plaintiff maintained all she received was a note saying the victim was brain dead. The plaintiff eventually signed a form consenting to surgery, although she later said she did not have a full understanding of the situation. She said a nurse informed her after the operation that the victim would not survive without life support. She later requested interpreter services an additional time but allegedly was told that the hospital had no means of obtaining the services. The next day, when the victim had not improved, the physician questioned the plaintiff about the interval between the heart attack and the arrival of the paramedics. Upon learning that fifteen minutes elapsed between the attack and efforts at resuscitation, he ordered a electroencephalogram, which showed the victim had no brain activity. Eventually, life support was discontinued and the victim died.

---

[56]　§ 36.302(c)(8).

[57]　§ 36.302(b)(1)–(2) (2011).

[58]　843 F. Supp. 1329 (N.D. Cal. 1994).

The court ruled that neither the plaintiff, nor the California Association for the Deaf, which also sought to participate in the suit as a plaintiff, had standing to demand injunctive relief under the allegations in the case. The court commented that "Mrs. Aikins has not shown that defendants' alleged discrimination is ongoing and that she is likely to be served by defendants in the near future. Mrs. Aikins's claims for injunctive relief are accordingly dismissed with leave to amend to show that Mrs. Aikins faces a real and immediate threat of future injury at the hands of defendants."[59] Similar problems barred the organization, and dismissal with leave to amend was ordered. The court further ruled that title III of the ADA did not apply to the emergency room physician, who as an independent contractor lacked the power to control hospital policy on interpreters. On the other hand, the hospital did not show that it complied with the ADA as a matter of law. The duty to furnish auxiliary aids and services applied, but the hospital relied on plaintiff to obtain her own interpreters, and miscommunication occurred. The question whether providing interpreters would have been an undue burden presented issues of fact. The court also ruled that plaintiff was an otherwise qualified individual under section 504, and that the physician and hospital did not show they complied with section 504 as a matter of law. Even if her husband would have received the same treatment had the communication been effective, her claim was valid because it related to her exclusion from meaningful participation in the decisions affecting the treatment. The plaintiff's ADA claims failed because injunctive relief is all that can be obtained under title III, and she lacked standing for injunctive relief in the absence of an amended complaint. However, damages would be available for the section 504 claim, so that claim stood. The court also held that the state law claims could proceed.

As noted below, the limits on relief under title III inevitably prevent some cases from going forward.[60] Where the plaintiff can show a sufficient likelihood of recurrence of the conduct to that plaintiff, however, claims based on denial of auxiliary aids and services can proceed, and are prone to generate fact-specific determinations about when the aids and services are needed to prevent discrimination and when the undue burden defense applies.

§ 5.04 ACCESSIBILITY STANDARDS AND BARRIER REMOVAL

As explained above, the major distinction to note regarding building accessibility is between new or altered construction and existing facilities. For new construction of places of public accommodation and commercial facilities, and for places of public accommodation and commercial facilities altered after January 26, 1992, the ADAAG apply, and only the most extreme circumstances can excuse compliance with the accessibility duty. However, for existing facilities, the obligation is to

---

[59] *Id.* at 1334; *see id.* at 1333–34 ("Mrs. Aikins has shown neither that she is likely to use the hospital in the near future, nor that defendants are likely to discriminate against her when she does use the hospital.").

[60] *See infra* § 5.07 (discussing remedies). *See generally* Adam A. Milani, *Wheelchair Users Who Lack "Standing": Another Procedural Threshold Blocking Enforcement of Titles II and III of the ADA*, 39 WAKE FOREST L. REV. 69 (2004) (discussing standing issues in accessibility cases).

remove barriers where doing so is readily achievable. When removal of a barrier is not readily achievable, alternative methods of service must be used if those are readily achievable. The removal of barriers duty applies to architectural barriers and to communication barriers that are structural in nature.

For new construction, one major controversy is whether an architect may be liable when a building the architect designed fails to comply with accessibility standards. In *Lonberg v. Sanborn Theaters, Inc.*, the court ruled title III did not impose liability on an architect firm that designed, but was not was not owner, lessee, lessor, or operator, of a movie theater said to violate the statute.[61] According to the plaintiffs, the wheelchair seating areas were too small to accommodate a wheelchair, did not have lines of sight comparable to other seating areas, did not have a companion seat next to them, and lacked transfer seats to provide persons in wheelchairs the ability to move to a regular seat. Moreover, the restroom stalls and emergency exits were too small to accommodate wheelchairs, and the emergency exit ramps were too steep to be used safely by persons in wheelchairs. The court quoted the general rule established by title III, 42 U.S.C. § 12182(a), which provides that no individual shall be discriminated against on the ground of disability in the full and equal enjoyment of the goods, services, and so on "of any place of public accommodation by any person who owns, leases (or leases to), or operates a place of public accommodation."[62] Nevertheless, the court acknowledged that § 12183(a) defines discrimination for purposes of the general rule as applied to public accommodations and commercial facilities to include the "failure to design and construct" facilities that are accessible.[63] If architects were not liable under this provision, and owners, lessees and lessors, and operators were liable only for inaccessible places of public accommodation, Congress would have created duties with regard to commercial facilities that are not places of public accommodation, that are applicable to nobody. Therefore, § 12183(a) has to be taken as creating a rule of liability beyond that of the general rule in § 12182(a).

The court, however, rejected this argument because it believed that establishing a rule imposing liability on those with significant control over the design and construction of a building created a standard not found in the statute. On the contrary, the court believed that § 12183(a) should be read in parallel with § 12182(a) to make owners, lessees and lessors, and operators liable for both public accommodations and commercial facilities that violate the law. The latter construction, it felt, fit better with the structure of the other titles of the ADA, in which a general rule of liability is specified, establishing who may be liable, and subsequent sections describe what constitutes discrimination. Moreover, injunctive relief, the remedy under title III, would make more sense applied to someone with ongoing responsibility for the facility, rather than the architect who is no longer responsible for the facility once it is in operation. The opinion lists various other courts that have lined up on one side or the other of the controversy over whether someone besides an owner, lessee or lessor, or operator can be liable under title III.[64]

---

[61] 259 F.3d 1029, 1036 (9th Cir.), *amended on denial of reh'g*, 271 F.3d 953 (9th Cir. 2001).

[62] 259 F.3d at 1032–33 (quoting 42 U.S.C. § 12182(a)).

[63] *Id.* at 1033 (quoting 42 U.S.C. § 12183(a)).

[64] *Compare* United States v. Days Inns of Am., Inc., 22 F. Supp. 2d 612, 615–16 (E.D. Ky. 1998)

Another controversy is the operation of what is sometimes called the "elevator exception," the provision of title III that says that except for shopping centers, shopping malls, the professional offices of health care providers, and categories of facilities designated by the Attorney General, facilities that are less than three stories or have less than 3,000 feet per story need not have an elevator installed to meet accessibility standards.[65] Congress apparently did not anticipate that many buildings are built with floor plans that have openings from one floor to another, and thus what some might deem a "story," others might deem a balcony or something else. The current regulations clarify matters somewhat, specifically the adoption of a 2004 ADAAG standard defining a story to include one or more mezzanines and further defining mezzanine as "an intermediate level or levels between the floor and ceiling of any story with an aggregate floor area of not more than one-third of the area of the room or space in which the level or levels are located."[66] This standard replaced one that defined a mezzanine simply as the portion of a story that is the intermediate level placed within a story and having occupiable space above and below its floor.

In *Laird v. Redwood Trust LLC*, the plaintiff contended that a nightclub with a basement level, a main floor level, and a large area above the main floor with an opening to the floor below was a three story building subject to elevator requirements.[67] The court disagreed, and affirmed a grant of summary judgment against the plaintiff on the ground that the facility instead was a two story building with a mezzanine, and thus was within the elevator exception. Applying the 1991 ADAAG standards, the court reasoned that the area above the main floor was less than a story by itself, because of an opening to the floor below that permitted persons above to look down on the main floor's dancing area. The second level's "portion" was "intermediate" between the main floor and the building roof. Completing the definition of mezzanine that the 1991 standards embodied, it had occupiable space above and below its floor. The court also ruled that there was no violation of the ADAAG restaurant and cafeteria guidelines requiring all new construction of those areas to make them accessible, because the conversion of the building from what it had previously been (a bank) to a nightclub constituted an alteration rather than new construction.

(finding no liability for franchisors); United States v. Days Inns of Am., Inc., 1998 U.S. Dist. LEXIS 21945 (E.D. Cal. 1998) (same); Paralyzed Veterans of Am. v. Ellerbe Becket, 945 F. Supp. 1, 2 (D.D.C. 1996) (finding no liability for architects), *with* United States v. Days Inns of Am., Inc., 151 F.3d 822, 827 (8th Cir. 1998) (finding liability for franchisor exercising control); United States v. Days Inns of Am., Inc., 997 F. Supp. 1080, 1084–85 (C.D. Ill. 1998) (same); United States v. Ellerbe Becket, Inc., 976 F. Supp. 1262, 1267–68 (D. Minn. 1997) (finding liability for architects); Johanson v. Huizenga Holdings, Inc., 963 F. Supp. 1175, 1177–78 (S.D. Fla. 1997) (same). *See generally* Adam A. Milani, *"Oh, Say, Can I See — And Who Do I Sue If I Can't?": Wheelchair Users, Sightlines Over Standing Spectators, and Architect Liability Under the Americans with Disabilities Act*, 52 Fla. L. Rev. 523 (2000) (discussing architect liability). An owner or other person who is liable may, of course, have common law remedies against the architect or other individual who is not subject to statutory liability.

[65] 42 U.S.C. § 12183(b) (2006).

[66] ADAAG § 106.5 (2004). The current design standards, including the 2004 ADAAG, may be found at http://www.ada.gov/regs2010/2010ADAStandards/2010ADAstandards.htm.

[67] 392 F.3d 661 (4th Cir. 2004).

Judge Duncan dissented, arguing that the majority's view would make any floor with an opening onto the floor below a "mezzanine," no matter how large the area without an opening and how much, functionally, the floor operated as a separate story of the building.[68] The dissent looked to representative building code definitions of mezzanine, and noted that the most common provision restricts the term to levels with a floor area no greater than one-third the area of the room in which the level was located. Under the facts of the case, what the majority termed a mezzanine was 5100 square feet compared to the main floor's 6400 square feet.[69] A concurrence by Judge Shedd responded that the Department of Justice regulations had not adopted an objective test such as the one-third-of-the-area rule, even though it obviously knew how to do so, having adopted a test identical to it for new construction dining areas.[70] This reasoning suggests that the case would come out differently under if the new ADAAG standards had applied.

Some important considerations apply to alterations of existing facilities, particularly with regard to paths of travel. The regulations call for alterations that affect the usability of or access to part of a facility that contains a primary function to be made so that, to the maximum extent feasible, the path of travel to the altered area and the restrooms, telephones, and drinking fountains serving the altered area are accessible to people with disabilities, including those who use wheelchairs, unless the cost and scope of the alterations would be disproportionate to the cost of the overall alteration. A "primary function" is a major activity for which the facility intended, as with the lobby of a bank or the dining area of a cafeteria, as opposed to areas such as mechanical rooms, boiler rooms, or supply storage rooms.[71] Alterations that affect the usability of access to an area include remodeling merchandise display areas or work areas of a department store, replacing an inaccessible floor surface in the customer service or employee work areas of a bank, and other similar examples, but do not include alterations to windows, hardware, controls, electrical outlets, and signage.[72]

As for existing facilities that are not being altered and the duty to remove barriers when that is readily achievable, the statutory definition for "readily achievable" is that which can be accomplished easily and carried out without much difficulty or expense.[73] Factors to be considered include the nature and cost of the removal, the overall financial resources of the facility or facilities involved in the action, the number of persons employed at the facility, the effect on expenses and resources, or the other impact on the operation of the facility. Also to be considered are the overall financial resources of the covered entity, the overall size of its business with regard to the number of employees, and the number, type, and location of its facilities, as well as the type of operation of the entity. This last topic includes the composition, structure, and functions of the work force of the entity, as

---

[68] *Id.* at 667 (Duncan, J., dissenting).

[69] *Id.* at 662 (majority op.).

[70] *Id.* at 666 (Shedd, J., concurring).

[71] 28 C.F.R. § 36.403(a)–(b) (2011). The regulation provides further examples.

[72] § 36.403(c).

[73] 42 U.S.C. § 12181(9) (2006).

well as the geographic separateness and administrative or fiscal relationship of the facility to the covered entity.[74]

The regulations flesh out these definitional matters by listing examples of steps to remove barriers. These include, but are not limited to: (1) installing ramps; (2) making curb cuts in sidewalks and entrances; (3) repositioning shelves; (4) rearranging tables, chairs, vending machines, display racks, and other furniture; (5) repositioning telephones; (6) adding raised markings on elevator control buttons; (7) installing flashing alarm lights; (8) widening doors; (9) installing offset hinges to widen doorways; (10) eliminating turnstiles or providing an alternative accessible path; (11) installing accessible door hardware; (12) installing grab bars in toilet stalls; (13) rearranging toilet partitions to increase maneuvering space; (14) installing lavatory pipes under sinks to prevent burns; (15) installing a raised toilet seat; (16) installing a full-length bathroom mirror; (17) repositioning a paper towel dispensers in a bathroom; (18) creating designated accessible parking spaces; (19) installing accessible paper cup dispensers at an existing inaccessible water fountain; (20) removing high pile, low density carpeting; or (21) installing vehicle hand controls.[75]

In order of priority, the first thing to be done is to provide access from the sidewalk, a parking area, or public transportation, for example, by installing ramps, widening entrances, and providing accessible parking spaces. Second priority is providing access to areas where goods and services are made available to the public, as by adjusting the layout of display racks, rearranging tables, providing signage usable by blind persons, widening doors, providing visual alarms, and installing ramps. Third priority is access measures for restroom facilities, and fourth is any other measures needed to provide full accessibility.[76] Construction undertaken to remove barriers should conform to the standards generally applicable to alterations of facilities, but where doing so would not be readily achievable, the public accommodation may take other measures to remove the barrier, for example, by installing a steeper ramp when there is no room for a ramp that fully complies with the alteration standards.[77] When the defendant can demonstrate that barrier removal is not readily achievable, it must make its goods and services available through alternative methods, such as curb service, home delivery, providing retrieval for merchandise in inaccessible areas or relocating activities to accessible locations.[78]

Not surprisingly, given these various regulatory specifications and other inter-pretative sources, courts have found that the term "readily achievable" is not unconstitutionally vague.[79] Perhaps the most common complaint of persons with disabilities with regard to public accommodations is that merchants fail to take even

---

[74] § 12181(9)(A)–(D).

[75] 28 C.F.R. § 36.304(b) (2011).

[76] § 36.304(c).

[77] § 36.304(d)(3). Portable ramps are to be used only when installation of a permanent ramp is not readily achievable. § 36.304(e).

[78] § 36.305(a)–(b). Personal devices and services need not be provided. § 36.306.

[79] Botosan v. Paul McNally Realty, 216 F.3d 827 (9th Cir. 2000) (also finding "disability" not vague);

the most basic steps of clearing items from aisles so that wheelchairs can pass through store areas. Courts have found violations of title III in cases brought over failure to remove barriers in retail spaces.[80]

States and localities have codes pertaining to environmental barriers, and in some instances these are more demanding than the ADAAG standards or the barrier-removal duty. The ADA does not preempt or in any way limit the operation of laws that provide protection for individuals with disabilities that equals or exceeds that provided under the ADA.[81] The Attorney General may certify a state or local code as meeting or exceeding title III standards, and when that occurs, certification is rebuttable evidence in a title III enforcement proceeding that the code meets or exceeds the standards.[82]

§ 5.05   PLACES OF PUBLIC EXHIBITION OR ENTERTAINMENT

Places of exhibition or entertainment such as arenas, auditoriums, and theaters a topic of special importance under the ADA. Issues courts have addressed include what facilities must do with regard to the sight lines for audience members in wheelchair locations and what they have to do to otherwise promote integration of persons with disabilities who attend performances and events. Necessary actions may include increasing accessibility of areas outside the main auditorium, guaranteeing the availability of companion seating, and providing auxiliary aids and similar accommodations to audience members who need them.

Major litigation has taken place over the issue of sight lines in auditoriums and theaters. The 1991 ADAAG provision adopted as part of the Department of Justice title III regulations, Department of Justice Standard 4.33.3, required "a choice of admission prices and lines of sight comparable to those for members of the general public."[83]

An early case involving a concert facility, *Caruso v. Blockbuster-Sony Music Entertainment Centre*, interpreted the standard to require large auditoriums to have several wheelchair locations with different views at prices corresponding to those for similarly priced fixed seats.[84] However, it rejected the plaintiff's reading

---

see Pinnock v. International House of Pancakes Franchisee, 844 F. Supp. 574 (S.D. Cal. 1993) (finding "readily achievable" not vague).

[80] *E.g.*, Lieber v. Macy's West, Inc., 80 F. Supp. 2d 1065 (N.D. Cal. 1999).

[81] 42 U.S.C. § 12201(b) (2006).

[82] § 12188(b)(1)(A)(ii).

[83] The standard provided:

Wheelchair areas shall be an integral part of any fixed seating plan and shall be provided so as to provide people with physical disabilities a choice of admission prices and lines of sight comparable to those for members of the general public. They shall adjoin an accessible route that also serves as a means of egress in case of emergency. At least one companion fixed seat shall be provided next to each wheelchair seating area. When the seating capacity exceeds 300, wheelchair spaces shall be provided in more than one location.

28 C.F.R. § 36, App. A, std. 4.33.3 (2006) (superseded).

[84] 193 F.3d 730 (3d Cir. 1999) (Alito, J.).

of the standard, which would have required elevated areas for wheelchairs to allow lines of sight over patrons standing in front of wheelchair locations. The court refused to defer to an interpretation in the Department of Justice Technical Assistance Manual supporting the plaintiff's position, saying that earlier materials showed that the standard meant to leave the views-over-standing-patrons issue open for future rulemaking, and that under the Administrative Procedure Act,[85] notice and comment rulemaking would be required to adopt any contrary interpretation. The court disagreed with *Paralyzed Veterans of America v. D.C. Arena L.P.*, which deferred to the interpretation in the Technical Assistance Manual and affirmed a district court decision requiring a facility to provide lines of sight over standing spectators for 78–88% of its wheelchair seating.[86] At the same time, the *Caruso* court held that the absence of wheelchair access to the lawn seating area of the facility violated the basic requirement of title III that facilities be readily accessible to and usable by individuals with disabilities.

In subsequent litigation involving stadium-style movie theaters, several courts interpreted standard 4.33.3 to require sight lines that are actually comparable to those of patrons in fixed-seating areas, deferring to the position of the Department of Justice that the *Caruso* court rejected.[87] The court in *United States v. Cinemark* said that the argument that notice and comment rulemaking was necessary to adopt the Department of Justice's current interpretation ignored the principle of administrative law that permits agencies to choose between proceeding by general rule or by individual litigation. It also said that even if the interpretation could not stand as a legislative rule, it deserved deference as an interpretive rule not subject to notice and comment.[88]

The Title III Department of Justice regulations that are effective in 2011 adopt the 2004 ADAAG. For facilities bound by the new standards, the law now requires. among other things, that "Wheelchair spaces shall provide spectators with choices of seating locations and viewing angles that are substantially equivalent to, or better than, the choices of seating locations and viewing angles available to all other spectators,"[89] and that when spectators are expected to remain seated during events and the audience members are afforded lines of sight over the heads of spectators in the first row in front of their seats, spectators in wheelchair spaces are to be afforded lines of sight over the heads of seated spectators in the first row in front of the wheelchair spaces. When spectators are expected to stand during

---

[85] 5 U.S.C. § 553 (2006).

[86] 117 F.3d 579 (D.C. Cir. 1997).

[87] United States v. Hoyt Cinemas Corp., 380 F.3d 558 (1st Cir. 2004) (affirming denial of motion for summary judgment for defendant by overturning sua sponte grant of motion for summary judgment by government); United States v. Cinemark, 348 F.3d 569 (6th Cir. 2003); Oregon Paralyzed Veterans of America v. Regal Cinemas, 339 F.3d 1126 (9th Cir. 2003). These courts take a position contrary to that of *Lara v. Cinemark USA, Inc.*, 207 F.3d 783 (5th Cir. 2000), which required comparability but said that the standard only required unobstructed (even if uncomfortable) lines of sight from the wheelchair locations. *See generally* John Hammerle, Note, Oregon Paralyzed Veterans of America v. Regal Cinemas, Inc.: *The Rise of Stadium Seating in Movie Theaters and the Disabled's Fight for a Comparable Seat in the House*, 54 DePaul L. Rev. 589 (2005) (discussing controversy).

[88] 348 F.3d 569, 580–81 & n.8 (6th Cir. 2003).

[89] ADAAG § 221.2.3 (2004).

events, those in wheelchairs are to be afforded lines of sight over the heads of spectators in the first row in front of their seats when standing spectators have that view, and afforded lines of sight over the shoulders and between the heads of standing spectators when that is the view provided standing spectators.[90] Since these provisions have been adopted as a final rule pursuant to notice and comment procedures, the question of the validity of the Department of Justice interpretation posed by the caselaw appears to be resolved.

The integration of individuals with mobility impairments with other persons seated in places of entertainment has also been the subject of litigation. As noted, *Caruso* required that the facility provide wheelchair access to the lawn seating area pursuant to the ADAAG standard adopted by the Department of Justice requiring at least one accessible route connecting accessible spaces on the same site unless a covered entity can demonstrate structural impracticability. The court emphasized that the structural impracticability exception is reserved for rare circumstances when the terrain prevents incorporation of accessibility features. A mere showing that the slope was over 12–15% was not sufficient, and the fact that the lawn did not contain fixed seating was irrelevant. The court said that the equal access obligation is not merely a technical requirement but rather an explicit duty imposed by the statute itself, embodied in the general provisions of the Department of Justice regulations. Access to audience areas occupied by persons without disabilities (in this case by up to 18,000 music fans) is important in breaking down the segregation of individuals with disabilities from other persons.

Companion seating is also important to enabling people in wheelchairs to attend events with friends who do not have mobility impairments, and sometimes to permit attendance at all when someone must provide attendant services to the person with a disability during an event or performance. In *Fortyune v. American Multi-Cinema, Inc.*, the court affirmed a grant of permanent injunctive relief requiring a theater to give priority to companions of customers who use wheelchairs in the seats adjacent to the wheelchair spaces, and requiring the moving of other patrons from those seats if necessary.[91]

The regulations adopted in 2010 provide that in stadiums, arenas, and grandstands to which the new standards apply, wheelchair spaces and companion seats must be dispersed to all levels that include seating served by an accessible route, and in areas that have seating encircling a playing field or performance space, the spaces and companion seats are to be dispersed around the field or space.[92]

An additional matter important to integrating people with disabilities into audiences in public entertainment spaces is auxiliary aids. As noted above, title III requires auxiliary aids and services, unless the entity can demonstrate that taking steps to provide the aides and services would cause a fundamental alteration or undue burden.[93] Auxiliary aids include interpreters, readers, and other means of facilitating communication, and may entail acquisition or modification of equipment

---

[90] § 802.2.1.1–.2.

[91] 364 F.3d 1075 (9th Cir. 2004).

[92] 28 C.F.R. § 36.406(f) (2011).

[93] 42 U.S.C. § 12182(b)(2)(A)(3) (2006).

or devices.[94] The Department of Justice regulations mention closed caption decoders and captioning as examples of auxiliary aids and services.[95] Whether captioning of movies is required for patrons who are deaf and audio descriptions for patrons who are visually impaired has been the subject of a number of disputes, with courts ruling that title III may require a theater to provide captioning under appropriate circumstances,[96] and at least one other court ruling that under the facts of the case it did not.[97] In the 2010 regulations, the Department of Justice said it was still studying movie captioning requirements and expected to engage in rulemaking specifically on the issue in the near future.[98]

§ 5.06 INSURANCE ISSUES

Title III may affect insurance in two ways. First, the accessibility and barrier-removal requirements apply to insurance offices. Second, the various obligations requiring title III entities to avoid discrimination regarding participation, benefits, eligibility criteria, policies and practices, and the like, may apply to insurance policies. The first topic has not been controversial. The second one has sparked significant dispute, and brings into play a provision of title V of the ADA often referred to as a safe harbor provision, which states that the rest of the ADA shall not be read to prohibit or restrict:

(1)   an insurer, hospital or medical service company, health maintenance organization, or any agent, or entity that administers benefit plans, or similar organizations from underwriting risks, classifying risks, or administering such risks that are based on or not inconsistent with State law; or

(2)   a person or organization covered by [the ADA] from establishing, sponsoring, observing or administering the terms of a bona fide benefit plan that are based on underwriting risks, classifying risks, or administering such risks that are based on or not inconsistent with State law; or

(3)   a person or organization covered by [the ADA] from establishing, sponsoring, observing or administering the terms of a bona fide benefit plan that is not subject to State laws that regulate insurance.[99]

Nevertheless, these provisions "shall not be used as a subterfuge to evade the

---

[94] 42 U.S.C.S. § 12103(1) (LexisNexis 2011).

[95] 28 C.F.R. § 36.303(b)(1) (2011).

[96] Arizona *ex rel.* Goddard v. Harkins Amusement Enters.,; 603 F.3d 666 (9th Cir. 2010) (further holding that audio description may be required but that open captioning is not required under current regulations); Ball v. AMC Entm't, Inc., 246 F. Supp. 2d 17 (D.D.C. 2003). One captioning mechanism is called "rear window captioning," and entails placing a screen behind the patrons that displays text for the dialogue or other sounds of the movie. Viewers may attach a transparent panel to their seats at an angle to catch the projected dialogue as though it were superimposed at the bottom of the movie image. *Id.* at 20 n.9.

[97] Cornilles v. Regal Cinemas, Inc., 2002 U.S. Dist. LEXIS 7025 (D. Or. Jan. 3, 2002) (magistrate judge recommendation), *adopted in principal part*, 2002 U.S. Dist. LEXIS 7023 (Mar. 19, 2002).

[98] ADA Title III Department of Justice Guidance on Revisions to ADA Title III Regulation, 28 C.F.R. § 36, App. A § 36.303 (2011).

[99] 42 U.S.C. § 12201(c)(1)–(3) (2006).

purposes of" titles I and III.[100] Because many individuals acquire insurance through work-based plans, title I may bear on insurance topics along with title III.[101]

A number of courts have found title III inapplicable to insurance policies, reasoning that while an insurance office may be a place of public accommodation, the sale of the policy itself is not.[102] Moreover, they say, the ADA does not require public accommodations to offer special goods, so the insurer need not provide coverage for a given condition or on any given terms.[103] Other authorities respond that Congress apparently contemplated including insurance in public accommodations, as suggested both by the existence of the safe harbor provision and by the ADA's legislative history.[104] What is more, they argue, discrimination in coverage can amount to unlawful exclusion, segregating, screening out, failing to modify rules, and other conduct that specifically violates title III.[105] Some of the cases that find insurance not to be a public accommodation may need to be reevaluated in light of 2001's *PGA Tour, Inc. v. Martin*, which applied a broad definition of that term to find that the intangible entity of a golf tournament series constituted a public accommodation.[106]

If title III applies to insurance policies, there still remains a question of what conduct it prohibits, given the safe harbor that title V provides for writing policies so as to classify risks.[107] Courts have generally given a narrow reading to the subterfuge exception to the safe harbor provision.[108]

---

[100] § 12201(c).

[101] Title I is discussed generally in Chapter 2, but the insurance-as-benefits topic is beyond the scope of this book.

[102] Weyer v. Twentieth Century Fox Film Corp., 198 F.3d 1104 (9th Cir. 2000); Ford v. Schering-Plough Corp., 145 F.3d 601 (3d Cir. 1998); Parker v. Metro Life Ins. Co., 121 F.3d 1006 (6th Cir. 1997).

[103] *See* sources cited *supra* previous note.

[104] ADA Title III Department of Justice Interpretive Guidance, 28 C.F.R. § 36, App. C § 36.212 (2011) ("Language in the committee reports indicates that Congress intended to reach insurance practices by prohibiting differential treatment of individuals with disabilities in insurance offered by public accommodations unless the differences are justified."); *see* Pallozzi v. Allstate Life Ins. Co., 198 F.3d 28 (2d Cir. 1999) (applying title III to insurance policy sold by insurance office), *amended on denial of reh'g*, 204 F.3d 392 (2d Cir. 2000); Carparts Distrib. Ctr., Inc. v. Automobile Wholesaler's Ass'n of New England, Inc., 37 F.3d 12, 19 (1st Cir. 1994) (holding that establishments of public accommodation are not limited to physical structures); *see also Parker*, 121 F.3d at 1019 (Martin, J., dissenting) (public accommodations not limited to physical structures), 1020 (Merritt, J., dissenting) (finding title III applicable to insurance policy).

[105] *See* sources cited *supra* previous note.

[106] 532 U.S. 661 (2001). *See generally supra* § 5.02 (discussing case).

[107] *Compare* Zamora-Quezada v. HealthTexas Med. Group of San Antonio, 34 F. Supp. 2d 433 (W.D. Tex. 1998) (denying summary judgment on claim based on defendant's failure to support risk assessments with actuarial and statistical data), *with* Weyer v. Twentieth Century Fox Film Corp., 198 F.3d 1104 (9th Cir. 2000) (finding safe harbor applicable). *See generally* Doe v. Mutual of Omaha Ins. Co., 179 F.3d 557 (7th Cir. 1999) (finding cap on lifetime benefits for AIDS or AIDS-related conditions not to violate title III despite absence of actuarial support for cap); Jeffrey W. Stempel, *An Inconsistently Sensitive Mind: Richard Posner's Cerebration of Insurance Law and Continuing Blind Spots of Econominalism*, 7 Conn. Ins. L.J. 7, 65–77 (2000–2001) (criticizing *Doe*).

[108] *See, e.g.*, Ford v. Schering-Plough Corp., 145 F.3d 601, 611 (3d Cir. 1998).

§ 5.07 REMEDIES

Lawyers often use the term "remedies" to refer to two different things: procedures or mechanisms that individuals can use to get relief in their cases, and the relief itself. In public accommodations cases, both "procedures" and the "relief" senses of the term need explanation.

Title III says that the "remedies and procedures set forth in section 2000a-3(a) of this title are the remedies and procedures this subchapter provides to any person who is subjected to discrimination on the basis of disability in violation of this subchapter . . . ."[109] The provision referred to, 42 U.S.C. § 2000a-3(a), is in title II of the Civil Rights Act of 1964, which prohibits discrimination on the basis of race, color, religion, or national origin in a somewhat narrower range of public accommodations than that covered by the ADA. Section 2000a-3(a) states that a victim of discrimination may file an action for preventive relief, including a temporary or permanent injunction, and that the Attorney General may intervene and the court may appoint an attorney for the plaintiff and waive fees, costs, and furnishing of security. Nevertheless, some courts have interpreted the title III provision to require compliance not just with § 2000a-3(a), but also with another subsection of § 2000a-3, subsection (c), which states that if a state or local authority may grant or seek relief or criminal proceedings for the alleged discrimination, "no civil action may be brought under subsection (a) of this section before the expiration of thirty days after written notice of such alleged act or practice has been given to the appropriate State or local authority by registered mail or in person," and that "the court may stay proceedings in such civil action pending the termination of State or local enforcement proceedings."[110] If this provision is applied, the plaintiff would at the minimum be required to give notice if the case arises in a jurisdiction that has a state or local entity that can act on public accommodations complaints. At the maximum, the suit could be stayed pending notice or pending the complete exhaustion of the state or local entity's proceedings.[111]

In *Botosan v. Paul McNally Realty*, the Ninth Circuit Court of Appeals ruled that title III of the ADA does not require notice or exhaustion pursuant to title II of the Civil Rights Act's § 2000a-3(c) provision.[112] The court reasoned that the ADA's language incorporates only § 2000a-3(a), and that the language is clear and unambiguous. Had Congress wanted to incorporate any of the other subsections of § 2000a-3, it could easily have done so, and its failure to do so implicated the maxim of statutory construction that inclusion of one statutory item to the exclusion of another has to be deemed meaningful. It quoted the language of the district court opinion that "[it is] unlikely that Congress would absentmindedly forget to adopt a

---

[109] 42 U.S.C. § 12188(a)(1) (2006).

[110] 42 U.S.C. § 2000a-3(c) (2006); *see, e.g.*, Daigle v. Friendly Ice Cream Corp., 957 F. Supp. 8 (D.N.H. 1997); Howard v. Cherry Hills Cutters, Inc., 935 F. Supp. 1148 (D. Colo. 1996). Various district court decisions from the Ninth Circuit also reach this conclusion.

[111] *See generally* Adam A. Milani, *Go Ahead. Make My 90 Days: Should Plaintiffs Be Required to Provide Notice to Defendants Before Filing Suit Under Title III of the Americans with Disabilities Act?*, 2001 Wis. L. Rev. 107 (cataloguing and evaluating arguments concerning applicability of notice and exhaustion requirement).

[112] 216 F.3d 827 (9th Cir. 2000).

provision that appears a mere two paragraphs below the subsection it adopted."[113] The court of appeals also said that the regulatory provisions and legislative history and Technical Assistance Manual issued by the Department of Justice "generally support the conclusion that Title III actions do not require state notification."[114] The court buttressed its conclusion by citing a significant number of lower court decisions that had found notice and exhaustion not to be required.

With regard to relief, title III's incorporation of the Civil Rights Act remedial provision restricts what may be obtained from a court to "preventive relief," specifically injunctions, restraining orders, and other orders.[115] The enforcement section of title III continues with language specifically addressing injunctive relief, stating that in case of failure to remove architectural barriers and communication barriers that are structural in nature from existing facilities, where removal is readily achievable, injunctive relief shall include an order to make the facilities readily accessible to and usable by individuals with disabilities to the extent that title III requires.[116] The same rule applies to violations of title III with regard to new construction and alterations in public accommodations and commercial facilities.[117] The section goes on to state that where appropriate, the injunctive relief shall also include requiring the provision of an auxiliary aids or services, modification of policies, or provision of alternative methods of making goods and services available.[118] An ADA plaintiff may in one lawsuit obtain an injunction against all accessibility barriers related to the plaintiff's disability that the plaintiff is likely to encounter upon returning to the public accommodation, but the barriers must relate to his or her disability.[119] Some criticism has emerged of "serial litigants," who bring many accessibility suits and are accused of exaggerating the injuries they claim,[120] though the practice of filing multiple actions does not by any means undermine the validity of any particular case.[121]

---

[113] *Id.* at 832 (quoting Botosan v. Fitzhugh, 13 F. Supp. 2d 1047, 1050 (S.D. Cal. 1998)).

[114] *Id.*

[115] 42 U.S.C. § 2000a-3(a) (2006).

[116] 42 U.S.C. § 12188(a)(2) (2006) (referring to 42 U.S.C. § 12182(b)(2)(A)(iv)). This remedy applies as well to failure to remove transportation barriers in existing vehicles and rail passenger cars (not including barriers that can be removed only by retrofitting vehicles or rail passenger cars or installing lifts), when the removal is readily achievable. *See* § 12182(b)(2)(A)(iv).

[117] § 12188(a)(2) (referring to § 12183(a)).

[118] § 12188(a)(2) (final sentence). Any injunctive action must, of course, contend with questions about whether the plaintiff is likely to again want or need goods or services from the defendant and so remain in a position to benefit from relief. As suggested by the *Aikins* case discussed above, this may present an obstacle in some instances. Aikins v. St. Helena Hosp., 843 F. Supp. 1329 (N.D. Cal. 1994) (discussed *supra* § 5.03[B]).

[119] Chapman v. Pier I Imports (U.S.), Inc., 631 F.3d 939 (9th Cir. 2011).

[120] *See* Molski v. Evergreen Dynasty Corp., 500 F.3d 1047 (9th Cir. 2007) (affirming order requiring that frequent ADA plaintiff and law firm obtain pre-filing approval for new title III suits).

[121] *See* Molski v. M.J. Cable, Inc., 481 F.3d 724 (9th Cir. 2007) (overturning judgment on jury verdict against frequent filer of title III cases in action concerning accessibility of restaurant washroom). State laws may allow for damages relief, creating more of an incentive to sue than the ADA does. *See id.* at 731 (describing treble damages remedy under California law).

As useful as injunctive relief may be to private litigants, title III conspicuously omits damages and other monetary relief from what may be obtained upon establishing a violation of the law. Damages are available only if the Attorney General brings suit in a case regarding a pattern or practice of discrimination or other case of general public importance.[122] In that instance, a court may award damages to persons who are aggrieved, when requested by the Attorney General.[123] Along with equitable relief, civil penalties of up to $50,000 for a single violation and up to $100,000 for subsequent violations may also be imposed, though punitive damages are otherwise excluded.[124]

As with actions under other titles of the ADA, the court may award attorneys' fees to prevailing claimants in public accommodations suits brought by private individuals.[125] Given the low likelihood that the Attorney General will take on a case and the fact that injunctive relief merely requires a defendant to do what it should have been doing all along, the attorneys' fees are both the only real incentive for defendants to comply with title III. They also serve as a major inducement for plaintiffs to bring title III enforcement actions. At the time the ADA was enacted in 1990, all the circuits that had passed on the matter ruled that claimants could obtain attorneys' fees under federal civil rights laws when they prevailed in achieving what they sought in the litigation, even if the case ended in a dismissal for mootness, voluntary dismissal, or other disposition that did not involve a final judgment in the claimant's favor. The court would find that plaintiff "prevailed" in the action and award fees if the action was the catalyst for the defendant's change of conduct.[126] The courts in these cases acted on the basis of legislative history pertaining to the original Civil Rights Attorneys' Fees Act of 1976, which was the model for subsequent federal civil rights fees statutes.[127] In 1987, the Supreme Court described the catalyst theory as "settled law."[128] A congressional effort to overturn it failed in 1985.[129]

---

[122] *See* 42 U.S.C. § 12188(b)(1)(B) (2006).

[123] § 12188(b)(2)(B).

[124] § 12188(b)(2)(A), (C) & (4).

[125] *See* § 12205.

[126] *See, e.g.,* Nadeau v. Helgemoe, 581 F.2d 275, 279–81 (1st Cir. 1978); *see also* Buckhannon Bd. & Care Home, Inc. v. West Virginia Dep't of Health & Human Res., 532 U.S. 598, 626 & n.4 (Ginsburg, J., dissenting) (collecting twelve additional courts of appeals decisions as of 1987). One court of appeals subsequently overturned the catalyst theory, but all the others to consider the matter reaffirmed the rule. *Compare* S-1 v. State Bd. of Educ., 21 F.3d 49 (4th Cir. 1994) (rejecting catalyst theory), *with* Stanton v. South Berkshire Reg'l Sch. Dist., 197 F.3d 574 (1st Cir. 1999); Morris v. City of W. Palm Beach, 194 F.3d 1203 (11th Cir. 1999); Payne v. Board of Educ., 88 F.3d 392 (6th Cir. 1996); Marbley v. Bane, 57 F.3d 224 (2d Cir. 1995); Kilgour v. City of Pasadena, 53 F.3d 1007 (9th Cir. 1995); Zinn v. Shalala, 35 F.3d 273 (7th Cir. 1994); Beard v. Teska, 31 F.3d 942 (10th Cir. 1994); Baumgartner v. Harrisburg Hous. Auth., 21 F.3d 541 (3d Cir. 1994); Little Rock Sch. Dist. v. Pulaski City Sch. Dist. No. 1, 17 F.3d 260 (8th Cir. 1994) (all reaffirming catalyst theory).

[127] *See, e.g.,* H.R. REP. No. 94-1558, at 7 (1976) ("[A]fter a complaint is filed, a defendant might voluntarily cease the unlawful practice. A court should still award fees even though it might conclude, as a matter of equity, that no formal relief, such as an injunction, is needed.").

[128] Hewitt v. Helms, 482 U.S. 755, 760 (1987). The Supreme Court itself never fully considered and approved the theory, however.

[129] *See* Mark C. Weber, *Litigation Under the Individuals with Disabilities Education Act After*

Nevertheless, in the 2001 case *Buckhannon Board & Care Home, Inc. v. West Virginia Department of Health & Human Resources*, the Supreme Court overturned the catalyst theory and ruled that in order to be a prevailing party entitled to attorneys' fees, the claimant had to achieve a judicially-sanctioned change in the legal relationship of the parties.[130] Although a consent decree or other settlement with a sufficient "judicial imprimatur" satisfies the judicially sanctioned-change test, change in the defendant's conduct after the filing of the suit which results in the case's voluntary dismissal or dismissal on the basis of mootness does not.[131]

Buckhannon puts title III plaintiffs at a disadvantage, because to avoid paying any attorneys' fees a defendant needs only to make the corrections to its facilities, policies, or other targeted accessibility conditions or practices that it should have made in the first place to comply with the ADA. It may then move to dismiss on the ground that the action is moot. The plaintiff has no claim for damages to keep the action alive and support the attorneys' fees award. If the court grants the motion, the plaintiff will have achieved accessibility, but will be out of pocket for the costs of the attorneys. A plaintiff will be unable to bring the action in the first place unless wealthy enough to pay an attorney in the event that the defendant decides to obey the law while the case is pending. It remains true that mootness dismissals are not to be granted when the defendant voluntarily ceases illegal activity but is free to return to its old conduct.[132] There has to be a probability that the defendant will return to its previous ways, however, and many courts are skeptical of plaintiffs' arguments about the likelihood of recurrence in deciding motions to dismiss for mootness.[133]

Buckhannon Board & Care Home, Inc. v. West Virginia Department of Health & Human Resources, 65 Ohio St. L.J. 357, 367–68 (2004) (collecting sources).

[130] 532 U.S. 598 (2001). The case involved the application of state laws and practices that kept a group home for persons with disabilities from operating. The action and claim for fees were brought under title II of the ADA and the Fair Housing Act Amendments of 1988.

[131] *Id.* at 605.

[132] United States v. W.T. Grant & Co., 345 U.S. 629, 635 (1953).

[133] *See, e.g.*, Preiser v. Newkirk, 422 U.S. 395, 401–02 (1975); *see also* Michael Ashton, Note, *Recovering Attorney's Fees with the Voluntary Cessation Exception to Mootness Doctrine After Buckhannon Board and Care Home, Inc. v. West Virginia Department of Health and Human Resources*, 2002 Wis. L. Rev. 965, 990–95 (discussing difficulties with relying on voluntary cessation doctrine).

Chapter 6

DISCRIMINATION IN GOVERNMENT SERVICES AND FEDERALLY FUNDED PROGRAMS

§ 6.01 OVERVIEW OF DISCRIMINATION IN GOVERNMENT AND FEDERALLY FUNDED PROGRAMS

The disability discrimination laws address wrongful conduct by government, whether federal or state and local. Title II of the ADA specifically covers services, programs, and activities of any state or local government or their departments, agencies, special purpose districts, and other instrumentalities.[1] Title II builds on section 504 of the Rehabilitation Act of 1973, which forbids disability discrimination by any program or activity receiving federal financial assistance.[2] Since all states and vast numbers of local government entities receive federal financial assistance, they were already subject to non-discrimination duties at the time the ADA came into effect. Title II extended section 504's obligations to the state and local government entities that were not receiving federal funds, and provided a new set of rules for all state and local government entities to follow. Congress simplified the task of following the law, however, for the provisions it enacted, apart from those relating to public transportation, are just a definitional provision,[3] a general prohibition on discrimination,[4] an incorporation by reference of section 504's remedies,[5] and a delegation to the Attorney General to promulgate regulations that are to be consistent with the regulations already promulgated to enforce section 504.[6] Although there are a few differences between title II and section 504, they are not significant for practical purposes in cases where both statutes apply.[7] This chapter will consider the topic of governmental discrimination and discrimination by federally funded programs, beginning with discrimination by federal agencies (which is governed in part by other provisions in section 504) and then proceeding to discrimination in state and local government activities and federally funded programs.

---

[1] 42 U.S.C. § 12131(1) (2006).

[2] 29 U.S.C. § 794 (2006).

[3] 42 U.S.C. § 12131 (2006).

[4] § 12132.

[5] § 12133 (incorporating 29 U.S.C. § 794a).

[6] § 12134.

[7] *See generally* Mark C. Weber, *Disability Discrimination by State and Local Government: The Relationship Between Section 504 of the Rehabilitation Act and Title II of the Americans with Disabilities Act*, 36 WM. & MARY L. REV. 1089 (1995) (explaining similarities and differences).

§ 6.02 DISCRIMINATION BY FEDERAL AGENCIES

Section 504 of the Rehabilitation Act bars disability discrimination under any program or activity conducted by an executive agency of the federal government or by the United States Postal Service.[8] In applying this provision, courts have generally drawn on the body of case law relating to section 504 for federal grantees or the ADA for the entities it covers.

One prominent recent case that arose from a non-employment context is *American Council of the Blind v. Paulson*, which held that the absence of accessibility features on paper currency constitutes a violation of the Rehabilitation Act.[9] The district court granted a declaratory judgment for the plaintiffs. It found that most people who are blind and most people with low vision — a combined group of more than 3.2 million — cannot look at American paper currency and distinguish one denomination from another. Although these individuals cope with the problem by having sales clerks identify bills and by folding the bills differently or placing them in separate pockets, they are constantly at risk of being cheated or making errors. Of the 180 nations that issue paper currency, only the United States makes its bills identical in size and color in all denominations; more than 100 countries have different sizes for different denominations, and all the others include at least some features by which persons with visual impairments can identify the bills, such as tactile features on the Canadian dollar, the Swiss franc, the yen, and Chinese currency. Many countries' bills, such as the euro, the pound, and the Australian dollar, contain both tactile features and sizes that vary by denomination. The United States Bureau of Engraving and Printing, which sells the currency and postage stamps it prints to other federal entities, has an annual revenue of $525 million on the sale of $8.8 billion in currency notes to the Federal Reserve and $6.1 billion in stamps to the Postal Service. Although a mid-2000s redesign of bills (which cost tens of millions of dollars) provided some features, such as larger numbers, to make the currency easier to read by persons with limited vision, the primary purpose of the redesign was to prevent counterfeiting. Recommendations by the National Academy of Sciences to have size and color vary with denomination were not followed.

The court first rejected a sovereign immunity defense. It noted that the case sought only injunctive relief, and construed section 504 to include a waiver of immunity for that remedy. It then analyzed whether the government failed to provide meaningful access to persons with disabilities by the design of the currency and whether forcing a change would impose an undue burden on the government. The court concluded that people who are blind lack meaningful access to currency if they cannot accurately identify paper money without the assistance of someone who can see. The government's duty extends only to reasonable accommodations, but plaintiffs proposed several that on their face appeared to be so: variation by size, or the use of embossed dots, foil, tiny perforations, or raised printing, all on bills other than the $1 bill, which could stay the same. The court rejected arguments that adding the features might facilitate counterfeiting, pointing out that the characteristics are viewed as enhancing security in other currencies. The court also rejected

---

[8] 29 U.S.C. § 794(a) (2006).

[9] 463 F. Supp. 2d 51 (D.D.C. 2006), *aff'd*, 525 F.3d 1256 (D.C. Cir. 2008).

as unsupported the assertion that a drastic change in American currency would undermine its acceptance internationally. Although the court was willing to credit an argument that adding accessibility features might increase costs by diminishing the usable life of the bills, the government could provide no evidence of such costs. Transition costs and some ongoing expenses from changing the bills could be considered, but even the government's figures showed less than a 5% increase in Bureau spending, and that might be diminished if accessibility were incorporated into a larger redesign such as those undertaken in 1996 and 2004. The court set for further proceedings the issue of the form of injunctive relief, but certified the decision as immediately appealable.

The District of Columbia Circuit affirmed. It ruled that forcing millions of visually impaired individuals to depend on "the kindness of others" in using currency, unless they purchased expensive electronic equipment, denied them "meaningful access to currency."[10] It placed the burden on the Treasury to show that the accommodations identified by the plaintiffs would impose an undue burden, and held the burden was not met. The court emphasized that the large majority of other currencies in the world have accommodated people with visual impairments, and the costs of changing American currency appeared manageable. On remand, the district court entered injunctive relief requiring accessibility but affording the Treasury Department choices about how to achieve it,[11] and in 2010, the Bureau of Printing and Engraving issued proposed design modifications including a "raised tactile feature" that would be part of the next currency redesign, large, high-contrast numerals consistent with recent bill redesigns, and a supplemental currency reader program by which electronic readers would be lent to blind and visually impaired persons at no cost.[12] The decision stands as an application of quite ordinary reasonable-accommodation analysis to cause a significant change in one of the most familiar features of daily life, one that the plaintiffs charged with needlessly excluding a large segment of the population from equal participation in daily life.

Section 504 also applies to federal employment. The standards to be used in employment cases under section 504 are the same as those applied in cases under title I (employment provisions) and title V (general provisions, such as the ban on retaliation) of the ADA.[13] However, there is also a separate provision in the Rehabilitation Act, section 791(b) of title 29, requiring provision of affirmative action for persons with disabilities in federal employment, and several courts have used that provision to elevate the requirements that the federal government has to satisfy over those applicable to other employers of persons with disabilities. The provision reads:

> Each department, agency, and instrumentality (including the United States Postal Service and the Postal Regulatory Commission) in the

---

[10] 525 F.3d 1256, 1259 (D.C. Cir. 2008).

[11] 581 F. Supp. 2d 1 (D.D.C. 2008).

[12] Meaningful Access to United States Currency for Blind and Visually Impaired Persons, 75 Fed. Reg. 28331 (May 20, 2010). The $1 bill and the newly redesigned $100 bill were excluded from the proposal.

[13] 29 U.S.C. § 794(d) (2006).

executive branch and the Smithsonian Institution shall . . . submit . . . an affirmative action program plan for the hiring, placement, and advancement of individuals with disabilities in such department, agency, instrumentality, or Institution. Such plan shall include a description of the extent to which and methods whereby the special needs of employees who are individuals with disabilities are being met. Such plan shall be updated annually, and shall be reviewed annually and approved . . . , if . . . such plan provides sufficient assurances, procedures and commitments to provide adequate hiring, placement, and advancement opportunities for individuals with disabilities.[14]

Section 791 contains a provision conforming standards for whether it has been violated to the standards under the ADA, but the provision makes an exception for complaints based on the affirmative action language of section 791(b):

The standards used to determine whether this section has been violated in a complaint alleging nonaffirmative action employment discrimination under this section shall be the standards applied under title I of the Americans with Disabilities Act of 1990 (42 U.S.C. 12111 et seq.) and the provisions of sections 501 through 504, and 510, of the Americans with Disabilities Act of 1990 (42 U.S.C. 12201–12204 and 12210), as such sections relate to employment.[15]

In its first case interpreting section 504 of the Rehabilitation Act, the Supreme Court distinguished the limited duties that section 504 creates from the more expansive duties created by this section. *Southeastern Community College v. Davis* upheld a decision of a community college not to modify its nursing program so as to allow a student who was deaf and used lip reading for communication to complete portions of the program during which doctors and other nurses would be wearing surgical masks or would otherwise be able to communicate only by voice.[16] The Court acknowledged that section 504 required some accommodations, but concluded that the requested accommodation of substituting or deleting the surgical or other clinical rotations would amount to affirmative action. The Court said that affirmative action was more than Congress wished to force upon states and localities. The Court explicitly contrasted the limited duty of reasonable accommodation with the greater affirmative action obligations imposed on federal agencies by § 791(b).[17]

In *Taylor v. Garrett*, Judge Pollak found that a rigger for the Navy who could no longer do the essential functions of his job because of a back injury could be entitled to reclassification into a permanent light-duty job, which the Navy had maintained

---

[14] 29 U.S.C.S. § 791(b) (LexisNexis 2011). This provision predated section 504's coverage of federal agencies. Section 504 initially addressed only federal grantees; federal agencies were included in section 504 in 1978. Pub. L. 95–602, title I, §§ 119, 122(d)(2), 92 Stat. 2982, 2987 (1978).

[15] § 791(g).

[16] 442 U.S. 397 (1979).

[17] *Id.* at 411 ("A comparison of these provisions demonstrates that Congress understood accommodation of the needs of handicapped individuals may require affirmative action and knew how to provide for it in those instances where it wished to do so.").

was beyond what the duty of reasonable accommodation required.[18] The court declared that § 791(b) puts higher standards on a federal employer than section 504 places on a federal grantee, and concluded that as long as the employee could perform the essential functions of a light-duty position, placing him permanently in that position could be required under § 791(b). At least one other district court case applied the statute in a similar way to impose an elevated duty on a federal employer.[19]

Some cases, however, appear to elide the provision. In *Fedro v. Reno*, the Seventh Circuit affirmed a decision that the Rehabilitation Act did not require the combining of two part-time positions into a full-time one in order to accommodate a United States marshal whose disability prevented him from returning to his previous job classification.[20] In dissent, Judge Rovner protested that the court had ignored the elevated responsibilities placed on federal employers by § 791(b).

§ 6.03   STATE AND LOCAL GOVERNMENT AND FEDERALLY FUNDED PROGRAMS: DISPARATE IMPACT DISCRIMINATION

The title II regulations bar disparate impact discrimination:

(3) A public entity may not, directly or through contractual or other arrangements, utilize criteria or methods of administration:

(i) That have the effect of subjecting qualified individuals with disabilities to discrimination on the basis of disability;

(ii) That have the purpose or effect of defeating or substantially impairing accomplishment of the objectives of the public entity's program with respect to individuals with disabilities; or

(iii) That perpetuate the discrimination of another public entity if both public entities are subject to common administrative control or are agencies of the same State.

. . . .

(8) A public entity shall not impose or apply eligibility criteria that screen out or tend to screen out an individual with a disability or any class of individuals with disabilities from fully and equally enjoying any service, program, or activity, unless such criteria can be shown to be necessary for the provision of the service, program, or activity being offered.[21]

---

[18] 820 F. Supp. 933 (E.D. Pa. 1993).

[19] Meissner v. Hove, 872 F. Supp. 507 (N.D. Ill. 1994); *see, e.g.*, Mantolete v. Bolger, 767 F.2d 1416, 1422 (9th Cir. 1985) ("In addressing federal employers and contractors, Congress chose to use the term 'affirmative action' and to require employers to make 'reasonable accommodation' whenever possible; it was clearly implying that a more active and extensive effort than 'non-discrimination' must be made to eliminate barriers to employment of the handicapped in federal agencies, departments, instrumentalities, and contractors.").

[20] 21 F.3d 1391 (7th Cir. 1994).

[21] 28 C.F.R. § 35.130(b) (2011); *see also* § 35.130(b)(4) (extending duty to avoid discriminatory effects

The regulation also bars surcharges for individuals with disabilities to cover the costs of auxiliary aids or other measures required to provide the individual or group of individuals with nondiscriminatory treatment.[22] Surcharges for those sorts of services needed by persons with disabilities would impose a disparate impact.

The seminal decision of the Supreme Court interpreting section 504 and its regulations pertaining to disparate impact is *Alexander v. Choate*.[23] In *Choate*, the Court upheld a state cost-cutting measure that imposed an annual limit on the number of days of Medicaid-covered hospitalization. The plaintiffs contended that the plan had a disproportionate negative impact on individuals with disabilities, and said that it was not a necessary measure to accomplish budget reductions, which could be achieved in less harmful ways.[24] Although the district court had dismissed the complaint, the court of appeals found the disparity to establish a prima facie case of discrimination, and required the state to put forward a justification. The Supreme Court reversed. It rejected the state's argument that section 504 reaches only intentional discrimination, and distinguished section 504 from title VI of the Civil Rights Act, which does not itself bar disparate impact discrimination but for which administrative regulations are the source of disparate impact duties. Not only had courts interpreted the Civil Rights Act to reach disparate impact at the time of adoption of section 504, and not only had Congress rejected an amendment to title VI to restrict it to disparate treatment cases, but "[d]iscrimination against the handicapped was perceived by Congress to be most often the product, not of invidious animus, but rather of thoughtlessness and indifference — of benign neglect."[25] Therefore, "much of the conduct that Congress sought to alter in passing the Rehabilitation Act would be difficult if not impossible to reach were the Act construed to proscribe only conduct fueled by a discriminatory intent."[26] The Court cited the example of architectural barriers, which Congress plainly meant to deal with. It also cited decisions from all the courts of appeals holding that section 504 reached at least some disparate impacts, and noted the regulations of 24 federal agencies, which incorporated bans on disparate impacts.

Nevertheless, the Court concluded that not all conduct that might be thought to have a negative effect on persons with disabilities was forbidden. The Court believed that it would be unwieldy and contrary to congressional intent to require an assessment of the impact on persons with disabilities of every proposed action of federal grantees, something it compared to the requirement for an environmental impact statement in the National Environmental Policy Act. It was willing to assume without deciding that some disparate impacts were covered, but ruled that a Medicaid plan that permitted meaningful access to hospitalization services was

---

to determining site or location of facilities); § 35.130 (b)(5) (duty to avoid using discriminatory criteria for selecting procurement contractors); § 35.130(b)(6) (duty to avoid discriminatory licensing requirements).

[22] § 35.130(f); *see* Klingler v. Director, Dep't of Revenue, 433 F.3d 1078 (8th Cir. 2006) (holding that collection of annual fee for placards for parking spaces reserved for persons with disabilities constituted unlawful surcharge).

[23] 469 U.S. 287 (1985).

[24] The Court noted undisputed statistics indicating that the 14-day limit on covered hospitalization would have a greater harmful effect on persons with disabilities than on other persons.

[25] *Id.* at 295.

[26] *Id.* at 296–97.

permissible. Section 504 did not require the state to alter its program to meet the greater medical needs of persons with disabilities than those without. *Choate's* language figures prominently in the legislative history of title II,[27] a fact that strongly suggests that the statute is intended to cover discriminatory impact even without the force of the implementing regulations, but a fact that also suggests that some disparate impacts will be treated differently from others.

The Supreme Court's recognition of the congressional purpose to reach unintentional discrimination in section 504, and the later congressional extension of that interpretation to title II, distinguishes disparate impact disability discrimination cases from those disparate impact race discrimination cases barred by *Alexander v. Sandoval*.[28] In *Sandoval*, the Supreme Court held that the regulations under title VI outlawing disparate impacts are not enforceable through a private right of action. Not only does *Choate's* approach imply that section 504's and title II's statutory terms were intended to reach some disparate impacts, but also Congress enacted title II's delegation of authority to adopt regulations barring discriminatory impact after the section 504 regulations barring discriminatory impact had been adopted and widely recognized to support a private right action. *Choate* stated that "too facile an assimilation of Title VI law to § 504 must be resisted."[29] Accordingly, several courts have refused to apply *Sandoval* to block claims based on violations of the title II and section 504 regulations.[30]

Cases concerning licensing of attorneys have had to confront seemingly neutral rules that may have a disparate impact on individuals with disabilities. In one such case, the district court upheld a claim of a bar applicant who, because of her record of mental illness, was required to undergo a psychological evaluation by one of two selected examiners at her own expense.[31] The court found that the applicant was a qualified individual with a disability, and that she had been intentionally singled out on account of her disability, even though some other classes of persons were also required to submit additional information at their own expense. It further applied the regulation prohibiting a public entity from using criteria that screen out or tend to screen out an individual with a disability or any such class unless the criteria can be shown to be necessary. It said that any necessity defense that might be advanced under the title II regulation pertaining to licensing would be an issue for later development.

---

[27] *See* H.R. REP. No. 101–485(II), at 84 (1990), *reprinted in* 1990 U.S.C.C.A.N. 267, 367 ("It is . . . the Committee's intent that section 202 [ADA title II] be interpreted consistent with *Alexander v. Choate*.").

[28] 532 U.S. 275 (2001).

[29] *Choate*, 469 U.S. at 294 n.7.

[30] *See* Mark H. v. Lemahieu, 513 F.3d 922, 935–39 (9th Cir. 2008); Robinson v. Kansas, 295 F.3d 1183, 1187 (10th Cir. 2002); Frederick L. v. Department of Pub. Welfare, 157 F. Supp. 2d 509, 537–38 (E.D. Pa. 2001). Courts, however, have disagreed on whether to apply *Sandoval* to bar a private right of action to enforce the specifics of 28 C.F.R § 35.150(d), which requires a transition plan for accessibility of public facilities. *Compare* Lonberg v. City of Riverside, 571 F.3d 846 (9th Cir. 2009) (no private right of action), *and* Iverson v. City of Boston, 452 F.3d 94 (1st Cir. 2006) (same), *and* Ability Ctr. of Greater Toledo v. City of Sandusky, 385 F.3d 901 (6th Cir. 2004) (same), *with* Chaffin v. Kansas State Fair Bd., 348 F.3d 850 (10th Cir. 2003) (upholding private right of action).

[31] Brewer v. Wisconsin Bd. of Bar Exam'rs, 2006 U.S. Dist. LEXIS 86765 (E.D. Wis. Nov. 28, 2006).

In another case, a court found that an inquiry in the bar questionnaire asking if the applicant had within the past five years been treated or counseled for any mental, emotional or nervous disorder, violated the ADA regulations pertaining to licensing and eligibility criteria by imposing a burden on persons with disabilities without adequate justification.[32]

Licensing of other professionals has been subjected to similar scrutiny. In *Medical Society of New Jersey v. Jacobs*, the district court found a high probability of success on the merits of a claim that the New Jersey Board of Medical examiners violated the ADA by making inquiries about psychiatric illness, alcohol and drug abuse, and other matters on the application for initial or renewal applications for medical licenses.[33] It found that the use of an answer to the inquiries to trigger further investigation operated as a screening device and that the inquiries substituted an impermissible inquiry into the status of the applicant for proper and necessary inquiries into the applicant's behavior.

§ 6.04 STATE AND LOCAL GOVERNMENT AND FEDERALLY FUNDED PROGRAMS: MODIFICATIONS OF POLICIES

The title II regulations contain a provision requiring covered entities to make reasonable modifications in policies, practices, and procedures when the modifications are necessary to avoid discrimination on the basis of disability, unless the entity can demonstrate that making the modifications would fundamentally alter the nature of the service, program, or activity.[34] A prominent case that applies this provision is *Dadian v. Village of Wilmette*, in which an elderly couple, one of whom had severe restrictions on walking due to her osteoporosis, prevailed on ADA title II and Fair Housing Amendments Act claims concerning the denial of a permit to put a front driveway on their property.[35] A local ordinance prohibited front or side driveways when fewer than 50% of the houses on the block had them; only six of sixteen houses on the plaintiffs' block had front or side driveways, so the plaintiffs applied for an exception. The village board of trustees denied the application after hearing from the plaintiffs that the alternative of a much longer rear driveway would create difficulties because of the plaintiff's inability to twist her head for the time needed to cover that distance, and that a rear driveway with a turnaround would result in almost complete paving of the plaintiffs' back yard. A jury found in

---

[32] Clark v. Virginia Bd. of Bar Exam'rs, 880 F. Supp. 430 (E.D. Va. 1995); *see also* Ellen S. v. Florida Bd. of Bar Exam'rs, 859 F. Supp. 1489 (S.D. Fla. 1994) (denying motion to dismiss). *But see* McCready v. Illinois Bd. of Admissions, No. 94 C 3582, 1995 U.S. Dist. LEXIS 791 (N.D. Ill. Jan. 24, 1995) (upholding question to references concerning applicant's mental health); Applicants v. Texas State Bd. of Law Exam'rs, No. A93 CA 740 SS, 1994 U.S. Dist. LEXIS 21290 (W.D. Tex. Nov. 11, 1994) (upholding inquiry concerning diagnosis of specific mental illnesses).

[33] No. Civ. A. 93-3670 (WGB), 1993 U.S. Dist. LEXIS 14294 (D.N.J. Oct. 5, 1993). The court nevertheless denied a preliminary injunction because the plaintiff, the Medical Society of the state, failed to show immediate and irreparable harm.

[34] 28 C.F.R. § 35.130(b)(7) (2011).

[35] 269 F.3d 831 (7th Cir. 2001). The Fair Housing Act Amendments are discussed at length *infra* Chapter 7.

favor of the plaintiffs and the court of appeals affirmed judgment on the verdict. The court found no need to discuss a burden-shifting framework; it said that after trial the issue is whether the jury's verdict is against the weight of the evidence. The court held there was adequate evidence to support the finding that one of the plaintiffs had a disability within the meaning of the law. It also held that sufficient evidence supported the claim that the defendant failed to reasonably accommodate the plaintiff's disabilities. The court called attention to the testimony about the need for the plaintiff to avoid either twisting and turning for too long or walking long distances; an architect and appraiser testified that a rear garage with a turnaround would produce a parking-lot feeling and loss of home value; moreover, with six of sixteen houses on the block already having drives cutting into the curb, the permit did not work at odds to the purpose of the ordinance or cause a fundamental or unreasonable change despite whatever concerns might exist about safety.[36]

One panel opinion of the Seventh Circuit Court of Appeals attempted to limit the application of the title II reasonable-modification duty to instances in which the policy, practice or procedure being challenged has a disparate impact on individuals with disabilities. In *Wisconsin Community Services, Inc. v. City of Milwaukee*, the panel decision vacated a district court order directing the city to issue a special use permit for the operation of a mental health clinic in a new location.[37] The panel said that the district court, in applying the reasonable accommodation requirement in the title II and section 504 regulations, had concluded that the city needed to accommodate the plaintiff because the existing clinic was overcrowded and the building where the plaintiff proposed to open the clinic was the most cost-efficient option; the district court held that the accommodation of a permit allowing operation at the new location was reasonable. The panel, however, took the position that it was error for the district court to rule that the plaintiff could prevail by showing disparate impact or failure to make reasonable accommodation. According to the panel, the accommodation requirement is not free standing; accommodation is the means by which disparate impact is eliminated, and in the absence of a rule that bears more heavily on persons with disabilities, there is no need for accommodation. A requirement that imposes equal costs on all persons lacks a disparate impact, according to the panel, and "the statutes do not require a city to be more forgiving when mental-health clinics want to bend the rules than when dental-health clinics make the same request."[38] The panel drew analogies to cases appearing to use such an approach with the Fair Housing Act Amendments.[39] It

---

[36] The court found no reversible error in a jury instruction on the direct-threat defense, though it commented that there was error in limiting the defense to the intentional discrimination claim. Title II does not contain a direct threat provision, but some courts have found such a defense to be implied. *See, e.g.,* Washington v. Indiana High Sch. Athletic Ass'n, 181 F.3d 840, 484 (7th Cir. 1999).

[37] 413 F.3d 642 (7th Cir. 2005), *vacated,* 465 F.3d 737 (7th Cir. 2006).

[38] 413 F.3d at 646.

[39] *See generally infra* Chapter 7 (discussing treatment of uniform rules imposing costs under Fair Housing Act Amendments). The panel's position is not entirely consistent with the relevant case law. As noted in Chapter 7, most of the housing discrimination cases recognize that a uniform rule such as one imposing costs on everyone may have a disparate impact on persons with disabilities because of economics or other matters, just as a uniform rule such as one imposing a high school graduation requirement for a job may have a disparate impact on African-Americans. *Cf.* Griggs v. Duke Power Co., 401 U.S. 424 (1971) (applying disparate impact theory in case under title VII of Civil Rights Act). This

found that there was inadequate evidence in the record of disparate impact or, alternatively, of discriminatory animus, a theory supported in part by the facts as developed so far, but which the district court did not reach; accordingly, the panel remanded the case to the district court. It stated, however, that if accommodation were required, requiring provision of the permit would be reasonable as an accommodation. One of the panel members dissented.

On rehearing en banc, the court of appeals concluded that section 504, the Fair Housing Amendments Act, and ADA title II all embodied a duty to accommodate. This duty is free standing: "[F]ailure to accommodate is an *independent* basis for liability under the ADA."[40] "[A] plaintiff need not allege either disparate treatment or disparate impact in order to state a reasonable accommodation claim under Title II of the ADA."[41] The accommodation must be provided when necessary to avoid discrimination on the basis of disability, that is, when the reason for the deprivation of the services or benefits desired is the disability. The accommodation must be reasonable, but there is no special deference to municipal zoning ordinances.

The court of appeals said that although the reasonable accommodation duty is free standing, the district court nevertheless committed error by failing to require an adequate showing that the accommodation was necessary, that is, that but for the disability of the plaintiff's clients, the services or benefits desired would have been provided. It said that on the record of what had happened before the city's decision-making body, the inability to meet the special use criteria appeared to be due not to the disabilities of the plaintiff's clients but to the city's desire to locate a commercial, tax-paying tenant in the proposed space. The court therefore remanded to the district court to allow the parties to develop the question whether the clinic had been prevented from occupying that location because of its clients' disabilities. The author of the panel opinion that was vacated wrote a brief concurring opinion stating that the disparate impact label need not be used or a statistical showing implied by the label used, as long as courts require that the accommodation be necessary because of the plaintiff's disability.

The upshot of this debate appears to be a reaffirmance that failure to provide reasonable modifications is indeed a free standing basis on which to make out a violation of title II and section 504, but that the language of the title II regulation "when the modifications are necessary to avoid discrimination on the basis of disability" is likely to be applied in a rigorous manner.[42]

---

does not mean, however, that the disparate impact is one that the ADA or section 504 is meant to address. As the *Choate* case indicates and the fair housing cases confirm, the disability discrimination statutes reach many disparate impacts, but not all of them.

[40] 465 F.3d at 751 (emphasis in original).

[41] *Id.* at 753.

[42] *See* 28 C.F.R. § 35.130(b)(7) (2011).

§ 6.05 STATE AND LOCAL GOVERNMENT AND FEDERALLY FUNDED PROGRAMS: INTEGRATED SERVICES

The preamble to the ADA includes the finding that "historically, society has tended to isolate and segregate individuals with disabilities, and, despite some improvements, such forms of discrimination . . . continue to be a severe and pervasive social problem."[43] To address the problem of segregation in public services, the title II regulations provide that "[a] public entity shall administer services, programs, and activities in the most integrated setting appropriate to the needs of qualified individuals with disabilities."[44]

In *Olmstead v. L.C.*, the Supreme Court gave a "qualified yes" to the question whether the ADA requires placement of individuals with mental disabilities in community settings rather than institutions.[45] Two women with mental retardation and mental illness lived for many years in state institutions, even though treating professionals concluded that they could be served in community-based residential programs that would allow them more freedom and greater opportunity to be integrated into society. The district court granted partial summary judgment on their claim that failing to place them in the community violated the ADA, and the court of appeals affirmed, though it remanded the case to the district court for consideration of a defense based on the cost to the state.

The Supreme Court cited the regulation quoted above, which it termed the "integration regulation,"[46] and declared that "[u]njustified isolation is properly regarded as discrimination based on disability."[47] It linked segregation to stereotyped thinking about persons with disabilities: "[I]nstitutional placement of persons who can handle and benefit from community settings perpetuates unwarranted assumptions that persons so isolated are incapable or unworthy of participating in community life."[48] Confinement in an institution severely limits everyday life activities, including family relations, social contacts, work opportunities, economic independence, education, and participation in cultural activity. The Court stressed that discrimination took place when services for persons like the plaintiffs were available only in institutions, noting that only persons with disabilities, not others, had to relinquish their freedom in order to obtain the medical services they needed. The Medicaid law, in its current form, did not impose a preference for institutional settings that contravened the nondiscrimination requirement.

Nevertheless, nothing in the ADA requires an end to institutional arrangements for anyone who cannot handle or benefit from a community setting; only "qualified" individuals are protected by the relevant provisions. Thus a state may rely on the reasonable assessments of its own professionals in determining whether a person

---

[43] 42 U.S.C.S. § 12101(a)(2) (LexisNexis 2011).

[44] 28 C.F.R. § 35.130(d) (2011).

[45] 527 U.S. 581, 587 (1999).

[46] *Id.* at 592.

[47] *Id.* at 597.

[48] *Id.* at 600.

meets the eligibility requirements for a community-based setting; moreover, the ADA does not impose community-based treatment on persons who do not desire it. Finally, consistent with the reasonable modification-fundamental alteration limits on what states must do, the obligation to provide community-based treatment is not boundless, but instead the state may show that in allocating available resources, immediate placement in a community setting for an individual would be inequitable given the responsibility the state has for the whole population of persons with mental disabilities. Thus, "[i]f . . . the State . . . demonstrate[d] that it had a comprehensive, effectively working plan for placing qualified persons . . . in less restrictive settings, and a waiting list that moved at a reasonable pace not controlled by the State's endeavors to keep its institutions fully populated, the reasonable-modifications standard would be met."[49]

Olmstead was foreshadowed by a decision of the Third Circuit, *Helen L. v. DiDario*, in which the court reversed the dismissal of an ADA claim brought by a nursing home resident with paralysis who alleged that she could live at home with her children rather than be segregated into the nursing home if she were furnished services under the state's attendant care program.[50] She was eligible for the services, but languished on a waiting list even though the cost of attendant care services was considerably lower than that of the nursing home. The court applied the integration regulation and held that providing the services would not constitute a fundamental alteration. No change in the eligibility requirements for attendant care or nursing home care was entailed, and the administrative convenience involved in not shifting funds from nursing home care to attendant care was not an adequate justification. If state law did not permit the movement of funds from one line to another, it was up to the state to find a funding mechanism to comply with the ADA's mandate. The court directed the entry of an order granting summary judgment to the plaintiff.

Not every case runs in that direction, however. In *Easley v. Snider*, another Third Circuit case, the court reversed the judgment of the district court and held that a "mental alertness" requirement for the individuals who are served consti-tuted a fundamental part of Pennsylvania's in-home attendant care services program, and so did not have to be modified in light of the ADA's nondiscrimination provisions.[51] *Easley* may be distinguished from *Helen L.* on the ground that program eligibility standards that the court felt justified by the nature of the program would have had to be modified to provide relief to the *Easley* plaintiffs, but it may also be true that *Easley* simply placed less priority on integration. *Easley* did

---

[49] *Id.* at 605–06. This portion of the opinion received four votes. Justice Stevens concurred, but said that the Court should not have discussed fundamental alteration because the court of appeals below had remanded that issue to the district court without making a decision on it. *Id.* at 607–08 (Stevens, J., concurring in part and concurring in the judgment). Justice Kennedy, joined by Justice Breyer, concurred with the majority, but added a caution about inappropriate deinstitutionalization; in a portion of the opinion not joined by Breyer he said he would have remanded the case for application of a narrower reading of the discrimination standard than the majority used. *Id.* at 608–15 (Kennedy, J., concurring in the judgment). Justice Thomas filed a dissenting opinion, which Chief Justice Rehnquist and Justice Scalia joined. *Id.* at 615 (Thomas, J., dissenting).

[50] 46 F.3d 325 (3d Cir. 1995).

[51] 36 F.3d 297 (3d Cir. 1994).

not even cite the integration regulation in its discussion of the ADA's requirements.

A continuing controversy in the wake of *Olmstead* and other cases is whether states may be required to furnish services to persons with mental or severe physical disabilities who are currently at home, often living with aging parents who provide some care for them, but who want to be served with publicly funded intermittent services furnished in the home or want to be moved to group home arrangements. These services may be paid for under Medicaid programs, but the state must apply for and allocate the funding. Otherwise, needed medical and other services are offered only if the individual is placed in a nursing home or state institution. Applying *Olmstead*'s principles, a number of courts have concluded that cost allocation arrangements that result in withholding publicly funded services unless the person goes into a nursing home or institution may violate the integration regulation.[52] Although the plaintiffs in these cases typically are not currently institutionalized, they claim that they will need to become so in order to access a full range of services; moreover, some claim they are virtual prisoners in their own homes (and jailers of their caretakers) due to a lack of any programs to serve them.[53]

§ 6.06 STATE AND LOCAL GOVERNMENT AND FEDERALLY FUNDED PROGRAMS: SPECIFIC ISSUES AND GENERAL ACCESSIBILITY DUTY

Some public services of state and local government are addressed in other chapters, for example, constitutional aspects of commitment for mental disability in Chapter 1 and government-provided transportation and web site communications in Chapter 7. A few specific government activities and services and the major legal issues they present may be noted here, however. These activities include employment, voting, courts, prisons, public benefits, and recreation. Moreover, discussion of the general accessibility duties for the operation of programs and facilities is in order.

[A] Employment

The regulations promulgated by the Department of Justice pursuant to the congressional direction to the Department to implement title II[54] state that "[n]o qualified individual with a disability shall, on the basis of disability, be subjected to discrimination in employment under any service, program, or activity conducted by a public entity."[55] Nevertheless, the Ninth Circuit Court of Appeals has rejected

---

[52] *See, e.g.*, M.A.C. v. Betit, 284 F. Supp. 2d 1298 (D. Utah 2003); Martin v. Taft, 222 F. Supp. 2d 940 (S.D. Ohio 2002); Makin v. Hawaii, 114 F. Supp. 2d 1017 (D. Haw. 1999). As these cases note, an ongoing controversy also exists whether the Medicaid statute creates enforceable rights to community treatment.

[53] *See generally* Mark C. Weber, *Home and Community-Based Services,* Olmstead *and Positive Rights: A Preliminary Discussion,* 39 Wake Forest L. Rev. 269 (2004) (discussing potential claims under 28 C.F.R. § 35.130(d)).

[54] *See* 42 U.S.C. § 12134(a) (2006) ("Not later than 1 year after the date of enactment of this Act, the Attorney General shall promulgate regulations in an accessible format that implement this title.").

[55] 28 C.F.R. § 35.140(a) (2011).

the validity of the regulations and has found title II not to cover employment cases.

In *Zimmerman v. Oregon Department of Justice*, the court affirmed the dismissal of the suit of a ADA title II employment discrimination plaintiff whose claim under title I, the part of the ADA specifically directed to employment, was not timely filed with the EEOC.[56] The court reasoned that it did not need to defer to the federal regulation's interpretation of title II on the ground that "Congress unambiguously expressed its intent for Title II not to apply to employment."[57] The court said that the wording of title II covers "services, programs, or activities of a public entity," and this referred to "outputs," not "inputs" such as employment.[58] The court further said that title II's disjunctive phrase covering being "subjected to discrimination by any such entity" could not be read independently of the "services, programs, or activities" language. It looked at the "public services" heading of title II and noted that the "qualified individual with a disability" term of title II relates to essential eligibility requirements for receipt of services or participation in programs or activities.[59] The court also argued that the structure of the ADA as a whole was unambiguously incompatible with the regulation for five reasons:

> (1) Congress placed employment-specific provisions in Title I, which it labeled "Employment," whereas Congress placed no employment-related provisions in Title II, which it labeled "Public Services." (2) Congress defined "qualified individual with a disability" differently in Title I than in Title II. In Title I, a person is "qualified" if the person can work, whereas in Title II a person is "qualified" if the person is eligible to receive services or participate in a publicly provided program. (3) Allowing employment discrimination claims under Title II would make Title I redundant as applied to public employees and would eviscerate the procedural require-ments of Title I for those employees. (4) Congress gave regulatory authority to different agencies for Title I and Title II. Congress gave authority over Title I to the EEOC, the agency that administers most federal employment-related statutes. (5) Congress expressly linked the employment-related provisions of the Rehabilitation Act to Title I of the ADA, not to Title II.[60]

The court also rejected an argument for coverage of employment based on language in title II expressly or implicitly incorporating the coverage of section 504 of the Rehabilitation Act.

The Eleventh Circuit took the contrary position in *Bledsoe v. Palm Beach Conservation District*.[61] The district court granted summary judgment for defen-dant in a title II employment discrimination case brought by the former employee of a local government entity that was not covered by title I of the ADA because it

---

[56] 170 F.3d 1169 (9th Cir. 1999).

[57] *Id.* at 1173.

[58] *Id.* at 1174 (citing 42 U.S.C. § 12132 with respect to services, programs, or activities).

[59] *Id.* at 1175 (citing 42 U.S.C. § 12131(2) with respect to qualified individual).

[60] *Id.* at 1176.

[61] 133 F.3d 816 (11th Cir. 1998).

had fewer than 15 employees. One ground for the district court's decision was that title II does not apply to employment; the court applied an analysis similar to that later adopted by *Zimmerman*. The court of appeals reversed. It relied on the legislative history of title II establishing that Congress intended title II to apply to employment:

> The Committee intends, however, that the forms of discrimination prohibited by section 202 [codified as 42 U.S.C. § 12132] be identical to those set out in the applicable provisions of titles I and III of this legislation. . . . In addition, activities which do not fit into the employment or public accommodations context are governed by the analogous section 504 regulations.[62]

In addition, the court noted the congressional intention to have title II work in the same manner as section 504, which up to the time of the ADA, was dominantly focused on employment. The court rejected the inputs-outputs argument later found persuasive by the Ninth Circuit in *Zimmerman*, relying on the general phrase at the end of the statutory term that outlaws discrimination by a public entity in all contexts. The court further relied on Supreme Court precedent establishing that considerable weight should be given to an enforcing agency's construction of a statutory scheme[63] and finally noted that precedent within the Eleventh Circuit and outside it supported extension of title II to employment.

The controversy over coverage of employment may be less important than it appears, because most entities covered by title II receive federal funding, making them subject to section 504, which, as the Eleventh Circuit noted, has always been construed to cover employment. The Ninth Circuit's approach does create a gap in coverage, however, for individuals employed by or seeking employment with public entities that do not receive federal funding and are not covered by title I because they have fewer than 15 employees.[64]

[B] Voting

Voting is a fundamental constitutional right, and elections are an important activity conducted by state and local government.[65] Nevertheless, many polling places are inaccessible to persons with mobility impairments, and persons with visual impairments and some manual impairments are typically unable to use voting machines without assistance, a condition that undermines the secrecy of their ballots.[66] Some people with mental impairments face categorical barriers to

---

[62] *Id.* at 821 (quoting H.R. Rep. No. 101-485(III), at 50 (1990), *reprinted in* 1990 U.S.C.C.A.N. 445, 473).

[63] *Id.* at 822–23 (citing Chevron, U.S.A. v. Natural Res. Def. Council, 467 U.S. 837, 844 (1984)).

[64] *See* 42 U.S.C.S. § 12111(5) (LexisNexis 2011) (defining employers covered by title I as those having 15 or more employees for specified time periods).

[65] *See* Harper v. Virginia State Bd. of Elections, 383 U.S. 663, 666 (1966) (describing right to vote as fundamental).

[66] Professor Michael Waterstone has done extensive, highly insightful work on the topic of voting rights of persons with disabilities. *See, e.g.,* Michael E. Waterstone, Lane, *Fundamental Rights and Voting*, 56 Ala. L. Rev. 793 (2005); Michael E. Waterstone, *Civil Rights and the Administration of*

exercising the right to vote.[67] The Help America Vote Act requires participating states and localities to provide all voters with a means of voting that furnishes the same opportunities for access and participation (including guarantees of privacy and independence) as other voters enjoy, but little litigation has emerged so far under that statute.[68]

Voting accessibility litigation under the ADA has proven only partially successful. Although one district court granted a preliminary injunction requiring a locality to comply with the ADA's accessibility guidelines with respect to its polling places and another issued a declaratory judgment regarding access to ballot secrecy,[69] two courts of appeals have rejected ADA claims brought by persons with disabilities seeking to alter existing voting procedures. In *Lightbourn v. County of El Paso*, the Fifth Circuit ruled that a claim for failure to provide accessibility did not lie against the Texas Secretary of Elections, reasoning that the office did not receive federal funds and so was not bound by section 504, and that an official whose obligations under state law extended only to enforcing election laws was not also bound to enforce the ADA.[70] The court's analysis suggests that there may be difficulties in finding a proper defendant for pressing a statewide claim for failure to provide accessibility.[71] In *Nelson v. Miller*, the Sixth Circuit Court of Appeals rejected a claim that Michigan inadequately protected the confidential voting rights of voters with visual impairments.[72] The court said that the Michigan Constitution did not guarantee a secret vote, and so the state was not discriminating in violation of the ADA or section 504.

[C]   Courts

The judiciary is a critical activity of state and local government, and access to justice is a fundamental right of Americans.[73] In *Tennessee v. Lane*, the Supreme Court ruled that a man with paraplegia who on one occasion had to crawl up two

---

Elections — Toward Secret Ballots and Polling Place Access, 8 J. Gender Race & Just. 101 (2004); Michael E. Waterstone, *Constitutional and Statutory Voting Rights for People with Disabilities*, 14 Stan. L. & Pol'y Rev. 353 (2003). These articles collect sources on inaccessibility of polling places and difficulties with securing a secret ballot for persons with visual impairments.

[67] *See* sources cited *supra* previous note.

[68] 42 U.S.C. § 15421(b) (2006). The Act in its entirety is found at 42 U.S.C. §§ 15301–15545. Regarding federal elections, see the Voting Accessibility for the Elderly and Handicapped Act, 42 U.S.C. § 1973ee-1(a) (2006) (requiring accessibility).

[69] New York *ex rel.* Spitzer v. County of Schoharie, 82 F. Supp. 2d 19 (N.D.N.Y. 2000) (issuing preliminary injunction); *see* American Ass'n of People with Disabilities v. Hood, 310 F. Supp. 2d 1226 (M.D. Fla. 2004) (issuing declaratory judgment); *see also* American Ass'n of People with Disabilities v. Smith, 227 F. Supp. 2d 1276 (M.D. Fla. 2002) (upholding claim).

[70] 118 F.3d 421 (5th Cir. 1997).

[71] The opinion indicates that plaintiffs settled their claim with the county. *See id.* at 424.

[72] 170 F.3d 641 (6th Cir. 1999); *see also* American Ass'n of People with Disabilities v. Harris, 647 F.3d 1093 (11th Cir. 2011) (ruling that voting machines did not qualify as facilities under ADA regulations); American Ass'n of People with Disabilities v. Shelley, 324 F. Supp. 2d 1120 (C.D. Cal. 2004) (denying preliminary injunction in claim regarding ballot secrecy).

[73] A variety of information is available about improving the accessibility of judicial services. *See, e.g.,* Alexandria Bosna, Implementing the Court-Related Needs of Older People and Persons with Disabilities: An Instructional Guide (1992); Office of the Illinois Attorney General, Opening the Bench & Bar to

flights of steps to reach an inaccessible courtroom to answer criminal charges, and on another refused to crawl or be carried in his wheelchair and so was arrested and jailed for failure to appear, could sue for monetary relief for a violation of the ADA.[74] The Court held that in light of the fundamental nature of the right to access to justice, Congress had the Fourteenth Amendment authority to abrogate the state's immunity from damages relief under the principles of the Eleventh Amendment. *Lane* develops the issue of Eleventh Amendment immunity more than the contours of the right to accessible courthouses, but its holding underlines the seriousness of the right to access to justice that the ADA guarantees by forcing states and localities to provide court facilities that can be used by persons with disabilities.[75]

A noteworthy decision concerning whether blind persons may be allowed to serve on juries is *Galloway v. Superior Court*.[76] In that case, the United States district court enjoined the District of Columbia Superior Court's policy of refusing to permit persons who are blind from serving on juries, stressing that uncontradicted evidence showed that sight is not necessarily required to assess veracity of witnesses, and that individuals who are blind rely on the same considerations of context, speech patterns, intonation, and syntax as sighted jurors do in determining credibility. At least ten states forbid blanket exclusion of persons who are blind from jury service, and permit exclusion only when required by the nature of the case; blind judges have conducted bench trials requiring assessment of credibility. The superior court itself had a blind judge and permitted deaf jurors to serve. The court further suggested that the reasonable accommodation of a person trained to describe physical movements, dress, and physical settings, or of a reader or a reading machine, could be furnished. Accordingly, the court ruled that the policy violated the ADA and that the service of a blind juror in each case would have to be addressed individually during the ordinary processes of juror selection.

[D] Prisons

After some period of uncertainty among the lower courts, the Supreme Court made clear in *Yeskey v. Pennsylvania Department of Corrections* that title II of the ADA covers prisons.[77] The Court affirmed the reversal of a district court decision

---

People with Disabilities, *at* http://www.illinoisattorneygeneral.gov/rights/Manual_ Court_Disability_Co-ordinators.pdf (last visited Feb. 8, 2007); Judicial Branch of Georgia, A Meaningful Opportunity to Participate: A Handbook for Georgia Court Officials on Courtroom Accessibility for Individuals with Disabilities, *at* http://www.georgiacourts.org/agencies/gcafc/handbook_toc.html (last visited Feb. 8, 2007).

[74] 541 U.S. 509 (2004).

[75] The breadth of the right is underlined by the Court's additional upholding of the claim of a court reporter with paraplegia who alleged deprivation of the opportunity to attend proceedings. *See id.* at 514. Some courts have rejected claims for particular auxiliary services to accommodate persons who are deaf or hearing impaired under the exigent circumstances of arrest or in various other phases of criminal proceedings. *See, e.g.*, Tucker v. Tennessee, 539 F.3d 526 (6th Cir. 2008); Bircoll v. Miami-Dade County, 480 F.3d 1072 (11th Cir. 2007).

[76] 816 F. Supp. 12 (D.D.C. 1993).

[77] 524 U.S. 206 (1998); *see also* Armstrong v. Schwarzenegger, 622 F.3d 1058 (9th Cir. 2010)

that had dismissed a prisoner's claim that he was denied the opportunity to serve his sentence in a boot camp setting because of his history of hypertension. The Court relied on the plain language of the statute, saying that the defendant was a public agency and provided a multitude of services and programs. Voluntary participation is not required for the program or service to be included.

[E] Public Benefits and Welfare

Alexander v. Choate, in which plaintiffs failed on a disparate-impact theory in their section 504 challenge to a limit on the number of hospital days covered by state Medicaid, suggests that disparate-impact attacks on public welfare policies will face difficulty. *Choate* figures prominently in the legislative history of the ADA, so there may be little reason to expect that title II cases alleging a disparate impact from welfare or benefits program rules would fare any better than ones brought under section 504, at least in the absence of any claim based on an integration theory.[78] Not surprisingly, then, plaintiffs have more frequently framed their cases challenging public welfare limits in terms of disparate treatment, claiming that programs explicitly use disability based classifications and that these classifications violate the ADA.

There have mixed results in these efforts. In *Does 1-5 v. Chandler*, the Ninth Circuit Court of Appeals affirmed the denial of a preliminary injunction when the plaintiffs claimed that changes in Hawaii's General Assistance program violated the ADA.[79] Before 1995, benefits were given to (1) needy persons with dependent children, (2) needy able-bodied adults 55 and over, and (3) needy persons with disabling conditions who were not otherwise provided benefits under state law or federal assistance programs. A 1995 law eliminated benefits for the able-bodied adults 55 and over, and limited the receipt of benefits by persons with disabling conditions to no more than one year. The court concluded that the change in the law did not deny benefits based on disability. The court reasoned that the state did not need to have any assistance program at all, and that it could have one providing help only to families with dependent children. Thus the state assistance program functionally was made up of two programs, one for needy families with children and another for needy persons with disabilities, and "[t]he ADA does not require equivalent benefits in different programs."[80] The fact that no benefits were available for needy persons who were neither part of a family with dependent children nor had a disability meant that there was not a single, unified program with an essential purpose of providing assistance based only on need.

In a contrasting case, *Weaver v. New Mexico Human Services Department*, the New Mexico Supreme Court affirmed a decision that a state regulation violated the

---

(upholding claims by class of state prisoners with disabilities to accommodations in county jails); Kinman v. New Hampshire Dep't of Corrs., 451 F.3d 274 (1st Cir. 2006) (vacating summary judgment against former prisoner on accommodations claim); *cf.* Pierce v. County of Orange, 526 F.3d 1190 (9th Cir. 2008) (determining that county failed to reasonably accommodate pretrial detainees with disabilities). *See generally* 28 C.F.R. § 35.152 (2011) (setting out nondiscrimination duties for jails and prisons).

[78] *See generally supra* § 6.05 (discussing benefits cases based on integration claims).

[79] 83 F.3d 1150 (9th Cir. 1996).

[80] *Id.* at 1155. The court also rejected a constitutional challenge to the state's policy.

ADA by imposing a duration limit on receipt of state assistance by persons eligible on the basis of disability.[81] The New Mexico General Assistance program provided aid to needy individuals who were (1) adults with permanent disabilities who were not eligible for federal assistance because their disabilities were not serious enough, (2) adults with temporary disabilities, and (3) caregivers acting on behalf of minor children ineligible for federally supported assistance because they were not living with a relation specified in the federal law. Due to budget shortfalls, the state limited the period of time during which an adult with a disability could receive benefits to 12 months. The court ruled that the plaintiff assistance recipients were covered under the ADA and the imposition of a duration limit on aid to them discriminated against them on the basis of their disability. Citing *Chandler*, the state contended that the assistance program was functionally three programs, one for persons with long-term disabilities, another for those with short-term disabilities, and a third for families with dependent children; the state argued that the ADA does not require different programs to have equivalent benefits. But the New Mexico court disagreed, saying that, as established by legislature, the program was a unified program of assistance with a single statutory purpose, a single statutory description, and a single budget line item. Finding the change to violate the ADA, the court declared: "While the ADA does not require equivalent benefits in different programs, . . . we understand the law to require equivalent benefits for disabled and non-disabled recipients of a single program."[82]

Whether an assistance program can be described as one or as several might seem to be a slender reed on which to place important decisions about allocations of public welfare, but it is hard to dispute the *Weaver* court's view that the logic of the *Chandler* decision invites the drawing of such distinctions.

[F] Recreation

An important function of state and local government is to provide opportunities for recreation. In *Concerned Parents to Save Dreher Park Center v. City of West Palm Beach*, the court granted a preliminary injunction against the cutting of recreational programs offered by a city for children and adults with disabilities.[83] These programs included a summer day camp for children with disabilities, club programs for children and adults with mental and other disabilities, a social program for adults with visual impairments, lip reading instruction, a quarterly outing club for teenagers with visual impairments, a leisure program for adults with mental disabilities, baseball and swimming for persons with disabilities, and other activities. About 300 persons with disabilities participated in a given year. Budget cuts in 1993 caused the termination of all the programs for persons with disabilities.

The court pointed out that no eligibility requirement applied to the city's recreation program, and that the program had to viewed as a whole to include an entire network of individual activities and services. Although the city was not

---

[81] 945 P.2d 70 (N.M. 1997).

[82] *Id.* at 75.

[83] 846 F. Supp. 986 (S.D. Fla. 1994).

obliged to offer a recreation program to the public, it had to use methods and criteria of administration of the program it offered that did not have the purpose or effect of impairing the objectives of providing recreation with respect to persons with disabilities. While there was no evidence of deliberate exclusion of persons with disabilities from the general recreational activities offered by the city, many of those activities could not offer the benefits of recreation to individuals with disabilities because of the nature of the activities and the physical or mental disabilities of those persons. Separate benefits and services are required when necessary to provide persons with disabilities with benefits and services that are as effective as those provided to others.[84] Moreover, the city could not account for the disparity of the budget cuts in the programs for persons with disabilities as opposed to those in other programs. The court thus found likelihood of success on the merits of the ADA claim, and further determined that irreparable injury would occur, that the balance of hardships favored the plaintiffs, and that the public interest favored injunctive relief.

[G]   Accessibility Requirements in General

A general obligation applies to state and local government entities to "operate each service, program, or activity so that the service, program, or activity, when viewed in its entirety, is readily accessible to and usable by individuals with disabilities."[85] The regulation goes on to state that this obligation does not necessarily require the entity to make each of its existing facilities accessible, nor require it to take action that would threaten or destroy the historic significance of historic property, nor require the entity to do things that it can demonstrate would result in a fundamental alteration in the nature of a service, program, or activity or result in undue financial and administrative burdens. Decisions that compliance would result in such an alteration or burden have to be made by the head of the public entity or that person's designee after considering all resources available for use in the funding and operation of the service, program, or activity. A written statement of the reasons for the conclusion has to accompany it. If the action were to result in a fundamental alteration or undue burden, the entity is to take other action that would not do so but would still ensure that individuals with disabilities receive the benefits or services provided by the entity. The regulation lists methods for compliance with the accessibility section, including "redesign of equipment, reassignment of services to accessible buildings, assignment of aides to beneficiaries, home visits, delivery of services at alternate accessible sites, alteration of existing facilities and construction of new facilities," and other measures.[86] Audio-visual presentations or assignment of guides may be used to provide accessibility to otherwise inaccessible historical sites.[87] Transition plans are required.[88]

---

[84] *See* 28 C.F.R. § 35.130(b)(1)(iv) (2011).

[85] § 35.150(a).

[86] § 35.150(b)(1).

[87] § 35.150(b)(2).

[88] § 35.150(d). As noted *supra* § 6.03, courts have disagreed about whether this provision is enforceable in private litigation.

Department of Justice regulations effective in 2011 establish a safe harbor regarding elements in existing facilities that have not been altered on or after March 15, 2012 and that comply with the technical and scoping specifications for those elements in the 1991 Americans with Disabilities Act Accessibility Guidelines ("ADAAG") or the Uniform Federal Accessibility Standards ("UFAS"). The provision states that these elements are not required to modified in order to comply with accessibility standards adopted in the revision of the Department of Justice regulations in 2010; however, it goes on to list a number elements covered by the 2010 standards that are not eligible for safe-harbor treatment.[89]

The requirement that a program, when viewed in its entirety, be accessible has a dual aspect. As the specifications in the regulation indicate, it excuses programs from making each and every facility immediately accessible. On the other hand, it also forces programs to establish accommodations, within the limits of fundamental alteration and undue hardship, to offer access to everyone. As the regulation suggests, this may mean rearranging activities, delivering services where they are currently not provided, altering equipment, and undertaking other measures that entail the use of creativity to make sure that persons with disabilities can benefit from public programs. Moreover, all newly constructed facilities and parts of facilities, as well as all facilities and parts of facilities that are altered, must be readily accessible to and usable by persons with disabilities.[90]

With respect to new construction and alterations begun after July 26, 1992 and before September 15, 2010, state and local government are permitted to conform either to the UFAS or the 1991 ADAAG.[91] Because states and large numbers of local government entities receive federal money, they were subject to accessibility obligations under section 504 the Rehabilitation Act of 1973 long before passage of the ADA and development of the ADAAG. There was thus some logic to letting them continue to follow the UFAS, which is very similar to the 1991 ADAAG, after passage of the ADA. The elevator exception in the 1991 ADAAG did not apply to state and local government entities, however.

The ADAAG standards were updated in 2004 and adopted by the Department of Justice in the 2010 Standards for Public Accommodations and Commercial Facilities. New construction and alterations must comply with the UFAS, the 1991 ADAAG, or the 2010 standards if the applicable date is on or after September 15, 2010, and before March 15, 2012.[92] New construction and alterations have to comply with the 2010 standards if the applicable date is on or after March 15, 2012.[93]

---

[89] § 35.150(b)(2). Examples of items not eligible for the safe harbor include amusement rides, exercise machines and equipment, fishing piers and platforms, and various others.

[90] § 35.151(a)–(b). The alteration provision covers each facility or part of facility altered in a manner that affects or could affect the usability of the facility or part of the facility, and it provides that the facility or part shall, to the maximum extent feasible, be altered in such a manner that the altered portion is readily accessible to and usable by individuals with disabilities.

[91] § 35.151(c)(1).

[92] § 35.151(c)(2).

[93] § 35.151(c)(3).

Accessibility cases against state and local governments have focused on some particularly public amenities, such as sidewalks and streets. One of the earliest ADA cases of this type was *Kinney v. Yerusalem*, in which the court of appeals affirmed a district court decision requiring Philadelphia to make curb cuts for wheelchairs on all streets resurfaced since the effective date of the ADA.[94] The case turned on whether resurfacing a street constitutes an alteration, so as to trigger the provision in the regulations that states, "[n]ewly constructed or altered streets, roads, and highways must contain curb ramps or other sloped areas at any intersection having curbs or other barriers to entry from a street level pedestrian walkway."[95] An alteration was defined in the title II regulations and the ADAAG as a change that affects the usability of the facility. The court concluded that when resurfacing is defined to include at least the laying of a new asphalt bed spanning the length and width of a city block, it clearly improves usability of the road. The language of the curb-cut regulation allows no undue burden defense, and the court rejected any argument that streets and curbs are separate "facilities," citing the express language of the regulation.

In *Barden v. City of Sacramento*, the plaintiffs contended that the city had to remove barriers such as benches, sign posts, and wires where they interfered with mobility of persons using wheelchairs on the city's sidewalks.[96] The district court ruled that sidewalks are not a service, program or activity within the meaning of title II, and so were not subject to accessibility requirements. The court of appeals reversed, applying a definition of service, program or activity that brings within the scope of title II anything a public entity does. It declared that providing and maintaining public sidewalks is a normal function of a city and thus falls within title II. The court further noted that section 504 defines "program or activity" to include "all the operations of" a qualifying local government,[97] and that the legislative history of title II supports the position that title II extends all the prohibitions on discrimination found in section 504 to all the actions of state and local governments.[98] It also relied on the Department of Justice's position that the accessibility regulations extend to public sidewalks.

The regulations that apply to state and local government activities also require accommodations such as auxiliary aids and services for communication[99] and facilitating the use of service animals.[100] These provisions harmonize with those that apply to public accommodations under the ADA title III regulations.[101]

---

[94] 9 F.3d 1067 (3d Cir. 1993).

[95] 28 C.F.R. § 35.151(e) (2006).

[96] 292 F.3d 1073 (9th Cir. 2002).

[97] *See* 29 U.S.C. § 794(b)(1)(A) (2006).

[98] *See* H.R. Rep. No. 101-485(II), at 84 (1990), *reprinted in* 1990 U.S.C.C.A.N. 303, 367.

[99] 28 C.F.R. § 35.160(b) (2011).

[100] § 35.136.

[101] *See supra* Chapter 5 (discussing duties of public accommodations).

§ 6.07 STATE AND LOCAL GOVERNMENT AND FEDERALLY FUNDED PROGRAMS: REMEDIES

Title II adopts the remedies applicable to section 504.[102] Remedial issues with regard to title II and section 504 include a number of topics. Among the more prominent are whether there is a need for administrative exhaustion; what the scope of injunctive relief is; when may damages relief be obtained; and whether Eleventh Amendment immunities operate to restrict otherwise available remedies in cases against state agencies.

[A] Exhaustion Issues

Section 504 has been held not to require exhaustion of administrative remedies.[103] For this reason, most courts have found that even employment claims, which if brought under title I would have to be exhausted through EEOC procedures, need not be filed administratively with the EEOC.[104] Of course, in the Ninth Circuit, which rejects the application of title II to employment, persons with employment cases must proceed under title I and file with the EEOC.[105] If the governmental employer receives federal funds, however, it appears the plaintiff could proceed solely under section 504 and bypass exhaustion.

[B] Injunctive Relief

The section 504 remedies incorporated by title II include injunctive relief. Voluntary compliance with an injunction does not necessarily justify vacating the injunction.[106]

---

[102] *See* 42 U.S.C. § 12133 (2006) ("The remedies, procedures, and rights set forth in section 794a of Title 29 shall be the remedies, procedures, and rights this subchapter provides to any person alleging discrimination on the basis of disability in violation of section 12132 of this title.").

[103] Tuck v. HCA Health Servs., 7 F.3d 465 (6th Cir. 1993); *see* Smith v. Robinson, 468 U.S. 992 (1984), *superseded by statute*, 20 U.S.C. § 1415(*l*) (2006) (recognizing general absence of exhaustion requirement for section 504 claims). An exception applies if a statute specifically subjects claims in a given area to an exhaustion requirement, as with some special education-related cases. *See supra* Chapter 4.

[104] *E.g.*, Bledsoe v. Palm Beach County Soil & Water Conservation Dist., 133 F.3d 816, 824 (11th Cir. 1998); Dominguez v. City of Council Bluffs, Iowa, 974 F. Supp. 732, 737 (S.D. Iowa 1997); Dertz v. City of Chicago, 912 F. Supp. 319, 324–25 (N.D. Ill. 1995); Petersen v. University of Wis. Bd. of Regents, 818 F. Supp. 1276, 1279 (W.D. Wis. 1993).

[105] Zimmerman v. Oregon Dep't of Justice, 170 F.3d 1169 (9th Cir. 1999).

[106] Sheely v. MRI Radiology Network, P.A., 505 F.3d 1173, 1184–89 (11th Cir. 2007) (holding that claims for declaratory and injunctive relief were not moot when policy was changed due to desire to avoid liability); Tandy v. City of Wichita, 380 F.3d 1277 (10th Cir. 2004) (refusing to vacate injunction after change in policy that previously permitted bus drivers to deny transportation to individuals with disabilities); *see also* authorities discussed *supra* § 5.07 (discussing injunctive relief and mootness in public accommodations cases).

[C]   Damages Relief

Section 504 remedies incorporated by title II include compensatory damages relief, at least for conduct that meets an intent standard.[107] The intentionality may include bad faith or gross misjudgment,[108] or deliberate indifference.[109] Courts that reject damages claims when intent has not been shown typically reason that precedent under title VI of the Civil Rights Act, whose language was the model for section 504 and whose remedies are incorporated by section 504, permits damages only for intentional discrimination.[110]

Punitive damages are not available under section 504 and title II. In *Barnes v. Gorman*, the Supreme Court reversed a court of appeals decision that reinstated a punitive damages award the district court had vacated.[111] The plaintiff, a person with paraplegia who used a wheelchair and lacked control over his urination, was arrested outside a bar. While waiting for a police van, he was denied permission to get to a washroom to empty his urine bag. When the van arrived, it could not accommodate his wheelchair, so the police took him out of the chair and strapped him to the van's bench. He loosened a strap to relieve pressure on the urine bag but as a result fell to the floor, rupturing the bag and injuring his back and shoulder. He later suffered a bladder infection, lower back pain, and uncontrollable spasms in his paralyzed areas, which forced him to miss work. The jury awarded him over $1 million in compensatory damages and $1.2 million in punitive damages in his suit under section 504 and title II.

Justice Scalia's opinion noted that the two statutes are enforceable through private causes of action, that title II incorporates the remedies of section 504, and that section 504 incorporates the remedies of title VI of the Civil Rights Act of 1964. The Court said that title VI invokes congressional power to place conditions on the grant of federal funds and declared that Spending Clause legislation is in the nature of a contract by which the recipient agrees to abide by federally imposed conditions in return for federal funds. As explained in *Pennhurst State School and Hospital v. Halderman*,[112] the contract must be voluntary, so the conditions must be unambiguous. A recipient is on notice that it is subject not only

---

[107] Sheely v. MRI Radiology Network, P.A., 505 F.3d 1173, 1204 (11th Cir. 2007) (holding that emotional distress damages are available for violations of section 504); *see* Barnes v. Gorman, 536 U.S. 181, 185 (2002) (noting in damages case that section 504 and title II provide private right of action).

[108] *E.g.*, Mark H. v. Lemahieu, 513 F.3d 922, 938–39 & n.15 (9th Cir. 2008) ("[T]o the extent that the district court concluded that the H. family, in order to recover damages, is required to demonstrate a mental state greater than deliberate indifference to the requirements imposed by the FAPE regulations, it erred."); M.P. v. Independent Sch. Dist. No. 721, 326 F.3d 975 (8th Cir. 2003); McKellar v. Pennsylvania Dep't of Educ., No. 98 CV 4161, 1999 U.S. Dist. LEXIS 2194 (E.D. Pa. Feb. 23, 1999); Walker v. District of Columbia, 969 F. Supp. 794 (D.D.C. 1997).

[109] *E.g.*, Bartlett v. New York Bd. of Law Exam'rs, 226 F.3d 69 (2d Cir. 2000); Scruggs v. Meriden Bd. of Educ., No. 3:03CV2224(PCD), 2005 U.S. Dist. LEXIS 19296 (D. Conn. Aug. 25, 2005), *vacated in part*, 2006 U.S. Dist. LEXIS 68120 (D. Conn. Sept. 22, 2006).

[110] *E.g.*, Ferguson v. City of Phoenix, 157 F.3d 668 (9th Cir. 1998). This position has been criticized. *See* Sande Buhai & Nina Golden, *Adding Insult to Injury: Discriminatory Intent as a Prerequisite to Damages Under the ADA*, 52 RUTGERS L. REV. 1121 (2000).

[111] 536 U.S. 181 (2002).

[112] 451 U.S. 1, 17 (1981).

to remedies explicitly provided for in the legislation but also to those traditionally available in suits for breach of contract. These include compensatory damages and injunctions, but do not generally include punitive damages. The Court saw no basis on which to imply a punitive damages remedy.

In a concurring opinion, Justice Souter, joined by Justice O'Connor, said that the analogy to contract remedies was appropriate in this case but cautioned that the analogy may not be applicable to questions such as the measure of damages. Justice Stevens, joined by Justices Ginsburg and Beyer, concurred in the judgment, but stated that the analogy to *Pennhurst* was inapt and a sounder basis for the decision was the well established principle that absent clear congressional intent to the contrary, municipalities are not subject to punitive damages. The reservations of five members of the Court about applying a contract approach to the measure of damages under title II would appear to gain support from the reality that courts awarding compensatory damages in title II and section 504 claims employ a tort measure of damages rather than the more restrictive one used in some categories of contract cases, and Congress was obviously aware of this interpretation of section 504 when it enacted title II.

[D] Eleventh Amendment Immunity

Under the principles embodied by the Eleventh Amendment to the Constitution, states and state agencies are generally immune from awards of damages by federal courts.[113] Nevertheless, Congress may abrogate the immunity when acting properly pursuant to its power to enforce the Fourteenth Amendment. Moreover, section 504 contains a provision abrogating the immunity; even if those provisions are not effective as written, it might be argued that receipt of federal funds under a statute that contains such an abrogation constitutes waiver of the immunity. Finally, title II of the ADA provides a means by which damages suits for unconstitutional disability discrimination may be brought without an Eleventh Amendment obstacle.

The Supreme Court considered the effectiveness of the ADA's abrogation of state immunity from suits for damages in two cases.[114] In *Board of Trustees of the University of Alabama v. Garrett*, the Supreme Court ruled that Congress did not validly abrogate state immunity from suit for damages in an employment case brought under title I of the ADA.[115] Two individuals with disabilities sued the defendant for damages when it refused to provide them reasonable accommodations. The district court dismissed, the court of appeals reversed, and the Supreme Court reversed and upheld the dismissal. Arguing from the Supreme Court's case law regarding the scope of congressional authority in section 5 of the Fourteenth Amendment to enforce the rights of equal protection and due process contained in section 1 of the Fourteenth Amendment, the state contended that the

[113] Eleventh Amendment immunity generally does not bar injunctive relief. *Ex parte* Young, 209 U.S. 123 (1908). In addition, it does not apply to local government entities. *See* Mt. Healthy City Sch. Dist. Bd. of Educ. v. Doyle, 429 U.S. 274, 280–81 (1977).

[114] A third case of significance is *United States v. Georgia*, 546 U.S. 151 (2006), discussed *infra* this section.

[115] 531 U.S. 356 (2001).

remedy provided in title I was not proportionate to and congruent with any violation of equal protection. Thus, the abrogation of the immunity was invalid. The Supreme Court agreed in an opinion by Chief Justice Rehnquist. It restricted its decision to employment claims under title I of the ADA, dismissing certiorari on the question whether state employers may be sued for damages under title II.[116] The Court reasoned that rational-basis scrutiny applies to claims that disability discrimination violates the Fourteenth Amendment, hence accommodations are not constitutionally required when denial of them can be rational. The Court also found that there was no congressional identification of a pattern of unconstitutional employment discrimination against people with disabilities by states, so title I was not proportional to and congruent with the constitutional violations as a prophylactic measure against unconstitutional discrimination. Justice Kennedy, joined by Justice O'Connor, concurred, noting among other things the continuing availability of actions brought by the United States against the states.

Justice Breyer dissented in an opinion joined by Justices Stevens, Souter, and Ginsburg. The dissent stressed the large amount of evidence in the legislative record of state-supported discrimination against persons with disabilities, evidence the majority rejected because it was not sufficiently tied to employment and not clearly enough identified as instances of irrational, therefore unconstitutional, discrimination. Justice Breyer noted that legislatures cannot be expected to develop evidence in support of their actions with the specificity one would expect from a court, and otherwise disputed the majority's characterizations. The opinion also rejected the requirement that the legislative record had to show irrationality with a level of scrutiny that would be required in constitutional litigation. It saw a need to defer to Congress in determining the necessary scope of laws to enforce the Fourteenth Amendment.

In the next opinion interpreting the scope of Eleventh Amendment immunity, the Supreme Court declined to extend *Garrett,* and found that the Family and Medical Leave Act was a valid exercise of congressional power as a prophylactic measure to combat unconstitutional sex discrimination.[117] The Court emphasized the elevated standard of equal protection review that applies to sex-based classifications and the recognition by Congress that gender stereotypes with regard to caregiving persist and that employers rely on them.

In *Tennessee v. Lane,* the Court took on the question whether title II validly abrogates Eleventh Amendment immunity, and held that title II does abrogate the immunity as applied to cases implicating the fundamental right of access to the courts.[118] As noted above, in *Lane,* the plaintiff was a man with paraplegia who on one occasion had to crawl up two flights of steps to reach an inaccessible courtroom to answer criminal charges, and on another refused to crawl or be carried in his wheelchair and so was rearrested and jailed for failure to appear. He sued for damages, and the court of appeals affirmed on interlocutory appeal a decision that

---

[116] The Court's decision to decline to decide the claim under title II stemmed from its observation that the parties had not developed the issue, and controversy existed whether title II even applied to employment. *Id.* at 360 n.1.

[117] Nevada Dep't of Human Res. v. Hibbs, 538 U.S. 721 (2003).

[118] 541 U.S. 509 (2004).

the case could proceed despite an Eleventh Amendment objection. The Supreme Court affirmed in an opinion by Justice Stevens.[119] It ruled that Congress unequivocally manifested its intent to abrogate the immunity, and that the abrogation fit within congressional power to enforce the Fourteenth Amendment. The Court noted that title II, like title I, seeks to enforce the Equal Protection Clause's ban on irrational disability discrimination, but it also seeks to enforce a variety of other constitutional guarantees that are subject to more searching judicial review. Access to the courts is one such guarantee, protected by the Sixth Amendment in criminal cases and the Fifth in civil proceedings, as well as by the First with respect to persons seeking to attend proceedings. The Court stressed the backdrop of pervasive discrimination by state government against persons with disabilities, including the deprivation of fundamental rights, and it noted the extensive materials in the legislative record of title II, including evidence related directly to access to courts. It drew an analogy to the Family and Medical Leave Act case and noted that the right of access to courts also calls for a review at least as searching, if not more so, than in gender discrimination cases. It also noted that the remedy provided in title II is a limited one, restricted by limits on the duty of reasonable modification and other duties. Justice Ginsburg, joined by Justices Souter and Breyer, filed a concurrence, questioning the wisdom of requiring extensive legislative records in order to find a valid abrogation of immunity.[120]

Chief Justice Rehnquist dissented in an opinion joined by Justices Kennedy and Thomas. The dissent portrayed the case as closer to *Garrett* than the majority let on. Justice Rehnquist doubted that the legislative record contained much evidence of unconstitutional discrimination by the states, particularly unconstitutional discrimination relating to access to courts. The dissent thought the coverage of title II's terms far too broad for any constitutional violations that might exist. Justice Scalia filed a separate dissent.

Subsequent to *Lane*, a number of courts have found title II to abrogate Eleventh Amendment immunity in suits alleging failure to provide accommodations in post-secondary education.[121] It remains to be seen how broadly the courts will apply *Lane*, or, conversely, what the ultimate reach of *Garrett* might be.

Even if title II were not to be found to work a valid abrogation of Eleventh Amendment immunity in a given field, a state might still be deemed to have waived the immunity in a suit under section 504, for states have accepted money from the federal government while aware of an abrogation of Eleventh Amendment immunity applicable to section 504. Several courts of appeals have adopted this view,[122] although the Second Circuit has rejected it with regard to the time period

---

[119] The Court also upheld the claim of a court reporter with paraplegia who alleged deprivation of the opportunity to attend proceedings. *See id.* at 514.

[120] Justice Souter, joined by Justice Ginsburg, also filed a concurring opinion.

[121] Bowers v. NCAA, 475 F.3d 524 (3d Cir. 2007); Toledo v. Sanchez, 454 F.3d 24 (1st Cir. 2006); Constantine v. Rectors & Visitors of George Mason Univ., 411 F.3d 474 (4th Cir. 2005); Association for Disabled Americans v. Florida Int'l Univ., 405 F.3d 954 (11th Cir. 2005).

[122] *See, e.g.,* Miller v. Texas Tech. Univ. Health Scis. Ctr., 421 F.3d 342 (5th Cir. 2005); Douglas v. California Dep't of Youth Auth., 271 F.3d 812, *amended, id.* at 910 (9th Cir. 2001); Nihiser v. Ohio Environmental Protection Agency, 269 F.3d 626 (6th Cir. 2001); Jim C. v. United States, 235 F.3d 1079

before the state had reason to believe it had any immunity to waive by accepting the funds.[123]

Title II of the ADA provides a cause of action, free of Eleventh Amendment immunity, for conduct that constitutes disability discrimination and is also an actual violation the Fourteenth Amendment, including any violation of the provisions of the Bill of Rights incorporated into the Fourteenth Amendment by operation of the Due Process Clause. In *United States v. Georgia*, a prisoner with paraplegia alleged that he was confined 23 to 24 hours a day in a narrow cell where he could not even turn his wheelchair.[124] He was denied assistance with showering and toileting, and injured himself attempting to transfer to the toilet and shower on his own. At times, he had to sit in his urine or feces when prison personnel refused to assist him. He claimed denial of needed physical therapy and medical treatment as well as denial of access to virtually all prison programs. The lower courts did not permit the plaintiff's title II damages claims to proceed, but the Supreme Court reversed. The Court assumed that the conduct alleged violated both title II of the ADA and the Eighth Amendment's prohibition on cruel and unusual punishment. It declared that section 5 of the Fourteenth Amendment empowers Congress to create a damages remedy for actual violations of the Fourteenth Amendment, such as those alleged by the plaintiff. "This [section 5] enforcement power includes the power to abrogate state sovereign immunity by authorizing private suits for damages against the States."[125] Accordingly, the plaintiff's damages claim could go forward. The Court's analysis would appear to extend to all violations of constitutional rights, such as equal protection, due process, or the provisions of the Bill of Rights incorporated into the Due Process Clause of the Fourteenth Amendment, when the government's conduct is also barred by title II.

(8th Cir. 2000); Koslow v. Pennsylvania, 302 F.3d 161 (3d Cir. 2002).

[123] *See* Garcia v. S.U.N.Y. Health Sci. Ctr., 280 F.3d 98 (2d Cir. 2001).

[124] 546 U.S. 151 (2006).

[125] *Id.* at 159; *see* Bolmer v. Oliveira, 594 F.3d 134, 145–49 (2d Cir. 2010) (holding title II's abrogation of immunity effective in case implicating substantive due process right to be free from unjustified civil commitment).

Chapter 7

HOUSING, TRANSPORTATION, TELECOMMUNICATIONS, AND ADDITIONAL DISCRIMINATION TOPICS

§ 7.01 HOUSING DISCRIMINATION

Although section 504 of the Rehabilitation Act[1] and titles II[2] and III[3] of the ADA forbid some residential discrimination on the basis of disability, the primary source of housing discrimination protection is the Fair Housing Act Amendments of 1988 (FHAA).[4] The 1988 Amendments to the original Fair Housing Act extended its reach from discrimination on the basis of race, color, religion, national origin, and sex to familial status and "handicap," the term for disability prevalent at the time.[5] The Act's protection of individuals with disabilities thus predated the ADA. Even though many years have elapsed since passage of the FHAA, accessible housing remains an unfulfilled goal for disability rights advocates. Topics relevant to housing discrimination may be examined by discussing the FHAA's terms themselves, their application to facial and disparate treatment discrimination, their application to cases alleging failure to provide reasonable accommodation and disparate impact discrimination, the interpretation of the various exemptions and defenses found in the statute, and then the remedies provided by the law.

---

[1] 29 U.S.C. § 794 (2006). This statute applies to federally funded activity, and so prohibits discrimination against persons with disabilities by municipal housing authorities, colleges operating dormitories, or other federal funds grantees.

[2] 42 U.S.C. § 12132 (2006). Title II of the ADA applies to state and local government activities, so it too applies to municipal housing authorities and to public colleges; it applies to other state and local government providers of housing, even if they do not receive federal funds.

[3] 42 U.S.C. § 12182 (2006). As a general matter, housing subject to the FHAA is not covered by title III, but development sales and rental offices not covered by the FHAA must meet title III accessibility requirements, and temporary-stay social service accommodations must meet title III standards as well.

[4] 42 U.S.C. §§ 3601–3619 (2006).

[5] The term is given the familiar definition so as to include "(1) a physical or mental impairment which substantially limits one or more of such person's major life activities, (2) a record of having such an impairment, or (3) being regarded as having such an impairment," but current illegal use of or addiction to a controlled substance is not included. 42 U.S.C. § 3602(h) (2006). Because the "handicap" language is currently viewed by many as stigmatizing, this chapter will generally refer to persons denoted in the FHAA as "handicapped" persons as persons or individuals "with disabilities" and substitute the term "disability" for "handicap" as appropriate. One prominent case, relying in part the congruence of purpose between the ADA and the FHAA, ruled that the definition extended to recovering drug addicts and other former drug users who had completed at least one drug-free year in a treatment program. United States v. Southern Mgmt. Corp., 955 F.2d 914 (4th Cir. 1992) (affirming injunctive relief but reversing monetary relief).

[A] Overview of the FHAA

The basic prohibition of disability discrimination in the FHAA forbids discrimination in the sale or rental, or otherwise making unavailable or denying, a dwelling to any buyer or renter because of the disability of the buyer or renter, the person intending to reside in the dwelling, or a person associated with that person.[6] The Act also forbids discrimination against any person in the terms, conditions, or privileges of sale or rental of a dwelling or services or facilities in connection with the dwelling because of the disability of the person, the person residing in or intending to reside in the dwelling, or any person associated with that person.[7] Advertising that indicates a preference, limit, or discrimination on the basis of disability is forbidden,[8] as is falsely representing to any person because of disability that a dwelling is not available for sale or rental.[9]

The FHAA also bars refusal to permit, at the expense of the person with a disability, reasonable modifications of existing premises that person occupies or will be occupying, if the modifications may be necessary for full enjoyment of the premises (although in a rental arrangement, the landlord may, if it is reasonable, condition the modification on an agreement by the renter to restore the interior premises to the condition before the modification).[10] A court applying this provision granted a preliminary injunction to compel a trailer park to permit a person living there to install a wheelchair ramp that wrapped around the front and side of her trailer and protruded out into her driveway, even though it would impede the removal of the trailer and diminish the usefulness of the driveway for parking.[11] The court placed the burden on defendant to show an undue burden.

An additional provision of the FHAA forbids refusal to make reasonable accommodations in rules, policies, practices, or services, when the accommodations are needed to afford equal opportunity to use and enjoy the dwelling.[12] The basic requirement of nondiscrimination and the additional provisions regarding such matters as reasonable accommodations in rules, policies, practices, and services are applicable to government conduct as well as that of private individuals and entities. Accordingly, discriminatory zoning decisions may be challenged under the Act.[13]

---

[6] 42 U.S.C. § 3604(f)(1) (2006).

[7] § 3604(f)(2).

[8] § 3604(c).

[9] § 3604(d). The Act also forbids anyone from, for profit, inducing or attempting to induce a person to sell or rent a dwelling by representations regarding the entry or prospective entry into the neighborhood of persons with a particular disability. § 3604(e). Discrimination in residential real estate related transactions, such as making of loans, is also forbidden, § 3605, as is discrimination in the provision of brokerage services, § 3606.

[10] § 3604(f)(3)(A).

[11] United States v. Freer, 864 F. Supp. 324 (W.D.N.Y. 1994).

[12] 42 U.S.C. § 3604(f)(3)(B) (2006).

[13] See, e.g., Oconomowoc Residential Programs, Inc. v. City of Milwaukee, 300 F.3d 775, 783 (7th Cir. 2002); see also H.R. REP. No. 100–711, at 24 (1988), reprinted in 1988 U.S.C.C.A.N. 2173, 2185 (noting applicability of FHAA provisions to state and local land use and health and safety regulations, laws, practices, and decisions).

For covered multifamily dwellings to be first occupied after March 19, 1991, the Act requires that they be designed and constructed so that (1) the public use and common use portions of the dwellings are readily accessible to and usable by persons with disabilities; (2) all the doors designed to enter the premises and within the premises and dwellings are wide enough to allow passage by persons in wheelchairs; (3) and the premises within the dwellings all have the following basic accessibility features: an accessible route into and through the dwelling; light switches, electrical outlets, thermostats and other environmental controls in accessible locations; reinforcements in bathroom walls to allow the later installation of grab bars; and kitchens and bathrooms made so that a person in a wheelchair can maneuver about the space.[14]

"Covered multifamily dwellings" has the specific meaning of buildings consisting of four or more units if the buildings have one or more elevators, and ground floor units in other buildings consisting of four or more units.[15] These provisions have been applied to require, for example, that an apartment complex be built so that ground floor units would have accessible front doors leading out to a landing that was a common use area, rather than front doors that were up a set of steps from the landing, even when accessible back patio doors were furnished.[16]

[B] Facial Discrimination and Disparate Treatment

Courts have reached a variety of conclusions in applying the FHAA's general prohibitions against discrimination. Many cases deal with municipal zoning or other governmental land use decisions that prevent group homes for people with disabilities from locating in one or another area. These cases frequently allege facial discrimination or other discrimination that may be classed as intentional, though issues of discriminatory impact and reasonable accommodation may also come into play. In *Larkin v. Michigan Department of Social Services*, the Sixth Circuit Court of Appeals affirmed a judgment in favor of a person who proposed to operate an adult foster care facility for up to four individuals with disabilities against a state agency that had denied her a license.[17] The agency had denied the operator the license after the municipality where the facility was to be located determined that the proposed location was within 1,500 feet of an existing adult foster care facility. State law required that the state agency notify the community where the proposed facility was to be located and that the agency not issue a license if another licensed residential facility existed within a 1,500 foot radius of the proposed location (unless permitted by local zoning ordinances) or if issuance of the license would lead to excessive concentration of residential facilities in the community.

The court of appeals ruled that the state law provisions were facially discriminatory, and so even if they were passed with a benign intent to benefit

---

[14] 42 U.S.C. § 3604(f)(3)(C) (2006).

[15] § 3604(f)(7).

[16] United States v. Edward Rose & Sons, 384 F.3d 258 (6th Cir. 2004) (upholding preliminary injunction).

[17] 89 F.3d 285 (6th Cir. 1996).

persons with disabilities, they could not stand unless justified by the defendants. Not adopting a simple rational-basis test for this determination, the court said that the defendants had to demonstrate that the statute's provisions were warranted by the unique and specific needs and abilities of the persons with disabilities to whom the regulations applied. The defendants failed to meet the burden. Although defendants justified the provisions on the ground they prevented clustering and the creation of ghettos or an institutional environment, the court said that integration did not justify the imposition of quotas, especially when the burden fell on the disadvantaged minority. The provisions limited the number of adult foster care facilities in an area rather than the number of persons with disabilities, but many persons with disabilities have no choice but to live in such a facility, and if that were not so, the provisions would not prevent clustering. Furthermore, no evidence was produced that the facilities would cluster without the operation of the statute. People with disabilities were permitted to choose to live near other people with disabilities. Though deinstitutionalization is a worthy goal, spacing of 1,500 feet was not needed to meet that goal. The *Larkin* court distinguished *Familystyle of St. Paul, Inc. v. City of St. Paul*[18] on the ground that in that case, the organization already housed 119 people with disabilities within a few city blocks, producing a much greater threat of recreating institutionalized settings in a local community. Even the notice requirements were held to lack justification.

The *Familystyle* case may be somewhat more difficult to reconcile with *Larkin* than the court let on. In *Familystyle*, the Eighth Circuit Court of Appeals affirmed a grant of summary judgment against an organization that operated residential group homes for mentally ill persons and had been denied special use permits to enable it to add three houses to its existing campus of group homes, expanding the capacity from 119 to 130. The court in that case declared that deinstitutionalization was a state priority, and that the priority was advanced by a requirement that new group homes be located at least a quarter mile from an existing residential program unless given a conditional use or special use permit by local authorities. The district court had determined that the dispersal requirements in their effect and on their face limited housing choices for persons with mental illness. The burden thus shifted to the defendant to show that the rules were necessary to promote a governmental interest commensurate with the level of scrutiny afforded the class of persons harmed by the rule. The court of appeals applied the rational basis test drawn from *City of Cleburne v. Cleburne Living Center*[19] to the case, and said that the governmental interest of deinstitutionalization was sufficiently advanced by the rule. Although *Familystyle* and *Larkin* are obviously distinguishable in that the *Familystyle* plaintiff was pushing for a concentration of persons with disabilities in a given location that ran a much greater risk of creating an institution-like environment, the cases appear to clash quite directly on whether an approximate quarter-mile dispersal rule can be upheld, and their methods differ in the extreme. *Larkin* imposed an exacting test of justification, where *Familystyle* imposed a lax one, and *Larkin* alone relied on the right of persons with disabilities to live wherever they chose and drew a close analogy between persons with

---

[18] 923 F.2d 91 (8th Cir. 1991).

[19] 473 U.S. 432 (1985).

disabilities and members of other minority groups protected by the Fair Housing Act. At least with regard to municipal defendants, the *Familystyle* case would appear to establish no higher duties than those already established by equal protection doctrine under *Cleburne*.[20]

Another case that provides a counterpoint to *Larkin*, this one on the issue of whether a zoning restriction ought to be viewed as facial discrimination against persons with disabilities, is the Third Circuit's *Community Services, Inc. v. Wind Gap Municipal Authority*.[21] In *Community Services*, the plaintiff for-profit corporation leased a house in which it provided care for three women with mental retardation. Initially, the house sheltered only one resident, whose family had established a trust to retain the house for her use. To make the arrangement continue to work economically, two other women with mental retardation moved into the house so all could receive services from the same caregivers. Although the municipality gave zoning approval to operate a group home on the premises, it changed the house's status from "residential" to "commercial," which entailed greatly increased sewer charges. The new commercial status was based on defendant's classification of the house as a "personal care home," which the relevant regulations did not define but which was included as an example in the regulations' "Commercial Unit" classification. Plaintiff sued under the FHAA, and the district court granted plaintiff's motion for summary judgment. The district court reasoned that since persons who need "personal care" are, by definition, persons with disabilities, "personal care home" status was a proxy for disability status under the Act and the classification therefore was facially discriminatory. It also found discriminatory impact discrimination and failure to afford reasonable accommodations.

The court of appeals reversed and remanded. The court identified the issue as whether different treatment of a personal care home was necessarily disability-based and thus facially discriminatory. The court concluded that it was not. The court noted that, on its face, the term "personal care home" has no relation to disabled status and could include facilities housing persons with or without disabilities. The court said the record lacked evidence of disparate treatment showing that an individual's need for a personal care home was a proxy for disability, and that it was possible that a shelter for battered women or neglected juveniles could be included in the category. Moreover, the court stated that, even if a personal care home could be equated with a home for persons with disabilities, in this case the house's new commercial status was based more on its commercial nature than on disability. The court distinguished what it termed "true 'proxy' cases" like *Larkin* on the ground that they included four elements:

> [F]irst, the alleged discriminatory classification was actually defined by the challenged regulation in terms that largely coincided with the FHAA

---

[20] A number of courts have labeled *Familystyle* an outlier. *See* Sierra v. City of New York, 552 F. Supp. 2d 428, 431 (S.D.N.Y. 2008) (noting that Sixth, Ninth, and Tenth Circuits "have applied more searching scrutiny"; finding rational basis scrutiny inappropriate); *see also* Jeffrey O v. Boca Raton, 511 F. Supp. 2d 1339, 1350–51 (S.D. Fla. 2007) (contrasting other courts' approaches with that of *Familystyle*).

[21] 421 F.3d 170 (3d Cir. 2005).

definition of "handicap"; second, the classification was used specifically to "single out" facilities for handicapped individuals for different treatment "because of" their disability; third, there was often direct or circumstantial evidence of discriminatory animus indicating an intent to discriminate "because of" the disabled status of the facilities' residents; and fourth, the defendant's purported reason for treating plaintiff's facility differently was predicated on a justification for treating disabled persons differently that was of questionable legitimacy.[22]

These elements were not present in this case, and so the theory was not available. In fact, with regard to the last, the court believed that commercial facilities, in general, might have greater needs for water and sewer services, justifying higher charges. The court said that the summary judgment for plaintiff on the issue should be reversed and summary judgment entered for defendant.

Finally, the court reversed plaintiff's grant of summary judgment on the disparate impact and reasonable accommodation claims. As to disparate impact, the court said the district court's ruling was based in large part on its erroneous finding that defendant failed to present legitimate reasons for the house's being reclassified as commercial, and too many material factual issues existed concerning this claim. As to reasonable accommodation, issues of fact existed there as well. The parties and the district court were more focused on the discriminatory classification claim, and the record was not adequately developed on such issues as whether accommodations had properly been requested and if so whether and why they were rejected.[23]

Facial discrimination remains a viable theory in cases involving municipal action against group facilities, but the *Community Services* case makes clear that the issue of whether facial discrimination exists will not necessarily be taken for granted, just as the *Familystyle* case makes clear that different approaches may be taken over whether differing treatment on the basis of disability is justified if the differing treatment can be shown to have taken place.

[C] Reasonable Accommodation and Disparate Impact

As the latter part of the *Community Services* opinion suggests, cases concerning zoning decisions for group facilities may also call into play the FHAA's requirement that reasonable accommodations be made in rules, policies, practices, or services, when the accommodations may be necessary to afford a person with a disability equal opportunity to use and enjoy a dwelling.[24] *Community Services* did

---

[22] *Id.* at 180.

[23] On remand, *Community Servs., Inc. v. Wind Gap Mun. Auth.*, No. CIV.A. 02-8366, 2006 U.S. Dist. LEXIS 54948 (E.D. Pa., Aug. 7, 2006), the district court dismissed the case on mootness grounds. Before trial, defendant changed the house's status back to residential, returned excess fee payments, and amended the regulation under which it had classified the property as commercial, to provide that home facilities that have residents who qualify under the FHAA would be charged residential sewer fees. *Id.* at *1–2.

[24] *See* 42 U.S.C. § 3604(f)(3)(B) (2006).

not develop the issue, but other cases have.[25]

The proponents of a group facility were successful in using the reasonable accommodation term of the statute to overturn a decision denying them a zoning variance in *Oconomowoc Residential Programs, Inc. v. City of Milwaukee*.[26] The plaintiff provider acquired a house for six adults with developmental disabilities or traumatic brain injury but was denied an occupancy permit because of a zoning requirement that community living arrangements not be located within 2,500 feet of each other. It applied for a variance, but the Board of Zoning Appeals, after hearing objections from neighbors, voted to deny the application. The provider and prospective residents sued, calling the vote a denial of a request for a reasonable accommodation. The district court granted a motion for summary judgment against the city, and the court of appeals affirmed. The court of appeals interpreted the statutory language regarding accommodations that are necessary to afford equal opportunity as requiring a showing that without the accommodation, the plaintiff will be denied the opportunity to choose to live in a residential neighborhood or will have less opportunity to do so than people without disabilities. The court noted that a community based residential facility often provides persons with disabilities the only means by which they can live in a residential neighborhood. It said that the mere availability of the zoning variance procedure is not itself an accommodation. The city gave various reasons that a variance for the specific location of the house was not a reasonable accommodation: the plaintiff provider had a history of some problems operating other group homes, the house was on a busy street without a sidewalk, and adjacent to a river that could flood. The court rejected the argument based on problems with the provider, given that they were not tied to the specific facility and the provider continued to maintain its state license to operate. There was no evidence of more police calls to the provider's other residences than to other neighborhood residences. Anecdotal evidence about the dangers of the road or the river or the behavior of the residents themselves was also inadequate and based on unfounded generalizations and stereotypes that the FHAA rejects. The plaintiffs met their burden of demonstrating that the variance was necessary to provide them an equal opportunity to use and enjoy a dwelling. One prospective resident's options were limited by the need for a wheelchair-accessible home, and two needed supportive services 24 hours a day and could not afford to live on their own. Others had similar needs. Accordingly, the plaintiffs prevailed.

In *Elderhaven, Inc. v. City of Lubbock*, the court reached a contrary result on facts similar, but not identical, to those of *Oconomowoc Residential Programs*.[27] The court affirmed a grant of summary judgment against a provider seeking to

---

[25] Other public decisions may also implicate the FHAA reasonable accommodation obligation. *See, e.g.,* Dadian v. Village of Wilmette, 269 F.3d 831 (7th Cir. 2001) (requiring municipality to permit persons with disabilities to put in driveway to street).

[26] 300 F.3d 775 (7th Cir. 2002). A contrasting case is *Harding v. City of Toledo*, 433 F. Supp. 2d 867 (N.D. Ohio 2006), in which the court denied a preliminary injunction against an ordinance requiring 500 feet of separation between adult group homes. The court distinguished *Oconomowoc Residential Programs* on the ground that 500 foot limit was less restrictive and had been adopted in accordance with a settlement agreement in another case. *Id.* at 873.

[27] 98 F.3d 175 (5th Cir. 1996).

open a shared living residence for several elderly adults with mental or physical disabilities. The plaintiff applied for a zoning variance and was denied; the city then passed an ordinance requiring that groups of five or more disabled persons could apply to the zoning board for a special exception. Plaintiff sought a special exception and was granted one for a ten-person residence, but not for the twelve-person residence it wanted to open, and so sued under the FHAA.[28] The court of appeals said that the plaintiff bears the burden of proof on reasonableness of the accommodation. Unlike the court in *Oconomowoc Residential Programs*, it did not look to ADA employment cases placing the burden of proving lack of reasonableness on the defendant after an initial showing by the plaintiff that the accommodation was needed and reasonable. It said that the plaintiff had not borne its burden to raise a genuine issue of fact as to whether the city failed to reasonably accommodate. The court noted that the city had shown flexibility and had granted almost all the permit and special exemption applications it received, and said that the plaintiff had failed to prove that the two additional residents it wanted to house at the one residence would be critical to making the arrangement feasible.

Oconomowoc Residential Programs and *Elderhaven* can be reconciled on their facts. The showing of need for the accommodation to open the house in *Oconomowoc Residential Programs* was stronger than that for the accommodation to permit two additional residents in the house in *Elderhaven*. *Elderhave* n found no occasion to discuss the competing interests or concerns of the municipality taken up in *Oconomowoc Residential Programs*, but the weakness of the municipality's objections discussed in *Oconomowoc Residential Programs* provided little counterweight to the plaintiff's showing of need. There is a clear contrast between the two cases, however, in the placement of the burden of proof, with the *Oconomowoc Residential Programs* case drawing the analogy to ADA title I and the *Elderhaven* case finding no basis for a shift. The court in *Elderhave* n also placed greater weight on the defendant's conduct in other instances in approving the opening of group homes.

In the view of some courts, a failure to make use of procedures to obtain accommodations may defeat a reasonable accommodation claim. *Oxford House-C v. City of St. Louis* involved the opening of group residences for recovering alcohol and drug abusers in neighborhoods zoned for single-family dwellings.[29] The city cited the houses for violating a rule that defined single family dwellings to include group homes with eight or fewer unrelated residents with disabilities. Oxford Houses sued under the FHAA, and prevailed in district court, obtaining an injunction against enforcement of the ordinance and denial of the city's counterclaim for enforcement of the zoning ordinance. The court of appeals, however, reversed the judgment, vacated the injunction, and remanded for further consideration of the city's counterclaim. The court of appeals upheld the FHAA against a challenge that it exceeded the congressional commerce power, and found that the zoning ordinance was not a maximum occupancy limit exempt from challenge under the Act. Nevertheless, the court ruled that the rule was not

---

[28] During the litigation, plaintiff provider acquired another house and received approval for eight-person occupancy there.

[29] 77 F.3d 249 (8th Cir. 1996).

discriminatory in violation of the FHAA. Turning first to facial discrimination claims, the court said the ordinance favored residents with disabilities, in that homes other than group homes for persons with disabilities could, under local law, have no more than three unrelated persons residing together. Expert testimony indicated that a home with eight residents would have therapeutic benefits, and the court dismissed the contention that an eight-person limit would destroy the financial viability of many houses of this type as financial hardship that does not violate the FHAA as long as the city has a rational basis for the ordinance. The court then ruled that the legitimate interest in decreasing congestion, traffic and noise in residential areas and that an ordinance limiting the number of unrelated people occupying a single family residence was reasonably related to that interest. The court also dismissed testimony tending to show that city officials involved in enforcement were tainted with prejudice and unfounded fears about recovering addicts as isolated comments, and further said that inspectors, for example, were not involved in making policy.

On the specific claim that the defendant failed to provide reasonable accommodations, the court said that refusal on the part of Oxford Houses to apply for a variance was "fatal to their reasonable accommodation claim."[30] It said that like other citizens, citizens with disabilities had to make use of ordinary mechanisms to resolve their grievances before going to court: "In our view, Congress also did not intend the federal courts to act as zoning boards by deciding fact-intensive accommodation issues in the first instance."[31] It said there was no demonstration of futility to avoid the operation of this rule. Although this disposition of the issue might be criticized as the engrafting onto the FHAA of an administrative or state-remedies exhaustion requirement found nowhere in that statute, it might be defended on the ground that denial of reasonable accommodation entails the proper making of a request and willingness on the part of the plaintiff to engage in an interactive process. It perhaps may also be defended on the ground that adverse action is not final unless the plaintiff has lost after making use of the available procedures or demonstrating futility, though in this case the plaintiff felt the adverse effect immediately.

Other cases developing the reasonable accommodation duty have to do with activities of private landlords and other non-governmental defendants. In two prominent cases from the courts of appeals, the courts affirmed orders requiring apartment complexes to provide parking availability as a reasonable accommodation for tenants with multiple sclerosis who experienced hardships getting either to a distant parking location or to on-street parking.[32] Both courts relied on analogies to section 504 cases in applying the reasonable accommodation obligation. Providing a contrast to those cases, a court of appeals rejected a reasonable accommodation claim and affirmed a grant of summary judgment for the defendant in a case challenging the threatened eviction of a man with mental

---

[30] *Id.* at 253.

[31] *Id.*

[32] Jankowski Lee & Assocs. v. Cisneros, 91 F.3d 891 (7th Cir. 1996); Shapiro v. Cadman Towers, Inc., 51 F.3d 328 (2d Cir. 1995); *see also* Astralis Condo. Ass'n v. Secretary, U.S. Dep't of Hous. & Urban Dev., 620 F.3d 62 (1st Cir. 2010) (enforcing order requiring parking space accommodation).

illness who had been the subject of complaints that he slammed doors and screamed throughout the night.[33] The apartment complex's agent had added soundproofing to a door and delayed action on the eviction so that a counselor could work with the tenant making the noise. Ultimately, however, the tenant received an eviction notice. The court placed the burden on the tenant to establish the reasonableness of the possible accommodations he proposed: relocating him or the neighbor who had complained, finding a hard of hearing tenant to live above him, making a standing arrangement to contact the tenant's social worker when complaints occurred, or adding more soundproofing. The court went through each proposal and found it either impractical or a fundamental alteration not required by the Act.

Fees imposed by landlords for services or amenities disproportionately needed by individuals with disabilities may create a disparate impact; if waivers are denied, the denial may constitute a failure to provide reasonable accommodation. In *United States v. California Mobile Home Park Management Co.*, the court reversed a judgment of dismissal in a case alleging a violation of the FHAA in charging and refusing to waive fees for the presence of a long-term guest and guest parking.[34] The plaintiff's young daughter had a respiratory disease and needed the presence of a home health aide. The management company demanded $1.50 a day for the presence of a long-term guest on the premises and $25 a month for parking. The court relied on the duty to reasonably accommodate, drawing on section 504 cases interpreting the obligation. It cited legislative history from the FHAA that expressed an intent to prohibit the application of otherwise neutral rules and regulations affecting health, safety, or land use in a manner that discriminates against individuals with disabilities.[35] It said that fees that affect residents with and without disabilities equally were proper, but that a highly fact-specific, case-by-case inquiry needed to be made on whether waiver would be a reasonable accommodation. Because the decision on a motion to dismiss did not include that inquiry, the court reversed.[36] Some courts have suggested that reasonable accommodation need only be provided to relieve people with disabilities from the burden of rules that hurt them by reason of their disabilities rather than by reason of things they have in common with others, such as scarcity of housing or limited resources.[37] Nevertheless, *California Mobile Home Park* and the various cases stressing the economic need for shared living arrangements demonstrate that economic concerns of persons with disabilities must be taken into account in disparate impact and reasonable accommodations cases under the FHAA and other laws bearing on disability discrimination claims.[38]

---

[33] Groner v. Golden Gate Gardens Apartments, 250 F.3d 1039 (6th Cir. 2001).

[34] 29 F.3d 1413 (9th Cir. 1994). The plaintiff complained to the Department of Housing and Urban Development, which determined that reasonable cause existed for a violation of the FHAA; the Department of Justice prosecuted the claim on the plaintiff's behalf.

[35] *Id.* at 1417 (citing H.R. Rep. No. 100–711, at 24 (1988), *reprinted* in 1988 U.S.C.C.A.N. at 2185).

[36] On remand, the court entered judgment for defendant following a bench trial, and the court of appeals affirmed. United States v. California Mobile Home Park Mgmt. Co., 107 F.3d 1374 (9th Cir. 1997).

[37] *See, e.g.,* Hemisphere Bldg. Co. v. Village of Richton Park, 171 F.3d 437, 440 (7th Cir. 1999).

[38] *See also* Giebeler v. M&B Assocs., 343 F.3d 1143, 1154 (9th Cir. 2003) (noting that *Hemisphere Building Co.* and similar case, Salute v. Stratford Greens Garden Apartments, 136 F.3d 293 (2d Cir.

Courts have considered whether landlords or other defendants might be forced to waive a no-animals policy for individuals who need service animals because of their disabilities. In *Bronk v. Ineichen*, the court considered a damages action brought by two women who were profoundly deaf against their landlord, who refused to allow them to have a dog that they said had been trained by the brother of one of them to assist them.[39] The court declared that, "Balanced against a landlord's economic or aesthetic concerns as expressed in a no-pets policy, a deaf individual's need for the accommodation afforded by a hearing dog is, we think, per se reasonable within the meaning of the statute."[40] In the actual case, however, there was evidence that the dog lacked the skills to be anything other than a pet. Rather than affirm a jury verdict against the plaintiffs, the court vacated the judgment and ordered a new trial because the jury instructions implied that the dog needed to have service animal school training to be considered a reasonable accommodation. Instead, the jury should have been instructed to weigh the degree to which the dog in fact aided the plaintiffs in meeting disability related needs against any harm from waiving the no-animals policy. In other instances, courts have engaged in similar reasoning and either found waiver of no-animals rules required[41] or decided that the rules need not be waived.[42]

[D] Defenses and Exemptions

The FHAA's coverage is broad, but it does have some limits. For example, sale or rental of a single-family house by its owner ordinarily is not covered (except with regard to the advertising provision), provided that the private owner does not own more than three single-family houses at any one time and does not make use of sales or rental facilities or services of any broker, agent, salesman or other person who is in the business of selling or renting dwellings.[43] Dwellings with four or fewer families living independently of each other where the owner occupies one of the units as the owner's residence are also exempt.[44] The FHAA also specifically permits religious organizations to give preference to co-religionists, and private clubs may restrict lodgings they own or operate to members or give them preference.[45] The Act also permits reasonable maximum occupancy rules

---

1998), "cannot be reconciled with the Supreme Court's analysis" of reasonable accommodations in U.S. Airways v. Barnett, 535 U.S. 391 (2002); holding that allowing provision of co-signer for lease should be considered reasonable accommodation for individual impoverished because of disability) The Seventh Circuit has adhered to its views. *See* Wisconsin Cmty. Servs., Inc. v. City of Milwaukee, 465 F.3d 737, 754–55 (7th Cir. 2006) (en banc).

[39] 54 F.3d 425 (7th Cir. 1995).

[40] *Id.* at 429.

[41] *E.g.*, Green v. Housing Auth., 994 F. Supp. 1253 (D. Or. 1998) (holding that housing authority could not require proof of training for hearing dog and granting summary judgment for plaintiff).

[42] *E.g.*, Access Now, Inc. v. Town of Jasper, 268 F. Supp. 2d 973 (E.D. Tenn.) (finding plaintiff not to be individual with disability and miniature horse not to be service animal). *See generally supra* § 5.03[A] (discussing current law regarding miniature horses and other service animals under ADA public accommodations provisions).

[43] 42 U.S.C. § 3603(b)(1) (2006). Additional conditions also apply. *See id.*

[44] § 3603(b)(2).

[45] § 3607(a).

established by federal, state, or local law.[46] The general antidiscrimination term of the Act contains a proviso that nothing in the subsection requires a dwelling to be made available to anyone whose tenancy would constitute a direct threat to the health or safety of other individuals or whose tenancy would result in substantial physical damage to the property of others.[47]

In *City of Edmonds v. Oxford House*, the Supreme Court construed the exemption that the FHAA establishes for state or local maximum occupancy laws.[48] Oxford House opened a group home for ten to twelve adults recovering from alcoholism and drug addiction. The home was in an area zoned for single-family residences and the municipality took action under a local rule stating that persons living in single-family dwelling units must compose a family, which, under local rule, meant an individual or two or more persons related by genetics, adoption, or marriage, or a group of five or fewer unrelated persons. Oxford House contended that a group home for recovering substance abusers needed eight to twelve residents to be financially and therapeutically viable, and sued the city for violation of the FHAA, but the city prevailed on summary judgment in the district court. That court ruled that the definition of the family in the local law amounted to a reasonable restriction on the maximum number of occupants permitted to occupy a dwelling, and thus it fell under the maximum occupancy exemption under the Act. The court of appeals reversed, and the Supreme Court affirmed that ruling.

The Court held that a family composition rule is different from a maximum occupancy restriction. A maximum occupancy restriction ordinarily applies uniformly to all residents of all dwelling units and is designed to protect health and safety by preventing overcrowding. A restriction of an area to single-family residences is designed to preserve the character of a neighborhood. The Court referred to *Moore v. City of East Cleveland*, which found unconstitutional a definition of family in a zoning ordinance that forbade extended families from living in the same residence.[49] The Court in that case drew a distinction between the zoning ordinance which it overturned and a separate ordinance specifying maximum occupancy for floor area, which was not challenged. The ordinance Oxford House was challenging was a classic example of a use restriction, and did not cap the number of people who could live in the dwelling. In fact, a separate ordinance specified the number of occupants per square footage of floor area. Accordingly, the definition of family did not provide an exemption to the municipality. The Court remanded for the lower courts to consider whether the city's enforcement of the family definition rule violated the FHAA.

As noted above, the FHAA does not ordinarily cover sale or rental of a single-family house by its owner, provided that the owner does not have more than three

---

[46] § 3607(b)(1).

[47] § 3604(f)(9). Courts in applying this provision have ruled that it applies only if the individual would be a direct threat if reasonable accommodations were provided, or no reasonable accommodation exists. Roe v. Housing Auth., 909 F. Supp. 814 (D. Colo. 1995) (denying defendants' motion for summary judgment); Roe v. Sugar River Mills Assocs., 820 F. Supp. 636 (D.N.H. 1993) (denying defendants' motion for summary judgment).

[48] 514 U.S. 725 (1995).

[49] 431 U.S. 494 (1977).

single-family houses at any one time, does not make use of sales or rental facilities or services of any broker, agent, salesman or other person who is in the business of selling or renting dwellings, and makes use of the exception only once in a 24-month period.[50] In *Michigan Protection & Advocacy Service, Inc. v. Babin*, the court found a defendant entitled to that exemption.[51] The court affirmed a grant of summary judgment against the plaintiffs in a case in which a real estate broker who was working for a seller of a house bought the house herself with the idea that a state agency would then lease it from her to operate a group home for mentally disabled adults. During a delay in finalizing the lease arrangements, people living near the home started a campaign against the group home. Petitions were presented and a town meeting held at which 100 persons showed up. Ultimately, someone offered to purchase the house for $5,000 more than the broker had bought the property for three months earlier. When the broker demanded $4,000 more, one of the neighbors provided the extra funds and then collected donations from other neighbors. Although the broker did not pay a commission to the brokerage agency she worked for, the closing documents bore that agency's logo and were preprinted listing the owner of the agency as broker for the sale. The court ruled that the broker fell within the exception of the FHAA because she did not own more than three homes, she had not made a similar sale in 24 months, she did not violate the advertising provision, and although she was a broker and the form papers listed the real estate agency, these facts were not for the court sufficient to take the transaction outside the statute's language.[52] Similarly, the broker whose name was on the papers and the agency prevailed because they were not actually involved in the sale. Although the neighbors, who were also defendants, might be said to have violated the "otherwise make unavailable" language of the FHAA, the court found that the term did not reach economic competition for the property, however unworthy its motivation.

[E] Remedies

Remedial avenues under the FHAA include (1) civil actions that may be brought by any aggrieved person to recover actual and punitive damages, injunctions, and attorneys' fees;[53] (2) administrative complaints filed with the Department of Housing and Urban Development (HUD) (or initiated by HUD itself), which may be referred to a state or local anti-discrimination agency, brought to court for the

---

[50] 42 U.S.C. § 3603(b)(1) (2006).

[51] 18 F.3d 337 (6th Cir. 1994).

[52] The court also said that the broker's earning of commissions on sales of other homes did not trigger the exception to the exception that applies when the owner has an interest in, or there is owned or reserved on that person's behalf, title to or any right to all or a portion of the proceeds from the sale or rental of more than three single family houses. The court said that provision would apply only to persons with a claim to proceeds of a sale because of their interest in the fee simple of the property. Although, as the court stated, commissions contracts do not affect the state of a property title, the interpretation might be criticized on the ground that the terms "title" and "right to" are separated by an "or," and it appears that the broker had a right to proceeds of sales of many houses. Perhaps the court was suggesting that there is an implied term in the statute that makes the sales matter only when the houses are owned by the person who would otherwise have the exemption, but the court did not explain why that term ought to be implied.

[53] 42 U.S.C. § 3613 (2006).

same relief as available in civil actions, or presented to an administrative law judge, who can award compensatory damages to the aggrieved person, injunctive relief, and civil penalties up to $55,000;[54] and (3) civil actions brought by the Attorney General if a defendant has engaged in a pattern or practice of resistance to rights protected by the statute or if a group has been denied rights and the denial raises an issue of general public importance, in which actions the government may recover injunctive relief, damages for aggrieved persons, and civil penalties up to $110,000.[55]

§ 7.02 TRANSPORTATION

Accessible transportation has been a major goal of the disability rights movement for more than a generation, but there are significant costs to changing a system that was created with little participation by or concern for persons with disabilities. The compromises in drafting the relevant legislation are evident, and the provisions have a highly technical character. For analysis, the topic may be divided into ground transport and air transport.

[A] Ground Transportation

With regard to public ground transportation operated by state and local government entities but not including intercity and commuter rail activities, title II of the ADA covers fixed-route systems (such as ordinary city buses that travel regular routes), paratransit service that supplements fixed-route systems, and demand-responsive systems (such as a publicly owned car service). Publicly operated commuter rail and intercity rail activities are also covered by title II, but in a separate set of provisions. Privately operated ground transportation, such as typical taxicab operations and intercity buses, are covered by title III of the ADA.

When government-operated fixed-route systems (such as those with ordinary city buses that travel regular routes) purchase or lease new vehicles, they must select only vehicles that are readily accessible to and usable by individuals with disabilities, including those who use wheelchairs.[56] If used vehicles are purchased or leased, a good faith effort to obtain accessible cars must be made.[57] Remanufactured vehicles are to be made accessible to the maximum extent feasible.[58] Exceptions apply for remanufactured vehicles that are of a historical

---

[54] §§ 3610–3612.

[55] § 3614. Remedial topics beyond the mere description of the statutory mechanisms include who has standing to sue as an aggrieved party, who is a proper defendant, when the various available relief should be awarded, statutes of limitations (particularly problematic in instances when the action is brought after new construction is completed) and a variety of other topics. For a valuable discussion of these matters in suits over accessibility of new construction, see Robert G. Schwemm, *Barriers to Accessible Housing: Enforcement Issues in "Design and Construction" Cases Under the Fair Housing Act*, 40 U. RICH. L. REV. 753 (2006).

[56] 42 U.S.C. § 12142(a) (2006).

[57] § 12142(b).

[58] § 12142(c)(1).

character.[59]

State and local government entities that operate a fixed route system other than one that provides nothing but commuter bus service also have to furnish paratransit and other special transportation services to persons with disabilities, including those who use wheelchairs.[60] These services are typically provided on a call-and-reserve basis and have accessible vans providing door to door travel. Under title II, the services have to be sufficient to provide persons with disabilities a level of service comparable to the level of designated public transportation services provided to individuals without disabilities. That includes, to the extent practicable, a response time comparable to the level of designated public transportation services provided to individuals without disabilities. Congress delegated many of the specifics of the paratransit requirements to the Department of Transportation for coverage in regulations, but also reserved a long list of things that the regulations had to say.[61] This list includes eligibility provisions; a service area definition restricting required services to the area of the public entity operating a fixed route system, other than any portion in which the entity solely provides commuter bus service; a provision allowing the public entity to escape obligations that impose an undue financial burden; a grant of authority to permit the Department of Transportation to require public entities to provide a level of services above that which the undue burden exception might otherwise allow; public participation provisions; requirements for submission of plans; and other measures.[62]

State and local governments that operate some form of demand-responsive public transportation system, such as a public car service operation or publicly operated taxi service, must purchase or lease only those new vehicles that are readily accessible to and usable by individuals with disabilities, including those who use wheelchairs, unless the system, when viewed in its entirety, provides a level of service to individuals with disabilities that is equivalent to the level of service the system provides to people who do not have disabilities.[63]

Publicly operated intercity rail and commuter rail passenger transportation systems have their own set of rules. Commuter rail passenger transportation means "short-haul rail passenger transportation in metropolitan and suburban areas usually having reduced fare, multiple-ride, and commuter tickets and morning and evening peak period operations."[64] Intercity rail refers to the operations of the National Railroad Passenger Corporation (Amtrak).[65] Commuter rail[66] and intercity rail[67] systems must provide one car per train that is readily

---

[59] § 12142(c)(2).

[60] § 12143(a).

[61] § 12143(b)–(c).

[62] § 12143(c).

[63] § 12144.

[64] 49 U.S.C.S. § 24102(3) (LexisNexis 2011) (incorporated by reference in 42 U.S.C. § 12161(2)).

[65] *See* 42 U.S.C. § 12161(3) (2006).

[66] § 12162(b). New cars must be accessible, although a few limits apply to the accessibility requirements for that equipment. If used cars are purchased or leased, a good faith effort to obtain

accessible to and usable by individuals with disabilities, including individuals who use wheelchairs, and new cars must be accessible. Station accessibility must also be provided, with a 20-year period (from 1990) for compliance for all existing intercity rail stations and a compliance period of three years (extendable to 20) for existing key stations in commuter rail systems.[68] Whenever facilities are altered, a "maximum extent feasible" accessibility requirement applies and will be enforced.[69] Courts interpreting title II have been reluctant, however, to find that the general nondiscrimination duties set out in Part A of the statute impose obligations that are greater than the specific duties applicable to public transit, which are found in Part B.[70]

A prominent case dealing with the gamut of paratransit issues is *Walter v. SEPTA*.[71] The issue was whether two individuals with mobility impairments who used wheelchairs were entitled to continued paratransit service when defendant Southeastern Pennsylvania Transportation Authority (SEPTA) changed the eligibility criteria for the service but when certain "key stations" on the defendant's rail lines were not yet accessible to individuals with disabilities. SEPTA operated several fixed-route transportation systems that included bus, subway, elevated-line, regional rail, and paratransit services. SEPTA informed plaintiffs in July, 2004, that because all buses were now equipped with wheelchair-accessible lifts or ramps, plaintiffs were no longer eligible for the paratransit service. The plaintiffs alleged that using the bus service would be much harder for them than using paratransit because, for example, they would have to transfer among several different bus routes rather than receive a single paratransit ride from one destination to another. They further alleged that some of the rail line stations were still not fully accessible for wheelchair users. If these key stations were fully accessible, it would be much easier for the plaintiffs to travel without the use of paratransit.

The deadline for SEPTA to make key stations on its rapid-transit and light rail lines fully accessible was July 26, 1993. If, however, SEPTA could show that it would incur extraordinarily expensive structural changes, it could obtain an extension until 2020, as long as two-thirds of key stations were made accessible by 2010. Likewise, the deadline for SEPTA to make key stations on its commuter rail

---

accessible cars must be made. § 12162(c). Remanufactured cars are to be made accessible to the maximum extent feasible. § 12162(d).

[67] § 12162(a)(1). New cars must be accessible, but there are some limits to the duty to purchase or lease accessible new cars with regard to wheelchair accessibility of some car types. § 12162(a)(2). The same obligations pertaining to used and remanufactured commuter train cars apply to intercity train systems.

[68] § 12162(e).

[69] Disabled in Action of Pa. v. Southeastern Pa. Transp. Auth., 635 F.3d 87 (3d Cir. 2011) (applying 42 U.S.C. § 12147(a)).

[70] *See, e.g.*, Abrahams v. MTA Long Island Bus, 644 F.3d 110, 121 (2d Cir. 2011) (finding that paratransit services are not covered by Department of Justice reasonable-modification regulation); Boose v. Tri-County Metro. Transp. Dist., 587 F.3d 997, 1001-03 (9th Cir. 2009) (upholding refusal to provide additional modifications to paratransit system); George v. Bay Area Rapid Transit, 577 F.3d 1005, 1013 (9th Cir. 2009) (denying claim for additional access features for riders with visual impairments and upholding Part B safe-harbor provision).

[71] 434 F. Supp. 2d 346 (E.D. Pa. 2006).

lines fully accessible was July 26, 1993, but it could obtain an extension for extraordinarily expensive structural changes.[72]

The plaintiffs claimed eligibility for paratransit under the Department of Transportation regulations, specifically those applicable to persons eligible for paratransit under what is termed the Category 2 definition:

> (2) Any individual with a disability who needs the assistance of a wheelchair lift or other boarding assistance device (and is able with such assistance) to board, ride, and disembark from any vehicle which is readily accessible to and usable by individuals with disabilities if the individual wants to travel on a route on the system during the hours of operation of the system at a time (or within a reasonable period of such time) when such a vehicle is not being used to provide designated public transportation on the route.[73]

The regulations pertaining to Category 2 designate specific situations in which a person is to receive paratransit services: "With respect to rail systems, an individual is eligible under this paragraph if the individual could use an accessible rail system, but — (A) there is not yet one accessible car per train on the system; or (B) key stations have not yet been made accessible."[74]

Plaintiffs argued that, because certain stations already designated by SEPTA as key stations and which they needed for their regular travel were not yet fully accessible, they remained eligible for paratransit service even though buses now were accessible. SEPTA responded that, under the statutory definitions relating directly to paratransit eligibility, plaintiffs were not eligible for paratransit service, and further contended that the regulations on which plaintiffs relied for their paratransit-eligibility theory were an unreasonable interpretation of the statute, that the plaintiffs were not eligible for paratransit service merely because not all key stations had been made fully accessible, and that paratransit eligibility did not include commuter rail lines, as one plaintiff argued.

The court denied the defendant's motion to dismiss with regard to one plaintiff and granted it with regard to the other. The court ruled that the United States Transportation Department's regulations were a reasonable interpretation of the paratransit eligibility statute. The court found that the statutory language was ambiguous regarding the applicability of paratransit obligations to rail operations within an urban area, and that the Category 2 eligibility standard was a reasonable interpretation of the statutory terms. According to the court, "it appears that in crafting the paratransit regulatory provisions, the DOT took a statute which was drafted with bus systems in mind, and applied it to rail systems by using the 'key stations' language found in other parts of the ADA," which was logical as a complement to the requirements of paratransit for bus systems.[75] Interpreting the regulations, the court said that they did not require paratransit only until a single

---

[72] *See* 42 U.S.C. § 12162(e)(2)(A)(ii)(I)–(II) (2006).

[73] 42 U.S.C. § 12143(c)(1)(A) (2006). The regulations recapitulate this statutory term.

[74] 49 C.F.R. § 37.123(e)(2)(iii) (2011).

[75] *Walter*, 434 F. Supp. 2d at 356.

key station was made accessible (as defendant argued), or until all or some specified fraction of stations achieved accessibility (as plaintiff apparently argued), but rather until those the individual seeks to use are made accessible, both at the beginning and end of the trip. The court, however, ruled that the paratransit provision, though it applies to rail systems other than long-distance commuter lines, does not apply to commuter rail lines. Since one plaintiff lived outside the city in a community served by SEPTA only through a long-distance commuter rail line, she was not covered by the paratransit provision, and the action was dismissed as to her. It continued as to the other plaintiff, who lived within the city.

There is little case law specifically on the intercity rail provisions of title II, but *Wray v. National Railroad Passenger Corp.* is one case of interest on the general topic of intercity rail travel.[76] There, the court considered whether the defendant violated the provision of the ADA that forbids coercion, threats, and intimidation of persons exercising rights under the ADA[77] when two passengers with disabilities who did not reserve disability-accessible seats on a train from Chicago to Memphis were directed to move from those seats to the seating area on the upper level of the car. One plaintiff alleged that because of medication she took for her arthritis, she needed to urinate frequently, and that due to being placed in the upstairs seating of the car, she urinated several times before reaching the bathroom, causing her discomfort and humiliation. Both plaintiffs alleged that they were injured when they received no help getting off the train and carrying their luggage. The court granted summary judgment for the defendant on the ADA coercion claim, ruling that the right to sit in the accessible seats without a reservation when demand for the seats exceeds capacity is not a right protected under the ADA. The court further noted that the conductor did not single the plaintiffs out because of their disabilities in directing them to move; instead, he chose them because they appeared somewhat less disabled than others who might have been asked to relocate. The court nevertheless ruled that the plaintiffs might have a claim under state negligence law, given Amtrak's knowledge of the disabilities and the potential ability to prevent harms to the plaintiffs by doing things other than allowing them to stay in the accessible seats.[78]

Title III of the ADA forbids discrimination on the basis of disability by privately operated public transit, such as city-to-city buses and taxicab companies. A private entity that operates a fixed route system that is not "specified public transportation" (defined as "transportation by bus, rail, and any other conveyance (other than aircraft) that provides the general public with general or special service (including charter service) on a regular and continuing basis") provided by a private entity primarily engaged in the business of transporting people, is subject to the general provisions of title III and is specifically forbidden from buying or leasing a vehicle

---

[76] 10 F. Supp. 2d 1036 (E.D. Wis. 1998).

[77] 42 U.S.C. § 12203(b) (2006). Thus, the case did not implicate the statutory provisions relating to intercity rail, and the court noted that no claim was being made that Amtrak violated the one-car-per-train rule. The court said, however, that a rule more clearly addressing the number of seats to be made accessible would be desirable. *Wray*, 10 F. Supp. 2d at 1040 n.1.

[78] The court rejected a different negligence theory based on the directive to move from the seats, citing the reservation of the right to move passengers in the railroad's tariff. *Wray*, 10 F. Supp. 2d at 1042.

that seats more than 16 (including the driver) unless the vehicle is readily accessible to and usable by individuals with disabilities, including those who use wheelchairs.[79] If the entity buys or leases a smaller vehicle after the ADA's effective date, it must operate its system so that, when viewed in its entirety, the system gives a level of service to people with disabilities, including wheelchair users, equivalent to that provided people without disabilities.[80] For private entities operating a demand responsive system that is not specified public transportation provided by a private entity primarily engaged in the business of transporting people, the system has to be operated so that when viewed in its entirety, it gives a level of service to people with disabilities, including wheelchair users, equivalent to that provided people without disabilities.[81] Vehicles with a seating capacity in excess of 16 (again, including the driver) must be accessible, unless the entity can demonstrate that, when viewed in its entirety, the system gives a level of service to people with disabilities, including wheelchair users, equivalent to that provided people without disabilities.[82] These specific provisions are not applicable to over-the-road buses (those that have an elevated passenger deck located over a luggage compartment).[83] Over-the-road buses bought or leased by private entities that provide transportation of individuals but that are not primarily engaged in the business of transporting people have to comply with regulations issued by the Department of Transportation.[84]

For "specified public transportation" provided by an entity primarily engaged in the business of transporting people, the essential obligations are: (1) not to impose eligibility criteria that screen out or tend to screen out individuals with disabilities from full enjoyment of the services unless the criteria can be shown to be needed for the provision of the services offered;[85] (2) to make reasonable accommodations consistent with title III's provisions;[86] (3) to provide auxiliary aids and services consistent with title III;[87] (4) to remove barriers, again consistent with title III;[88] (5) not to buy or lease a new vehicle other than an automobile or van with a seating capacity of less than eight passengers (including the driver) or an over-the-road bus used to provide the specified public transportation, that is not readily accessible to and usable by individuals with disabilities, including those using wheelchairs, except that the new vehicle does not need to be accessible if it is to be used solely in a demand responsive system and the entity can show that the system, when viewed in its entirety, provides a level of service to individuals with disabilities equivalent to the level of service provided the general public;[89] (6) not to buy or lease an

---

[79] 42 U.S.C. § 12182(b)(2)(B)(i) (2006).

[80] § 12182(b)(2)(B)(ii).

[81] § 12182(b)(2)(C)(i).

[82] § 12182(b)(2)(C)(ii).

[83] § 12182(b)(2)(D)(i).

[84] § 12182(b)(2)(D)(ii).

[85] § 12184(b)(1).

[86] § 12184(b)(2)(A).

[87] § 12184(b)(2)(B).

[88] § 12184(b)(2)(C).

[89] § 12184(b)(3).

over-the-road-bus that fails to comply with regulations issued by the Department of Transportation, and not to disobey any other of the regulations;[90] (7) not to buy or lease a new van with seating for fewer than eight, including the driver, that is used to provide specified public transportation unless it is readily accessible to and usable by individuals with disabilities, including those using wheelchairs, except that the new van does not need to be accessible if it is to be used solely in a demand responsive system and the entity can show that the system, when viewed in its entirety, provides a level of service to individuals with disabilities equivalent to the level of service provided the general public;[91] (8) not to buy or lease a new rail passenger car used to provide specified public transportation unless it is readily accessibly to and usable by individuals with disabilities, including those who use wheelchairs;[92] and (9) not to remanufacture a rail passenger car that is to be used for specified public transportation so as to extend its usable life for ten or more years or to buy or lease such a car unless, to the maximum extent feasible, the car is made readily accessible to and usable by individuals with disabilities, including those using wheelchairs.[93] There is a limited exception for historical or antiquated rail passenger cars or rail stations served exclusively by those cars.[94]

One noteworthy case discusses the obligations of taxi companies with respect to the purchase or lease of new vehicles under 42 U.S.C. § 12184(b)(3). In *Toomer v. City Cab*, the plaintiffs contended that the defendant cab operators were out of compliance because used vehicles they acquired were manufactured after the effective date of the ADA provision.[95] The used vehicles were thus "new" in the sense of being post-ADA, and, of course, they were new acquisitions. The district court granted the defendants' motion for summary judgment, concluding that the term meant vehicles with no prior use rather than those made after the ADA's effective date. The Tenth Circuit Court of Appeals affirmed the judgment. It held that word "new" was ambiguous and referred to the relevant regulations. The Department of Transportation's definition of a "new vehicle," that is, one offered for sale or lease after manufacture without any prior use,[96] was held to be consistent with one of the common usages of "new," identical to the Architectural and Transportation Barriers Compliance Board's definition, and consistent with the ADA's purpose of providing for accommodation with certain limitations. Thus, the definition was not arbitrary, capricious, or contrary to congressional intent.

---

[90] § 12184(b)(4).

[91] § 12184(b)(5).

[92] § 12184(b)(6).

[93] § 12184(b)(7).

[94] § 12184(c).

[95] 443 F.3d 1191 (10th Cir. 2006).

[96] 49 C.F.R. § 37.3 (2011).

[B]   Air Transportation

In 1986, the Supreme Court ruled that section 504 does not cover air carriers, despite federal financial support for airport operations and the maintenance of an air traffic control system.[97] Congress responded by enacting the Air Carrier Access Act of 1986 (ACAA), which establishes that air carriers must not discriminate against otherwise qualified individuals with disabilities.[98] The Department of Transportation has promulgated regulations fleshing out the obligations imposed by the Act. The regulations define qualified individuals as those who have or try to obtain a ticket and meet reasonable, nondiscriminatory contract of carriage requirements applicable to all passengers, and those accompanying or meeting them; the definition of an individual with a disability includes actual impairment, record of impairment, and being regarded as having an impairment.[99] The regulations specify that covered individuals must not be discriminated against, must not be forced to accept special services they do not want (other than preboarding as a condition of receiving certain seating or in-cabin stowage accommodations), must not be denied the benefit of air transportation or related services, and must not be penalized for asserting rights under the law.[100]

The regulations further specify that newly purchased aircraft have to meet accessibility standards, although airplanes currently in use do not need to be retrofitted. Nevertheless, those planes must have accessibility features added when they are refurbished.[101] Airport facilities must be readily accessible to persons with disabilities, including those who use wheelchairs.[102] A qualified individual with a disability must not be denied transportation because of appearance or involuntary behavior that offends, annoys, or inconveniences crewmembers or passengers.[103] The number of persons with disabilities on a given flight cannot be limited.[104] Although airlines may refuse to provide transportation on the basis of safety and may require 48 hours advance notice and one hour advance check-in for specified classes of passengers, the ability of the airlines to do so is limited.[105] Airlines may require a person with a disability to be accompanied by an attendant, but only if the passenger is traveling on a stretcher or in an incubator, so mentally disabled as to be unable to understand or respond appropriately to safety

---

[97] United States Dep't of Transp. v. Paralyzed Veterans of America, 477 U.S. 597 (1986).

[98] 49 U.S.C. § 41705 (2006). Congress declined to duplicate this coverage when writing title III of the ADA, and placed language in title III's definition of "specified transportation" excluding conveyance by aircraft. 42 U.S.C. § 12181(10) (2006).

[99] 14 C.F.R. § 382.3 (2011).

[100] § 382.11(a) (2011).

[101] § 382.21 (2006).

[102] § 382.23. Under this provision, compliance with ADA title III regulations suffices.

[103] § 382.31(b).

[104] § 382.31(c).

[105] §§ 382.31(d) (safety); 382.33 (notice and check-in). The notice and check-in provision applies to a passenger who wants to use medical oxygen on flight, carry an incubator, use a respirator, accompany a passenger on a stretcher, carry an electric wheelchair in a plane with under 60 seats, carry a wheelchair battery that needs hazardous material packing, be part of a group of ten or more individuals with disabilities traveling as a group, or use a wheelchair on an aircraft that has no accessible lavatory.

instructions, so impaired in mobility as to be unable to assist in his or her own evacuation, or both severely visually impaired and severely hearing impaired if the passenger is unable to establish some means of communication with the personnel of the air carrier.[106] There is a limited prerogative on the part of the airlines to restrict seating of passengers with disabilities, for example to comply with exit-seating rules.[107]

With regard to what assistance must be provided by airline personnel, the regulations specify that help must be furnished, if needed, for entering and leaving the plane, moving to and from seats when boarding and deplaning, preparing meals (as with unwrapping or identifying food), accessing the lavatory with an on-board wheelchair, accessing the lavatory for passengers who are semi-ambulatory but do not need to be lifted or carried, and loading and retrieving carry-ons, including mobility aids.[108] Medical services need not be furnished, nor assistance with feeding, nor assistance in the lavatory.[109] Airlines, in cooperation with or under contractual arrangements with larger airports, are required to provide boarding assistance for all but the smallest aircraft.[110] Accommodations must be provided to communicate with passengers with hearing and visual impairments.[111] A provision generally requiring similar treatment for persons with disabilities and others applies to security screening of persons with disabilities.[112] A direct-threat test applies for refusing to transport passengers with contagious conditions.[113] The regulations also address the transport of service animals, and they cover several other topics.[114] The Act contains a process by which complaints must be investigated by the Department of Transportation, then reviewed and made the subject of an annual report to Congress.[115]

The key legal controversy with regard to the ACAA is whether an individual may sue to obtain relief for a violation, or whether the administrative enforcement mechanism that the Act provides is an exclusive remedy.[116] *Love v. Delta Air Lines* holds that the statute does not create a private right of action for a passenger who has been harmed by violation of the law.[117] The case involved a passenger who used a wheelchair for mobility who alleged that the airline failed to provide an accessible call button, an aisle chair, a fully accessible lavatory, and personnel adequately

---

[106] § 382.35.

[107] § 382.37. Some seating accommodations must be provided such as, for example, companion seating in some situations. § 382.28.

[108] § 382.39(b).

[109] § 382.39(c).

[110] §§ 382.40–40a.

[111] §§ 382.45(c), 382.47.

[112] § 382.49. Assistive devices that could conceal a weapon may be examined.

[113] § 382.51.

[114] *E.g.*, § 382.559(a) (service animals).

[115] 49 U.S.C.A. § 41705(c) (2006).

[116] *See generally* Curtis D. Edmonds, *When Pigs Fly: Litigation Under the Air Carrier Access Act*, 78 N. Dak. L. Rev. 687 (2002) (discussing private right of action and other issues, including limitations and preemption).

[117] 310 F.3d 1347 (11th Cir. 2002).

trained to provide needed assistance to her. She sued for monetary and equitable relief, but the district court, while denying a motion for summary judgment on the ACAA claim, ruled that the Act permitted only injunctive and declaratory relief. On interlocutory appeal, the Eleventh Circuit reversed the district decision to allow the ACAA claim to proceed, reasoning that *Alexander v. Sandoval*, the Supreme Court's decision finding no private right of action to enforce regulations barring disparate impact discrimination under title VI of the Civil Rights Act, demands that only limited considerations be looked to in determining whether Congress intended creation of a private right to sue.[118] Applying the considerations used in *Sandoval*, the court found no explicit right of action in the ACAA, and instead found an administrative remedy in the requirements that the Department of Transportation receive and investigate complaints and that courts of appeals entertain private individuals' petitions to review enforcement decisions of the Department.[119] The right of action to petition to review "powerfully suggests that Congress did not intend to provide other private rights of action."[120] In *Boswell v. Skywest Airlines, Inc.*, the Tenth Circuit followed *Love* and held that the ACAA does not carry a private right of action.[121]

The analysis engaged in by these courts might be criticized on the ground that it diverts attention from the most obvious indication of what Congress was attempting to do in enacting the ACAA. Congress was acting to fill the void that the Supreme Court created when it found that section 504 did not cover air travel. The language it chose mimics that of section 504. Both section 504 and the statute on which it is modeled, title VI of the Civil Rights Act of 1964, embody a private right of action. *Sandoval* did nothing to undermine the position the Supreme Court has always embraced that the whole cluster of civil rights acts modeled on title VI carry a private right of action, at least to redress intentional conduct, nor did it purport to overrule *Alexander v. Choate*,[122] which stated that an individual's claim under section 504 could address at least some disparate impacts. Two circuits have held that there is a private right of action for violations of the ACAA, though the court in *Love* found the decisions unpersuasive because they predated *Sandoval*.[123]

---

[118] 532 U.S. 275 (2001).

[119] The court also pointed to a requirement that the carriers themselves receive complaints and establish a mechanism to resolve them. *See* 14 C.F.R. § 382.65 (2006).

[120] *Love*, 310 F.3d at 1357.

[121] 361 F.3d 1263 (10th Cir. 2004).

[122] 469 U.S. 287, 296–97 (1985) ("Discrimination against the handicapped was perceived by Congress to be most often the product, not of invidious animus, but rather of thoughtlessness and indifference-of benign neglect. . . . In addition, much of the conduct that Congress sought to alter in passing the Rehabilitation Act would be difficult if not impossible to reach were the Act construed to proscribe only conduct fueled by a discriminatory intent."); *see* Cannon v. University of Chicago, 441 U.S. 677 (1979) (ruling that private right of action exists to enforce title IX of Education Amendments of 1972). Title VI, section 504, and title IX all provide administrative enforcement mechanisms as well, although the mechanisms are not identical to that of the ACAA.

[123] Shinault v. American Airlines, Inc., 936 F.2d 795, 800 (5th Cir. 1991); Tallarico v. Trans World Airlines, Inc., 881 F.2d 566, 568 (8th Cir. 1989); *see also* Newman v. American Airlines, Inc., 176 F.3d 1128 (9th Cir. 1999) (ruling on merits of private action for violation of ACAA).

Resolving another issue regarding air transport, the Third Circuit has ruled that the Federal Aviation Act does not preempt state law tort claims based on the alleged failure to provide adequate assistance to a passenger who needed crutches to walk and could not safely navigate a narrow set of stairs when disembarking from a plane, resulting in a fall and serious injuries.[124] It also ruled that the ACAA does not control the standard of care in such a tort case.[125]

§ 7.03   TELECOMMUNICATIONS

The topic of telecommunications embraces technologies such as relay systems, which are covered by ADA title IV, as well as Internet sites, potentially covered under title III.

[A]   Telecommunications Relay Systems

Title IV of the ADA, the only portion not codified in the civil rights portion of the United States Code (it is codified as an amendment to the telecommunications laws), charges the Federal Communications Commission to use its regulatory powers "to make available to all individuals in the United States a rapid, efficient nationwide communication service. . . ."[126] The mechanism to achieve that goal is a telecommunications relay service, by which one caller communicates by voice to an operator who transmits what the caller said to the person on the other end of the line by electronically transmitted text. The person on the other end of the line communicates by text, and the operator reads it to the person using voice. The statute requires that telephone companies provide relay services that enable an individual with a hearing impairment or speech impairment to engage in communication with a hearing individual in a manner functionally equivalent to the ability of an individual who does not have a hearing impairment or speech impairment to communicate using voice communication services.[127] The regulations adopted by the Commission must, under the statute, require that the relay services operate every day for 24 hours a day, require that users of the relay services pay rates no greater than the rates paid for functionally equivalent voice communication services, prohibit operators from refusing calls or limiting the length of calls, prohibit operators from disclosing the content of any relayed conversation or keeping records of the content of the conversation, and prohibit operators from intentionally altering a relayed conversation.[128] Complaint procedures are specified in the statute as well.[129]

---

[124] Elassaad v. Independence Air, Inc., 613 F.3d 119, 131 (3d Cir. 2010) (discussing 49 U.S.C. §§ 40101–40129 and applicable regulations).

[125] *Id.* at 133.

[126] 47 U.S.C.S. § 225(b)(1) (LexisNexis 2011).

[127] § 225(c); *see* § 225(a)(3) (defining telecommunications relay services). *See generally supra* § 5.03[B] (discussing public accommodations' obligation to provide auxiliary aids and services, including communication through relay systems).

[128] 47 U.S.C. § 225(d) (2006).

[129] § 225(g).

[B]   Internet Sites and Other Means of Telecommunication

It should come as no surprise that the ADA, a statute drafted in the 1980s and passed in 1990, makes no mention of the Internet. Accessibility of web sites is important, however, if the goal is to allow persons with visual disabilities and some other forms of sensory disability to participate in the mainstream of contemporary American life. Moreover, making a web site accessible to persons with visual impairments may be a very easy accommodation to provide, as by making text readable by electronic reading software rather than unreadable because of the nature of the graphic display. An alternative text of invisible code may be embedded beneath graphics, and electronic reader and voice synthesizer software can convert that text into spoken words.

The principal subject of litigation in web site accessibility cases has been whether title III of the ADA, the title that covers public accommodations offered by private enterprise, extends its reach to web sites. Title III prohibits discrimination "on the basis of disability in the full and equal enjoyment of the goods, services, privileges, advantages, or accommodations of any place of public accommodation" by anyone owning, leasing, or operating a place of public accommodation.[130] Hence, the question frequently has been whether a web site is one of the goods, services, privileges, advantages, or accommodations of a place of public accommodation.

In *National Federation of the Blind v. Target Corp.*, plaintiffs alleged that the Target.com web site was inaccessible to persons with visual disabilities.[131] The defendant moved to dismiss, and the court denied the motion in significant part. The court stressed that the statute applies to the goods, services, etc. *of* a place of public accommodation, rather than *in* a place of public accommodation. It found no requirement that a plaintiff needs to allege that the physical space of the stores were inaccessible. Although the defendant argued that if title III does apply, an accessible web site should be viewed as an auxiliary aid for which the covered entity may substitute other methods of communication, such as shopping by telephone, the court regarded this argument as an affirmative defense that would be premature to consider on the motion to dismiss. Thus the motion was denied, except to the extent that the web site offered information and services unconnected to the stores of the defendant, which would not affect the enjoyment of goods and services offered in the stores. The court also denied the motion to dismiss regarding the state law claims, discussing at length a constitutional objection to the application of state law to web sites. The court denied the plaintiffs' motion for preliminary injunction without prejudice to its refiling, noting factual disputes and incomplete discovery on the merits of the case.

Rendon v. Valleycrest Productions, Ltd., though not a case over a web site, further supports the proposition that accessibility duties related to telecommunications do not begin and end at a physical space.[132] In *Rendon*, the

---

[130] 42 U.S.C. § 12182(a) (2006). *See generally supra* § 5.03[B] (discussing public accommodations' obligation to provide auxiliary aids and services, including telecommunications in general).

[131] 452 F. Supp. 2d 946 (N.D. Cal. 2006).

[132] 294 F.3d 1279 (11th Cir. 2002).

plaintiffs alleged that the automated telephone-keypad selection process for the show "Who Wants To Be A Millionaire" violated title III because it screened out individuals with hearing impairments and upper-body mobility impairments. The process depended on quickly keying in answers to questions using a touch-tone phone, disadvantaging those who cannot hear or cannot move their fingers rapidly, no matter how good they might be at answering the questions. The plaintiffs said they could be reasonably accommodated by the use of telephone relay services. The defendants responded that they did not operate a place of public accommodation subject to title III. The court of appeals reversed a district court's dismissal of the case. The court of appeals relied on the fact that the plaintiffs were seeking to compete in a contest held in an actual place, that is, a television studio. The court said that "off-site screening appears to be the paradigmatic example contemplated in the statute's prohibition of 'the imposition or application of eligibility criteria that screen out or tend to screen out an individual with a disability.' "[133]

Access Now v. Southwest Airlines rejected a title III claim challenging the accessibility of an airline's web site.[134] The plaintiffs alleged that the site was inaccessible by blind persons who used screen readers and that it lacked other accessibility features. The court, however, determined that the web site was not a place of public accommodation within the meaning of title III, reasoning that a web site is not among the twelve listed categories of public accommodations in the statute. It further held that there was no nexus between the web site and any physical space that was a public accommodation; hence the case was unlike *Rendon*, which considered a mechanism for accessing a concrete space. Although the court did not note the fact, *Access Now* is indeed different in that the web site of an airline is not in any way a service of a place of public accommodation. Airlines occupy physical space for their customer operations, but they are explicitly excepted from coverage in title III of the ADA.[135]

Plaintiffs have thus had success in making accessibility claims on the theory that web sites are services of stores or other entities that are places explicitly covered by title III.[136] Nevertheless, it might still be possible to question whether an approach to coverage of web sites that requires a physical space somewhere that is governed by title III is a proper interpretation of the statute. In *PGA Tour, Inc. v.*

---

[133] *Id.* at 1285 (quoting 42 U.S.C. § 12182(b)(2)(A)(i)).

[134] 227 F. Supp. 2d 1312 (S.D. Fla. 2002), *app. dismissed*, 385 F.3d 1324 (11th Cir. 2004).

[135] *See* 42 U.S.C. § 12181(10) (2006).

[136] *See also* Guidance on Revisions to ADA Regulation on Nondiscrimination on the Basis of Disability by Public Accommodations and Commercial Facilities, 28 C.F.R. § 36, App. A, 75 Fed. Reg. 56259, 56316 (Sep. 15, 2010) ("Although the language of the ADA does not explicitly mention the Internet, the [Justice] Department has taken the position that title III covers access to Web sites of public accommodations."); Letter from Assistant Attorney General Deval L. Patrick to Senator Tom Harkin (Sep. 9, 1996), at http://www.justice.gov/crt/foia/readingroom/frequent_requests/ada_tal/tal712.txt (discussing web sites in context of auxiliary aids and services requirement of title III, stating: "Covered entities under the ADA are required to provide effective communication, regardless of whether they generally communicate through print media, audio media, or computerized media such as the Internet. Covered entities that use the Internet for communications regarding their programs, goods, or services must be prepared to offer those communications through accessible means as well.").

Martin, the United State Supreme Court applied a broad definition of title III's coverage to find that the intangible entity of a golf tournament series constituted a public accommodation.[137] Although the Court noted that golf courses are themselves physical spaces,[138] the PGA Tour is not a golf course, but instead a series of competitions among golfers, which can hardly be compared to the fixed physical space of a store or office. If the intangible entity of PGA's tour is subject to title III, a parallel argument might be made that the virtual space of the Internet is covered as well.[139]

Government conduct is outside the coverage of title III and so must be analyzed separately. The Rehabilitation Act requires accessibility of the web sites of federal agencies. Section 508 of the Rehabilitation Act is a 1998 amendment to that law which forbids federal agencies from purchasing, maintaining, or using electronic and information technology, such as federal web sites, telecommunications, and software that is not accessible to individuals with disabilities, unless providing accessibility is an undue burden.[140] Since title II of the ADA covers all activities of state and local government and does not contain a "place of" term, it would appear to require accessibility of those entities' web sites.[141]

§ 7.04   ADDITIONAL DISCRIMINATION ISSUES

The purpose of this section is to discuss in brief a number of disability discrimination issues that are not discussed in a systematic way elsewhere in this book. The topics are retaliation claims, disability harassment claims, and international and comparative law topics.

[A]   Retaliation

Title V of the ADA forbids discrimination against any individual (not just an individual with a disability) because the individual has opposed any act or practice that the ADA makes unlawful, or because the individual made a charge, testified, assisted, or participated in any way in an investigation, proceeding, or hearing

---

[137] 532 U.S. 661 (2001). *See generally supra* Chapter 5 (discussing case).

[138] *P.G.A. Tour, Inc.*, 532 U.S. at 677. The PGA appears to have made an argument in the lower courts that its tour is not a place of public accommodation because the competitors' spaces are not open to the general public during the competition, but it abandoned the argument in the Supreme Court. *Id.* at 677–78.

[139] Some cases suggest that a place of public accommodation governed by title III may be something other than physical space. *See* Doe v. Mutual of Omaha Ins. Co., 179 F.3d 557, 559 (7th Cir. 1999) (stating in dicta that title III covers web sites, which exist in "electronic space"); Carparts Distribution Ctr. v. Automotive Wholesalers Ass'n, 37 F.3d 12, 19–20 (1st Cir. 1994) (considering businesses that operate by telephone and mail). *But see* Young v. Facebook, Inc., No. 5:10-cv-03579-JF/PVT, 2011 U.S. Dist. LEXIS 52711 (May 17, 2011) (holding that social networking service lacked sufficient nexus to physical place of public accommodation to support coverage under ADA title III).

[140] 29 U.S.C. § 794d (2006).

[141] *See* Martin v. Metro Atlanta Rapid Transit Auth., 225 F. Supp. 2d 1362 (N.D. Ga. 2002) (requiring accessibility for local government web site); *see also* U.S. Dep't of Justice, Accessibility of State and Local Government Websites to People with Disabilities (June 2003), *available at* www.ada.gov/websites2.htm.

under the ADA.[142] Most cases concern employment. In that context, rarely is there direct evidence that a given action by a defendant was retaliation for the plaintiff's opposition to an unlawful practice or other participation in ADA proceedings. Accordingly, courts often rely on inferences from temporal proximity between the conduct of the plaintiff and that of the defendant,[143] or they use an adapted *McDonnell Douglas Corp. v. Green*[144] inferential framework: The employee shows that he or she was treated differently than a similarly situated employee who did not file a discrimination charge; the employer responds to the evidence of different treatment; and the employee rebuts the evidence presented by the employer.[145] As long as the actions of the plaintiff are in good faith and relate to conduct that actually violates the ADA, the claim for retaliation is valid, even if the underlying proceeding is ultimately unsuccessful.[146] Precedent from the Supreme Court on the analogous retaliation provision in title VII of the Civil Rights Act establishes that the retaliatory action must be materially adverse but that it need not be employment- or work-related.[147] The Supreme Court has also upheld a retaliation cause of action under title IX of the Education Amendments of 1972, a statute similarly worded to and usually construed in the same fashion as section 504.[148]

The remedies and procedures available under the respective provisions of title I, title II, and title III are available for violations of the prohibition on retaliation.[149] This would permit equitable relief in all categories of cases, as well as compensatory damages without limit in title II actions and compensatory and punitive damages up to the statutory limits for title I cases. Nevertheless, the Court of Appeals for the Seventh Circuit has ruled that no compensatory and punitive damages remedy exists for employment cases under the ADA retaliation provision.[150] The court reasoned that although the provision incorporates by reference the remedies and procedures available under title I, it does not explicitly incorporate the damages provision, 42 U.S.C. § 1981a, which applies to title I cases.

Several other courts have rejected this reasoning. The court in *Edwards v. Brookhaven Science Associates* pointed out that the incorporation by reference itself eliminates the need for the statute doing the incorporation — the ADA retaliation provision — to specify what the incorporated-by-reference statute — title I — also incorporates:

---

[142] 42 U.S.C. § 12203(a) (2006).

[143] *See* Shellenberger v. Summit Bancorp, 318 F.3d 183 (3d Cir. 2003).

[144] 411 U.S. 792 (1973).

[145] *See* Stone v. City of Indianapolis Pub. Utils. Div., 281 F.3d 640 (7th Cir. 2002) (critically evaluating various adaptations of *McDonnell Douglas* in retaliation scenarios and applying test to summary judgment decision).

[146] Weissman v. Dawn Joy Fashions, Inc., 214 F.3d 224, 234 (2d Cir. 2000).

[147] Burlington N. & Santa Fe Ry. Co. v. White, 548 U.S. 53 (2006).

[148] *See* Jackson v. Birmingham Bd. of Educ., 544 U.S. 167 (2005).

[149] 42 U.S.C. § 12203(c) (2000).

[150] Kramer v. Banc of Am. Sec., LLC, 355 F.3d 961 (7th Cir. 2004). *Accord* Alvarado v. Cajun Operating Co., 588 F.3d 1261 (9th Cir. 2009).

In the Court's view, the omission of § 12203 in § 1981[a] is of no consequence when § 1981[a] is read in conjunction with the relevant provisions of the ADA. . . . [T]he retaliation provision of the ADA contains no remedy of its own. Rather, it is clear that the "remedies and procedures . . . available to aggrieved persons" for violations of § 12203 are the *same* as the "remedies and procedures available under" Title I of the ADA. . . . Considering that the remedies available for retaliation under the ADA are commensurate with those available under Title I, it was unnecessary for Congress to separately mention retaliation in § 1981[a]. Thus, it is fair to assume that the expansive effect of § 1981[a] applies equally to claims under Title I as it does to retaliation claims by virtue of the fact that the remedies available for retaliation claims incorporate, and are coextensive with, the remedies available under Title I.[151]

Taking away a damages remedy removes any effective judicial response in the very common situation in which the plaintiff does not want or is not entitled to injunctive or other equitable relief. That might occur, for example, when the an employee obtains a similar-paying job at another employer following a retaliatory discharge and so is not entitled to back pay and does not want a reinstatement order.[152]

A number of courts, noting that section 12203 applies to all acts of retaliation, not just those of covered entities, have upheld personal liability of the individuals violating the statute.[153]

[B] Disability Harassment

In 2001, two decisions from the federal courts of appeals affirmed judgments in ADA title I cases based on allegations of disability harassment.[154] In *Fox v. General Motors Corp.*, the Fourth Circuit Court of Appeals affirmed a judgment on a jury verdict in favor of an assembly worker whose supervisors and co-workers constantly ridiculed him and swore at him on account of his back injuries.[155] One supervisory blocked another supervisor's efforts at accommodation, and at one

---

[151] 390 F. Supp. 2d 225, 236 (E.D.N.Y. 2005); *see* Ostrach v. Regents of the Univ. of Cal., 957 F. Supp. 196 (E.D. Cal. 1997) (adopting same interpretation).

[152] The Seventh Circuit's interpretation of ADA title I creates an inconsistency with title VII caselaw, which permits damages remedies for retaliation. *See* Sink v. Wal-Mart Stores, Inc., 147 F. Supp. 2d 1085, 1101 (D. Kan. 2001) (following Seventh Circuit approach but noting inconsistency with title VII and questioning logic of approach).

[153] *E.g.*, Shotz v. City of Plantation, 344 F.3d 1161, 1178 (11th Cir. 2003); Regional Econ. Cmty. Action Program, Inc. v. City of Middletown, 294 F.3d 35, 45 n.1 (2d Cir. 2002); Coleman v. Town of Old Saybrook, No. 3:03CV01275(RNC), 2004 U.S. Dist. LEXIS 7442 (D. Conn. Apr. 28, 2004). *Contra, e.g.*, Baird v. Rose, 192 F.3d 462, 471 (4th Cir. 1999); Hiler v. Brown, 177 F.3d 542, 545 (6th Cir. 1999).

[154] Disability harassment has been a major topic of inquiry for the author of this book. A list of sources includes: Mark C. Weber, Disability Harassment (2007); *Exile and the Kingdom: Integration, Harassment, and the Americans with Disabilities Act*, 63 Md. L. Rev. 162 (2004); *Workplace Harassment Claims Under the Americans with Disabilities Act: A New Interpretation*, 14 Stan. L. & Pol'y Rev. 241 (2003); and *Disability Harassment in the Public Schools*, 43 Wm. & Mary L. Rev. 1079 (2002). Regarding state common law remedies for, among other things, disability harassment, see Mark C. Weber, *The Common Law of Disability Discrimination*, Utah L. Rev. (forthcoming, 2012).

[155] 247 F.3d 169 (4th Cir. 2001).

point the plaintiff was placed at a work table that so low that it exacerbated his disability. He developed depression, anxiety, and suicidal ideation. In sustaining the claim, the court reasoned that, like title VII of the Civil Rights Act, the ADA bars discrimination regarding terms, conditions, and privileges of employment, and the bar extends to the creation of a hostile environment. The court noted that Congress enacted the ADA after the Supreme Court had already determined that harassment violates the similar language of title VII.[156]

In *Flowers v. Southern Regional Physician Services*, the Fifth Circuit affirmed the entry of judgment on a jury verdict in favor of an employee infected with HIV.[157] After the plaintiff's supervisor learned about the condition, the supervisor shunned her, refusing to go to lunch with her or socialize with her, and instead began an eavesdropping campaign. The president of the company avoided her and would no longer shake her hand.[158] She had to submit to four drug tests in a week, was twice written up for disciplinary reasons, was placed on probation, called names and humiliated, then ultimately fired. The court of appeals noted the identity in language and purpose of title VII and the ADA, and used the comparison to find that an ADA claim existed for hostile environment harassment. It affirmed the jury verdict for the plaintiff.[159]

Harassment may occur in places other than the workplace. A number of courts have upheld damages claims for harassment in violation of section 504 and ADA title II. Most of the cases have to do with teacher or peer harassment at school. In *Baird v. Rose*, a child who was being treated for depression alleged that after her teacher learned about the diagnosis, she excluded her from activities of a musical performance class and humiliated her before her classmates.[160] The court upheld a damages claim under title II of the ADA. Courts have also upheld claims for school administrators' failure to respond adequately to peer harassment of students with disabilities.[161]

Many disability harassment claims fail, with courts often holding that the conduct of the defendant lacked the severity or pervasiveness that the title VII case law has established as the standard for a hostile environment violates that statute.[162] Nevertheless, harassing conduct, even that which might not rise to that of an environment permeated with discrimination actionable under a title VII

---

[156] *Fox*, 247 F.3d at 175–76 (citing Patterson v. McLean Credit Union, 491 U.S. 164, 180 (1989), and Meritor Bank v. Vinson, 477 U.S. 57, 64–66 (1986)). The court overturned an award of $4,000 for unpaid overtime on the ground that it was inconsistent with the jury's finding that General Motors had not intentionally discriminated against the plaintiff. *Id.* at 181.

[157] 247 F.3d 229 (5th Cir. 2001).

[158] *Id.* at 237.

[159] *Id.* at 236. The court nevertheless ruled that the plaintiff had not presented adequate evidence of a specific emotional injury, and vacated the damages award, remanding for entry of an award of nominal damages. *Id.* at 239.

[160] 192 F.3d 462 (4th Cir. 1999).

[161] *E.g.*, M.P. v. Independent Sch. Dist. No. 721, 326 F.3d 975 (8th Cir. 2003); K.M. v. Hyde Park Cent. Sch. Dist., 381 F. Supp. 2d 343 (S.D.N.Y. 2005).

[162] *E.g.*, Vollmert v. Wisconsin Dep't of Transp., 197 F.3d 293 (7th Cir. 1999) (finding trainer's unfavorable actions not so severe or pervasive as to establish hostile environment); Walton v. Mental

standard, has the very definite and intended effect of forcing people with disabilities to go away, that is, to segregate themselves for their own self-protection, undermining the central goal of the ADA. An alternate approach to the problem of harassment, particularly harassment that does not meet a title VII test, might make use of 42 U.S.C. § 12203(b), which provides:

> It shall be unlawful to coerce, intimidate, threaten, or interfere with any individual in the exercise or enjoyment of, or on account of his or her having exercised or enjoyed, or on account of his or her having aided or encouraged any other individual in the exercise or enjoyment of, any right granted or protected by this chapter.[163]

Like the retaliation term of title V of the ADA, this statute applies to all areas covered by the ADA. Title I has regulations further defining the application of the statutory language to employment: "[I]t is unlawful to . . . coerce, intimidate, threaten, harass, or interfere with any individual in the exercise or enjoyment of . . . any right granted or protected in this part."[164] Section 12203(b) derives from the Great Depression-era federal labor laws, rather than from title VII, and does not have any analogue in title VII. In other fields in which similar prohibitions apply, courts have upheld claims based on threats and insults, without requiring harassment that meets a severe-or-pervasive standard of the type applied in title VII cases.[165]

In addition, in many instances, including some where ADA claims may not apply, plaintiffs claiming harassment have been successful making claims under state common law, often using intentional infliction of emotional distress causes of action. For example, in *Baird v. Rose*, the court ruled that plaintiff stated a claim for intentional infliction of emotional distress under Virginia law.[166] Courts have also upheld state common law intentional infliction claims in disability harassment cases concerning employment[167] and public services.[168]

Health Ass'n, 168 F.3d 661 (3d Cir. 1999) (finding conduct not pervasive or severe enough to meet standard for liability).

[163] 42 U.S.C. § 12203(b) (2000). Some courts, however, have limited the remedies available under § 12203 in employment cases. *See supra* § 7.04[A].

[164] 29 C.F.R. § 1630.12(b) (2011).

[165] *E.g.*, Sofarelli v. Pinellas County, 931 F.2d 718 (11th Cir. 1991) (upholding liability under Fair Housing Act coercion provision for one incident of threatening note and other incident of neighbors shouting obscenities); *see* N.Y.U. Med. Ctr. v. NLRB, 156 F.3d 405 (2d Cir. 1998) (upholding liability under labor law coercion provision for threatening to fire employees). *See generally* Robert G. Schwemm, *Neighbor-on Neighbor Harassment: Does the Fair Housing Act Make a Federal Case Out of It*, 61 Case W. Res. L. Rev. 865 (2011) (collecting and analyzing Fair Housing Act harassment cases).

[166] 192 F.3d 462, 472–73 (4th Cir. 1999).

[167] *E.g.*, Robel v. Roundup Corp., 59 P.3d 611 (Wash. 2002) (also upholding state statutory claim in case involving co-worker harassment of employee with disabilities).

[168] *E.g.*, Williams v. Tri-County Metro. Transp. Dist., 958 P.2d 202 (Or. App. 1998) (upholding claim of bus passenger with disabilities alleging harassment by driver for bringing service dog on bus).

[C]   International and Comparative Law Issues

Three international and comparative law-related issues have garnered attention in connection with disability discrimination law: extraterritorial effects of the Americans with Disabilities Act, the anti-discrimination duties found in the laws of other nations, and the development of a United Nations convention on the rights of persons with disabilities. These topics will each receive a brief discussion here.

On the extraterritoriality of United States law, the key source is the 2005 United States Supreme Court decision *Spector v. Norwegian Cruise Line Ltd.*[169] There, the Court ruled that title III of the ADA applies to foreign flag cruise ships operating in United States waters. Plaintiffs claimed that the defendant charged passengers with disabilities higher fares, had inaccessible evacuation programs and equipment, required them but not other passengers to waive potential medical liability, required them to travel with a companion, reserved the right to remove passengers with disabilities from the ship if their presence threatened the comfort of other passengers, offered inaccessible cabins, particularly cabins of the most desirable type and location, and had raised doorsills and other inaccessible structural features in many areas of the ships. The defendant responded by arguing, among other things, that title III did not apply to its ships, which in this case were registered in the Bahamas. The portion of Justice Kennedy's opinion that constitute the opinion of the Court said that the ships were places of public accommodation and specified public transportation under title III of the ADA. It went on to rule, however, that the duty to remove barriers established by title III would not apply if the removal of the barrier were to violate the International Convention for the Safety of Life at Sea or any other international legal obligation; barrier removal in that circumstance would not be readily achievable, as would barrier removal creating significant safety or health risks that could not be eliminated by modifying policies, practices, and procedures. Separate opinions disputed, among other things, how much of a clear statement, if any, needed to be made for title III to govern matters that might be viewed as falling within the internal affairs and operation of a ship.

Extraterritoriality issues may also arise in other contexts, such as the provision of accessibility and auxiliary aids and services in a study-abroad program operated by a United States university.[170] In addition, a few extraterritoriality issues are addressed explicitly in the ADA's statutory language. The employment provisions state that a covered entity may take an action that would ordinarily constitute discrimination with respect to an employee in a workplace in a foreign country if obeying nondiscrimination duties would cause the entity to violate the law of the country where the workplace is located.[171] If an employer controls a corporation that is incorporated in a foreign country, any discriminatory practice that the

---

[169] 545 U.S. 119 (2005).

[170] *See* Bird v. Lewis & Clark Coll., 303 F.3d 1015, 1021 n.1 (9th Cir. 2002) (reserving issue). *See generally* Arlene S. Kanter, *The Presumption Against Extraterritoriality as Applied to Disability Discrimination Laws: Where Does It Leave Students with Disabilities Studying Abroad?*, 14 STAN. L. & POL'Y REV. 291 (2003) (discussing extraterritoriality of American disability discrimination law with respect to study abroad).

[171] 42 U.S.C.S. § 12112(c)(1) (LexisNexis 2011).

corporation engages in is presumed to be engaged in by the employer; the determination as to control is to be based on the interrelation of operations, the common management, the centralized control of labor relations, and the common ownership or financial control of the employer and the corporation.[172] That presumption does not apply with regard to foreign operations of an employer that is a foreign person not controlled by a United States employer.[173]

Many foreign countries now have disability discrimination laws that parallel the ADA in one or more respects. The Canadian Human Rights Act broadly forbids discrimination on the basis of disability, and there is a separate Employment Equity Act forbidding discrimination in private and public employment.[174] The United Kingdom and many other nations also have extensive statutory provisions outlawing disability discrimination in employment and public services, and often in other settings as well.[175]

On December 13, 2006, the United Nations General Assembly adopted the Convention on the Rights of Persons with Disabilities.[176] The Convention is open for signatures by member nations and regional integration organizations (entities exercising the right to vote of nations that are members of a given international organization). The treaty covers topics such as education, employment, and participation in politics and cultural life, and it affirms rights that include freedom of movement, freedom from exploitation and violence, and access to health, habilitation and an adequate standard of living.[177] The United States signed the Convention on July 7, 2009, but has not yet ratified it. The Convention's adoption and implementation is likely to be a major topic of interest for disability law students and practitioners in the current decade.

---

[172] § 12112(c)(2)(A), (C).

[173] § 12112(c)(2)(B).

[174] Canada Human Rights Act, R.S.C. 1985, c. H-6, § 3(1); Canada Employment Equity Act, S.C. 1995 c. 44 § 5.

[175] See Equality Act, 2010, c. 15 Pt. 2 c. 1 § 6 (U.K.). Regional organizations of nations have also adopted anti-discrimination measures. For an extremely valuable analysis and compilation of enactments throughout the world, see Theresia Degener & Gerard Quinn, A Survey of International, Comparative and Regional Disability Law Reform, available at http://www.dredf.org/international/degener_quinn.html, and country-by-country index, available at http://www.dredf.org/international/lawindex.shtml (last visited Aug. 27, 2011).

[176] Convention on the Rights of Persons with Disabilities, available at http://www.un.org/disabilities/documents/convention/convoptprot-e.pdf (last visited Aug. 27, 2011).

[177] Additional information on the Convention is found on the U.N.'s Enable web site, at http://www.un.org/disabilities/ (last visited Aug. 27, 2011). As of August 27, 2011, the Convention had 149 signatories and 103 ratifications.

TABLE OF CASES

[References are to pages]

A

Ability Ctr. of Greater Toledo v. City of Sandusky 165
Abrahams v. MTA Long Island Bus. 202
Access Now, Inc. v. Southwest Airlines, Co.. . . .212
Aikins v. St. Helena Hosp.. 143
Aka v. Washington Hospital Center. 71
Albertson's, Inc. v. Kirkingburg 18; 28; 59
Alexander v. Choate 40; 164, 165; 209
Alexander v. Gardner-Denver Co. 90
Alexander v. Sandoval 165; 209
Alvarado v. Cajun Operating Co.. 214
Am. Council of the Blind v. Paulson. 160-161
Am. Ass'n of People with Disabilities v. Harris . 174
Am. Ass'n of People with Disabilities v. Hood. .174
Am. Ass'n of People with Disabilities v. Shelley.174
Am. Ass'n of People with Disabilities v. Smith . 174
AMTRAK v. Morgan 84
Anderson v. Little League Baseball, Inc.. 136
Applicants v. Texas State Bd. of Law Exam'rs. .166
Arlington Cent. Sch. Dist. Bd. of Educ. v. Murphy 116
Armstrong v. Schwarzenegger. 175
Astralis Condo. Ass'n v. Secretary, U.S. Dep't of Hous. & Urban Dev.. 195
Atkins v. Virginia 10

B

Baird v. Rose. 216, 217
Ball v. AMC Entm't, Inc.. 152
Barden v. City of Sacramento. 180
Barnes v. Gorman 182
Barth v. Gelb 64
Belk v. Southwestern Bell Tel. Co.. 60
Bircoll v. Miami-Dade County 175
Bledsoe v. Palm Beach County Soil & Water Conservation Dist.. 172
Board of Education v. Rowley. 103; 105
Board of Trustees v. Garrett 8; 94; 183
Bodenstab v. County of Cook. 90
Bolmer v. Oliveira 186
Boose v. Tri-County Metro. Transp. Dist.. 202
Borkowski v. Valley Cent. Sch. Dist.. 65
Boswell v. Skywest Airlines, Inc.. 209
Botosan v. Paul McNally Realty. 154
Bowers v. NCAA. 185

Bragdon v. Abbott. 23; 27; 31
Breece v. Alliance Tractor-Trailer Training II. . .140
Bronk v. Ineichen 197
Brown v. Board of Educ.. 97
Brownfield v. City of Yakima. 79
Buck v. Bell 10
Buckhannon Bd. & Care Home, Inc. v. W. Va. Dep't of Health & Human Res.. 157

C

California Mobile Home Park Management Co.; United States v.. 196
Cannon v. University of Chicago 209
Carr v. Reno. 52; 68
Caruso v. Blockbuster-Sony Music Entertainment Centre. 149
Cedar Rapids Community Sch. Dist. v. Garret F. by Charlene F.. 108
Chaffin v. Kansas State Fair Bd.. 165
Chalk v. United States Dist. Court Cent. Dist.. . . .95
Chapman v. Pier I Imports (U.S.), Inc.. 155
Chevron U.S.A. Inc. v. Echazabal 87, 88
Chevron U.S.A. Inc. v. NRDC 87
Cinemark USA, Inc.; United States v.. 150
City of (see name of city). . . . .
Clark v. Virginia Bd. of Bar Exam'rs. 166
Cleburne, City of v. Cleburne Living Ctr., Inc.. . .5; 190
Cleveland v. Policy Mgmt. Sys. Corp.. . . . .53, 54
Cmty. Servs. v. Wind Gap Mun. Auth.. . . .191-192
Concerned Parents to Save Dreher Park Ctr. v. City of W. Palm Beach. 177
Conroy v. New York State Dep't of Corr. Servs.. . 77; 79
Cornilles v. Regal Cinemas, Inc.. 152
County of (see name of county). . . . .
Cripe v. City of San Jose 58

D

D'Angelo v. ConAgra Foods, Inc 39; 74; 79
Dadian v. Vill. of Wilmette. 166; 193
Dalton v. Subaru-Isuzu Auto., Inc.. 70
Daniel R.R. v. State Bd. of Educ.. 110
Daugherty v. City of El Paso 70
Den Hartog v. Wasatch Academy 81, 82; 89

[References are to pages]

Dennin v. Connecticut Interscholastic Ath. Conf. 108-109

Dewitt v. Proctor Hosp. 83

Disabled in Action of Pa. v. Southeastern Pa. Transp. Auth. 202

Doe v. National Bd. of Med. Exam'rs 130

Does 1-5 v. Chandler. 176

Douglas v. California Dep't of Youth Auth. 185

E

Easley by Easley v. Snider. 170

Edmonds, City of v. Oxford House 198

Edwards v. Brookhaven Sci. Assocs., LLC. . . .215

EEOC v. Humiston-Keeling, Inc. 70

EEOC v. Wal-Mart Stores. 86; 89

EEOC v. Watkins Motor Lines 27

Elassaad v. Independence Air, Inc. 210

Elderhaven, Inc. v. City of Lubbock 193

Estate of (see name of party) . . . .

Ex rel. (see name of relator). . . . .

F

Familystyle of St. Paul, Inc. v. St. Paul 190

Fedro v. Reno 69, 70; 163

Florence County Sch. Dist. Four v. Carter by & Through Carter 114

Flowers v. S. Reg'l Physician Servs. 56, 57; 216

Forest Grove Sch. Dist. v. T. A. 115

Fortyune v. Am. Multi-Cinema, Inc. 151

Fox v. GMC 56, 57; 215, 216

G

Galloway v. Superior Court of Dist. of Columbia 175

George v. Bay Area Rapid Transit. 202

Georgia; United States v. 186

Giebeler v. M&B Assocs. 196

Giles v. GE 54

Gilmer v. Interstate/Johnson Lane Corp. 90

Goddard, Arizona ex rel. v. Harkins Amusement Enters. 152

Griffin v. Steeltek, Inc. 77

Guckenberger v. Boston Univ. 127

H

Hankins v. Gap, Inc. 70

Harding v. City of Toledo. 193

Harlow v. Fitzgerald. 126

Harrison v. Benchmark Elecs. Huntsville, Inc. . . .80

Helen L. v. DiDario 170

Hoffman v. Caterpillar, Inc. 54

Honig v. Doe. 117

Huber v. Wal-Mart Stores, Inc. 71

Humphrey v. Memorial Hosps. Ass'n 52

I

Int'l Union, United Auto., etc. v. Johnson Controls. 88

Irving Independent School Dist. v. Tatro 108

Iverson v. City of Boston 165

J

Jeffrey O v. Boca Raton. 191

Johnson v. Gambrinus Company/Spoetzl Brewery. 141

K

Kaplan v. City of N. Las Vegas. 74

Kelly v. Metallics West, Inc. 74

Kinman v. New Hampshire Dep't of Corrs. . . . 175

Kinney v. Yerusalim 180

Klingler v. Director, Dep't of Revenue 164

Kramer v. Banc of Am. Sec., LLC 214

L

Laird v. Redwood Trust LLC 146

Lane v. Pena 123

Larimer v. IBM Corp. 82

Larkin v. Michigan Dep't of Social Servs. 189

Lee v. City of Columbus, Ohio. 79

Leonel v. Am. Airlines, Inc. 76

Lightbourn v. County of El Paso 174

Lonberg v. City of Riverside 165

Lonberg v. Sanborn Theaters, Inc. 145

Love v. Delta Air Lines 208, 209

Lowe v. Am. Eurocopter, LLC 27

Lucas v. W.W. Grainger, Inc. 72

Lyons v. Legal Aid Soc'y 68

M

Mark H. v. Lemahieu. 165; 182

Mauro by & Through Mauro, Estate of v. Borgess Med. Ctr. 88, 89

McBride v. BIC Consumer Prods. Mfg. Co. 72

McCready v. Illinois Bd. of Admissions 166

[References are to pages]

McDonnell Douglas Corp. v. Green . . . 54; 82; 214

McGregor v. Louisiana State Univ. Bd. of Supervisors 122

McKellar v. Pennsylvania Dep't of Educ.. 182

Medical Soc'y v. Jacobs. 166

Mengine v. Runyon. 72

Michigan Protection & Advocacy Serv. v. Babin.199

Miller v. Ill. DOT. 51

Miller v. Public Storage Mgmt., Inc. 92

Mills v. Board of Education. 98

Mobley v. Allstate Ins. Co.. 72

Molski v. Evergreen Dynasty Corp.. 155

Molski v. M.J. Cable, Inc.. 155

Moore v. East Cleveland. 198

Mt. Healthy City Sch. Dist. Bd. of Educ. v. Doyle 183

Murphy v. UPS 19; 34, 35

N

Nat'l Fed'n of the Blind v. Target Corp. 211

Nelson v. Miller. 174

Nelson v. Thornburgh. 62

New York ex rel. Spitzer v. County of Schoharie 174

New York State Bd. of Law Exam'rs v. Bartlett. .15

Newberry v. East Tex. State Univ. 74

O

O'Connor v. Donaldson. 9

Oberti v. Board of Educ.. 110

Oconomowoc Residential Programs, Inc. v. City of Milwaukee. 193

Ohio Civil Rights Comm'n v. Case Western Reserve Univ.. .121

Olmstead v. L. C. by Zimring. 56; 169

14 Penn Plaza LLC v. Pyett. 90

Oxford House-C v. City of St. Louis 194

P

Padilla v. School Dist. No. 1 116

Pallozzi v. Allstate Life Ins. Co.. 153

Paralyzed Veterans of Am. v. D.C. Arena L.P. . . 150

Parker v. Metropolitan Life Ins. Co.. 153

Pennhurst State Sch. & Hosp. v. Halderman . . . 182

Pennsylvania Ass'n for Retarded Children v. Pennsylvania. 98

Pennsylvania Dep't of Corrections v. Yeskey. . .175

PGA Tour, Inc. v. Martin. 137– 139; 153; 213

Pierce v. County of Orange 175

Pottgen v. Missouri State High Sch. Activities Ass'n 109

Pushkin v. Regents of University of Colo. 125

R

Raytheon Co. v. Hernandez. 60; 74

Rendon v. Valleycrest Prods. Ltd.. 211

Roberts by & Through Rodenberg Roberts v. KinderCare Learning Ctrs. 140

Roe v. Providence Health Sys.-Oregon 142

Roncker on behalf of Roncker v. Walter 110

Rooney v. Sprague Energy Corp.. 16

Rose v. Springfield-Greene County Health Dep't.142

Rowley v. Board of Education. 105

S

Sacramento City Unified Sch. Dist., Bd. of Educ. v. Rachel H. by & Through Holland 109

Salute v. Stratford Greens Garden Apartments . . 196

Schaffer v. Weast. 113

School Bd. of Nassau County v. Arline. .22; 35; 88; 123

School Committee of Burlington v. Department of Education 114

Scruggs v. Meriden Bd. of Educ. 182

Shaywitz v. American Bd. of Psychiatry & Neurology. 130

Sheely v. MRI Radiology Network, P.A. . . 181, 182

Sierra v. City of New York 191

Smith v. Midland Brake, Inc.. 72

Southeastern Community College v. Davis . 39; 120; 141; 162

Spector v. Norwegian Cruise Line Ltd.. 218

Sutton v. United Air Lines, Inc.. .16, 17; 33, 34; 37, 38

T

Taylor v. Garrett. 163

Tennessee v. Lane 175; 184

Timothy W. v. Rochester, School Dist. . . . 103, 104

Toomer v. City Cab 206

Toyota Motor Mfg. v. Williams. 29; 32–34

Trujillo v. PacifiCorp 83

Tucker v. Tennessee 175

Tyndall v. Nat'l Educ. Ctrs.. 52

TABLE OF CASES

[References are to pages]

U

United States v. (see name of defendant). . . . . .
US Airways, Inc. v. Barnett . . . 63, 64; 66; 68; 196

V

Vande Zande v. Wisconsin Dep't of Admin. . 52; 56; 65, 66
Village of (see name of village). . . . .
Vitek v. Jones. 9

W

Walter v. SEPTA. 202
Weaver v. New Mexico Human Servs. Dep't. . . .177
Weber v. Strippit, Inc. 39; 67; 71; 74
Williams v. Philadelphia Hous. Auth. Police Dep't. .74

Winkelman v. Parma City Sch. Dist. 114
Wisconsin Cmty. Servs., Inc. v. City of Milwaukee. 167; 196
Wong v. Regents of the Univ. of Cal.. .30; 126; 129
Wray v. AMTRAK. 204
Wright v. Universal Maritime Serv. Corp. 91
Wynne v. Tufts University School of Medicine. .124

Y

Young v. Facebook, Inc.. 213
Youngberg v. Romeo. 9

Z

Zimmerman v. Oregon DOJ. 172
Zukle v. Regents of the Univ. of Cal.. 125

TABLE OF STATUTES

[References are to pages]

FEDERAL STATUTES, RULES, AND REGULATIONS

United States Constitution

Amend.	Page
amend.:1	127, 128
amend.:1:to:10	6; 186
amend.:5	5
amend.:6	185
amend.:8	5; 10, 11; 186
amend.:11	5; 8; 94; 119; 175; 181; 183–186
amend.:14	1; 5; 8; 97; 99; 175; 183–186
amend.:14:1	183
amend.:14:5	183; 186

United States Code

Title:Sec.	Page
5:553	150
20:1400 to 1487	97
20:1401(3)(A)(ii)	100
20:1401(3)(B)	101
20:1401(26)	108
20:1411(b)	42
20:1411(h)(2)	42
20:1411(i)	42
20:1412(a)(1)	104
20:1412(a)(1)(A)	117
20:1412(a)(5)(A)	109, 110
20:1412(a)(10)(C)(ii)	115
20:1412(a)(10)(C)(iii)(I)	115
20:1412(a)(10)(C)(iii)(II) to (III)	115
20:1412(a)(10)(C)(iv)	115
20:1414(b)(2)(B)	102
20:1414(b)(6)(A)	101
20:1414(d)	113
20:1415	99; 181
20:1415(b)(3)	112
20:1415(c)(1)	112
20:1415(d)	112
20:1415(i)(3)(B) to (G)	114
20:1415(i)(3)(B)(i)	115
20:1415(i)(3)(B)(i)(II) to (III)	116
20:1415(j)	113
20:1431 to 44	104
21:801	24
29:705(9)(B)	35

United States Code—Cont.

Title:Sec.	Page
29:705(10)(B)	24
29:705(20)(C)(i)	24
29:705(20)(C)(ii)	25
29:705(20)(C)(iii)	25
29:705(20)(E)	27
29:706(7)(B)(ii)	22
29:791	92
29:791(b)	49; 162
29:794	39; 159; 187
29:794(a)	49; 160
29:794a(b)	95
29:794(b)(1)(A)	180
29:794(b)(3)(B)	48
29:794(d)	47; 161
29:794d	213
42:791	93
42:1973ee-1(a)	174
42:1981a	92
42:1981a(a)(2)	61; 92
42:1981a(a)(3)	63; 72
42:1981a(b)(2)	93
42:1981a(b)(3)	93
42:1983	99
42:2000a-3(a)	155
42:2000a-3(c)	154
42:2000a(b)	137
42:2000e-5	85
42:2000e-5(c)	85
42:2000e-5(e)	84
42:2000e-5(e)(3)	84
42:2000e-5(f)(1)	85
42:2000e-5(g)(1)	94
42:3601 to 3619	187
42:3602(h)	187
42:3603(a) to (b)	42
42:3603(b)(1)	197; 199
42:3604(f)(1)	188
42:3604(f)(3)(B)	188; 192
42:3604(f)(3)(C)	189
42:3613	199
42:12101	20
42:12101(a)(2)	169
42:12102(1) to (3)	129
42:12102(2)	129

United States Code—Cont.

Title:Sec.	Page
42:12102(2)(A)	31
42:12102(2)(B)	24; 31
42:12102(3)	36
42:12102(3)(B)	38
42:12102(4)(B)	28
42:12102(4)(D)	29
42:12102(4)(E)(i)(I)	20
42:12102(4)(E)(iii)(I)	20
42:12102(4)(E)(iii)(II)	21
42:12103(1)	152
42:12111(2)	41; 48
42:12111(5)	173
42:12111(6)	24
42:12111(8)	50
42:12111(9)(B)	68
42:12111(10)(B)(iv)	62
42:12112	37
42:12112(a)	21; 45
42:12112(b)(1)	46; 56
42:12112(b)(3)(A)	57
42:12112(b)(4)	81
42:12112(b)(5)(A)	62
42:12112(b)(6)	78
42:12112(c)(1)	218
42:12112(d)(2)(A)	75
42:12112(d)(3)	77
42:12112(d)(4)(B)	78
42:12113(b)	83; 86
42:12113(c)	21
42:12113(d)	49
42:12114	24
42:12114(a)	73
42:12114(c)(1)	25
42:12114(c)(2)	25
42:12114(d)(1)	80
42:12117(a)	84; 92
42:12131	159
42:12131(1)	159
42:12131(2)	123
42:12132	39; 47; 120; 187
42:12133	181
42:12134(a)	47; 171
42:12142(a)	200
42:12143(c)(1)(A)	203
42:12147(a)	202
42:12161(2)	201
42:12161(3)	201

United States Code—Cont.

Title:Sec.	Page
42:12162(e)(2)(A)(ii)(I) to (II)	203
42:12181	137
42:12181(9)	147
42:12181(10)	207; 212
42:12182	187
42:12182(a)	133; 211
42:12182(b)(1)(A)(iv)	138
42:12182(b)(2)(A)(3)	151
42:12182(b)(2)(B)(i)	205
42:12182(b)(3)	136
42:12183(b)	136; 146
42:12187	99; 138
42:12188(a)(1)	154
42:12188(a)(2)	155
42:12188(b)(1)(B)	156
42:12189	119; 130
42:12201(b)	149
42:12201(c)(1) to (3)	152
42:12201(h)	39; 74
42:12203(a)	214
42:12203(b)	204
42:12205	95
42:12210	24
42:12210(b)	25
42:12210(c)	25
42:12210(d)	24
42:12211(a)	27
42:15301 to 15545	174
42:15421(b)	174
42 U.S.C. 12102	13; 20
42 U.S.C. 12103	20
47:225(b)(1)	210
47:225(d)	210
49:24102(3)	201
49:40101 to 40129	210
49:41705	207

Code of Federal Regulations

Title:Sec.	Page
14:382.3	207
28:35.104	26, 27
28:35.130(b)	163
28:35.130(b)(1)(iv)	178
28:35.130(b)(7)	166; 168
28:35.130(d)	169
28:35.140(a)	47; 171

[References are to pages]

Code of Federal Regulations—Cont.

Title:Sec.	Page
28:35.140(b)(1)	47
28:35.140(b)(2)	47
28:35.150(d)	165
28:35.152	175
28:35.160(b)	180
28:36	138; 142; 152, 153; 212
28:36.104	26, 27; 142
28:36.207(a)	139
28:36.303(b)(1)	152
28:36.304(b)	148
28:36.309	130
28:36.403(a) to (b)	147
28:36.404(a)	136
28:36.406	134
28:36.406(f)	151
29:2(o)(4)	74
29:32.3	26, 27
29:32.15	78
29:35.1630.2(h)	26
29:1601.1 to 34	86
29:1601.27	86
29:1630	15; 27; 30; 35; 37; 51; 67, 68; 71; 74, 75; 83; 89; 129
29:1630.2(i)(1)(i)	31
29:1630.2(i)(1)(ii)	31
29:1630.2(i)(2)	33
29:1630.2(j)(1)	29
29:1630.2(j)(2)	29
29:1630.2(j)(3)(iii)	24; 31

Code of Federal Regulations—Cont.

Title:Sec.	Page
29:1630.2(j)(4)(i)	30
29:1630.2(k)(1)	36
29:1630.2(n)	50
29:1630.2(n)(3)	51
29:1630.2(o)(3)	71
29:1630.2(o)(4)	39
29:1630.4	46
29:1630.12	46
29:1630.12(b)	217
29:1630.14(a)	75
29:1630.14(b)(3)	78
29:1630.15(f)	38
29 C.F.R. 1630.2	14, 15
34:104.33(b)(1)	104
34:104.42(b)(4)	123
34:104.44(a)	123
34:300.8(c)(9)	102; 104
34:300.116(b)(3)	111
34:300.116(c)	111
34:300.300(a) to (b)	113
34:300.324(a)(2)(i)	117
49:37.3	206
49:37.123(e)(2)(iii)	203

Federal Rules of Civil Procedure

Rule	Page
68	115

INDEX

[References are to sections.]

A

ACTUALLY IMPAIRED
Generally . . . 2.02
Major life activities
    Generally . . . 2.02[C]
    Working, of . . . 2.02[D]
Mental impairment . . . 2.02[A]
Physical impairment . . . 2.02[A]
Substantially limits . . . 2.02[B]

**AMERICANS WITH DISABILITIES ACT
(ADA)**
Amendments Act of 2008 . . . 2.01[C]
Coverage . . . 2.06[A]
Covered entities under . . . 3.01[B]

ATTORNEYS' FEES
Employment discrimination . . . 3.10[C]

AUXILIARY AIDS AND SERVICES
Public accommodations discrimination . . . 5.03[B]

B

BACKPAY
Employment discrimination . . . 3.10[B]

C

CIVIL RIGHTS MODELS
Medical models and . . . 1.01[A]

COMPARATIVE LAW
Generally . . . 7.04[C]

COMPENSATORY DAMAGES
Employment discrimination . . . 3.10[A]

CONSTITUTIONAL ISSUES
Generally . . . 1.03
Due process . . . 1.03[B]
Eighth Amendment . . . 1.03[C]
Eleventh Amendment immunity . . . 6.07[D]
Equal protection . . . 1.03[A]

CONTAGIOUS DISEASES
Disability, as . . . 2.01[D]

D

DAMAGES
Employment discrimination
    Compensatory damages . . . 3.10[A]
    Punitive damages . . . 3.10[A]
Government services and federally funded programs
    . . . 6.07[C]

DEFENSES
Employment discrimination (See EMPLOYMENT
    DISCRIMINATION)
Housing discrimination . . . 7.01[D]

DISABILITY
Actually impaired (See ACTUALLY IMPAIRED)
Alternative definitions . . . 2.01[B]
Contagious diseases . . . 2.01[D]
Definition . . . 2.01
Exclusions
    Generally . . . 2.01[F]
    Illegal drugs, exclusion for current users of
        . . . 2.01[E]
Federal statutory provisions . . . 2.01[A]
Illegal drugs, exclusion for current users of
    . . . 2.01[E]
Mitigating measures
    Americans with Disabilities Act Amendments
        Act of 2008 . . . 2.01[C]
    Sutton trilogy . . . 2.01[C]
Record of impairment . . . 2.03
Regarded as having impairment . . . 2.04

DISABILITY DISCRIMINATION
Generally . . . 1.01[B]; 1.02
Additional discrimination issues . . . 7.04
Comparative law . . . 7.04[C]
Constitutional issues (See CONSTITUTIONAL IS-
    SUES)
Educational discrimination (See EDUCATIONAL
    DISCRIMINATION)
Employment discrimination (See EMPLOYMENT
    DISCRIMINATION)
Entities bound by (See STATUTORY COVERAGE,
    subhead: Disability discrimination laws, entities
    and individuals bound by)
Federally funded programs (See GOVERNMENT
    SERVICES AND FEDERALLY FUNDED PRO-
    GRAMS)
Forms of discrimination . . . 1.02[A]
Government services and federally funded programs
    (See GOVERNMENT SERVICES AND FEDER-
    ALLY FUNDED PROGRAMS)
Harassment as . . . 7.04[B]
Housing discrimination (See HOUSING DISCRIMI-
    NATION)
Individuals bound by (See STATUTORY COVER-
    AGE, subhead: Disability discrimination laws,
    entities and individuals bound by)
International law . . . 7.04[C]
Public accommodations discrimination (See PUB-
    LIC ACCOMMODATIONS DISCRIMINATION)
Retaliation . . . 7.04[A]
Sources of law . . . 1.02[B]
Statutory coverage (See STATUTORY COVERAGE,
    subhead: Disability discrimination laws, entities
    and individuals bound by)
Telecommunications (See TELECOMMUNICA-
    TIONS)

[References are to sections.]

DISABILITY DISCRIMINATION—Cont.
Transportation (See TRANSPORTATION)

DISABILITY LAW
Generally . . . 1.01
Civil rights models, medical models and
. . . 1.01[A]
Discrimination . . . 1.01[B]
Medical models and civil rights models
. . . 1.01[A]
Public benefits . . . 1.01[B]
Torts . . . 1.01[B]

DISCRIMINATION (See DISABILITY DIS-
CRIMINATION)

DISPARATE IMPACTS
Employment discrimination (See EMPLOYMENT
DISCRIMINATION, subhead: Disparate impacts)
Government services and federally funded programs
. . . 6.03
Housing discrimination . . . 7.01[C]

DISPARATE TREATMENT
Employment discrimination (See EMPLOYMENT
DISCRIMINATION, subhead: Disparate treat-
ment)
Housing discrimination . . . 7.01[B]

DUE PROCESS
Generally . . . 1.03[B]

E

EDUCATIONAL DISCRIMINATION
Post-secondary education (See POST-SECONDARY
EDUCATION)
Primary and secondary education
Generally . . . 4.01
Appropriate education . . . 4.01[C]
Eligibility . . . 4.01[B]
Evaluation . . . 4.01[B]
Individuals with Disabilities Education Act
. . . 4.01[A]
Least restrictive environment . . . 4.01[D]
Procedures . . . 4.01[E]
Remedies . . . 4.01[E]
Student discipline . . . 4.01[D]
Secondary education (See subhead: Primary and
secondary education)

EIGHTH AMENDMENT
Generally . . . 1.03[C]

ELEVENTH AMENDMENT IMMUNITY
Generally . . . 6.07[D]

EMPLOYMENT DISCRIMINATION
Generally . . . 3.01
Americans with Disabilities Act, covered entities
under . . . 3.01[B]
Associational discrimination . . . 3.08
Attorneys' fees . . . 3.10[C]
Backpay . . . 3.10[B]
Compensatory damages . . . 3.10[A]

EMPLOYMENT DISCRIMINATION—Cont.
Contractual arrangement, discrimination by
. . . 3.07
Covered entities under Americans with Disabilities
Act . . . 3.01[B]
Defenses
Generally . . . 3.09
Administrative remedies, exhaustion of
. . . 3.09[B]
Direct threats . . . 3.09[C]
Exhaustion of administrative remedies
. . . 3.09[B]
Limitations . . . 3.09[A]
Mandatory arbitration . . . 3.09[D]
Disparate impacts
Criteria . . . 3.04
Methods of operation with . . . 3.04
Standards . . . 3.04
Disparate treatment
Classification . . . 3.03
Limitation . . . 3.03
Segregation . . . 3.03
Injunctions . . . 3.10[B]
Inquiries (See subhead: Medical examinations and
inquiries)
Medical examinations and inquiries
Generally . . . 3.06
Conditional job offer, medical examination
after . . . 3.06[B]
Current employees . . . 3.06[C]
Drug testing and related issues . . . 3.06[D]
Pre-employment inquiries . . . 3.06[A]
Punitive damages . . . 3.10[A]
Qualified individual
Generally . . . 3.02
Essential functions . . . 3.02[B]
Judicial estoppel . . . 3.02[C]
Reasonable accommodation and, relationship
. . . 3.02[A]
Reasonable accommodations
Generally . . . 3.05
Alcoholism . . . 3.05[E]
Burdens . . . 3.05[A]
Illegal drugs, use of . . . 3.05[E]
Interactive process . . . 3.05[D]
Job restructuring and reassignment to vacant
position . . . 3.05[C]
Persons regarded as disabled, for . . . 3.05[F]
Qualified individual and, relationship
. . . 3.02[A]
Reassignment to vacant position, job restruc-
turing and . . . 3.05[C]
Undue hardship standards and . . . 3.05[B]
Reinstatement . . . 3.10[B]
Remedies
Generally . . . 3.10
Administrative remedies, exhaustion of
. . . 3.09[B]
Attorneys' fees . . . 3.10[C]
Backpay . . . 3.10[B]
Compensatory damages . . . 3.10[A]
Exhaustion of administrative remedies
. . . 3.09[B]

[References are to sections.]

EMPLOYMENT DISCRIMINATION—Cont.
Remedies—Cont.
    Injunctions . . . 3.10[B]
    Other equitable relief . . . 3.10[B]
    Punitive damages . . . 3.10[A]
    Reinstatement . . . 3.10[B]
Selection criteria, tests and . . . 3.04
Statutory provisions . . . 3.01[A]
Tests and selection criteria . . . 3.04
Undue hardship standards and reasonable accommodations . . . 3.05[B]

ENTERTAINMENT
Public accommodations discrimination . . . 5.05

EQUAL PROTECTION
Generally . . . 1.03[A]

ESSENTIAL FUNCTIONS
Employment discrimination . . . 3.02[B]

EXHIBITION
Public accommodations discrimination . . . 5.05

F

FACIAL DISCRIMINATION
Housing discrimination . . . 7.01[B]

FAIR HOUSING ACT AMENDMENT (FHAA)
Housing discrimination . . . 7.01[A]

FEDERALLY FUNDED PROGRAMS (See GOVERNMENT SERVICES AND FEDERALLY FUNDED PROGRAMS)

FHAA (See FAIR HOUSING ACT AMENDMENT (FHAA))

G

GOVERNMENT SERVICES AND FEDERALLY FUNDED PROGRAMS
Generally . . . 6.01
Federal agencies, discrimination by . . . 6.02
General accessibility duty (See subhead: Specific issues and general accessibility duty)
Local government (See subhead: State and local government)
Remedies
    Generally . . . 6.07
    Damages relief . . . 6.07[C]
    Eleventh Amendment immunity . . . 6.07[D]
    Exhaustion issues . . . 6.07[A]
    Immunity under Eleventh Amendment . . . 6.07[D]
    Injunctive relief . . . 6.07[B]
Specific issues and general accessibility duty
    Generally . . . 6.06
    Accessibility requirements . . . 6.06[G]
    Courts . . . 6.06[C]
    Employment . . . 6.06[A]
    Prisons . . . 6.06[D]
    Public benefits and welfare . . . 6.06[E]
    Recreation . . . 6.06[F]

GOVERNMENT SERVICES AND FEDERALLY FUNDED PROGRAMS—Cont.
Specific issues and general accessibility duty—Cont.
    Voting . . . 6.06[B]
    Welfare, public benefits and . . . 6.06[E]
State and local government
    Disparate impact discrimination . . . 6.03
    General accessibility duty (See subhead: Specific issues and general accessibility duty)
    Integrated services . . . 6.05
    Modifications of policies . . . 6.04
    Remedies (See subhead: Remedies)
    Specific issues and general accessibility duty (See subhead: Specific issues and general accessibility duty)

H

HARASSMENT
Disability discrimination. as . . . 7.04[B]

HOUSING DISCRIMINATION
Generally . . . 7.01
Defenses . . . 7.01[D]
Disparate impact . . . 7.01[C]
Disparate treatment . . . 7.01[B]
Exemptions . . . 7.01[D]
Facial discrimination . . . 7.01[B]
Fair Housing Act Amendment . . . 7.01[A]
Reasonable accommodation . . . 7.01[C]
Remedies . . . 7.01[E]

I

IDEA (See INDIVIDUALS WITH DISABILITIES EDUCATION ACT (IDEA))

IMMUNITY
Eleventh amendment . . . 6.07[D]

IMPAIRMENT (See DISABILITY)

INDIVIDUALS WITH DISABILITIES EDUCATION ACT (IDEA)
Generally . . . 4.01[A]

INJUNCTIONS
Employment discrimination . . . 3.10[B]
Government services and federally funded programs . . . 6.07[B]

INQUIRIES (See EMPLOYMENT DISCRIMINATION, subhead: Medical examinations and inquiries)

INSURANCE
Public accommodations discrimination . . . 5.06

INTERNATIONAL LAW
Generally . . . 7.04[C]

J

JUDICIAL ESTOPPEL
Employment discrimination . . . 3.02[C]

[References are to sections.]

M

MAJOR LIFE ACTIVITIES
Generally . . . 2.02[C]
Working, of . . . 2.02[D]

MEDICAL EXAMINATIONS (See EMPLOY-
MENT DISCRIMINATION, subhead: Medical
examinations and inquiries)

MEDICAL MODELS
Civil rights models and . . . 1.01[A]

MENTAL IMPAIRMENT
Generally . . . 2.02[A]

P

PHYSICAL IMPAIRMENT
Generally . . . 2.02[A]

POST-SECONDARY EDUCATION
Generally . . . 4.02
Academic deference . . . 4.02[C]
Courses . . . 4.02[E]
Examinations . . . 4.02[E]
Higher education discrimination . . . 4.02[A]
Learning disabilities, specific issues regarding
. . . 4.02[D]
Qualifications . . . 4.02[B]
Reasonable accommodation . . . 4.02[B]

PRIMARY EDUCATION
Discrimination in (See EDUCATIONAL DISCRIMI-
NATION, subhead: Primary and secondary educa-
tion)

**PUBLIC ACCOMMODATIONS DISCRIMINA-
TION**
Generally . . . 5.01
Accessibility standards . . . 5.04
Auxiliary aids and services . . . 5.03; 5.03[B]
Barrier removal . . . 5.04
Definitions . . . 5.02
Entertainment, places of . . . 5.05
Exhibition, places of . . . 5.05
Fundamental alterations . . . 5.03[A]
Insurance issues . . . 5.06
Reasonable modifications . . . 5.03; 5.03[A]
Remedies . . . 5.07
Services, auxiliary aids and . . . 5.03; 5.03[B]
Undue burden . . . 5.03[B]

PUBLIC BENEFITS
Generally . . . 1.01[B]

PUNITIVE DAMAGES
Employment discrimination . . . 3.10[A]

Q

QUALIFIED INDIVIDUAL
Generally . . . 2.05
Employment discrimination (See EMPLOYMENT
DISCRIMINATION)

R

REASONABLE ACCOMMODATIONS
Employment discrimination (See EMPLOYMENT
DISCRIMINATION)
Housing discrimination . . . 7.01[C]
Post-secondary education . . . 4.02[B]
Public accommodations discrimination . . . 5.03;
5.03[A]

RECORD OF IMPAIRMENT
Generally . . . 2.03

REGARDED AS HAVING IMPAIRMENT
Generally . . . 2.04

REINSTATEMENT
Employment discrimination . . . 3.10[B]

REMEDIES
Employment discrimination (See EMPLOYMENT
DISCRIMINATION, subhead: Remedies)
Federally funded programs (See GOVERNMENT
SERVICES AND FEDERALLY FUNDED PRO-
GRAMS, subhead: Remedies)
Government services and federally funded programs
(See GOVERNMENT SERVICES AND FEDER-
ALLY FUNDED PROGRAMS, subhead: Rem-
edies)
Housing discrimination . . . 7.01[E]
Primary and secondary education . . . 4.01[E]
Public accommodations discrimination . . . 5.07

RETALIATION
Generally . . . 7.04[A]

S

SECONDARY EDUCATION
Discrimination in (See EDUCATIONAL DISCRIMI-
NATION, subhead: Primary and secondary educa-
tion)

SERVICES, AUXILIARY AIDS AND
Public accommodations discrimination . . . 5.03[B]

STATUTORY COVERAGE
Actually impaired (See ACTUALLY IMPAIRED)
Americans with Disabilities Act . . . 2.06[A]
Disability (See DISABILITY)
Disability discrimination laws, entities and individu-
als bound by
Generally . . . 2.06; 2.06[C]
Coverage
Americans with Disabilities Act
. . . 2.06[A]
Other provisions, of . . . 2.06[C]
Section 504, of . . . 2.06[B]
Qualified individual . . . 2.05
Record of impairment . . . 2.03
Regarded as having impairment . . . 2.04
Section 504, of . . . 2.06[B]

SUBSTANTIALLY LIMITS
Generally . . . 2.02[B]

[References are to sections.]

SUTTON TRILOGY
Generally . . . 2.01[C]

T

TELECOMMUNICATIONS
Generally . . . 7.03; 7.03[B]
Internet sites . . . 7.03[B]
Relay systems . . . 7.03[A]

TORTS
Generally . . . 1.01[B]

TRANSPORTATION
Generally . . . 7.02
Air transportation . . . 7.02[B]
Ground transportation . . . 7.02[A]

U

UNDUE BURDEN
Public accommodations discrimination . . . 5.03[B]

UNDUE HARDSHIP STANDARDS
Reasonable accommodations and . . . 3.05[B]